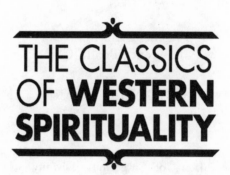

THE CLASSICS
OF **WESTERN**
SPIRITUALITY

THE CLASSICS OF WESTERN SPIRITUALITY
A Library of the Great Spiritual Masters

Seyyed Hossein Nasr—Professor of Islamic Studies, George Washington University, Washington, DC

Raimon Panikkar—Professor Emeritus, Department of Religious Studies, University of California at Santa Barbara, CA

Sandra M. Schneiders—Professor of New Testament Studies and Spirituality, Jesuit School of Theology, Berkeley, CA

Michael A. Sells—John Henry Barrows Professor of Islamic History and Literature, Divinity School, University of Chicago, Chicago, IL

Huston Smith—Thomas J. Watson Professor of Religion Emeritus, Syracuse University, Syracuse, NY

John R. Sommerfeldt—Professor of History, University of Dallas, Irving, TX

David Steindl-Rast—Spiritual Author, Benedictine Grange, West Redding, CT

David Tracy—Greeley Professor of Roman Catholic Studies, Divinity School, University of Chicago, Chicago, IL

The Most Rev. and Rt. Hon. Rowan D. Williams—Archbishop of Canterbury

Early Protestant Spirituality

EDITED AND TRANSLATED BY
SCOTT H. HENDRIX

PAULIST PRESS
NEW YORK • MAHWAH

Cover art: "Lutheran Eucharist," a sixteenth-century print showing the Eucharist being administered under both kinds, an important point in Martin Luther's eucharistic theology. Courtesy of the Richard C. Kessler Reformation Collection, Pitts Theology Library, Candler School of Theology, Emory University.

Cover and caseside design by Cynthia Dunne, www.bluefarmdesign.com
Book design by Lynn Else

Library of Congress Cataloging-in-Publication Data

Early Protestant spirituality / [edited by] Scott H. Hendrix.
    p. cm. — (The classics of western spirituality)
  Includes bibliographical references and index.
   ISBN 978-0-8091-4211-8 (alk. paper)—ISBN 978-0-8091-0566-3 (alk. paper)
  1. Church history—16th century. 2. Christian literature. I. Hendrix, Scott H.
  BR305.3.E27 2009
  248.088'2804—dc22

                                                                        2009005384

Published by Paulist Press
997 Macarthur Boulevard
Mahwah, New Jersey 07430

www.paulistpress.com

Printed and bound in the
United States of America

CONTENTS

CONTENTS

CONTENTS

CONTENTS

CONTENTS

Editor and Translator of This Volume

SCOTT H. HENDRIX is professor emeritus of Reformation history and doctrine at Princeton Theological Seminary in New Jersey. He received his doctorate from Tübingen University in Germany and taught church history at three Lutheran seminaries before going to Princeton Seminary in 1998. A former president of the Society for Reformation Research, Professor Hendrix serves on the editorial committees of several periodicals and monograph series in the field of Reformation history and theology. He has published extensively on the Reformation and is the author of *Recultivating the Vineyard: The Reformation Agendas of Christianization.*

ACKNOWLEDGMENTS
AND PERMISSIONS

This anthology suggested itself to me soon after 1998, when I published an essay on the spirituality of Martin Luther and began to teach courses on the Reformation at Princeton Seminary. Since then I have used the anthology in unpublished form in two courses with the same title as this collection. First and foremost, therefore, I wish to thank the students in those courses who provided me with invaluable feedback about improving the texts and the introductions. Many people have assisted me by making sources available, especially the staffs of Speer and Luce libraries at Princeton Seminary and, in particular, Joan Harden, who made access to many texts more convenient during my sabbatical in 2005 when much of the initial work was done. To them all I wish to extend my deep appreciation. My research assistant, Sandi Podoll, applied her proofreading and editorial skills to a penultimate version and helped to smooth out many rough spots. My wife, Emilee Hendrix, also assisted with proofreading and offered good-natured and persistent encouragement. Finally, Bernard McGinn and the staff of Paulist Press graciously welcomed this collection into their series and shepherded it to publication.

The texts offered here have been revised in order to allow for inclusive forms of the English language; in many cases that meant changing nouns and verbs from the singular to the plural, especially when the texts are translations of my own. I have made every effort, however, to preserve the original meaning of the text even when some forms have been altered. When a selection is said to have been translated from a non-English source, that translation has been made by the editor. In some cases I have made new translations of non-English sources even though English translations were available.

A number of the texts have been translated or adapted from publications that are in the public domain. For the rest, I am grateful to the following rights holders for permission to use selections from their material:

American Society of Church History, for Ulrich Zwingli, *Commentary on True and False Religion*. Ed. Samuel Macauley Jackson and Clarence Nevin Heller. Durham, NC: Labyrinth Press, 1981.

Baker Publishing Group, for *Ulrich Zwingli: Early Writings*. Ed. Samuel Macauley Jackson. Durham, NC: Labyrinth Press, 1987.

Baker Publishing Group, for *The Complete Sermons of Martin Luther*. Ed. J. N. Lenker. 7 vols. Grand Rapids, MI: Baker, 2000.

Continuum International Publishing Group, for *A Woman's Voice in the Reformation*. Ed. Peter Matheson. Edinburgh: T & T Clark, 1995.

David F. Wright, Edinburgh, for *Common Places of Martin Bucer*. Trans. and ed. David Wright. Appleford, UK: The Sutton Courtenay Press, 1972.

Elsie Anne McKee, Princeton, for *Reforming Popular Piety in Sixteenth-Century Strasbourg: Katharina Schütz Zell and Her Hymnbook*. Studies in Reformed Theology and History 2:4 (1994).

Evangelische Kirche Deutschland, Rechtsabteilung, for *Evangelisches Kirchengesangbuch*. Ausgabe für die evangelisch-lutherischen Kirchen Niedersachsens. Hannover: Schlütersche Verlagsanstalt/Göttingen: Vandenhoeck & Ruprecht, 1956, 1994.

Evangelische Kirche Deutschland, Rechtsabteilung, for *Ich rufe zu dir: Gebete des Reformators Philipp Melanchthon*. Ed. Martin H. Jung, Gerhard Weng, Klaus-Dieter Kaiser. 2nd ed. Frankfurt: GEP Buch, 1997.

Evangelische Verlagsanstalt, Leipzig, for *Melanchthon Deutsch*. Ed. Michael Beyer, Stefan Rhein, Günther Wartenberg. 2 vols. Leipzig: EVA, 1997.

Evangelische Verlagsanstalt, Leipzig, for *Reformatorenbriefe: Luther, Zwingli, Calvin*. Ed. Günter Gloede. Berlin: EVA, 1973.

Gütersloher Verlagshaus, Gütersloh, for *Martin Bucers Deutsche Schriften*, vol. 1. Ed. Robert Stupperich. Gütersloh: GVH/Paris: PUF, 1960.

Herald Press, for *The Essential Carlstadt: Fifteen Tracts*. Trans. and ed. E. J. Furcha. Scottdale, PA: Herald Press, 1995.

Hes & De Graaf Publishers, Netherlands, for Gunther Franz, *Huberinus–Rhegius–Holbein*. Nieuwkoop: B. de Graaf, 1973.

Marquette University Press, for *Preaching the Reformation: The Homiletical Handbook of Urbanus Rhegius*. Trans. and ed. Scott Hendrix. Milwaukee: Marquette University Press, 2003.

Neukirchener Verlag, Neukirchen-Vluyn, for *Supplementa Calviniana*, vol. 8. Ed. Willem Balke and Wilhelmus H. Th. Moehn. Neukirchen-Vluyn: Neukirchener Verlag, 1994.

N. T. Wright, Durham, UK, for *The Work of John Frith*. Trans. and ed. N. T. Wright. Appleford, UK: The Sutton Courtenay Press, 1978.

Theologischer Verlag, Zürich, for *Huldrych Zwingli Schriften*. Ed. Thomas Brunnschweiler, Samuel Lutz, Hans Ulrich Bächtold. 4 vols. Zürich: TVZ, 1995.

Truman State University Press, for Peter Martyr Vermigli, *Sacred Prayers Drawn from the Psalms of David*. Trans. and ed. John Patrick Donnelly, SJ. The Peter Martyr Library, vol. 3. Kirksville, MO: Truman State University Press, 1996.

University of Chicago Press, for *Church Mother: The Writings of a Protestant Reformer in Sixteenth-Century Germany, Katharina Schütz Zell*. Ed. and trans. Elsie Anne McKee. Chicago: University of Chicago Press, 2006.

University of Virginia Press, for *The Book of Common Prayer 1559: The Elizabethan Prayer Book*. Ed. John E. Booty. Charlottesville: University of Virginia Press, 1976.

ABBREVIATIONS

ALMA	Archivum Latinitatis Medii Aevi
AKG	Archiv für Kulturgeschichte
ARG	Archiv für Reformationsgeschichte
BS	Heinrich Bullinger Schriften. Ed. Emidio Campi, Detlef Roth, Peter Stotz. 6 vols. Zürich: Theologischer Verlag Zürich, 2004–6.
Calvin, Inst.	John Calvin, Institutes of the Christian Religion. Ed. John T. McNeill, trans. Ford Lewis Battles, 2 vols. Philadelphia: Westminster Press, 1960.
CChr-SL	Corpus Christianorum. Series Latina
CH	Church History: Studies in Christianity and Culture
CHR	Catholic Historical Review
Clemen	Luthers Werke in Auswahl. Ed. Otto Clemen & Albert Leitzmann. 8 vols. Berlin: De Gruyter, 1959–67.
CSEL	Corpus Scriptorum Ecclesiasticorum Latinorum. Ed. Kommission zur Herausgabe des Corpus der lateinischen Kirchenväter. 95 vols. Vienna, 1866–.
D–S	Enchiridion symbolorum definitionum et declarationum. Ed. Henricus Denzinger and Adolfus Schönmetzer. 34th ed. Freiburg: Herder, 1967.
FC	Fathers of the Church. 113 vols. Washington, DC: Catholic University of America Press, 1947–.
JEMH	Journal of Early Modern History
LCC	Library of Christian Classics. 26 vols. Louisville, KY: Westminster John Knox, 1953–90.
LQ	Lutheran Quarterly
LuJ	Lutherjahrbuch
LW	Luther's Works. American Edition. Ed. Helmut Lehmann and Jaroslav Pelikan. 55 vols. Philadelphia: Fortress/St. Louis: Concordia, 1955–86.

Mansi	Mansi, G. D. Sacrorum conciliorum nova et amplissima collectio. Florence: Expensis Antonii Zatta, 1761–62; reprinted Graz, 1960–61.
MPG	Migne, Patrologiae cursus completus, Series Graeca, ed. J.-P. Migne. Paris, 1857–66.
MPL	Migne, Patrologiae cursus completus, Series Latina, ed. J.-P. Migne. Paris, 1844–64.
NDB	Neue Deutsche Biographie
NPNF	Nicene and Post-Nicene Fathers, Series 1 and 2, 14 vols. each. Ed. Philip Schaff et al. Grand Rapids, MI: Eerdmans, 1956.
NRSV	The HarperCollins Study Bible, New Revised Standard Version, ed. W. A. Meeks et al. New York: HarperCollins, 1993.
OER	The Oxford Encyclopedia of the Reformation, ed. Hans J. Hillerbrand. 4 vols. New York/Oxford: Oxford University Press, 1996.
OS	Joannis Calvini Opera Selecta. Ed. Peter Barth and Wilhelm Niesel. 5 vols. Munich: Chr. Kaiser, 1926–70.
REPrThK	Realenzyklopädie für protestantische Theologie und Kirche
RQ	Renaissance Quarterly
RS	Renaissance Studies
SC	Supplementa Calviniana. Neukirchen: Neukirchener Verlag, 1961–.
SCES	Sixteenth Century Essays and Studies. 83 vols. Kirksville, MO: Truman State University Press, 1981–.
SCJ	The Sixteenth Century Journal
StA	Martin Luther Studienausgabe, ed. Hans-Ulrich Delius. 6 vols. Berlin: Evangelische Verlagsanstalt, 1979–99.
SVRG	Schriften des Vereins für Reformationsgeschichte
TRE	Theologische Realenzyklopädie
Vulg.	Biblia sacra iuxta vulgatam versionem. Ed. R. Weber et al. 2 vols. Stuttgart: Württembergische Bibelanstalt, 1969.

ABBREVIATIONS

WA	D. Martin Luthers Werke. Kritische Gesamtausgabe. Schriften. 69 vols. Weimar: Böhlau, 1883–.
WABr	D. Martin Luthers Werke. Kritische Gesamtausgabe. Briefwechsel. 18 vols. Weimar, 1930–85.
WADB	D. Martin Luthers Werke. Kritische Gesamtausgabe. Deutsche Bibel. 12 vols. Weimar, 1906–61.
WATR	D. Martin Luthers Werke. Kritische Gesamtausgabe. Tischreden. 6 vols. Weimar, 1912–21.
ZKG	Zeitschrift für Kirchengeschichte
Z	Huldreich Zwinglis Sämtliche Werke. 14 vols. Berlin/Leipzig/Zürich, 1905–.
ZS	Huldrych Zwingli Schriften. Ed. Thomas Brunnschweiler, Samuel Lutz, Hans Ulrich Bächtold. 4 vols. Zürich: Theologischer Verlag, 1995.

INTRODUCTION

To some ears *Protestant spirituality* will sound like an oxymoron. Although the term *spirituality* has become a popular alternative to words like *religion* and *theology*, it is still frequently associated with mysticism and personal devotion in non-Protestant traditions. Since the Reformation of the sixteenth century, however, Protestant churches have spawned their own spiritual movements with distinct patterns of revival and agendas for renewal. If the net is cast widely within Europe and North America, it will turn up strange and familiar names like illuminists, Anna Maria van Schurman (1607–78), pietism, Methodism, Brethren, evangelical awakenings, Pentecostalism, and charismatics. If the net is cast into the sixteenth century itself and spirituality is defined as piety and devotion, then the usual suspects will appear alongside some less familiar ones, as attested by the volumes in this series on John Calvin, Martin Luther, Anabaptists, and Valentin Weigel.

Early Protestants

The existence of a Protestant spirituality depends wholly, therefore, on how the terms *Protestant* and *spirituality* are defined. For the purpose of this book, *spirituality* means the way in which members of a religious community nurture and practice their faith. Since this volume is about Protestants, it deals with the manner in which certain Christians since the fifteenth century have lived out their convictions; and because it is restricted to *early* Protestants, the Christians whose spirituality is exemplified in this volume are those who left behind written evidence of their devotion between 1517, the traditional beginning of the Reformation, and 1560, the

1

year by which Protestant churches existed on firm legal footing in Germany, Switzerland, and England.

According to tradition, the epithet *Protestant* was applied to those German princes and city delegates who, at the Diet of Speyer in 1529, protested the rescinding of their right to reform Christianity in their cities and local regions. That right had been granted to them just three years earlier, and German reformers, who called themselves evangelicals (*die Evangelischen*), made the most of that breathing period to expand and consolidate the changes they had made. They were not, however, thinking of themselves as Protestant in the sense of a permanent type of Christianity defined by its opposition to the Church of Rome. The evangelicals, who adhered to the Augsburg Confession of 1530 and for the most part adopted the name Lutheran, were not given legal status within the Holy Roman Empire until 1555, just four years before the Elizabethan settlement made Protestantism the established form of Christianity in England. In the English-speaking world, the term *Protestant* was used increasingly to describe not only the new English religious establishment but the dissenters from Rome who gained some form of legitimacy elsewhere in Europe. We are using the term in this common way, even though non-English, sixteenth-century "evangelicals" would be surprised to hear it applied to them.

They would be surprised for another reason. Early Protestant reformers did not think of their religious world as their descendants describe it. Their century was not an age of Reformation over against a Catholic or Roman Catholic Middle Ages. Instead, the 1500s marked another century in the course of Western Christendom, but it was a Christendom that was no longer subject exclusively to the Roman bishop or the pope. Protestant reformers like Martin Luther referred to the centuries preceding the Reformation as Christendom under the papacy and to his own century as Christendom under the gospel or, more urgently, as the last days of Christendom in which its survival was threatened by demonic forces. Early Protestants knew that Christendom did not cover the entire world and that new lands and customs were being discovered. Their world was still, however, a cluster of small, European societies that were subject to a Christian view of history that pitted attacks of the devil against the divine plan for their ultimate salvation. For early

Protestants, the pope was not the head of one church among others; he was the antichrist that had allowed Christendom to teeter on the brink of ruin. Reformers conceived of their agenda as saving Christendom or, if that was no longer possible, as rescuing a faithful remnant before the end.

Against that background, *spirituality* could take on an urgent and polemical character that the modern usage of the word does not convey. Instead of connoting quiet meditation and ecumenical openness, the spiritual life for early Protestants meant recapturing the resources of their ancestors in order to strengthen their faith for the eschatological conflict they faced. Some of the selections in this volume, therefore, seem more polemical than spiritual texts ought to be. Besides, early Protestants were wrong about the last days and the pope. European Christendom did not end by 1560 or even by 1600. It happened much later, and some of its features are still detectable. The pope was not the antichrist and the papacy did become the chief authority for one kind of Western Christianity among others, the modern Roman Catholic Church. In spite of their short-sightedness, however, those early reformers did leave behind texts of lasting value that still enhance the spiritual life of their descendants.

Spirituality

It is not easy to find the precise meaning of *spirituality* either in the late Middle Ages or during the Reformation. Although the Latin word *spiritualitas*, from which the English term "spirituality" is derived, was in existence long before the sixteenth century, the form of the word indicates a way of being rather than a way of acting, or, to put that distinction in medieval terms, spirituality implies a closer relationship to the contemplative life than to the active life. For that reason, perhaps, spirituality has been more closely associated with medieval mystical experience and private devotion than with more active forms of piety. Personal contemplation of things divine can be, of course, a strenuous activity, especially if one practices it regularly as religious meditation, but it is more an activity of the mind than of the five senses or the body. In the late Middle Ages the senses

3

were also very much involved in the piety of the laity, especially the sense of sight. The mass was celebrated as a spectacle, and, in England, visions of all kinds played an extensive role in piety and served in diverse ways to reinforce belief in Christian teaching and to connect people to the eternal world they hoped to reach.[1]

In early Christian literature, however, the first occurrence of *spiritualitas* would not have restricted its meaning to contemplation or to visions. When it appears in a letter of Pelagius (d. after 418 CE) or one of his disciples, *spirituality* means the religious or spiritual life and even, perhaps, that spiritual discipline or asceticism for which Pelagius was an advocate. According to Aimé Solignac, the spiritual life was only one meaning of spirituality prior to the Reformation. It also had a philosophical sense that designated a mode of being opposed to corporality; and it took on a juridical definition that contrasted matters of the spiritual realm to matters of the temporal realm.[2] In reference to the spiritual life, however, spirituality meant a mode of practicing the faith that protected believers from temptations of the flesh and the world. Since Pelagius is best known as a heretic, it may seem odd to regard him as the father of spirituality, especially for Protestants who were so ardently Augustinian; nevertheless, whether their beliefs were judged heretical or orthodox, all Christians practiced the faith, and that included early Protestants. Although Martin Luther argued that saving righteousness was passive because it was received as a gift, the faith that received and lived out that gift, according to him, was hyperactive. In his preface to the Pauline Epistle to the Romans, written for the translation of the Bible into German, Luther described it as follows:

> Faith…is a divine work in us which changes us and makes us to be born anew of God (John 1:12–13)….O it is a living, busy, active, mighty thing, this faith. It is impossible for it not to be doing good works incessantly. It does not ask whether good works are to be done, but before the question is asked, it has already done them….Thus it is impossible to separate works from faith, quite as impossible as to separate heat and light from fire.[3]

Luther was trying to make the same case for active faith that many Protestants after him, like Ernest Campbell, a pastor at Riverside Church in New York, echoed: "The aim of faith is to *refine* life where it is coarse, to *soften* it where it is hard, to *reconcile* it where it is lost, to *value* it where it is debased, to *celebrate* it where it is doubted, to *free* it where it is hung up, and to *illumine* it where it is in darkness."[4]

It is erroneous, therefore, to distinguish early Protestants from their late medieval predecessors by contrasting a passive life of faith with an active life of good works. Faith and works were active in the spirituality of both communities; the meaning of faith and works and their relationship to each other were the decisive points of disagreement. That difference was both theological and practical, but matters of practice caused the sparks that ignited the Reformation. In Wittenberg it was the well-known custom of offering and acquiring indulgences that in 1517 provoked Luther's ninety-five theses. In 1522 friends of Ulrich Zwingli flouted the Lenten fasting rules in Zürich, and Zwingli supported them in a sermon that defended their freedom at any time to choose the foods they ate. The next year in Strasbourg, Martin Bucer, a former Dominican who had married a nun, officiated at the wedding of the evangelically minded priest Matthew Zell and Katharina Schütz, intensifying thereby the debate over clerical celibacy, which prompted Katharina herself to defend in writing their right to marry. Although theological disagreements between early Protestants and their opponents should not be minimized, those disagreements may not have led to a reformation unless the different ways of practicing the faith had not led to actual conflict and the defiance of church authorities.

For early Protestants, we have included under spirituality ways of practicing the faith, because the active expression of their faith was of equal or greater consequence than the theological justification for that practice. One can even say that the Reformation, in their eyes, was a reformation of spirituality, since the unresolved issues that led to a permanent separation of Protestant confessions from obedience to the pope were mainly matters of worship and piety: cult of the saints; celebration of the mass as a sacrifice, also in private, with the cup withheld from laity; the sacrament of penance with indulgences; involuntary monastic vows; compulsory celibacy for priests, monks, and nuns; required fasting at certain times; aspects of Marian piety. All Protestants did not object to these practices to the same degree, but all of them did make drastic changes to late medieval piety, and they insisted on those changes as stubbornly as Catholic theologians defended them.

That insistence and the division that resulted meant that new evangelical churches had to reconstruct spiritualities of their own for both pastors and laity. This reconstruction was the main task of reform, and it led to hard debates and finally to division among Protestants themselves. The issue was the faithful and beneficial practice of the Christian faith, that is, the designing of a spiritual life in the sense of Pelagius that, although not ascetic to an extreme, would nevertheless keep evangelical believers strong in faith, responsible in morals, assiduous in worship and prayer, and active in love toward others. In order to create and implement that design, reformers had to be confident in their own faith and calling (Part One), interpret scripture with clarity and certify its authority (Part Two), preach clearly and convincingly (Part Three), admonish and console the faithful (Part Four), teach them principles to live by (Part Five), compose and publish new songs of faith (Part Six), instruct people why they should pray and provide them with examples (Part Seven), redefine the sacraments and explain their purpose (Part Eight), and arrange new orders of worship and instruction (Part Nine). Early reformers had to guide and nurture their flocks, and, in order to do this, they had to be in action most of the time, fortifying their convictions and encouraging evangelical believers to do the same.

Authors

Limiting Protestant spirituality to the first forty-three years of its history is admittedly arbitrary, but this limitation does serve a constructive purpose: to introduce the reader to a variety of early Protestant writers who are not widely known. Most surveys of the Reformation fail to mention the reformers who were important colleagues of Martin Luther, Thomas Cranmer, Ulrich Zwingli, and John Calvin. Although well known to scholars who have written books and articles about them, these reformers have escaped notice because they do not appear as readily in history books and their writings have not been either translated or properly edited. Yet they, too, served on the frontline of the Reformation and contributed richly to the spirituality of early evangelical believers. Some of their texts are included in this collection, and their presence makes it possible for twenty-five different writers to be represented:

Albert, Duke of Prussia (1490–1568): Last grand-master of the Teutonic Order; adopted the Reformation in his duchy.

Martin Bucer (1491–1551): Reformer in Strasbourg who died in England.

Henry Bullinger (1504–75): Ulrich Zwingli's successor in Zürich.

John Calvin (1509–64): Reformer in Geneva.

Wolfgang Capito (1478–1541): Humanist and reformer in Strasbourg.

Miles Coverdale (1488–1568): English reformer, Bible translator, and bishop.

Thomas Cranmer (1489–1556): Archbishop of Canterbury and English reformer.

Elisabeth Cruciger (1500?–35): Early evangelical hymn writer in Wittenberg.

Johann Freder (1510–60?): Lutheran pastor and translator in North Germany.

John Frith (1503–33): One of the first Protestant martyrs in the English Reformation.

Argula von Grumbach (c.1492–undocumented): Bavarian noblewoman who wrote on behalf of the Reformation.

Caspar Huberinus (1500–53): South German reformer in Augsburg and Hohenlohe.

Leo Jud (1482–1542): Associate of Zwingli and Bullinger in Zürich.

Andrew Karlstadt (1486–1541): Luther's colleague who broke with the Wittenberg reformation.

Martin Luther (1483–1546): Reformer in Wittenberg.

Philip Melanchthon (1497–1560): Lay reformer in Wittenberg, humanist scholar, theologian.

Urbanus Rhegius (1489–1541): Lutheran reformer in Augsburg and Lower Saxony.

Caspar Schwenckfeld (1489–1561): Silesian nobleman, lay reformer, spiritual theologian.

Paul Speratus (1484–1551): Reformer and hymn writer in East Prussia.

William Tyndale (c.1494–1536): Translator of the Bible into English.

Peter Martyr Vermigli (1499–1562): Italian Reformed theologian who lived in England, Strasbourg, and Zürich.

Michael Weisse (c.1488–1534): Pastor among the Bohemian Brethren and
editor of their first German hymnbook.
Katharina Schütz Zell (c. 1498–1562): Author and advocate of reform in
Strasbourg.
John Zwick (c.1496–1542): Reformer in Constance.
Ulrich Zwingli (1484–1531): Reformer in Zürich.

More about these authors will be said in the introductions that
precede each of their writings in this book; taken together, they are
a small but impressive sample of the many contributors to the formation of early Protestant spirituality.

PART ONE

Personal Voices

Introduction

Expressions of spirituality are always personal, even when they are shared with others. The convictions people have about God and their relationship to the holy are often unarticulated until they are drawn out by a crisis or by challenges they feel must be addressed. The early Reformation was a time of crisis and challenge to the religious convictions and practices of an entire generation of men and women. For that reason their letters and pamphlets exhibit statements that articulate their faith in a variety of ways: viewing their age as a turning point in history, a *kairos*, when God is doing a new thing, sensing they have been called personally by God to a particular role, declaring steadfastness in the face of opposition and persecution, defending their actions as consistent with scripture and their new convictions, revealing a new religious identity and how it is changing their lives.

The statements collected in Part One illustrate all these dimensions of personal spirituality. Before the Reformation humanists like Ulrich Zwingli and Oswald Myconius were already sensing that the renewed study of letters and ideas would cast fresh light on a dark world, and the earliest stirrings of religious renewal in Germany and Switzerland intensified their longing for a new age. Martin Luther also had humanist sensibilities, but he had to wrestle with a complex monastic and family background before finding an unambiguous role for himself in the evangelical movement that formed around his conflict with Rome. The letter to his father is a remarkable disclosure of how that took place. Women's voices were just as personal but mostly undisclosed to a wider audience, because they could not occupy public roles or issue their opinions in print. All the more precious, therefore, are the published statements by Argula von Grumbach, which demonstrate unsurprisingly that immersion in scripture and religious self-confidence was not restricted to men.

The occasions for the statements by Martin Bucer and John Frith are different from the others. They are more obviously public and political and, because the Reformation was always a political matter, they show how personal faith had to mix with politics and how different the consequences could be. Bucer is making a case for permanent residence in Strasbourg for him and his wife, both of whom had left the religious orders to which they had belonged. Clerical marriage was the hot-button issue in that town, where the bishop and city council had a long history of conflict over who controlled the religious life of its citizens. Bucer, therefore, had to defend his personal integrity while, at the same time, arguing for the right of clergy to be married and encouraging the city council to exercise its authority. Bucer, however, remained in Strasbourg almost as long as John Frith was alive and became its leading reformer, while Frith, after declaring his faith and courage from jail in the tower of London, became a martyr at age thirty, a victim in England of the most politically convoluted and hazardous of all the reformations.

1. Ulrich Zwingli, Letter to Oswald Myconius, July 24, 1520

Ulrich Zwingli had been preaching at the Great Minster in Zürich eighteen months when he wrote the following letter to Oswald Myconius, a fellow humanist and a teacher in Lucerne. Myconius (1488–1552), who had instigated Zwingli's call to Zürich, returned to the city in 1523 and remained a close friend and supporter of reform. After Zwingli's death in 1531, Myconius became a pastor and teacher in Basel, where he penned the first biography of Zwingli.

This letter was written almost two years before eating meat during Lent broke the fasting regulations of the church and ignited the Reformation in Zürich. It betrays Zwingli's disappointment with humanism as a reform movement and expresses hope for a christocentric reformation. Martin Luther's conflict with Rome was already under way; he had been threatened with excommunication a month before Zwingli's letter.

Translation based on the German version in *Reformatorenbriefe*, 196–202, with reference to the Latin text in CR 94, 341–45.

My dear Myconius,

Your spirit is weighed down by anxiety over where our age is headed, and with so much tumult and confusion everywhere it is true that no one can make out its character. Amid such perplexity no one dares to take any initiative because exactly the opposite will raise its head. Even if some sharp-eyed spirit summons up new hope, it is still mixed with fear that lingers in the air.

Those who appreciate the splendor of good letters begin to hope for the return of those erudite times in which almost everyone, it seems, was learned. This hope is being undermined, however, by the stubborn ignorance, not to mention the shamelessness, of many people who would put up with anything rather than welcome a trace of erudition or refinement. Their reluctance is understandable, since otherwise they could not conceal the stain of their own ignorance. The helper of such people is power, the constant enemy of truth that itself cannot be conquered.

There is also fervent hope for a rebirth of Christ and the gospel, since many good and learned people have begun to steer, as they say, with rudder and sails toward the goal of making the seed bear ripe fruit. This hope is diminished, however, as soon as one sees the tares sown by the enemy while the workers slept and failed to keep watch. Since the tares have grown deep roots, I am afraid they are so entwined with the roots of the wheat that they cannot be separated without risk to the wheat. What can we do, you ask? Listen to what Christ advises: "Let both of them grow together until the harvest" (Matt 13:30). So, my cautious Myconius, gold must be purified with fire and silver cleansed of its tarnish. Accordingly, Christ told the apostles: "In the world you will face persecution" (John 16:33); and another time he said: "You will be hated by all because of my name" (Matt 10:22); and again: "The hour is coming when those who kill you will think that by doing so they are offering worship to God" (John 16:2). Even after they were finally permitted to live in the land promised to them, the children of Israel were never free of the Philistines, who molested them, led them into idolatry and disobedience to the commandments, and turned the Israelites into pagans.

We Christians will never lack people who persecute Christ in us, even though they make a show of coming themselves in the name of Christ. Genuine Christians, however, are those who have the mark by which Christ indicated he would acknowledge his own, when he said that everyone will recognize that you are my disciples when you keep my commandments (John 13:35; 15:14). Those who obey human law more than the divine plainly lack the sign of Christ, because they give priority to their own commandments over those of Christ. When you are molested by those people, then, it is grist for your mill; think of them as the flies of Egypt, as the Canaanites, the Perizzites, the Amorites, the Hittites, and the Jebusites who wish to draw you over to their side. They allow you to win the crown when you fight against them. Human life on earth is like military service. Armed with the weapons of Paul, those who will earn honor for themselves must fight bravely in the frontline if, with three bright stones, they wish to dash to the ground a world that has elevated itself like Goliath (1 Sam 17:49).

Now you will object and ask: "What shall we teach those who are given into our care when we see that all loving efforts are in vain and that no one, or at least only a few, obeys the gospel and apostolic teaching?" Here is my answer: you must work even harder to show as many as possible this pearl, which most people either scorn or ignore but which gleams with a unique beauty, so that they find it precious and sell all they have to obtain it (Matt 13:46). Did not Christ speak about different kinds of seeds, only some of which fall upon good ground (Matt 13:3–9)? Did he not say that he had come to bring fire to the earth and that he wished it were already kindled (Luke 12:49)? There is no better interpretation of that fire than steadfastness against temptation, a steadfastness that our parents hate when they lure us back to unfaithfulness and that commands the brother about to kill us to be still. Is not this the fire that exposes the deeds of everyone and reveals whether they enter the battle for the honor of the world or the honor of Christ? If for worldly honor, they are like the stubble that goes up in smoke as soon as the fire of judgment touches it (Matt 3:12); memory of it is gone as soon as the crackling can no longer be heard. If for the honor of Christ, however, they are like a smart householder who builds his house upon the rock (Matt 7:24), that is, Christ, and cannot be singed when it catches on fire. All who are built upon the same rock, that is, who fight for the honor of Christ and not for their own, remain unharmed for eternity. Neither death nor life nor sword nor anything else the apostle names can separate them from his love (Rom 8:35–39); they have been admonished to seek after the same victory to which he referred: "But take courage; I have conquered the world" (John 16:33).

What does it mean for Christ to say I have conquered the world? Does it mean that in some fashion I have also conquered it? To be sure, we have conquered it in him because he has conquered, but we conquer only in him. "Not that we are competent of ourselves to claim anything as coming from us; our competence is from God" (2 Cor 3:5). The one who is true said "take courage," as if he wanted to say, "If you place all your confidence in me, you will also conquer just as I have conquered, so take courage."

I say all this in order to hasten the battle that is already under way and hurries toward its end, to win for Christ as many soldiers as possible who will then fight boldly for him. Admonish them long and hard, so that the more cruelly they are persecuted the less shamefully they will respond. For this I tell you plainly: just as the church was born through blood, only through blood can she be renewed. Therefore, always teach Christ to those who belong to you. The more ignorance you see in his church, the better you should equip people, so that like Hercules they can shovel out the manure of many steers without being put off or vexed by the swarms of flies that buzz around them.[1] In this world, of course, they can expect no reward, nor can they complain when they bitterly offend people. They have to keep quiet and say to themselves, "If I wanted to please other people, I would not be a servant of Christ," or, to sum it up, "Blessed are those who are persecuted for righteousness' sake, for theirs is the kingdom of heaven" (Matt 5:10). The world will never be on good terms with Christ; persecution [of the faithful] has been promised even for the time when Christ will exact payment. He sent his own like sheep among wolves (Matt 10:16). My brother, consider how you can be a sheep of Christ. You will be one for certain when you do everything for the honor of Christ, even when the fiercest band of wolves threaten you with death or when they crush you with their teeth and flay you with their claws.

I have no fear for Luther's life and none whatsoever for his soul even if he is struck by the ban, the lightning bolt of that Jupiter.[2] I do not belittle the ecclesiastical ban, but if a condemnation is unjust, I believe it affects the body more than the soul. It is not for us to decide whether Luther is being treated justly or unjustly. You know already what my views are. In the next few days I will approach the papal commissary, William,[3] and as soon as he brings it up, I will advise him to urge the pope not to place Luther under the ban because it would be a serious mistake. If he does excommunicate Luther, the Germans will despise not only the ban but also the pope.

You, however, take courage. Our age will always have people who teach Christ purely and are willing to risk their life for him. What does it matter if they are defamed after this life by those who say (not for the first time in our day): "They were heretics, seducers, charlatans"? Those who talk like that also consider people of integrity to be seducers. As far as my reputation is concerned, for a long time I have reconciled myself to slander from all sides, clerical and lay. I ask for only one thing: that Christ enable me to bear it all with a stout heart and that he break or harden me, his vessel, as it suits him. If I am placed under the ban, I will remember Hilary, the learned and holy man who was forced to leave France and go to Africa,[4] and Lucius, who was chased from his see in Rome and was nevertheless able to return home in high esteem.[5] Not that I am comparing myself to them, but I would take comfort in their example since they, who were much better than we are, had to endure so much indignity. If I might boast a little, I would rejoice to suffer shame for the sake of Christ. But let those who think they are standing take heed lest they fall (1 Cor 10:12).

We have read almost nothing more by Luther, but in our opinion what we have seen so far does not depart from evangelical teaching. You understand if you remember the main reason I commended him in the first place: he supports what he says with solid evidence.

You ask about the meaning of the Greek word *oikonomia*, but I should ask you about it instead. So that you will not think I am denying you a favor, I will give you my opinion, although I have only briefly looked into it. Since I have not read the *Rhetoric* of Melanchthon from beginning to end,[6] I deserve to be forgiven if what I say sounds like my own imaginings. Melanchthon first describes three levels of elocution: elegant, ordinary, and humble. Then he identifies some characteristics that would enable us to recognize each level not only from its style but also from its subject matter. In his opinion classical writers were such prudent stewards of speech and diction that they avoided as best they could describing sublime matters with an ordinary style or flat locution. Nor did they ever forget themselves to such an extent that instead of explaining a simple matter they obliterated it with a pretentious style or suffocated it with grandiose and arrogant language. Accordingly, I think *oikonomia*, which otherwise means an orderly arrangement or distribution, stands here for that which is proper, fitting, and appropriate, so that one might refer to an *oikonomia* of style that is appropriate to the subject. Moreover, those with less rhetorical training could discern the style from the subject matter to which writers fit the style.

I have decided to resume in the next few days the study of Hebrew; then, if Christ wills, next December and the following Lent I will lecture on the Psalms to a group of beginners. Please ask Xylotectus[7] to return to me the *Rudimenta* of Reuchlin[8] within a month. I have no idea whether or not I can attend the *Primiz*,[9] now that Utinger has left for therapy in the waters at Baden. Nevertheless, commend me to Xylotectus, the musician, and to all of those with you.

Forgive this very confused letter. It has grown so noisy around my house that most of the time I cannot concentrate and am on the verge of moving somewhere else (anywhere in the world would suit me), if I cannot carry on my work in more suitable conditions. But keep quiet about this!

Farewell in Christ.
Zürich, the day before the feast of James,
the son of Zebedee, 1520.

2. Martin Luther, Letter to His Father, Hans Luther, November 21, 1521

This letter of dedication, written to his father in 1521, was printed in 1522 as the preface to Luther's *Judgment on Monastic Vows,* one of the major works that flowed from Luther's pen during his exile at the Wartburg Castle in 1521 and 1522. After he was declared an outlaw at the Diet of Worms, his sympathetic prince, Elector Frederick of Saxony, had Luther kidnapped and taken to the Wartburg in order to protect Luther and to give himself time to decide how to react. Back in Wittenberg, where Luther had lived at the Augustinian monastery and taught at the university, Luther's colleagues made changes to the mass while some monastic brothers broke their vows and left the cloister.

At the Wartburg Castle Luther was forced to rethink the nature of monastic vows and his own identity as a monk. His conclusions about vows in general were prefaced by the following letter, in which he pronounced judgment on his life as a monk and recounted his father's strong opposition and its impact on him. Sixteen years after he entered the Augustinian order, Luther gives credit to God's foresight and to his father for being right after all and caring about his future. He also articulates a new religious role for himself that requires neither monastic vows nor papal obedience.

Translation of the Latin text in WA 8, 573–76.

Greetings in Christ from his son, Martin Luther, to his father, Hans Luther.

I have not dedicated this book[10] to you, dearest father, in order to make you famous or to glory in the flesh against the teaching of Paul (Gal 6:13). Instead, I am seizing this occasion to recall in a short prologue what happened between you and me in order to illustrate for pious readers the reason for writing this book.

To begin with, I wish you to know that your son is now persuaded there is nothing holier, nothing more important, nothing more religiously to be observed than the divine commandment.[11] You will say: "Did you at one time doubt this, poor soul, and only now realize it to be true?" Even worse, I not only doubted it, but I was also completely unaware of it. Now let me show you that this ignorance was shared by us both.

16

Almost sixteen years have passed since I became a monk[12] without your knowledge or approval. Your fatherly affection made you worry about my vulnerability, because I was by then a young man entering my twenty-second year (in the words of Augustine, I was still "clothed in fervent youth"[13]), and in many cases you had seen how the monastic life led to an unfortunate end. You resolved therefore, to tie me down in a respectable and wealthy marriage. This fear of yours was an expression of your care [for me], and for a while your anger at me could not be placated. Friends attempted to persuade you without success to give your most precious possession if you wanted to offer something to God. Meanwhile, the Lord was drumming into your head this verse: "The Lord knows our thoughts, that they are but an empty breath" (Ps 94:11), but it fell on deaf ears.

At last you gave up and submitted your will to God, but without laying aside your fears on my behalf. As if it were yesterday,[14] after you had calmed down and were speaking to me again, I remember telling you that I had been summoned by terrors from heaven. I did not become a monk because I wanted to, even less for reasons of the flesh, but because I was besieged by the fear and agony of sudden death and felt compelled to take the vow.[15] Your reply was: "I hope it was not an illusion or a trick." Those words penetrated my soul and stayed deep within, as if God had spoken through you; nevertheless, as much as possible, I hardened my heart against you and your words. You said something else. When like a trusting son I reproached you for having been angry, you came back at me with a sudden retort so timely and so pertinent that in all my life I have never heard anything that was more powerful and stuck with me so long. "Have you not also heard," you said, "that parents should be obeyed?" But convinced of my own rectitude I heard in you only a man speaking and I ignored you with disdain, although in my heart I could not disregard what you had said.

See now whether or not you also failed to realize that the commandments of God take priority over everything else. If you had known that I was still obliged to obey you, would you not have used your paternal authority to strip the cowl from me? At the same time, if I had known it, I would never have become a monk without your knowledge and consent, even though I had to die a thousand deaths. My vow was worth nothing, since by taking it I withdrew myself from parental authority and direction that are commanded by God; more than that, it was an ungodly vow, not only because I sinned against your authority, but because it was not free and voluntary. Moreover, it was taken in harmony with human teaching and the superstition of hypocrites, none of which God has commanded. But God, whose mercies are innumerable and whose wisdom is infinite (Lam 3:22; Rom 11:33), brought so much good, as you can see, out of all these errors and sins! Would you not rather have lost a hundred sons than to have missed seeing this blessing?

From my childhood Satan must have anticipated some of the things that he now has to bear. He therefore tried all sorts of mad tricks to destroy or hinder me, so that I often wondered if I was the only person in the world under attack. But it was the Lord's will, I see now, that I should experience firsthand (through many sins and impieties, as it were) the wisdom of the schools and the holiness of the monasteries, so that wicked people would have no occasion, when I became their opponent, to boast that I was condemning things that were foreign to me. Hence I lived faultlessly as a monk, but of course not without sin; for in the kingdom of the pope godlessness and sacrilege are scarcely thought of as crimes but regarded as the highest forms of piety.

What do you think now, father? Would you still strip the cowl from me? You are still my father and I am still your son and vows carry no weight. On your side is the authority of God, on my side only human presumption. The sexual abstinence that they crow about avails not a thing without obedience to what God commands. Abstinence is not commanded but obedience is, yet the mad and foolish papists will not suffer any virtue to be put on the same level with abstinence and virginity. They exalt both with such shameless lies that their obsession with lying and the enormity of their ignorance, one or both, ought to render suspect everything they do or think. How intelligent can they be when they twist the words of the wise man, "No scales can weigh the value of her chastity" (Sir 26:15), to mean that one should prefer virginity and abstinence to anything else and that such vows may not be recanted or annulled? In fact, a Jew wrote these words about a chaste wife to other Jews, for whom virginity and abstinence were not virtues. The papists even apply to virgins another verse that praises the faithful wife "who has not entered into a sinful union" (Wis 3:13). In short, although scripture only approves virginity without praising it, those who are willing to endanger salvation by inflaming the soul dress up virginity, as it were, with fancy feathers by applying to it the praise given to a chaste marriage.[16]

Is it not true, however, that an obedient soul is also of great value? Accordingly, a chaste soul (that is, a faithful wife), has inestimable value, not only because it is commanded by God but also because, as the familiar saying has it, nothing in the world is more desirable than a faithful wife.[17] But those so-called faithful interpreters of scripture take what is said about the continence that is commanded (that is, fidelity in marriage) and apply it to the continence that is not commanded (that is, abstinence), thereby turning [their own] human opinion into God's view. The papists grant dispensations from everything, even from obedience to God, but they grant no dispensation from vows of abstinence that are unlawful because they were taken against parental authority. What petty doctors and teachers you are, truly deserving of the label papistic! Virginity and chastity should indeed be praised, but in such a way that their heavy demands scare us off instead of attracting us. That is how Christ spoke about it. When the disciples were praising abstinence, saying, "If such is the case of a man with his wife, it is better not to marry," he corrected them at once and said, "Not everyone can accept this teaching" (Matt 19:10–11). People should be aware of this precept, but Christ wanted it to be fully understood by only a few.

Let me come back to you, father: would you still take me out of the monastery? To keep you from boasting of it, the Lord anticipated you and has himself withdrawn me. What difference does it make whether I keep the cowl and tonsure or do away with them? They do not make a monk, do they? "All belong to you, and you belong to Christ," says Paul (1 Cor 3:22–23). Shall I then belong to the cowl, or does it not rather belong to me? My conscience has been liberated, and that is by far the greatest freedom I can have. I am thus still a monk and yet not a monk. I am a new creature, not of the pope but of Christ. The pope also creates, but he can only construct cardboard puppets, masks, and idols that are like him. I used to be one of them, deceived by different ways of speaking that brought even the wise man to the brink of death before he was delivered by God's grace (Sir 34:12–13).

Am I not robbing you again of your rightful authority? Not at all, because you still have authority over me as far as the monastic life is concerned; but that life means nothing to me anymore, as I said. Now that God has pulled me out of the monastery, his authority over me is greater than yours. You see, I have not been left in the made-up cult of the monastery but have now been placed in the true service of God. Who could doubt that I am in the ministry of the word? Parental authority must clearly defer to God's service, for Christ says: "Whoever loves father or mother more than me is not worthy of me" (Matt 10:37). This verse does not overturn parental authority, for the apostle insists that children should obey their parents (Eph 6:1; Col 3:20), but if it clashes with the authority or calling of Christ, then Christ's authority shall alone hold sway.

I am now convinced that the only way my refusal to obey you could not have endangered my conscience is for the ministry of the word to have superseded my monastic profession. Before that happened, as I said, neither you nor I realized that God's commandments must take priority over everything else. Virtually the whole world still suffers from this same ignorance while error holds sway under the detestable rule of the pope. Paul predicted this very situation when he said that children would become disobedient to their parents (2 Tim 3:2). That prediction squares exactly with the monks and priests of today, especially those who feigning piety and pretending to serve God pay no heed to the authority of parents, as if there were another way to serve God than to keep the commandments, including obedience to parents.

I am sending you, then, this book,[18] in which you can see by what prodigious feats Christ has absolved me from the monastic vow and endowed me with such abundant freedom that, although he made me a servant of everyone, I am nevertheless subject to no one but him. He is himself my immediate bishop (as they call it), abbot, prior, lord, father, and teacher. I acknowledge no other superior. Christ has therefore taken from you one son, I hope, so that through me he may begin to help many more of his children. You should not only tolerate this willingly, but you ought to be greatly pleased, as I am quite certain you will be. So what if the pope should kill me or damn me to the depths of hell! He will not raise up the one he has killed to slay me a second and third time; nor do I, having been once condemned by him,[19] have any desire ever to be pardoned. I am confident we have arrived at the day on which that kingdom of abomination and perdition will be destroyed. Before that happens, I wish we were worthy enough to be burned or slain by him, so that our blood might cry out even more loudly to hasten the day on which he is judged! If we do not deserve to bear witness with our blood, then let us at least pray for enough mercy to testify with life and voice that Jesus Christ alone is the Lord our God, who is blessed forevermore. Amen.

Farewell in the Lord, dearest father, and greet my mother, your Margaret,[20] and all our relatives in Christ. From the wilderness,[21] November 21, 1521.

3. Argula von Grumbach, To the Noble and Honorable Adam von Thering, the Count Palatine's Administrator in Neuburg...An Open Letter from Argula von Grumbach, née von Stauff, 1523

Argula von Stauff was the first German woman to defend the Protestant Reformation in print. Born around 1492 of nobility in the upper Palatinate, she was sent as a young girl to the court of the Bavarian duke in Munich where she became a lady-in-waiting to Duchess Kunigunde, sister of Emperor Maximilian. She eventually married Friedrich von Grumbach, the ducal deputy in Dietfurt, and they had four children. After her letters favoring the Reformation appeared in print in 1523 and 1524, nothing further was published, but she did visit Luther at the Coburg (northern Bavaria) in 1530. Her death is undocumented, reported as between 1554 and 1568.

In 1523 she defended publicly the evangelical beliefs of Arsacius Seehofer, an instructor at the University of Ingolstadt (Bavaria) who was accused of being Lutheran. When her outspokenness offended Adam von Thering (Törring), her mother's cousin, she defended herself in the following letter. It demonstrates both her knowledge of the Bible and the strength of her evangelical convictions.

From *Argula von Grumbach: A Woman's Voice in the Reformation*, 141–49. The title of the printed letter is slightly different from the original address.

To the noble and honorable lord Adam von Thering, my gracious lord the Count Palatine's administrator in Neuburg,…my dear lord and cousin.

The grace and peace of God and the presence of his Holy Spirit be with you, my beloved lord and cousin. I have been told that you were informed of my letter to the University of Ingolstadt and that this made you more than a little angry with me. Perhaps you thought it unbecoming of me as a foolish woman—which is, of course, exactly how I see myself. However, the wisdom needed to confess God does not derive from human reason but is to be seen as a gift of God. From this has come—and more may yet come—much malicious gossip on the part of the worldly wise, tending to my disgrace, shame, or ridicule.

As my family friend, you also paid careful attention to this [gossip]. I conclude from this that you love me as your family friend, and for this I express to you my deep and sincere thanks. For it is obvious to me that if you did not mean me well, you would have paid little heed to any gossip about me, whether good or evil. In recognition of what is clearly your friendship to me, I have been moved to write to you to advise you of the truth of the matter. I am therefore sending you a copy of what I have written, which I beseech you to read faithfully and to judge me according to the Spirit of God.

For the wisdom of the world cannot comprehend God's Spirit, as Hosea shows: there is nothing good in human nature, but what is in us is sin; I will change their glory into shame (Hos 4:7).[22] And Paul says, human wisdom is foolishness to God (1 Cor 1:25; 3:19). If I have acted wrongly I will, of course, gladly endure the punishment. But do not think you should be criticizing me, for no one should criticize us for doing what God has commanded us to do. In this case, too, I am not under constraint to obey anyone at all, for I vowed at baptism to believe in God, to confess him, and to renounce the devil and all his illusions. I can never hope to fulfill such a lofty vow until I am born anew through death. For while we live in the flesh we are sinners. As it says in the Book of Proverbs: "Who can say 'I have made my heart clean; I am pure from my sin'?" (Prov 20:9). And in Jeremiah: "Cursed are those who trust in mere mortals," but "blessed are those who trust in the Lord" (Jer 17:5, 7).

Now you well know that we all make the same vow: I believe, I renounce, et cetera. Which doctor has made a greater vow in baptism than I have? Which pope, or emperor, or prince? Every day I pray God for grace to be able to fulfill the vow that was made on my behalf by my godfather. Now that I have come to understand it, having been instructed in the Christian faith, I have accepted and affirmed it, and [my vow] is confirmed by my faith.

Therefore do not be astonished, my dear lord and cousin, that I confess God; for whoever does not confess God is no Christian, though he be baptized a thousand times. We must all give an account of ourselves at the last judgment. Neither pope, king, prince, nor doctor will settle my account. That is what I keep in mind. Nor will wealth be any help, as Ezekiel says: "Their silver and gold cannot save them on the day of the wrath of the Lord," and "When anguish comes, they will seek peace but there shall be none" (Ezek 7:19, 25). And Hosea: "For they sow the wind, and they shall reap the whirlwind" (Hos 8:7). Such is the fate of those who trust in riches and all its works.

So, my beloved lord and cousin, I beg you not to be vexed if you hear that I am being abused or ridiculed because I confess Christ. Be alarmed only if you hear that I have denied God (which may God forfend). I count it a great honor to be abused for the sake of God's honor; and it is a trifle to be cursed by those whom God has shamed and blinded for trusting in their human wisdom. For it says in Isaiah: "All people are grass, their constancy is like the flower of the field,...the flower fades,...but the word of our God will stand forever" (Isa 40:6–8). I speak as Paul did in his first chapter to the Galatians: "If I were still pleasing people, I would not be a servant of Christ" (Gal 1:10). For God says in Hosea: "You know no God but me, and besides me there is no savior" (Hos 13:4). And John: "The one who rejects me and does not receive my word has a judge" (John 12:48).

It is our preachers who prevent us from recognizing God, for the Lord says in Jeremiah: "My people have been lost sheep; their shepherds have led them astray" (Jer 50:6), and "The word of the Lord is to them an object of scorn; they take no pleasure in it" (Jer 6:10), and "For the shepherds are stupid and do not inquire of the Lord; therefore they have not prospered, and all their flock is scattered" (Jer 10:21), and "You pervert the words of the living God,... and I will bring upon you everlasting disgrace and perpetual shame, which will not be forgotten" (Jer 23:36, 40). Paul says in Second Timothy: "They will accumulate for themselves teachers to suit their own desires, and will turn away from listening to the truth and wander away to myths" (2 Tim 4:3–4). How often did our faithful shepherd Christ warn us to beware of false prophets and their teaching (Matt 7:15)! He calls it sour yeast, a little of which can leaven a large amount of dough, as in Matthew (Matt 16:6; 1 Cor 5:6).

In Matthew, when [Christ] is transfigured, it says: "This is my Son, the beloved; with him I am well pleased; listen to him" (Matt 17:5). In Isaiah: "My glory I give to no other" (Isa 42:8). And in John: "But to all who received him..., he gave power to become children of God" (John 1:12). I am called a follower of Luther, but I am not. I was baptized in the name of Christ; it is him I confess and not Luther. But I confess that Martin, too, as a faithful Christian, confesses him. God help us never to deny him, whether faced by disgrace, abuse, imprisonment, breaking on the wheel, and even death. God helps and enables all Christians in this matter. Amen.

You are reported to have said that if my own husband would not do it, some friend or relative should act and wall me up. But do not believe him.[23] Alas, [my husband] is doing far too much to persecute Christ in me. In Second Corinthians Paul says that we endure all things without complaint for the name of the Lord (2 Cor 4:8–11). So it is no difficulty for me, and I am not liable to obey my husband in this matter, for God says in Matthew that we must forsake father, mother, brother, sister, children, life and limb (Matt 10:21, 37). And then says in Mark: "For what will it profit them to gain the whole world and forfeit their life? Indeed, what can they give in return for their life" (Mark 8:36–37)?

That's the way it is; otherwise, God says he will not acknowledge us. But forsaking friendship, honor, property, and life does not appeal to the flesh. Of ourselves we are as feeble as St. Peter, who promised to die with the Lord, then denied him three times (Matt 26:35, 75). God allowed him to see what it means to be human, but finally God gave him the Spirit that enabled him to die joyfully for the sake of the Lord. God must give this Spirit, not flesh and blood. What does the Lord say in Matthew: Whoever asks God for a good spirit will be given it from the Father?[24]

I cannot pity our authorities enough, who are not taking this to heart at all. I have yet to meet one, either in the clerical or the secular realm, who was prepared to undertake the reading of the Bible so he could discover with certainty God's command. Instead they all curse, kill, and rage away, devoid of all knowledge and grounding in scripture. And still no one denounces such behavior as unchristian.

What Christian could keep silence in this situation? To say that God has spoken means no more to them than if some fool or grotesque figure had spoken. All this is because they are as well informed about the Bible as a cow is about chess. It is certainly not my task to deal with their stock retort: "I believe what my parents believed." But that is not the end of the matter. All Christians do have a responsibility to know the word of God. Paul says that faith comes from hearing (Rom 10:17). The princes and much of the nobility are the same. I have heard many say: If my mother and father are in hell, I do not want to go to heaven. Not me! Even if all my friends were there (God forbid), I fear they could not do much to entertain me!

It is the fault of the parents for failing to have their children taught. If by chance they have been to school, they are taught Terence[25] and Ovid[26] because it has always been done. But what is in these books? How to make love, be lechers and whores, and so forth. That is an option, for sure, and every level of society is full of people like that, whether married or not, who boast about it rather than being ashamed of it. Sadly, it has come to the point where whores and their partners often show more fidelity to each other than occurs in marriage.

This surely fulfils the words of St. Paul in First Corinthians: "It is actually reported that there is sexual immorality among you, and of a kind that is not found even among pagans" (1 Cor 5:1).

From this arises whining, quarreling, fighting, and violence. No peace, day or night; prosperity and morale plummet. There is no way out whatever a woman does, and so often it leads her to disaster. May God preserve all who fight against it and help those who have fallen to rise again. Everyone turns a blind eye, and if one complains to friends about it, one meets with laughter. It does no good to criticize; even the authorities have cut their cloth from the same bolt.[27]

I have scant enthusiasm or expectation about this meeting of the imperial diet[28] that has been summoned. May God send his Spirit to teach them to recognize the truth when they see it, so that this diet deserves its name and we become rich[29] in soul and body, all be governed in true Christian faith, and the wealth of land and people no longer be dissipated, making us poorer still. If as much attention were given to God's word as to eating, drinking, banqueting, gambling, masques, and the like, things would soon improve. I can remember hundreds of thousands of florins being wasted in such diets, and to what purpose? You know better than I! What deliberation is possible when they are so busy gorging themselves day and night that they can hardly sit upright?

I have seen it all at Nuremberg myself; that childish behavior on the part of the princes will be before my eyes as long as I live.[30] But, oh, how difficult it will be when the Lord says: "Give me an accounting of your management, because you cannot be my manager any longer" (Luke 16:2). And what does God say in Hosea: "They made kings, but not through me; they set up princes, but without my knowledge" (Hos 8:4)? May God remedy matters, so that they do not perish like Pharaoh for all their splendor. May the princes in their deliberations comprehend the word of God—not that the word of God should be subject to them, but rather that they may be subject to the same sure and steadfast word of God.

Therefore, my beloved lord and cousin, I plead with you as a friend to devote yourself to holy scripture. You have long been a counselor of princes; it is now time for you to take counsel for your own immortal soul by at least reading through the four Gospels before you die. May God grant, however, that you may read the whole Bible, the book that contains all the commands of God. It was never Luther's intent, after all, that one should have faith in his books; they should serve simply as guidebooks to the word of God. You could do a great deal of good in your territory, especially if you were to see to it that the posts of pastor and preacher were occupied by learned men. For all salvation is wrought by the word of God, as it says in Isaiah: For as the rain gives food and seed to the sower, and makes the earth green, so does the word that goes out from my mouth; it does not return to me without fruit.[31] And in Jeremiah: "Is not my word like fire, says the Lord, and like a hammer that breaks a rock in pieces?" (Jer 23:29).

I have been told they wish to deprive my husband of his office. I cannot help that; I weighed all the consequences carefully beforehand. It will not stand in the way of my salvation, as was the case with Pilate.[32] I am prepared to lose everything, even life and limb. May God stand by me! Of myself I can do nothing but sin. Pray to God earnestly for me, that he may increase my faith. Even if it should mean the end of me, do not regard that as a disgrace but rather praise God. Had I the grace, my soul would be like a precious jewel to the Lord God.

The property they can take from me is almost nothing. You know that my father was ruined under the princes of Bavaria and his children became beggars, although they have treated me and my children well by giving employment to my husband. May God be their reward. Although the priests of Würzburg have devoured my husband's property,[33] God will surely care for my four children and send the birds of the air to feed them and clothe them with the flowers of the field.[34] He has said it; he cannot lie.

I had intended to keep my writing private; now I see that God wishes to have it made public. That I am now abused for this is a good indication that it is of God, for if the world were to praise it, it would not be of God. Therefore, my beloved lord and cousin, I commend you now and forever to the grace of God; may it be with you now and forever. Grunbach [*sic*].

Argula von Grunbach, née von Stauffen

4. Martin Bucer, Answer to the Bishop's Accusations against Him Addressed to the City Council of Strasbourg, 1523

In the sixteenth century Strasbourg was a prominent German-speaking city in the Holy Roman Empire and the see of a Roman bishop. Martin Bucer (1491–1551) was the leading reformer of that city, who also attempted to reconcile Zwinglians and Lutherans during the early years of the Reformation.

Alsatian by birth, Bucer entered the Dominican Order as a teenager and was chosen to study in Heidelberg. Bucer's initial interest in evangelical ideas was confirmed by Martin Luther's defense of his famous theses in Heidelberg in 1518. By 1523, Bucer had left the cloister, married Elisabeth Silbereisen, tried his hand as a reformer in the town of Wissembourg (north of Strasbourg), and was excommunicated by the bishop of Speyer. His move to Strasbourg in 1523 involved him in a stiff but successful campaign to sway the city council toward reform against both the bishop and the emperor. In 1549, Bucer was forced to leave Strasbourg because he refused to accept the city's decision to comply with the interim agreement, imposed by Emperor Charles V, that would reverse changes made by the Reformation. Bucer accepted an invitation to Cambridge from Archbishop Thomas Cranmer, but he died after only two years in England.

In 1523 Bucer arrived in Strasbourg as a married and excommunicated ex-monk. The bishop of Strasbourg wanted to take action against him and asked the city council, with which he was already in conflict, to revoke the safe conduct it had granted to Bucer and his wife. When the council invited Bucer to defend himself, he composed the following statement that was read to the council on June 20, 1523. In addition to protesting that he sought "to maintain a true and sound faith and a devout way of life in the calling to which the Almighty calls me," Bucer delivered a spirited and multifaceted defense of clerical marriage, the issue that ignited the Reformation in Strasbourg.

Translated from the German text in *Martin Bucers Deutsche Schriften*, vol. 1: *Frühschriften 1520–1524*, 293–301.

My distinguished, wise, and gracious lords, I am forever your willing and diligent servant.

At your direction the wise and noble city officials, Egenolff Röder and Niclaus Kniebis, read to me the detestable letter that my gracious lord [the bishop] of Strasbourg sent to you on my account. He indicates that he has received various reports accusing me of improper and offensive behavior and requests that you withdraw the safe conduct granted to me so that he can take action and banish me from this diocese. Since it was too difficult for me to answer his letter in person, the officials allowed me to put my response in writing and address it to your graces, the worthy magistrates of my homeland, whom I am willing and obligated by divine law to obey in all external matters that concern honor, body, or possessions. This is my response to the bishop's charges and my own humble and truthful conviction. And I thank God almighty with particular diligence that he has given me cause to present a short account of my teaching and life. I have always sought the light and never avoided it, but until now I have received no public hearing, although here and elsewhere I have been slandered and criticized as if my character did not conform to Christian teaching.

(1) On the first point—that my gracious lord of Strasbourg claims he has heard from several sources that I lead an improper life that causes offense to the common and unlearned folk—my lord has been misled. God is my witness that I intend nothing other than to maintain a true and sound faith and a devout way of life in the calling to which the Almighty calls me, and with the gifts that he has bestowed on me to serve my neighbor as faithfully and diligently as I can in this place or wherever God might call me, as indeed I am obligated to do. If anyone can present words or actions that show I have a different intention, I would deserve a threefold punishment from your gracious lords for every just charge against me. I have not and cannot now profitably serve the people who support me by any means other than preaching and lecturing, and I promised some folk to do that in German. When both parties became aware that you gentlemen were not pleased with this arrangement, perhaps because it would have drawn too large a crowd to an unsuitable location, we dropped the plan and I decided to lecture in Latin on St. Paul's Epistle to Timothy for those who could understand the language. I only did this, however, on the condition that I would give myself over to death (Deut 13:5) if anyone discovered that I

taught something that was not expressed in scripture or failed to increase faith, to enkindle love, or to implant and strengthen true humility, patience, peace, obedience, and submission.

In no way do I wish to offend anybody, educated or uneducated. I am a burgher's son and a poor Christian, and to my knowledge I have never insulted anyone or engaged in improper behavior that could justly be held against me or unjustly affect my reputation. With all that I have learned and received from God that is divinely good and useful, I have undertaken to serve the welfare of my neighbors, so that I am not supported in vain by them or by others. People who are not willing to work in the community but allow their idle ways to be supported by it are called busybodies by St. Paul and commanded to earn their own living (2 Thess 3:11–12).

(2) The second charge that my lord bishop brought against me—that I have a wife—I have admitted to his vicar, but at the same time I defended my divine and human right in the matter so well that he was not able to refute me. I have also offered to uphold my marriage as legal and just before the bishop himself or any suitable judge who does not place human law over divine. If God wills that I should defend my marriage in front of your graces against all those who think it is illegal, it would certainly meet with your approval and not bring displeasure. For none can deny that in Genesis God has given to all people and also planted in nature his command to "be fruitful and multiply" (Gen 1:28; 9:7). Only those who have received from God the exceptional gift and capacity to live chastely apart from marriage (barely one in a thousand as one can see) and, thus freed from everything else, to cleave to God and divine things alone are exempt from this command. The rest are unable to live apart from marriage without falling into sin and disgrace.

Therefore, St. Paul says: "It is better to marry than to be aflame with passion" (1 Cor 7:9); and none can escape marriage except those who belong to the small number whom God himself has exempted. For according to Christ these matters can be grasped only by those to whom it is given: "Let anyone accept this who can" (Matt 19:12). God gave no commandment or vow on this matter but left it free. No Christian authority can rob me of this freedom, because all Christian authority is given by God to use for our benefit and for God, not against God or to our ruin (2 Cor 10:8). Marriage, therefore, is not only a choice for some but a command for all those whom God has not exempted. For that reason St. Paul also writes: "To avoid whoredom each man should have his own wife and each woman her own husband" (1 Cor 7:2). On the advice of pious, wise, and learned people I have tried also in this case to follow the divine commandment. No human law has stood in the way, as indeed it cannot, since I have never in my life taken a valid vow not to marry; this fact was acknowledged by the papal instructor, the worthy father and lord Anton Engelbrecht,[35] doctor of holy scripture and bishop coadjutant of Speyer. And even though I had already taken a vow, because it was against God's commandment and impossible for me to obey, it did not have power to bind me, and I had to obey God rather than human authority (Acts 5:29). According to divine law we should not only avoid evil but even the appearance of evil, and in God's eyes a fornicator is so contemptible that by command of the Holy Spirit, if the fornicator happens to be called a Christian, other Christians are forbidden to eat with that person (1 Cor 5:11).

In order for me and everyone, therefore, to be conscientious and to protect ourselves not only from unchastity but even from the suspicion and appearance of immorality, it would have been impossible for me to remain unmarried, since God had not exempted me. In every sense it was fitting for me to ignore human law, custom, and opinion, and not to presume that I was greater than I am or wish to appear holier than St. Peter and the other apostles of Christ, who took their wives around with them as they preached the Christian faith (1 Cor 9:5). At two places where he describes the qualifications of a Christian bishop and priest, Paul requires that he be above reproach and the husband of one wife (1 Tim 3:2). As a result, in order to arrange my life in a way that would please God and sincerely pious believers, I have taken a Christian spouse. I did keep my marriage secret for a while, as did Abraham and Isaac (Gen 12:11–20; 20:1–18; 26:6–11), so that those who were against God's word would hinder me as little as possible in the preaching of that word, but I never denied that I was married. To avoid having my behavior interpreted as a sign that I regarded my marriage as shameful and ungodly and thereby offending others and setting a bad example for those who have not received the gift of living chastely apart from marriage, I did not wish to keep my marriage secret any longer because that which is right and just does not shun the light. I had reason to expect that so many clear evangelical sermons would have been preached in this town and that knowledge of God's word had come so far here that, as a result, the good majority would rather see me lead my life according to God's command and the way the Holy Spirit describes it through Paul (namely, for a priest to marry) than for me to appear holier than others and yet live under suspicion or in open immorality as unfortunately we see on all sides. I sincerely hope that your gracious lords will not be troubled by the outcry of badly informed people who oppose God's word out of custom and long usage that are not against my actions but against God's command, especially since Christ and the apostles so often predicted that in these last days many damaging customs, laws, and commands would rise up under the false appearance of doing good (Matt 24:24–26; 2 Pet 2:1–3). St. Paul says specifically: "In later times some will renounce the faith by paying attention to deceitful spirits and teachings of demons, through the hypocrisy of liars whose consciences are seared with a hot iron. They forbid marriage" (1 Tim 4:1–3).

In addition, I will obey the recently published imperial mandate that requires all priests who marry and all monks and clergy who leave their orders to renounce all benefices and clerical exemptions. I desire to have no special privilege that other Christians and laypeople do not have, and like a layperson I will recognize civil authority in all matters, obey it as far as I can in those things that affect my honor, body, and property, just as I and others like me are obligated to do by divine law. If I am justly accused by you of refusing obedience in these matters, I wish to be punished. I ask only one thing: Allow me to serve my neighbors with the gifts God has given me and like everyone else to support myself by what I do. My marriage should not in any way keep me from preaching and teaching what is godly and good, just as St. Paul would have every bishop or supervisory cleric be a person who is married (1 Tim 3:2; Titus 1:5–6). Nor do I desire any benefices; my spiritual service will be beneficial for everyone, and I have no doubt that God, who feeds even the birds (Matt 6:26), will see to it that I have all the worldly goods I need. If benefices and exemption from ordinary duties belong to those who are not married, then they are justly withdrawn from me and all those who have married. Since, however, marrying is not a sin for anyone, I hope that I am not denied the common privilege that all enjoy, that is, to serve my neighbor and earn my living with what I have learned, because I am not trained for anything else.

Even harsh papal decrees go no further, and those that are somewhat Christian, like the decrees of the Synod of Gangra, place under the ban all those who would drive a married priest from the altar.[36] I was encouraged to make my marriage public here and to follow the Christian example of Nuremberg, Worms, and many other Christian towns and territories where priests, monks, and nuns have married, because their citizens have found clerical marriage much more acceptable, as they should, than the public adultery and immorality of the clergy they previously had to endure.

The fact that my wife also took vows need not offend any sincere Christian; that she is my legitimate spouse is demonstrated by God's command and the freedom that is given and available to everyone, and no vow can thwart that. She also had good Christian and urgent reason to marry. By means of incredible tricks and incessant hounding that she, as a young, unknowing, innocent, and fearful daughter could not avoid, she was forced into a cloister by some of her relatives for the sake of her maternal and paternal inheritance. In the cloister she never had a healthy day, nor did she learn anything Christian because only seldom was there preaching. Her life was so dreadful that it was right and necessary and would have been more Christian if the doctors had told her that she would never recover her health in the cloister. She also received credible warning of other dangers to her life that she would have to overcome. She has always led such an innocent and humble life that by God and my own soul I swear that anyone with a drop of fairness left in them, once they realized the situation and learned of her innocence, would thank me and in no way be offended. God is my witness that I married her not out of impure lust or inordinate affection, but because some Christian, wise, and God-fearing people counseled and implored me to do so. For if I had wanted only to satisfy my desire, I could have found someone who would have caused less gossip and fewer disadvantages.

My gracious lords, if anyone thinks that I have sinned by taking this woman as my wife at her pleading, out of urgent need and not out of improper desire (as her life and morals have already demonstrated and will continue to prove), I will answer the accuser in the presence of your lords and of every Christian authority, and if I am found to have sinned according to divine law, I will let myself be executed (Deut 13:5). I only know that your lordships, if you knew the whole story, would feel deep pity for my wife, who must have been robbed of her paternal and maternal inheritance in the amount of well over a thousand gulden and who was held so long in that ungodly prison that she will never fully recover. By your special gracious order allow us to live here as a married couple, and we will offend no one but, as God wills, use what we have to provide some service and be diligent always in doing good.

(3) The third matter alleged against me by my lord, the bishop, in his letter to you is that I am under the ban and was expelled by the clerical chapter at Speyer. My lord is also poorly informed in this matter, and I am astounded at this, especially in view of the fact that I gave a sufficient report to his vicar and even offered to substantiate my account. Since then the vicar has seen my lord bishop, so that I could have been brought before him. It is true that my lord official or vicar of Speyer excommunicated me and the pastor of St. John parish in Wissembourg, where I was the preacher, for allegedly refusing to obey a citation, although this action went against a promise made by the bishop of Speyer to the leaders of Wissembourg, who can testify to this. Although the excommunication was null and void, we appealed to the archbishop of Mainz and again to the diet of the cities held at Speyer.[37] The delegates of the free imperial cities bargained so intensively with my gracious lord, the bishop of Speyer, that he postponed the trial and promised to cite us to Speyer (as is right) and to provide us with safe passage also in the Palatinate. After we were notified of the agreed-upon date under the seal of the vicar of Speyer, too little time was left to obtain from the Palatinate the necessary safe conduct, and we were cited to Udenheim and not to Speyer. Not one, however, of the sensible and intelligent people whom we consulted advised us to proceed to Udenheim in these uncertain times without a safe conduct. Consequently, in order not to cause trouble for anyone, we decided on our own to leave Wissembourg and the entire diocese of Speyer and to come here to my fatherland, where I have already offered to be held accountable

and to answer before your graces for my preaching and life at Hagenau or Wissembourg. Going to Speyer was just too risky.

Since the previous proceedings, though amounting to nothing, have been delayed and we have not been cited again, and since we know of no other proceedings against us (nor can there be any against me for I am no longer under the jurisdiction of Speyer), it is clear that I am not under the ban and was not banished from the diocese of Speyer. I offered to present and prove all this before your graces just as I also offered to the vicar. Therefore, I plan to wait here in my fatherland until someone comes to my support. If God wills that I should, before your graces and every Christian authority, answer all those who wish to malign my teaching and life, I will do so under one condition: if I am found guilty of preaching or teaching anything that divine scripture does not clearly contain (not counting all the subjects for debate), I will submit to stoning and death in accord with divine law (Deut 13:5), and if anyone can show that I have ever lived in a way other than Christian, then I shall accept three punishments instead of one. I was obligated to offer this to the vicar of my lord bishop and therefore voluntarily sought him out. I knew ahead of time that he would not grant what I asked, and he dismissed me without any obligation. I cannot understand, therefore, on what grounds my lord bishop would banish me from his diocese, since I have not been accused of any misdeed, in fact have not even been summoned or interrogated, and since I appeared before his vicar who afterward saw his grace. Having offered and submitted to the above, I am obviously not guilty of anything, and, although the bishop has not recognized and favored me as one of his own, there is no just cause for dismissing me.

Your graces are famous for being champions of justice and defenders of the unjustly oppressed, and I submit to you my humble and conscientious plea through Christ Jesus and his holy gospel that you graciously accept my answer, which (God be my witness) is the certain and complete truth in all its details. As the magistrates of my fatherland, to whom the Almighty has granted special power to protect those who are threatened with violence and injustice, look with favor on me, the son of your citizen, and my wife. No one should separate us because I know for certain that God has joined us together (Matt 19:6). We ask no greater favor than to receive the same divine justice that is valid for everyone else, that is, for all Christians, and wish only to be shielded fairly from the use of force. After Christ I know of no authority to which I owe a special obligation except to you, the gracious lords and magistrates of my fatherland, and I ask God that he may allow me to defend all my teaching and behavior in your presence. I have no doubt that afterward you will no longer be lords but fathers to me and my wife. If, however, it is not fitting for me to defend myself before you, I offer to appear before any Christian judge, whoever he may be, who favors divine justice, and in the meantime I hope (especially since I request only what is just and godly) that your graces will pay no attention to the voices of opposition or to old ungodly custom and usage or make me pay for the time I spent unfairly in the unchristian prison of human regulations and from which I am now justly acknowledged to be free. By the divine justice that can never cause offense, bad counsel, and anything harmful, continue to provide merciful leadership as before, and Christ our Savior will richly reward your graces with the long-term welfare and blessed government of my fatherland. My wife and I will in turn forever do all we can to repay you by living as your obedient subjects, and humbly in Christ we await your reply.

Your obedient subject,
Martin Bucer

5. John Frith, Letter unto the Faithful Followers of Christ's Gospel, While He Was Prisoner in the Tower of London for the Word of God, 1532

John Frith (1503–33) was an ardent member and defender of the early Protestant movement, who at age thirty became one of the first martyrs of the English Reformation. Though educated at Cambridge, Frith was apparently not among the young men who gathered at the White Horse Inn to read Luther. Instead, he appears to have been converted to the Protestant cause by William Tyndale in London around 1525. That same year he received a position at Oxford in Cardinal College, which had been founded by Thomas Wolsey, cardinal archbishop of York and lord chancellor of England until 1529. When Wolsey embarked upon a campaign to prohibit Lutheran writings and to arrest suspected Protestants, Frith escaped to the continent where he met with William Tyndale, married, and began to write. All of his works written abroad were published in Antwerp.

In 1532 Frith returned to England in order to serve the small Protestant community. After being hounded for several months, he was arrested before he could return to the continent and imprisoned in the Tower of London. There he continued to write in spite of two official trials and private interviews with bishops Thomas Cranmer and Stephen Gardiner. He remained deaf to their pleas to recant and was finally burned at the stake on July 4, 1533. The letter that he wrote from the tower to his far-flung supporters summarizes his view of suffering for the sake of Christ and illustrates the strong correlation between his faith and his life.

From *The Work of John Frith*, ed. N. T. Wright, 257–60.

Grace and Peace from God the Father, through our Savior Christ Jesus, be with all them that love the Lord unfeignedly. Amen.

It cannot be expressed, dearly beloved in the Lord, what joy and comfort it is to my heart to perceive how the word of God has wrought and continually works among you, so that I find no small number walking in the ways of the Lord, according as he gave us commandment, willing that we should love each other as he loved us. Now have I experience of the faith that is in you and can testify that it is without simulation that you love not in word and tongue only but in work and verity.

What can be more trial of a faithful heart than to adventure not only to aid and succor through others (which without danger may not be admitted unto us), but also personally to visit the poor oppressed and see that nothing be lacking to them, but that they have both ghostly[38] comfort and bodily sustenance, notwithstanding the strait inhibition and terrible menacing of these worldly rulers, ever ready to abide the extreme jeopardies that tyrants can imagine. This is an evidence that you have prepared yourselves for the cross of Christ according to the counsel of the wise man who says: "My son, when you shall enter into the way of the Lord, prepare yourself for tribulation" (1 Thess 3:4). This is an evidence that you have cast your accounts and have wherewith to finish this tower that you have begun to build (Luke 14:28). And I doubt not but that the one who has begun to work in you shall for his glory accomplish the same even unto the coming of the Lord (Phil 1:6).

And, albeit God of secret judgments for a time keep the rod from some of them that ensue his steps, yet let them surely reckon upon it, for there is no doubt that all which will devoutly live in Christ must suffer persecution; for whom the Lord loves he corrects and scourges every child that he receives. For what child is that whom the father chastises not (Heb 12:6–7)? If you be not under correction of which we are all partakers, then you are bastards and not children.

Nevertheless, we may not suppose that our most loving Father should do that because he rejoices in our blood or punishment, but he does it for our singular profit, that we may be partakers of holiness, and that the remnants of sin, which through the frailty of our members rebel against the spirit and will, causing our works to go imperfectly forward, may someday be suppressed, lest they should subdue us and reign over us—as I have sufficiently declared in the epistle of my book that entreats of purgatory,[39] to which I remit them that desire to be further instructed in this matter.

Of these things God had given me the speculation before; now it has pleased him to put it in use and practice upon me. I ever thought, and yet do think, that to walk after God's word would cost me my life at one time or another. And, albeit that the king's grace should take me into his favor and not suffer the bloody Edomites[40] to have their pleasures upon me, yet will I not think I am escaped but that God has only deferred it for a season, to the intent that I should work somewhat that he has appointed me to do and so to use me unto his glory.

I beseech all the faithful followers of the Lord to arm themselves with the same supposition, marking themselves with the sign of the cross, not from the cross as the superstitious multitude do, but rather to the cross in token that they be ever ready willingly to receive the cross when it shall please God to lay it upon them. The day that it comes not, count it clear won, giving thanks to the Lord that has kept it from you; and then when it comes, it shall nothing dismay you, for it is no new thing but even that which you have continually looked for.

And doubt not that God, who is faithful, shall not suffer you to be tempted above that which you are able to bear, but shall ever send some occasion by which you shall stand steadfast (1 Cor 10:13). For either he shall blind the eyes of your enemies and diminish their tyrannous power or else, when he has suffered them to do their best and the dragon has cast a whole flood of waters after you, he shall cause even the very earth to open her mouth and swallow them up (Rev 12:15–16). So faithful is he and careful to ease us when the vexation should be too heavy for us.

He shall send a Joseph before you in case you should come into Egypt;[41] yea, he shall so provide for you that you shall have a hundred fathers for one, a hundred mothers for one, a hundred houses for one, and that in this life as I have proved by experience, and after this life everlasting joy with Christ our Savior (Mark 10:30). Notwithstanding, since this steadfastness comes not of ourselves, for (as St. Austin says[42]) there was never one so weak or frail, no, nor the greatest offender that ever lived, but that every person by nature should be as frail and commit as great enormities except he were kept from it by the power of God. I beseech you all in the Lord Jesus Christ and for the love of his Spirit to pray with me (Rom 15:30) that we may be vessels to his laud and praise, what time soever it pleases him to call upon us.

The Father of glory give us the Spirit of wisdom, understanding, and knowledge and lighten the eyes of our mind that we may know his ways, praising the Lord eternally (Eph 1:17–18). If it please any to write unto us of any such doubts as peradventure may be found in our books, it should be very acceptable unto us and, as I trust, not unfruitful for them. For I will endeavor myself to satisfy them in all points by God's grace. To whom I commit to be governed and defended forever, Amen.

John Frith, a prisoner of Jesus Christ,
at all times abiding his pleasure

PART TWO

Interpreting Scripture

Introduction

For sixteenth-century Protestants nothing shaped their personal devotion or spirituality more than the Bible, or so it is often said. In fact, that statement has to be qualified in two important ways. First, in the earliest decades of the Reformation, most people heard the Bible read and taught in church instead of studying their personal copy at home. It took time for vernacular translations from the Hebrew and Greek to be published. True, Martin Luther's German New Testament and William Tyndale's English translation appeared in the 1520s, but complete bibles in German, French, and English were not printed until the 1530s. Even then, the cost of a personal copy and the inability to read prevented many people from buying their own bibles. For the earliest Protestants, sermons and catechisms were more likely to serve as the sources of their religious formation than privately owned bibles.

Second, Protestant methods of teaching and interpreting the Bible varied widely from place to place. The Bible was the chief authority for Protestant doctrine, and in principle believers guided by the Holy Spirit could interpret the text for themselves without deferring to the official teaching of the clergy. In practice, however, Protestant ministers insisted that their training and their office qualified them to interpret the Bible for their flocks. It is well known that Protestant reformers disagreed among themselves over the meaning of important passages, and those disagreements led to the distinctive devotional and worship practices that characterized emerging Protestant churches. The Bible did indeed influence the spirituality of the laity, but less through the private study of scripture than through their participation in public rituals and instruction where the impact of the Bible was less direct and immediate.

For all Protestants the Bible was *scripture*, that is, not just a religious book but sacred text whose authority was to be honored and whose meaning for the community of believers was vital. Most reformers believed the meaning of scripture was clear but, as the texts below illustrate, sundry criteria were offered for establishing that clarity. In one of his earliest sermons Zwingli sought to prove from scripture itself that its meaning was clear to everyone who was enlightened by the Holy Spirit. His statement is a bold defense of the priesthood of believers, the principle stated by Luther in 1520 as he sought to refute the claim that the right to interpret scripture authoritatively belonged to the papacy. According to Zwingli, the Holy Spirit enabled believers to find the clear word of God in scripture, but that word of God might or might not be the most literal interpretation of the text. After he and Luther disagreed about the correct meaning of "this [bread] is my body," the clarity of scripture seemed less clear than before; which interpretation offered more clarity and therefore carried more weight, the literal or the spiritual?

One champion of the spiritual interpretation, the Silesian nobleman Caspar Schwenckfeld, defended his position in a crisp letter to the Lutheran pastor Cordatus. Schwenckfeld is often called a spiritualist because, like Zwingli, he clashed with Luther over the words of institution and because he made a more sweeping claim than did Zwingli for the superiority of spiritual interpretation. Although Luther defended the literal meaning of Jesus' words at the Last Supper, he could hardly be called a literalist, especially when it came to interpreting the Old Testament. Fully aware of the challenge that the Hebrew scripture presented to Christian interpreters and drawing on the venerable tradition of spiritual interpretation, Luther did not hesitate to find Christ and Christian teaching in the Hebrew scripture, as he does below in his favorite psalm. His colleague in Wittenberg, Philip Melanchthon, unabashedly applied the prophecy of Jeremiah to the crisis faced by German Protestants after Luther's death, and indeed that is what it meant for the Hebrew scripture to become sacred text also for Christians. If it could not be applied to the churches of the sixteenth century, then why not leave it out of the Bible?

Unexpectedly, it is the English reformer and translator William Tyndale who offers a different proposal for determining the clear and useful meaning of scripture. "The knowledge of our baptism is the key and the light of the scripture," he wrote. If we would not merely claim to be enlightened by the Spirit but learn and take to heart what our baptism means before we set out to interpret the Bible, then the meaning of the text would become clear. His proposal, which Luther also could have made, applies scripture directly to personal devotion, because it requires interpreters to ponder their baptism and hence to ask how the text of scripture nurtures their Christian identity. Instead of presupposing a priesthood of believers, it emphasizes, as it were, a priesthood of the baptized as the community in which scripture can most effectively do its work of shaping spirituality.

6. Ulrich Zwingli, The Clarity and Certainty of the Word of God, 1522

The following text comes from the published version of a sermon that Zwingli delivered at the Oetenbach convent in Zürich probably in July 1522, after the breaking of Lenten fasting rules ignited controversy over evangelical teaching and practice. Zwingli had been appointed by the city council to replace the Dominican friars as instructors of the nuns at the convent. In July he engaged other friars in debate over the invocation of Mary and the saints and then over the more basic issue of how to interpret scripture. Zwingli and his followers had invoked the authority of the Bible for the changes they wanted to make, but, like all reformers, they had to defend their claim to have a truer understanding of scripture than their opponents.

According to his sermon at the convent, Zwingli argued not only that scripture was clear in the plain and simple sense, but also that a true understanding of the word of God was available to every person whose spirit, created in the image of God, was enlightened by God's Spirit and the word itself. Zwingli supported this spiritual clarity of scripture with texts from both testaments, but he did not discuss the relationship between scripture and the word of God or the issue that would soon confront Protestants: conflicting interpretations that all

43

claimed divine illumination as their source. Zwingli's views nevertheless convinced the city council; it appointed Zwingli's fervent supporter, Leo Jud, pastor at the convent until the cloister was dissolved in 1524.
Translation from the modern German version in ZS 1, 128–54.

Now let us consider the meaning of clarity and light as they pertain to the word. God be praised! May he put the right words into our mouth so that we can make the matter clear and convincing. Amen.

When the word of God shines on human understanding, the mind is enlightened to such an extent that it understands and confesses the word and becomes certain of it. That was the experience of David, who exclaimed: "The unfolding of your words gives light; it imparts understanding to the simple" (Ps 119:130). Simple ones are those who can do nothing for themselves but resemble the child whom Jesus set in the midst of the disciples to teach them humility, saying: "Truly I tell you, except you change and become like children, you will never enter the kingdom of heaven" (Matt 18:3). This prevenient clarity that guides our understanding is presented to us at the birth of Christ, when the shepherds were surrounded by light before the angel began to speak with them, and the shepherds believed the words of the angel and found all things as it had said (Luke 2:8–20).

We will demonstrate the clarity of the word with some illustrations first from the Old Testament and then from the New. When God commanded him to build the ark, Noah believed that God would indeed destroy the whole earth with the flood (Gen 6:11–22). No human insight alone would have convinced him; otherwise, all who paid no heed but kept on building their houses and marrying and following their desires would make Noah, alone against the crowd, doubt and say to himself: "Ah, what you heard was merely a delusion caused no doubt by a demon." You can see, then, how the word of God emitted its own light that enabled Noah to recognize that no other than God was speaking to him....

These seven passages[1] from the Old Testament are sufficient to demonstrate that God's word can be understood by us without any human instruction—owing not to our understanding but to the light or Spirit of God, shining and breathing through the words in such a way that in the Spirit's own light we perceive the rays of divine teaching, as the psalm says: "For with you is the fountain of life, in your light we see light" (Ps 36:8), and likewise in John (John 1:4).

We will now turn to the New Testament passages.

In John it says that the word, or Son, of God was the true light which enlightens everyone that comes into the world (John 1:9).[2] But if the light enlightens everyone, it must be clarity itself, for however bright and clear a thing may be, it cannot enlighten everyone unless it is clarity itself; and if it is to continue enlightening everyone, it must necessarily be eternal. For all things that are clear must be illuminated by clarity. Listen, you quibblers who have no trust in the scriptures:[3] the word of God, which is God himself, enlightens everyone. Away then with your own clarifications that you would bestow upon the word of God through your interpreters. John the Baptist says: "No one can receive anything except what has been given from heaven" (John 3:27). If everything we are to receive and understand must come from above, then no human interpreter can give it to me. The comprehension and understanding of divine doctrine comes, then, from above and not from your interpreters, who are just as weak in the flesh and liable to err as Balaam was (2 Pet 2:15–16).

The Samaritan woman was clever enough to say to Christ: "'I know that Messiah is coming' (who is called Christ); 'when he comes, he will proclaim all things to us'" (John 4:25). Our theologians have not yet learned that lesson. Ask them if they understand the words: Christ is *caput ecclesiae*, that is, Christ is head of the congregation or church that is his body. They will answer yes, they understand them very well, but they are not allowed to do so without the approval of human authorities. Poor creatures! Rather than yielding to the truth, they deny that they are human, as if they lacked ordinary intelligence and did not know the meaning of *caput*. All that in order to subject divine truth to so-called just judges like Caiaphas and Annas.[4] It does not matter in the least to them what Christ said.

He says, however: "And they shall all be taught by God" (John 6:45), using the words of Isaiah (Isa 54:13). But if all Christians are taught by God, why not allow them to have that teaching with certainty and freedom according to the understanding God has imparted? From the words of Christ that follow we learn that God himself is the teacher of believing hearts: "Everyone who has heard and learned from the Father comes unto me" (John 6:45). None comes to the Lord Jesus Christ except those who have learned to know him from the Father. Note who the teacher is: not doctors or fathers of the church, not popes, not theologians or councils of the church, but the Father of Jesus Christ. You dare not ask if you can be taught by human instructors as well. No, for he has just said: "No one can come to me except drawn by the Father who sent me" (John 6:44). Even if you hear the gospel of Jesus Christ from an apostle, you cannot act upon it unless the heavenly Father teaches and draws you by the Spirit. The words are clear; divine teaching illuminates, instructs, and grants certainty without the need for human wisdom. When believers are taught by God, the teaching they receive is precise, clear, and convincing. If other teachers had to confirm the teaching and reassure us, believers would have to be described as taught by human beings rather than by God....

Now if you ask yourself when you are called by God: how am I to prepare myself, so that I may be certain to attain grace? I reply: put all your trust in the Lord Jesus Christ, that is, rest assured that he suffered for us and is the atoning sacrifice that has freed us for all eternity (1 John 2:2). The moment you believe, know that you are drawn by the Father and that which you regard as your own work is the Spirit of God secretly at work within you. For Christ says: "No one can come to me unless drawn by the Father who sent me" (John 6:44). Listen: when you seek him and find him and hold fast to him, you are being drawn by the Father; otherwise you could never have come to him....

You are likely to say: Our preachers today are only human teachers. Should we refrain from inquiring of them? Answer: No matter who they are, if they teach you their own thoughts, their teaching is false; but if they teach you according to the word of God, it is not they who teach you but God who teaches them. As Paul says, what are we other than "servants of Christ and stewards of God's mysteries" (1 Cor 4:1)? I know for certain that God teaches me, because I have come to know the mysteries. Do not deny me this expression, but try to understand on what basis I know that God teaches me. When I was in school, I made good progress in human subjects, like others in my day. But about seven or eight years ago, when I undertook to devote myself entirely to the scriptures, philosophy and theology always got in my way. Led by the word and Spirit of God I eventually realized I had to put aside all those things and learn the doctrine of God directly from his own lucid word. I began to ask God for light, and the scriptures became far clearer to me, even though I read nothing else, than when I was consulting many commentators and expositors. That must be a sign that God was leading me, for I could never have come so far by my own feeble intelligence. You can see that my progress did not come from overestimating myself but from humbling myself.

You were about to interrupt me, but I will forestall you. You intended to say it is a great error for people to think they understand a matter perfectly without needing any advice or instruction. Answer: Yes indeed, if they rely on their own understanding. You do that yourselves, for you cling to human interpretation and try to make divine knowledge conform to it. Hear the words of Paul: "Those who are unspiritual do not receive the gifts of God's Spirit, for the gifts are foolishness to them and they are unable to understand them because they are spiritually discerned. Those who are spiritual discern all things, and they are themselves subject to no one else's scrutiny. 'For who hath known the mind of the Lord, so as to instruct him'" (1 Cor 2:14–16). These words of Paul are more precious than all the gold in the world (Ps 19:10). Unspiritual persons are those who import their own understanding. Spiritual persons do not trust any interpretation that is not given by God; they are pure and simple and do not reek of ambition, covetousness, or carnal lusts. Those who judge in a spiritual way see at once whether the doctrine is of God or not. They are not judged by anyone, for even if they are judged—something they cannot avoid—they will not let themselves be torn away or turned aside from God's word....

Now, at last, to make an end of answering objections, our view of the matter is this: We should hold the word of God in the highest possible esteem and acknowledge only that which comes from the Spirit of God. We should trust it in a way that we cannot trust any other word. For the word of God is certain and can never deceive. It is clear and never leaves us groping in the dark. The word of God interprets itself and offers the correct understanding. It illumines the soul with full salvation and grace, fills the soul with sure trust in God, and it humbles the soul, so that the soul loses and even condemns itself while taking God into itself. The soul lives in God, yearning diligently for him and rejecting all creaturely consolation. God alone is the soul's salvation and assurance. Without him it has no rest; it rests in him alone, as the psalmist testifies: "My soul refused to be consoled, my thoughts turned to God and I felt delight" (Ps 76:3–4 Vulg.).[5] Blessedness begins in this present age, not in reality, but nonetheless in certainty offered by our trustworthy hope. May God increase this hope in us, and never allow us to lose it. Amen.

I think it is good at this point to summarize how we come to a true understanding of the word of God and to a personal experience of our illumination by God. Or how those who are not well versed in scripture can tell whether or not a priest is teaching them the pure truth that is unsullied by his own sinful desires.

First, we must inwardly ask God to kill off the old self that sets such great store by its own wisdom and ability.

Second, when the old self is slain and removed, pray that God will graciously flow into us so richly that we believe and trust only in him.

Third, when that is accomplished in us, we will be filled to overflowing with joy and comfort. We must constantly repeat the words of the prophet: "Show us your strength, O God, as you have done for us before" (Ps 68:28). For Paul says: "So if you think you are standing, watch out that you do not fall" (1 Cor 10:12).

Fourth, the word of God does not overlook anyone, least of all those who stand tallest among us. When God called Paul, he said to Ananias: "He is an instrument whom I have chosen to bring my name before Gentiles and kings" (Acts 9:15). Again, he says to the disciples: "And you shall be dragged before governors and kings because of me, as a testimony to them and the Gentiles" (Matt 10:18).

Fifth, it is the property of the word to humble the high and mighty and make them like the lowly. After all, the Virgin Mary sang: "He has brought down the powerful from their thrones, and lifted up the lowly" (Luke 1:52). And John proclaimed concerning Christ: "By him shall all the hills be brought low and the valleys filled" (Luke 3:5).

Sixth, the word of God always seeks out and helps the poor. It also encourages the comfortless and despairing but opposes those who trust in themselves, as Christ testifies.

Seventh, the word of God does not seek its own advantage; for that reason Christ commanded his disciples to carry neither bag nor purse (Luke 10:4).

Eighth, the word of God seeks only to make God known, so that the obstinate fear him and the lowly find comfort in him. Those who preach the word in that manner no doubt preach correctly. Those who are careful to seek their own advantage, however, defending human teaching instead of faithfully holding up the doctrine of God, are false prophets. You can recognize them by their words. They make a clever appeal: "The holy fathers! Shall we despise what they prescribed?" They make a big deal about such things instead of complaining about the lukewarm preaching of the gospel.

Ninth, when you find that the word of God renews you and begins to be more precious to you than formerly when you listened to human doctrines, then be certain it is the work of God.

Tenth, when you find that it gives you assurance of the grace of God and eternal salvation, it comes from God.

Eleventh, when you find that the word of God squeezes and crushes you while God is magnified in you, then God himself is at work.

Twelfth, when you find that the fear of God constantly gives you more joy than sorrow, it is definitely the operation of God's word and Spirit.

May God grant us this Spirit. Amen.

7. Caspar Schwenckfeld, A Letter of Caspar Schwenckfeld concerning the Course of the Word of God, March 4, 1527

If anyone in the sixteenth century could be said to have had spirituality, it was Caspar Schwenckfeld (1489–1561). He is usually classified as a radical reformer because that spirituality led him away from the Lutheran movement in his native Silesia and prevented him from finding a home in another Protestant party. Even so, Schwenckfeld was an early Protestant, rejecting the medieval church and earning sympathy from Swiss reformers. He was forced out of Silesia in 1529, but his followers survived and in 1734 five hundred of them emigrated to Pennsylvania, where they established a Schwenckfelder church very much like other Protestants. Schwenckfeld himself spent most of his later life in southern Germany around Ulm, where he died.

His break with Luther was based on personal spiritual experiences (*Heimsuchungen*) and on a spiritual reading of scripture that valued the internal word more highly than the external word that Lutherans preferred. The superiority of a spiritual reading is best described in a letter to Conrad Cordatus (1480–1546) that is presented here. Cordatus was an Austrian humanist, priest, and supporter of Luther who fled to Wittenberg in 1524. After a stint in prison in Hungary, he lived in Silesia in late 1526 and early 1527, where he exchanged theological views with Schwenckfeld. After 1527 Cordatus served as a Lutheran pastor in several locations and recorded Luther's 1532 and 1533 table talks while living in Wittenberg.

The letter was edited and published by the reformer of Basel, John Oecolampadius (1482–1531), after he received a copy from Schwenckfeld's colleague who was traveling in southwestern Germany.

Translated from the Latin text in *Corpus Schwenckfeldianorum*, 2, 590–99.

"Be prepared always to respond to everyone who asks" (1 Pet 3:15).
Greetings in Christ Jesus, our true and only salvation.
My dear father Cordatus,...

The sum and the basis of your teaching, if I have understood correctly, is this: God justifies and effects salvation by no agreement or arrangement other than by the preached word. Consequently, external preaching always takes precedence because "faith comes from hearing" (Rom 10:8–10) or in your exegesis, "external hearing," that is, hearing through the external word. That is your teaching and the foundation (were it not hay and stubble) on which you build.

By arguments and examples from scripture I will try to show you, as God permits, that you rely on that foundation completely in vain, for it is a hollow reed that weakens the hand of the one relying on it (2 Kgs 18:21). God grant that I may not race with you in vain and that he be in our midst. Amen.

Listen patiently, I ask, and consider carefully both scripture and the rule of faith.

(1) No one doubts that faith belongs to the order of spiritual and internal things, for it comes from God and, what is more, it is a work of God. Faith cannot originate in bodily things like the external word and external hearing; to remain firmly planted within the spiritual order where it belongs, faith derives from the internal word and precedes all ministerial actions. Because the natural human being is not able to perceive the things that belong to God (1 Cor 2:14), it is necessary first to be prepared through the word, to become spiritual and a fitting dwelling place of the word. Faith therefore does not come *from* the external word but *through* the external word.

(2) Whatever is not done out of faith is sin (Rom 14:23), and therefore even the external hearing of the gospel is subject to sin if it happens without faith already present.

(3) Christ who renewed us said the following: "No one comes to me unless drawn by the Father" (John 6:44). Again: "Everyone who learns from the Father" (John 6:45). Again: "Those whom the Father has given me" (John 17:9). You have the drawing, and you have the teaching of God the Father, without whom we can do nothing at all, neither speaking nor hearing in a visibly fruitful way.

(4) All preaching is empty unless a faithful heart and open ears are present as Christ speaks. "Those who have ears to hear, let them hear" (Matt 13:9). The word of God cannot be comprehended except by minds that have been illuminated by the light of faith and prepared by divine grace through Christ. Even if you bombarded unfaithful ears with the word of God a thousand times, they would receive nothing but noise or at most the carnal impulse of a simulated and false faith. By their own free will they will not acquire a faith that endures.

(5) If faith came from external hearing, then its origin would lie in the ministry or in the minister, and thus Apollo would be something and Paul would be something. But what are they in reality? Paul says they are servants of him whom you believed (1 Cor

3:5), and they believed God alone through Christ. Hence faith did not come from external hearing.

(6) The Lord alone gives increase (1 Cor 3:7), and faith is increase. Hence it does not come from an external source. As a lord is different from his servants, heaven different from earth, truth from falsehood, and God from that which belongs to God, so is it necessary for the creator to arrange things within one order and creatures within another. Human matters should not be compared to divine ones or to our God. The spiritual person knows this above all else and judges accordingly (1 Cor 2:15).

(7) If faith were the result of external hearing, it follows that God's word would be tied to the "elemental spirits of the universe" (Col 2:20), and, what is more, as soon as they heard the word preached, they would believe. The verse from Isaiah, "My word will not return to me empty" (Isa 55:11), which you customarily apply to the external word, was spoken about the living word of God. Those who hear this living word know it, appropriate it, direct their hearts toward God, and faithfully adhere to him.

(8) Whoever is from God hears the words of God (John 8:47). It follows that a divine operation comes first, as the psalm reports: "Coming before with blessings of goodness" (Ps 20:4 Vulg.),[6] that is, before the external word can be heard and bear fruit. Consider what Christ said to the Jews in John: "Why do you not hear what I say? Because you are not able to hear my words" (John 8:43). But surely they were able to hear him externally. Then he says: "You do not hear because you are not of God" (John 8:47).

(9) One is our teacher Christ, the cornerstone upon which the spiritual house is built. Like a lord he lays out the work of a servant, and the servant follows his command. Christ teaches the inner person not through externals but through his Spirit. When he writes to the Ephesians, therefore, Paul dares not claim anything for himself but rather refers everything to Christ when he says: "You did not so learn Christ; indeed you have heard about him and were taught in him, as the truth is in Jesus" (Eph 4:20–21). Here you see the true teacher and true teaching, eternal truth itself, which requires nothing fleeting or transitory to prop it up.

(10) If faith were to come by the word or from the preached word and external hearing, it would follow that justification comes

from a work or by the work of our hands, or at least it could not happen without human aid. Who does not realize how absurd that would be? Abraham, the type and model of our justification, believed God and not the preached word (since neither preachers nor the law yet existed), and it was reckoned to him as righteousness (Rom 4:3; Gen 15:6). Read all of Romans 4 and you will learn that internal things always take precedence.

(11) In justification, if external things necessarily come first, then the first stone would be set in place by us and not by God. Experience shows, however, what kind of building is erected when we again embrace the notion of historical faith; it is a certain kind of thinking or the assent of reason that comes from the literal word. We believe what scripture says will happen to us, just as the impious Jews of old believed the Messiah would be born to them (Matt 2:4–6).

(12) Christ says: "What is born of the flesh is flesh, and what is born of the spirit is spirit" (John 3:6). Those who think that faith comes from external hearing teach that the spirit is born from the carnal letter and heaven from earth, especially when they call the letter a vehicle of the spirit and claim that the letter becomes spirit through their faith. Faith, however, is a heavenly gift; it is righteousness looking down from heaven, purifying and cleansing the heart which, prepared thus beforehand by grace, not only believes the literal word but is seized and raised outside itself into the word of God, that is, God himself to whom it adheres through the Holy Spirit.

(13) Just as happiness does not come from external things, neither does faith. Thomas saw and even touched Christ, but it did not make him blessed (John 20:29). Flesh and blood did not reveal Christ to Peter, but the heavenly father (Matt 16:17). Therefore faith does not come from external hearing but from divine inspiration. God, who is the Spirit, does not magnify external things, but through Jesus Christ esteems and approves the internal and the spiritual.

(14) There is nothing to the objection that we are abolishing the letter of scripture. We do no such thing. We do not abolish the letter; we establish the letter in its proper place, namely, for the purpose of educating the flesh. Thus we obey him who says: "Examine the scripture" (John 5:29).

(15) God deals with the new person, or Christian, in a twofold way, internally and externally, since the new person is flesh and

spirit. God acts internally through the word of spirit and life, externally through the word of the letter or the preached word and through symbols. It is necessary for both flesh and spirit to be restored, taught, and edified so that we may be sanctified by the God of peace (1 Thess 5:23).

(16) Those who pay no heed do not furnish spiritual people with spiritual things or apply spiritual discernment (1 Cor 2:13, 15); instead they confuse and mix the carnal with the spiritual and miss completely the target of truth.

You will perhaps respond: We know faith is a divine work and confess with Paul that cultivation and edification come from God, for all things come from God (2 Cor 5:18). But God does this through the external word, and he ordained it this way when he commissioned the disciples to go forth into all the world and preach the gospel: "Those who believe and are baptized,..." (Mark 16:15–16). They are ministers and coworkers with God. At this point I am sure you will not fail to cite that verse in Matthew, "I will go before you into Galilee" (Matt 26:32), and "The gospel is the power of God unto salvation to every one who believes" (Rom 1:16), preached and to be preached on account of the elect, because "those whom he chose beforehand he also called, and those whom he called he also justified" (Rom 8:30). If preaching is to the elect, however, and unto salvation for everyone who believes, then grace indeed comes first and accomplishes its work by its own method and sequence: first on the inner person, whose coworkers and ministers then inform the outer person by the preached word.

Manifestly, therefore, without the grace of God it is impossible fruitfully to hear the word of God or to contemplate anything at all, as the popular hymn says: "Without your aid there is nothing in us."[7] You see, then, if there is nothing in us without the Spirit and divine aid, how can the natural person hear the word? For that very reason we say a prayer prior to the sermon and our soul is made ready by the living word. "Let not old things come from your mouth, for our thoughts are prepared by him" (1 Sam 2:3). "Those who fear God will prepare their hearts" (Sir 2:21), that is, let them listen to what the Lord says to them.

Now you will perhaps answer: "Hear in faith." But whoever hears in faith already has faith preceding, otherwise that person always hears in vain and without fruit. That is why we say that in the matter of salvation nothing can be done without the grace of God. If you do nothing without grace, then without it you will also not hear the word of God, which is spirit and life. If you have pre-venient grace, you already have faith, and by the order set down by God it follows that the word of God is heard, and heard in a fruit-ful way. Otherwise God would not desire our well being or be able to complete his work without us. Everyone can see how absurd it would be to say such things.

To summarize: The course of the living word of God is free; it is not bound to visible things, to a minister or the ministry, not tied to place or time, but it resides in invisible things although it is adumbrated to us through visible things. Believers do not seize upon the letter and the syllables of the preached word, but instead they apprehend God himself through these verbal symbols. As a result, you should see that godly people and believers are always led from the ministry of the word to the Word himself....

Consider finally what the Lord says: "Either make the tree good and its fruit good, or make the tree bad and its fruit bad" (Matt 12:33). Do you think it is an easy matter to hear the spoken gospel with fruit? Not so fast! Let us not forget all the unfaithful kings and prophets who desired to see and hear what the disciples saw and heard, but did not hear it (Matt 13:17). Not to mention the "many righteous persons" who, Christ said, desired the same (Matt 13:17). How can you now say that faith comes through the external word and outward hearing?

Regard instead, Cordatus, the course of the gospel, the apos-tolic ministry, and the order of Paul's words, including what he means when he says: "This is the word of faith that we preach" (Rom 10:8). Many errors have already been made in these matters. Interpret spiritual things for those who are spiritual and use spiri-tual discernment (1 Cor 2:13, 15). Then you will understand special matters through grace. Meanwhile, be very careful not to connect free will with faith more eagerly than the papists have connected it with works. That is enough for now.

My learned Cordatus, the objections raised against your teach-ing (which fails to promote the glory of God) have fallen during the time of carnival,[8] but if they could be brought up thoughtfully and openly, then without a doubt they could be discussed more fully and vigorously since they strive to settle things with the full engagement of scripture. They are not meant to provoke further debate, but I urge you to consider and discuss them with your colleagues (may God advance it in the best way possible). Then you also will have something from the letters and thoughts of Schwenckfeld, who is criticized, as you said, for always holding forth on some topic. Let them say what they will. Through the grace of God he [Schwenckfeld] knows that what is not forgotten will yet turn into dust and ashes and nothing more.

Farewell, my Cordatus, and pray to the Lord for me. Greet Luther in my name. If you wish to write back about this subject or about my books, it will be welcome, but I demand of you nothing you do not wish to do. Again farewell.

From Wohlau,[9] March 4, 1527.
Caspar Schwenckfeld

8. Martin Luther, The Beautiful *Confitemini* (Psalm 118:16–18), 1530

When Luther wrote this exposition of Psalm 118 in 1530, he was staying at the Coburg Castle on the border between Saxony and Bavaria. Ever since the Diet of Worms in 1521 had pronounced him an outlaw, Luther was not allowed to leave Saxony, but he wanted to be as near as possible to Augsburg, where his Wittenberg colleagues and other Protestants were presenting their confessions of faith to Emperor Charles V at a new diet called for that purpose. For Protestants it was a time of opportunity and apprehension. Lutherans were hoping the emperor would accept their confession and recognize their right to teach and practice their evangelical faith in Germany. It was also possible that the emperor and his forces would reject the confession and try to crush the Protestant movement.

Through letters Luther kept abreast of what was happening in Augsburg and offered advice and consolation to his colleagues. He also used the time to write essays and expositions like the one from which the following text is taken. Psalm 118 was called by Luther "the beautiful *confitemini*" from the first word of the psalm (no. 117 in the

Vulgate), and it was his favorite psalm. He took verse 17 as his personal motto, and verses 16–18 must have provided necessary strength during the difficult days at the Coburg. Indeed, on the advice of the Roman theologians, Emperor Charles V did reject the Augsburg Confession in 1530 and Lutherans remained in defiance of the imperial mandates.

Our translation is based on the 1530 German text in WA 31/1, 140–55.

16. "The right hand of the Lord is exalted, the right hand of the Lord does valiantly!
17. I shall not die, but I shall live and recount the deeds of the Lord.
18. The Lord has punished me severely, but he did not give me over to death."

These verses are the joyful song of the just that is sung by all the saints in their tents (Ps 118:15), that is, where they dwell together. The psalmist specifically means righteous persons in the era of the New Testament, when now and again the good news of Christ's wondrous works is preached in the churches. These verses are a song of the just, namely of the faithful, not a song of the godless. Those who do not believe but put their trust in human powers cannot sing this song; inwardly they will not understand a word, although they may babble it in clerical chapters and cloisters, where every Sunday this beautiful song is shamefully bawled and dishonored.[10] The godless sing in their hearts: "Our right hand does valiantly; the right hand of princes is exalted." They can only sing as they were taught, for leopards cannot change their spots.

"Singing" includes not only chanting or belting out a tune but also every sermon or public confession in which God's work, counsel, grace, help, comfort, victory, and salvation are openly praised. The Holy Spirit refers to such singing wherever the psalms and the rest of scripture mention singing, hymns, and psalms, as earlier in this psalm: "The Lord is my strength and my psalm; he has become my salvation."[11] God desires to be praised, honored, and acknowledged by us for his wondrous works. Faith does this and cannot be silent. It must declare and teach what it believes and knows about God for the sake of God's honor and of our instruction. As the psalm says: "I believed, therefore have I spoken."[12] If faith did not speak up and declare itself, it would not be genuine faith, even

57

though speaking up means it has to suffer misfortune and persecution, as the same psalm confirms: "I am greatly afflicted" (Ps 115:10
Vulg.). Against misfortune, however, faith has a helper who is its
salvation. Verse 14 teaches that persecution does not harm our salvation but rather advances it, for it so defies and blasphemes God
that he is forced to help and the just are compelled to call on God
and to pray to him. Persecution, therefore, makes things turn out
right....

Verse 17 of the psalm ("I shall not die, but I shall live")
describes the trouble, namely death, from which God's hand delivers the saints. To be sure, they still feel death when they are in mortal danger. Standing toe to toe with death is a bitter experience for
the flesh, for death is never alone but always shows up in the company of sin and the law. The saints therefore are really martyrs,
because they constantly face the threat of death and wrestle with it
all the time. Even if they are not assailed by tyrants and the ungodly
with fire, sword, prison, and similar persecutions, the devil himself
is still at work. He cannot abide the word of God or those who keep
and teach it. He plagues them as they live and as they are dying. As
long as they are healthy, he launches assaults on their faith, hope,
and love for God. He besieges and then storms a heart with terror,
doubt, and despondency until God seems like an enemy whom it
detests and avoids. As a result the tormented conscience is convinced that God has joined the devil, death, sin, hell, and all creatures to form a single unending and unrelenting enemy. Neither
Turk nor emperor could ever muster as much deadly force against
a city as the devil throws against a conscience.

The devil can also attack with force as the saints are dying, if
God allows it. At the deathbed he is very good at exaggerating sin
and reminding them of God's wrath. He must be an astoundingly
mighty spirit who can cause one small sin to produce terrible dread
and awful visions of hell. True, human beings rarely take note of
their serious sins, like unbelief and contempt for God, which prevent them from fearing, loving, and trusting God as they should,
and comparable sins of the heart, which are the real stumbling
blocks. Perhaps that is for the best, because I suspect that no faith
anywhere could withstand the sight without despairing. That is why
God allows us to commit other sins. Using them the devil can eas-

ily create hell and damnation for you, for instance, if you drink too much or oversleep. He makes you so sick with sadness, regret, and a bad conscience that you would rather die.

Even worse, the devil seizes on the best things you have done and hammers them into your conscience until they seem so shameful and worthy of damnation that none of your sins pains you as much as your best works, which are in fact good. You wish you had committed heinous sins instead of them. The devil wants you to disown your best works as if they were not done with divine aid, so that you end up blaspheming God as well. Then death and hell would not be far away. But who can recount all the devil's tricks by which he sets us on the road to sin, death, and hell? He has been at this trade for more than five thousand years, and he can do it better than any master. For the same length of time he has been the prince of death, and he has enough experience to know how to grant a frail conscience a foretaste of death. The prophets, especially our precious David, have felt and tasted it; they complain and speak about it, using terms like the gates of death, hell, and God's wrath, as if they had frequently been in the same situation.

Regardless of when or how it may happen, we hear that the saints must wrestle with the devil and grapple with death. He will supply the persecutors or pestilence, other illnesses and mortal danger. In this battle the best strategy for victory is to sing this song of the saints, that is, to disregard self and adhere to the right hand of God. Then the devil is fooled and arrives too late to do any harm. Sing like this: "I will not try to be strong; the only strength I have is the Lord." When I do this, I am completely drained and stripped of everything that is mine. Then I can say: "Devil, what are you contesting? If you wish to condemn my good works and my own holiness before God, I have none to condemn. My strength is not mine; the Lord is my strength. You cannot extract money from an empty purse, no matter how hard you try! If you plan to accuse me of my sins, I have none to attack. There is nothing here but God's might; try attacking it until you are satisfied. I am aware of no sins or holiness in me, in fact, of nothing in me but God's power."

It would be a fine thing if we could disregard ourselves to that degree and ridicule the devil like the poor householder with empty pockets, who mocked a thief whom he seized at night in his house.

"You fool," he said to the thief, "do you imagine you will find something here at night when I cannot find anything in the daytime?" What will the devil do when he finds a soul so bare that it refuses to argue with him about its sin or its holiness? The devil's skill at inflating sin and disparaging good works will be worth nothing, and he [the soul] will be directed to the right hand of God, to which he [the devil] must yield. If you forget this song, however, and the devil traps you in an argument with him about your sins and good works so that you take him seriously, then he can easily bend you to his will so that you forget God with his right hand and lose him and everything.

It is a real art to disregard oneself (as we heard), and we must keep working on it throughout our life, as all the saints before us, with us, and after us have to do. Just as we still experience sin, we must also experience death; just as we struggle to free ourselves of sin and cling to God's right hand as proclaimed to us by his word, we must also fight back against death and its prince and custodian, the devil, until we at last are completely free. Note how this verse presents the struggle. The devil, or persecutor, bears down on the saints with death. How do they respond? They avert their eyes and even turn their back, and then, renouncing themselves and all they have, they cling to God's hand and say: "I shall not die, you devil or tyrant, I shall not die, as you pretend. You are lying; I shall live. I will not bring up any good deeds I have done or any human works at all. I claim nothing for myself or any holiness of my own. I keep my eyes focused on the works of the Lord. I will praise only them and on them alone will I rely. Only the Lord can save us from sin and death. If you can override his work, then you have overcome me, too."

The comfort and help enjoyed by the just and the godly, mentioned already in verses 6 and 7,[13] are explained more fully here. Now you see how God's right hand raises up the heart and comforts it so profoundly in the midst of death that it says: "Although I die, yet I do not die; although I suffer, still I do not suffer; although I fall, I am not defeated; although I suffer indignity, I do not remain in disgrace." That is the comfort mentioned earlier. The help is further explained when the psalmist says: "I shall live." Now that is marvelous help, is it not? The dying live; those who suffer are joyful; the fallen rise up; honor and respect come to those who were disgraced. It is as Christ says: "Those who believe in me, even though they die, will live" (John 11:25). Paul likewise: "We are afflicted in every way, but not crushed; perplexed, but not driven to despair" (2 Cor 4:8). By itself no human heart can grasp these words....

This verse is truly a masterpiece for the way in which the psalmist removes death from our sight and refuses to acknowledge dying and sin. Instead, he admits nothing but life, so unbroken and indelible are the images he presents. Moreover, whoever does not see death lives forever, as Christ says: "Very truly, I tell you, those who keep my word will never see death" (John 8:51). They immerse themselves so deeply in life that death is swallowed up (1 Cor 15:54) and vanishes because with strong faith they hang onto the right hand of God. In this sense have the saints all sung this verse and will keep singing it forever. It applies to the martyrs above all. In the eyes of the world they die, but their hearts strong in faith declare: "Now I shall not die, but live."

We should learn the rule that whenever in the psalter and in scripture the saints are pressed to ask God for comfort and help, they mean eternal life and the resurrection of the dead. All these texts pertain to the doctrine of resurrection and eternal life; in fact, they concern the entire third article of the creed and what it says about the Holy Spirit, the holy Christian church, the forgiveness of sins, resurrection, and everlasting life. All that is a consequence of the first commandment where God says: "I am your God" (Exod 20:2). The third article of the creed confirms this verse. Although Christians lament the fact that they must suffer and die, they take comfort in another life, namely, in God himself, who reigns above and beyond this life. It is impossible, therefore, for them to die completely and not to enjoy eternal life. After all, the God on whom they rely and depend for comfort cannot die, and they must live in him. Furthermore, Christ says: "He is God not of the dead, but of the living" (Matt 22:32), [not a God] of those who exist no more. Thus Christians must live forever; otherwise he would not be their God, and they could not rely on him without being alive. Accordingly, for this small flock of the faithful, death will be none other than sleep....

9. Philip Melanchthon, The Lessons of Jeremiah's Prophecy, 1548

At the age of twenty-one the precocious humanist scholar Philip Melanchthon (1497–1560) was brought to Wittenberg from southern Germany to teach Greek at the university. He and Martin Luther, fourteen years his elder, soon developed deep respect for each other, and after 1520, as the Reformation unfolded, Melanchthon became his closest faculty colleague and the co-leader of the Lutheran movement. After Luther's death in 1546, Melanchthon remained at Wittenberg even though he became the lightning rod for controversies over Luther's theological legacy and the political stance of Lutheranism.

Although Melanchthon is best known for his classical scholarship and his theological and confessional writings, he also lectured on biblical books and published short expository works like the guide to reading Jeremiah presented here. Written and published during the 1540s, when German Protestants faced grim threats to their survival, this guide conveys the way in which Melanchthon extracted from Jeremiah's prophecy at the time of the Babylonian exile essential lessons for the precarious situation of his church. It turned out that German Lutherans would be granted legal standing in the Holy Roman Empire in 1555, but during the preceding decade, when Luther died and Emperor Charles V defeated the Protestant forces and took Wittenberg, such a happy ending was still unimaginable.

Translated from Philip Melanchthon, *Argumentum in Ieremiam Prophetam,* Frankfurt: Peter Brubach, 1548.

This prophecy includes many important and beneficial subjects, and it is useful to keep the chief topics in mind as one reads through the book.

(1) The sum and substance of the prophecy is a portrayal of how the church was preserved in a new and marvelous way through the people of Judah. The prophet also teaches how we should await the fulfillment of divine promises in extraordinary ways with a faith that is different from the way in which human reason ordinarily makes judgments.

The subject matter itself describes the new manner in which the church was preserved. Earlier leaders and prophets, like Moses,

Joshua, Samuel, David, and Isaiah, protected the people with glorious victories. But here Jeremiah looks out for the people by advising surrender that appeared to augur their destruction. It was impossible, was it not, to hope for their return after the whole nation had been scattered? Is there any record of a people so dispersed that regained their old territory after so long a time? In fact, their recovery of the land is a greater miracle than their initial occupation of it.

It was even more difficult to persuade the people to accept surrender since, after the capitulation and exile of King Jehoiachin, eleven years passed before Jerusalem was besieged (2 Kgs 24:12, 15–16; 25:2). Meanwhile, those who remained behind were cursing the prophet, claiming that he had misled them and that he was an impostor and a false prophet. Jeremiah nevertheless stood by his words in the face of everyone's judgment and the apparent course of events. Grave matters of this kind, when a serious crisis envelops kingdom, homeland, the people of God, the temple, and its worship, ought to be deliberated by wise counselors as best they can, but they cannot easily be put in plain words.

Jeremiah was under pressure because of promises that seemed to contradict him; for example, "The scepter shall not depart from Judah...until Shiloh comes" (Gen 49:10), and likewise [others that indicate] the temple and its cult will endure until the messiah appears. In this case Jeremiah needed spiritual wisdom to interpret the promises. God fulfills them, but not in the way that human reason thinks. He gives posterity to Abraham, but not in the manner he expected. Likewise, in this case, God does preserve this people and their worship, but not in the way their human reason anticipated. First he scatters the entire people, then he thoroughly destroys the temple and abolishes its cult, but in spite of everything God fulfills his promise when the people return from exile.

We ought to learn from these things that we should give preference to the word of God over everything else: what we experience as well as our opinions and deliberations. The apostles were promised that the church would be preserved, but they and all who listened to them were killed. In the meantime, however, the church consistently grew and flourished. Throughout our life, therefore, let us remember that divine promises are fulfilled in wondrous ways.

Moses never dreamed that he would wander forty years in the wilderness, and during that sojourn many Israelites gave up in despair and cursed Moses as an impostor, a traitor, and a tyrant. Nevertheless, God finally completed all that he had begun through Moses. We should diligently pay attention to this example, because God fulfills promises in ways that human reason does not understand.

(2) Now let us incorporate promises of the messiah into this interpretation of temporal promises concerning the return of the people from exile, for everyone agrees that all temporal promises should be referred to the promise of the messiah. It is the chief promise that also teaches the righteousness of faith and the new and eternal testament.

Accordingly, like all the prophets, Jeremiah sometimes preaches law and sometimes he declares promises of that righteousness which has been pledged for the sake of the messiah. His name, God our justifier, is stated by Jeremiah, for the noblest duty of the prophets is to preach about the coming messiah and the benefits he brings.

(3) The entire prophecy is a frightening example of the punishments awaiting impious priests, kings, and all those in the church who defend idolatry, commit adultery, or violate the sabbath, that is, disdain the office of ministry. Jeremiah refers to these very sins, and without doubt his prophecy portrays the last days of the church. The whole earth will be punished on account of idolatry, lust, and contempt for the office of the gospel.

(4) In his own person the prophet is an outstanding model of church leadership, the ministry of the gospel, and of Christ himself. The church is governed, liberated, and preserved not by human strength but by divine power operating through weak human beings, and consequently they perform great deeds so that the power of God may be recognized, as Paul says: "My power is perfected in weakness" (2 Cor 12:8).

Jeremiah accomplishes a remarkable thing that surpasses every human way of thinking. In contrast to all previous stories of great leaders and prophets, he persuades the king and the people to surrender, and in this new way he predicts that the kingdom, the cult, and the people will be saved. Moreover, he preaches against false worship and other sins, and indeed the people are finally saved through him. What is Jeremiah doing in the meantime? Forty years he wanders around like a deserter, he is ridiculed as a fool, put in jail, released, and imprisoned again. Unlike Isaiah, Elijah, or Elisha he performs no glorious unexpected miracles; rather, he appears weak because through him God will do great things and save the elect.

By considering this example carefully, we learn that the church is governed by God's wisdom and direction alone, not by our own, and we should take our hardships in good part and not let the power of our enemies cause us to despair.

(5) This useful prophecy teaches us that the church is governed differently from human affairs. In earthly realms the will of the majority rules, but in the church one person having the word of God prevails, just as Jeremiah contradicts kings, priests, and the majority of the people. Today this prophecy confirms us most of all against judgments rendered by the pope, bishops, and all the regular jurisdictions. They say that we dissent from the church because we disagree with the majority and the ordinary authorities. Let us study Jeremiah and learn from him that we should give precedence to the divine commandment over the authority of pontiffs and bishops. It is hard indeed to dissent from legitimate authority that adorns itself with the promises of God. But the shining example of Jeremiah brings us profound consolation. The prophet sharply opposed his own kings and pontiffs on matters of deportation and false worship just as we now quarrel with the pontiffs.

We spoke above about the miraculous preservation and guidance of the church. Let us now look at the prophet himself. Not only does he teach, foretell the exile, scare, and scold the ungodly and then console the godly and direct them by his own counsel, but he also prays frequently for the people and thus performs all the duties of the priestly office. His prayers contain passionate complaints and manifest a keen awareness of divine wrath.

Through their trials true prophets taste the sufferings of Christ, which the attacks on Jeremiah also signify. They know well the wrath of God against sin, how God is provoked to horrible anger by the idolatry of the people and the audacity of hypocrites, who were teaching lies and boasting that they were divinely sent prophets. They see the world's contempt for God on all sides, but they also know their own uncleanness and fear they may be rejected together with the people. Indeed, they are afraid that God's wrath might swallow the entire church without any remnant being saved. So it happened in the flood, in the fiery obliteration of Sodom, the destruction of Egypt, and later in the defeat of the Canaanites. The prophets keep these examples before their eyes, mourning and pleading that the church not be utterly destroyed and themselves with it. Hence the cry in chapter 10: "Correct me, O Lord, but in just measure; not in your anger, or you will bring me to nothing. Pour out your wrath on the nations that do not know you, and on the peoples that do not call on your name" (Jer 10:24–25).

We learn many things from these examples, namely, that we ought to be affected by the common lament for the sins of the people and simultaneously acknowledge our uncleanness. Even now the atrocious sins of idolatry, blasphemy, irreligious ideas, and degeneration of every kind are on the increase. Let us not witness these things without sorrow and fear of the horrible wrath of God. We should be mindful of the punishment to come and beseech God that we do not all perish.

The prophet's prayer teaches something else that deserves consideration. It is necessary for the church to be chastised, as he says here: "Correct me" (Jer 10:24). He also says: "You chastised me, O Lord, and I took the discipline; I was like a calf untrained" (Jer 31:18). These are not light chastisements but indicate that we are thoroughly rejected and damned by God.

In this trial the church receives consolation and teaches that discipline is imposed so that we may be called back to repentance. It is not the will of God that we perish. For that reason the prophet asks to be corrected in judgment, not in anger, lest he perish utterly (Jer 10:24). Again: "Therefore I am deeply moved for him; I will surely have mercy on him, says the Lord" (Jer 31:20). Also: "For surely I know the plans I have for you, plans for your welfare and not for harm, to give you a future with hope. When you call upon me and come and pray to me, I will hear you. When you search for me, you will find me; if you seek me with all your heart, I will let you find me, says the Lord" (Jer 29:11–14).

We ought to keep in mind, therefore, the prophet praying and his prayers, which are filled with teachings about sin, the wrath of

God, punishment, and that faith which accepts the remission of sins based on the unwavering promise of a coming savior.

(6) In the case of Jeremiah we should also take note of specific trials. Because his prophecy was not fulfilled right away, hypocrites took occasion to ridicule his predictions. Jeremiah had convinced King Jehoiachin and the great multitude that they should go far away into exile. Almost ten years later, however, when the city was still standing and fairly peaceful, many inhabitants were hoping that the danger was past. Those who had stayed behind were congratulating themselves on their decision and mocking those who had taken the advice of Jeremiah. They accused him of deceiving the people, and some put themselves forward as prophets against Jeremiah, like Hananiah (Jer 28) and others (Jer 29:15–23). Both kings and princes welcomed the rosy forecasts of these flatterers and thus they persecuted Jeremiah.

During this interim, Jeremiah keeps the faith that has been entrusted to the prophet, but not without great conflict: "If I say, 'I will not mention him or speak any more in his name,' then within me there is something like a burning fire shut up in my bones; I am weary with holding it in, and I cannot" (Jer 20:9). At this point he almost succumbs to his distress, but soon he is raised up again, saying: "But the Lord is with me like a dread warrior; therefore my persecutors will stumble, and they will not prevail" (Jer 20:11). Then a powerful impatience wells up in him again so that he appears to lose hope and to rage against the will of God.

These struggles are peculiar to the saints, and through them they discern the magnitude of sin in human nature. They match what Paul describes in Romans 7 and agree with what he says elsewhere (2 Cor 12:7) about torments or thorns being given to him in the flesh, that is, extreme fear and trepidation. In the midst of these torments, however, the Spirit yearns for help "with sighs too deep for words" (Rom 8:26), and it prevails.

(7) Since the exile did in fact last seventy years as foretold (Jer 25:11–12) and since other predictions about different kingdoms came true, we have solid testimony that the teaching of Jeremiah to this people is the word of God. No other nation can claim such exact predictions as the seventy years foretold here.

The return of the people and the complete restoration of Israel were no small matters, and no parallel can be found in the history of the world. No state that was thoroughly destroyed has been thus reestablished, especially after so long a time. This entire story is full of impressive miracles and works of God. Even the prophecy itself is a miracle, because it confirms that these lessons were given by God; moreover, the prophet also includes the full doctrine of the gospel (Jer 31:31–34).

(8) The great calamity that befell the people appears to be a prophecy of the devastation awaiting the church in the last days, for example, as the Turks are ravaging the churches in Asia and in Greece. When Judea was laid waste, a remnant did remain, and thus we know that remnants will now be saved when the coming grave devastations occur.

Following the example of Jeremiah, therefore, whose prayers mitigated those evils, let us stir up ourselves to repentance and call upon God; let us appoint Jeremiah our preacher in the present danger as if he is preaching to us indeed at the end of the age.

(9) These stories are also worth remembering because the prophet was so wonderfully protected amid harsh persecution; afterward he was freed by the Babylonian king, who gave to him some of the people. They were kept safe by Jeremiah, but later they killed him.[14] That is the end of the severe hardships he endured for forty years in his remarkable calling. Through it God used both new and familiar means to preserve the people by the word and the ministry of Jeremiah.

10. William Tyndale, Prologue to the Exposition of the First Epistle of St. John, 1531

William Tyndale (c. 1494–1536) is best known for translating most of the Bible into English. In 1515 he received the Master of Arts degree from Oxford and may have studied at Cambridge prior to serving as a tutor in his native Gloucestershire. After the bishop of London refused him permission to translate the New Testament, Tyndale fled to the continent, where his English translation from the Greek was printed in 1525 at Worms. He was working on the Old Testament when he was imprisoned near Brussels, condemned by the University of Louvain, and finally executed in 1536.

In addition to his translations Tyndale wrote Protestant tracts, a response to the Catholic humanist Thomas More, and commentaries on biblical books, such as his exposition of 1 John. In the prologue to this work Tyndale argues that "the knowledge of our baptism is the key and the light of the scripture," refuting the notion that interpreting the Bible without approval of the church and its teachers leads to heresy. Nevertheless, Tyndale believes that the Bible, even in English, has to be interpreted in the light of Christian doctrine and that laity should seek the help of preachers and theologians when they do not understand the text.

Adapted from the 1849 Parker Society edition of *Expositions and Notes on Sundry Portions of the Holy Scriptures together with the Practice of Prelates,* 136–44.

Unless we have the profession of baptism in our hearts, we cannot understand the scripture.

As we can by no means read, unless we are first taught the letters of the crossrow,[15] even so it is impossible for us, of whatever degree or name we are, to understand aught in the scripture to the honor of God and health of our souls unless we are first taught the profession of our baptism and have it also written in our hearts.

This profession consists of two things. The one is knowledge of the law of God, understanding it spiritually, as Christ expounds it in Matthew 5—7, so that the root and life of all laws is this: "You shall love the Lord your God with all your heart, and with all your soul, and with all your mind,...and your neighbor as yourself" (Matt 22:37, 39), for the neighbor's sake. And "love is the fulfilling of the law," as Paul teaches (Rom 13:10), so that whatever deed we do that is not of that love fulfills no law in the sight of God.

The other is to know the promises of mercy that are in our Savior Christ—understanding them also purely without all leaven[16] after the most merciful fashion in which scripture expresses them, and according to all fatherly love and kindness of God—unto all that repent toward the law and believe in Christ....

We, being all children of one God and servants of one Christ, must nevertheless agree among ourselves, and those who have offended must meekly acknowledge their faults and offer to make amends unto the utmost of their power. If they cannot make amends, [let them] ask forgiveness for Christ's sake and the other is bound to forgive them. Neither, without reconciling themselves with others, may they at first be received into the profession of Christ's faith, or continue therein, or be received again if they were expelled for their open offenses. For how can they love their neighbors as well as themselves and be sorry that they have hurt them unless they offer to make amends?

And we must henceforth walk in the life of penance (if you want to call it that) and according to the doctrine of Christ tame our flesh with prayer, fasting, and continual meditations on Christ's penance and passions for us, and on the holy saints, and with such abstinence and manner of living as each of us thinks is most meet for our constitution. The younger may confess their infirmities to the elder, who are more discreet and better learned, and ask their advice and wholesome counsel for the repressing of their diseases. But we should all tame the flesh and serve the neighbor without any superstitious mind.[17]

In God's eyes there is no satisfaction for sin save faith in Christ's blood out of a repenting heart. For our outward deeds cannot be applied to God, as if to perform service to his own person or through them to make him better. We can do no more with them, even if they were perfect and done with all love, than satisfy the law for the present time, do our duty unto our neighbors, and tame our own flesh; but they cannot make satisfaction to God for sin that is once past. The sin that is once committed must be forgiven by God freely out of divine love for Christ's sake.

When God visits us with sickness, poverty, or any adversity whatever, he does it not from a tyrannous mind—as if to satisfy a lust that we should suffer evil in order to make satisfaction for the past sin that we repent and regret—but from a fatherly love, in order to make us know ourselves and feel his mercy, to tame our flesh, and to keep us from sinning again....

The knowledge of our baptism is the key and the light of the scripture. Again, just as those who know their letters well and can spell perfectly cannot help but read, if they are diligent; and as those who have clear eyes without impediment or let[18] and walk in the light and open day cannot help but see, if they attend and take heed; even so those who have the profession of baptism written in their hearts cannot help but understand the scripture, if they exercise themselves therein, compare one place to another, mark the manner of speech, and ask here and there the meaning of a sentence from those who have more training and experience.

The doctrine that we should be taught before we are baptized, but for lack of age is deferred until the years of discretion, is the key that binds and looses, locks and unlocks the conscience of all sinners. By the same token that very lesson, where it is understood, is alone the key that opens all the scripture as if it were the whole scripture in itself, gathered together in a narrow compass and brought into a compendium. And until you are taught that lesson, so that your heart feels the sweetness of it, the scripture is locked and shut up for you and so dark that you could not understand it, even if Peter, Paul, or Christ himself did expound it to you—no more than the blind could see, even if you set a candle before them, or show them the sun, or point your finger at whatever you want them to espy.

Now we are all baptized; but alas not one person, from the highest to the lowest, ever taught what it means or how to profess it. And therefore we all remain blind—both our great rabbis,[19] in spite of the high learning they seem to have, and the laypeople. Yea, and so much the more blind are our great clerks[20] that the laypeople, except for a great number of them who are taught nothing at all, are all wrongly taught, and the doctrine of their baptism is all corrupted with the leaven of false glosses before they start to read the scripture. As a result, the light that the clergy bring with them to understand the scripture is utter darkness and as contrary to the scripture as the devil is to Christ. For this reason the scripture is locked up and becomes so dark that they grope for the door and can find no way in. It has become a maze in which they wander as in a mist, or (as we say) as if led by Robin Goodfellow,[21] so that they cannot come to the right way, no, even though they turn their caps.[22] The brightness thereof[23] has blinded their eyes with malice so that, although they do not believe the scripture to be false, yet they per-

71

secute the right understanding of it and cannot believe it to be true in the plain sense in which it speaks to them. It has become a turn-again lane[24] to them, which they cannot go through or make three lines agree together. Finally, the sentences of scripture are nothing but riddles to them, at which they cast [stones] as the blind man does at a crow, and expound by guess, a hundred doctors a hundred ways. One preacher in twenty sermons alleges one text after twenty fashions,[25] having no sure doctrine to cleave to, and all for lack of the right knowledge of the profession of our baptism.

Those who have the profession of their baptism written in their hearts cannot be heretics. Another conclusion is this: those who always creep along by the ground and never climb cannot fall from on high; likewise those who have the profession of their baptism written in their hearts cannot stumble in the scripture and fall into heresies or become makers of division and sects and defenders of wild and vain opinions. For the entire and only cause of heresies and sects is pride. Now the law of God, truly interpreted, robs those in whose hearts it is written and makes them as bare as Job of all things that can move them to pride. They have utterly forsaken themselves, with all their high learning and wisdom, and become the servants of Christ only, who has bought them with his blood. They have promised in their hearts unfeignedly to follow him and to take him alone for the author of their religion and only his doctrine for their wisdom and learning, to maintain it in word and deed, to keep it pure, and to build no strange doctrine thereupon; to be never at the highest but rather equal with their neighbors, and in that fellowship to wax ever lower and lower and every day to become more servant than other[26] to the weaker ones, after the example and image of Christ and in accord with his commandment and ordinance, not in feigned words of the pope.

This must be said because of our opponents who say that the scripture makes us heretics and corrupts us with false opinions, contrary to the profession of our baptism. [They claim that] the light by which we should expound the scripture is turned into darkness in our hearts, and the door of the scripture locked, and the wells stopped up before we come at it....

Is it not a greater blindness [for them] to say at the outset that the whole scripture is false in the literal sense and kills the soul? To prove that pestilent heresy, they abuse the text of Paul, which says that "the letter kills" (2 Cor 3:6), because that text was a riddle to them and they did not understand the meaning of the word *letter*. By this word Paul meant that the law given by Moses condemns all consciences, robs them of all righteousness, and drives them to the promises of mercy that are in Christ.

Heresy springs not from the scripture any more than darkness from the sun. Heresy is rather a dark cloud that springs out of the blind hearts of hypocrites, covers the face of scripture and blinds their eyes, so that they cannot behold the bright beams of the scripture.

The sum of all this is: If our hearts were taught the appointment made between God and us in Christ's blood when we were baptized, we would have the key to open the scripture and light to see and perceive the true meaning of it, and the scripture would be easy to understand. But we are not taught that profession, [and that] is the cause why the scripture is so dark and so far passing our capacity. The reason our expositions are heresies is that we are wrongly taught and corrupted by false opinions and made heretics before we ever come at the scripture. We have corrupted it (not it us) just as the sick person's taste turns wholesome and well-seasoned meat bitter, wearish,[27] and unsavory. The scripture, however, abides pure in herself and bright, so that those who are sound in the faith at once perceive that the judgment employed by heretics in their expositions is corrupt, just as a healthy person, after smelling the good meat, realizes at once that it must be the taste buds of the sick that are infected. The sound in faith can always use scripture to improve[28] heresies and false expositions; for the scripture purges herself even as the water once a year casts all filthiness to the sides. You see that is true by the authority of Paul: "All scripture is inspired by God and is useful for teaching, for reproof, for correction, and for training in righteousness" (2 Tim 3:16); and by the example of Christ and the apostles: how they confounded the Jews with the same scripture that had been corrupted and made obscure by their own darkness. You see it now by our example, how we have manifestly refuted the hypocrites in a hundred texts that they had corrupted in order to support their false opinions brought in apart from scripture....

Finally, the scripture is the light and life of God's elect and that mighty power by which God creates them and shapes them according to the similitude, likeness, and very fashion of Christ. It is therefore sustenance, comfort, and strength to encourage them, that they may stand fast, endure, and merrily maintain their souls' health, with which the lusts of the flesh are subdued and killed and the spirit made soft to receive the imprint of the image of our Savior Jesus. The scripture is so pure of itself that it can corrupt no one but the wicked who are infected beforehand and corrupt it with the heresies they bring with them. And the complaint of hypocrites that the scripture makes heretics is vain and feigned, and the reasons they would use to prove that laypeople ought not to read the scripture are false, wicked, and the fruit of rotten trees. Therefore, faithful servants of Christ and faithful ministers and dispensers of his doctrine, who are true-hearted toward their comrades and have given themselves into the hand of God, putting themselves in jeopardy of persecution and having their very life despised, have translated the scripture purely and with good conscience, submitting themselves and desiring those who can to amend their translation, or (if it please them) to translate it themselves after their best manner.[29]...

God has seen to it through them that a great part [of scripture] is translated. Yet, as it is not enough that the father and mother have begotten the child and brought it into this world unless they care for it and bring it up until it can help itself, even so it is not enough to have translated even the whole scripture into the vulgar and common tongue unless we have also recovered the light to understand it and to expel that dark cloud which the hypocrites have spread over the face of scripture so as to blind its right sense and true meaning. For that reason various introductions have been ordained to teach you the profession of your baptism, the only light of the scripture: one built upon the epistle of Paul to the Romans[30] and another called *The Pathway into the Scripture*.[31] For the same cause I have taken in hand to interpret this Epistle of St. John the evangelist, in order to edify the laypeople and teach them how to read the scripture and what to seek therein, and [to give them what they need] to answer the hypocrites and stop up their mouths.

PART THREE

Preaching

Introduction

Since most early Protestants were not clergy, it may seem restrictive to think of preaching as spirituality. For our purposes, however, preaching refers not only to the delivery of sermons but also to their reception. Although we do not have reliable figures for church attendance or adequate feedback from laity about the sermons they heard, we do know that preaching was the main feature of most Protestant services and that communal worship replaced to a large extent the private piety (like that described by Thomas Cranmer below) that had dominated late medieval religion. Insofar as spirituality by our definition is the way people practice the faith, going to church and hearing sermons was a prominent feature of the spiritual life of early Protestants.

Nevertheless, printed sermons do reveal more about the preacher than about the hearers: their theology of course, occasionally their daily lives, but also their reactions to current events and especially the expectations of clergy for the laity. The texts chosen here are not representative sermons in any sense of the word and are not to be understood as homiletical exemplars. The text by Urbanus Rhegius is an excerpt from a homiletical manual, but even he is more concerned about the content of Protestant sermons than about rhetoric and style. All three texts are, however, rich examples of homiletical texts that urged early Protestants in Germany, Geneva, and England to practice the faith in a new way that was more in accord with scripture and Reformation theology. In that sense these sermons express and advocate a Protestant spirituality.

They also express the high expectations of their authors and a certain disappointment that those expectations have not been met. Rhegius is disappointed not only in the laity but also in the young Protestant clergy, who are not teaching people clearly enough the consequences of their beliefs. Because concepts like law, good works, and election are presented to them in a simplistic and one-sided manner, laity appear to believe that being Protestant means they can ignore the commandments and other spiritual resources such as catechism, prayer, and worship. Calvin's standard is unusually lofty; the sermon text from Acts 4 to which his listeners are held accountable is one of the texts on which the monastic life had been founded. Religious reformers always have high ideals, of course, but the challenge faced by early Protestant preachers was especially daunting, because they were attempting to change in one generation a spirituality that had been building in Europe for centuries. They were attempting a revolution, and it is therefore miraculous that they succeeded at all.

11. Urbanus Rhegius, A Guide to Preaching about the Chief Topics of Christian Doctrine Carefully and without Giving Offense, for Young Ministers of the Word in the Duchy of Lüneburg, 1535

When the Lutheran reformer Urbanus Rhegius wrote this preaching manual for young Protestant clergy in northern Germany, he had been overseeing their work for more than four years. Originally from southern Germany, Rhegius was born Urban Rieger (1489–1541), but like other young humanists he changed his name after acquiring a classical and theological education that led to the priesthood. In 1520 he lost his job as the cathedral preacher in Augsburg for demonstrating too much sympathy with Martin Luther. In 1524 he returned to Augsburg as a Protestant preacher, married a prominent daughter of the town, and became an avid proponent of the Reformation.

When the imperial diet met at Augsburg in 1530, Rhegius was invited by Duke Ernest of Lüneburg to move north and assume leadership of the nascent Protestant church in the duke's lands. Until his death in 1541, Rhegius served energetically as the church superintendent of the territory. The training of young clergy, a task that had always been close to his heart, was one of his main responsibilities, but after he heard their sermons and the distorted messages that laypeople were receiving, he realized that a concerted campaign of clerical education was needed. One result of the campaign was this manual, the extensive title of which describes Rhegius's goal: a nuanced presentation of the Protestant message that would lead to a correct and balanced understanding by laity.

Adapted from *Preaching the Reformation,* trans. and ed. Scott Hendrix, 25–41 and 81–85.

Urbanus Rhegius desires the full knowledge of Christ for the novices in sacred letters in the duchy of Lüneburg who are preaching the gospel of Jesus Christ.

All sensible people, not to mention Christians, should watch with the greatest care what they say, lest their tongue get ahead of their mind and babble forth before they have organized their thoughts. It is especially incumbent upon ministers of the gospel to attend with the greatest diligence to what they will proclaim in the church of God and to deliver it in the most orderly manner possible, so that they give no offense to the uneducated members.

As scripture testifies, to speak in the church of the living God is a very difficult charge full of dread and danger. The children of God, served by angels, are sitting there listening, and the Lord God himself, the inspector of all things, is present as if in his tabernacle, with his angels and all creatures looking on and listening to the word of God with great reverence. For piety enjoins us to believe that all things render the highest reverence to God's word through which they have been created (John 1:3), with the exception of human beings and the devil, who have been made deaf by the despicable vice of ingratitude.[1]

St. Jerome correctly understood and said this very thing: "It is a great danger to speak in church, lest a perverse interpretation turn the gospel of Christ into a human gospel or, what is worse, into the gospel of the devil."[2] Earnest admonitions of the apostle refer to this: "When you come together,…let all things be done for building up" (1 Cor 14:26). "Let your speech always be gracious, seasoned with salt" (Col 4:6). "Do your best to present yourself to God as one approved by him, a worker who has no need to be ashamed, rightly explaining the word of truth" (2 Tim 2:15). What else does Paul teach here than how the awe-inspiring mysteries of the word of God should be treated with the greatest care and piety? Ambrose gives the same advice: one should speak about the faith at the right time and place, letting modesty be the mistress.[3] For if our thoughtlessness causes us to present the doctrines of our faith to people in a form that is distorted or defiled, then we do not rightly explain the word of God, and for such temerity we will surely suffer severe punishment at the day of the Lord, when we have to give account of our stewardship before the supreme judge.

In order that young, unpracticed novices in theology may avoid offending anyone with their teaching, I have written for you a short explanation, as it were, of how to speak carefully about the most important articles of Christian doctrine. I use something like this myself when I preach. For years now, with great distress, I have seen in many parts of Germany how often laity have been seriously offended by that confused, inept, and imprudent way of speaking when certain thoughtless know-it-alls, with an inflated estimate of their own knowledge, take no notice of what they say, how they say it, or to whom they are speaking. I will give a few examples of these offensive formulations that corrupt the minds of the laity and drive many away from the gospel.

Part One

Some rarely preach about repentance at all, but only about faith and remission of sins, as if people who do not repent could believe the gospel and receive the forgiveness of sins. Quite to the contrary, the gospel embraces both repentance and forgiveness of sins, as you find in the last chapter of Luke: "It was necessary that repentance and forgiveness of sins be proclaimed in the name of Christ unto all the nations beginning at Jerusalem" (Luke 24:46–47). Here you see the order established by Christ: repentance should be preached first followed by the proclamation of the forgiveness of sins.

Some do an adequate job of urging repentance and terrifying consciences by vehemently applying the law, but they are unable to comfort those same consciences with the gospel. Consequently, they teach a maimed and defective repentance. I am convinced by my own experience that a pastor who ignores the article of repentance is no more useful to the flock of Christ than a wolf is to the sheepfold.

Whenever the clear and firm doctrine of faith and good works is to be laid before the people, some preach as follows: "Our works are nothing. They are of no use. They stink before God. He does not want them. They only produce hypocrites. Faith alone does it. If you believe, then you will be godly and blessed."

These phrases slip out of some preachers without any salt. They add nothing but instead babble forth a truncated teaching about faith and works without giving these words the necessary clarification. No wonder, then, that such words offend simple laity, especially those who have rarely heard a sermon on the gospel. They think that everything is attributed to faith in such a way as to reject works completely and make them useless. Soon they start to realize: the preacher must be lost in a fog to condemn out of hand good works that Christ himself performed and also requires of us. Then they begin to look down on all our teaching.

With similar imprudence some speak about the mass without any explanation of so great a matter. They carry on frivolously like this: "The mass is an abomination before God. One must absolutely avoid it or lose eternal salvation. The priests crucify Christ again in the mass. The mass is no sacrifice at all. It is the teaching and invention of the pope." They leave it at this without further clarification.

When simple laity hear nothing but these words, which merely tear down without building up, what else will they conclude but that everything that happens in the mass is of no importance? They also neglect the supper of the Lord as something unnecessary. The authors of such impious negligence are those insipid and brash people who do not know how to distinguish the abuse of a thing far and wide from the thing itself, but throw away the thing itself because of the abuse. They act like people who find a pearl in the dirt and then throw it away as if it were completely worthless

79

because of the dirt sticking to it instead of removing the dirt and keeping the pearl.

Here one should proceed with caution, and the supper of the Lord ought to be separated from those inventions that were added by the superstition or greed of the papists. Then people will clearly understand that we condemn only human additions that conflict with faith. We do not condemn the mass of Christ and the apostles, that is, the supper of the Lord or the most venerable sacrament of the altar.

In striving to present Paul's teaching about the law and its office, some preachers brazenly teach the following: "The ten commandments were not given for us to obey." Here they abruptly stop the sermon and move on to another topic, although they should explain in detail why the law was given at all, since it cannot justify the sinner. Unless they already understand Paul perfectly, people who hear such things cannot avoid taking offense. Right away they think that meditating upon the law, keeping it, and doing good works are unnecessary and that it is permitted to steal and to commit adultery and murder. For one hears these things said publicly by people who have listened to such foolish sermons.

Some preachers rattle on carelessly and crudely about free will as follows: "We have no free will at all. Whatever we do we are compelled to do." At this point they add nothing that would make such talk bearable; instead they leave these darts lodged in the minds of simple people who immediately think: "If I do everything out of necessity and nothing freely, how am I any better than the beasts? And how can I then avoid sinning? If I am compelled to sin, why am I accused of transgression?" In this way reckless preachers give the masses reason to believe that God is the author of sin, and that is nothing but blasphemy. God is not the cause of sin. On the contrary, in the law God has revealed to us his own will, showing that he hates sin, indeed that he forbids and punishes it with great severity both in this life and in eternity.

In like fashion, without taking the laity into consideration at all, some preachers present an exceedingly offensive message about the difficult article of predestination, although they could moderate their speech and remain within the limits of Pauline teaching. Sometimes they even say: "If you are predestined by God to salvation, you cannot be damned no matter what you do, evil or good." People who hear this either lose all restraint and despise every law, or they despair and utter impieties like: "Why should I bother to fast, pray, give alms, forgive my neighbor and torment myself with good works like these? Our pastor says it does no good. I will be a good fellow and not worry about anything. If I am predestined, I will be saved. If not, I will go the way of the masses. I will do whatever I want; it makes no difference." Human reason cannot avoid this blasphemy when it hears such a superficial preacher who babbles about the sacred mystery of election with a mouth so defiled and words so disgraceful. No, it does matter what you do. We see that Christ says: "Come, you that are blessed by my Father, inherit the kingdom prepared for you from the foundation of the world; for I was hungry and you gave me food, etc." (Matt 25:34–35). Here you have it: whoever does good will be saved; whoever does evil and persists in it will be damned.

The same thing happens in the article concerning Christian freedom. The untrained preachers treat this topic in such ignorant and godless fashion that the uncivil masses imagine Christians have no obligation to anyone, are free from all laws, and owe no obedience to magistrates. They are convinced that everything should be held in common by everyone: forests, fields, vineyards, lakes, personal property, and houses. No one should have to pay tithes or interest. To sum it up: they think anyone can do anything they want. Ignorance of this doctrine gave rise to the Peasants' War in 1525, in which 100,000 people were killed in Swabia, Franconia, Thuringia, and Alsace. I myself knew a master from Paris who tried to defend a peasant before the abbess at Lindau. The peasant was her servant, bound to perform duties of public service. "Kind lady," he said, "it is not right for you to burden poor people like that and demand service from them, for Christ has redeemed us and made us free through his blood."

Note how this old master, who had been a preacher for forty years, still did not understand the freedom we have in Christ. He confused the political kingdom of the world with the spiritual kingdom of Christ by thinking it was a great honor for Christ to have freed us from our public duties and acquired for us a carnal freedom. This master understood nothing of sin and justification, nor

81

did he teach about it, just like his own school [Paris], which still today serves the antichrist.

I speak from experience. Such stupid, godless, and seditious sermons about Christian freedom have scared away from the gospel capable and educated people. After they heard these know-it-alls extol the gospel as a pretext for such terrible errors, they were soon looking askance at the entire doctrine of the gospel, even though it was not the gospel of Christ that those fanatics were declaring, but their own dreams. For the gospel does not abolish civil authority and laws but confirms them. They have spoken falsely about civil office and failed to commend the function of magistrates as a good and necessary work; instead, they have reproached it as if it were tyranny and violence.

Furthermore, some preachers have heard that all Christians are taught by God (John 6:45), and right away they defend their laziness. They condemn all liberal education as useless, strut about, and boast they can do everything. The more uneducated a person is, the more grandly he brags about the spirit, as if the Holy Spirit would repudiate his own gifts, namely, learning and knowledge (Isa 11:2; 1 Cor 12:8). Such error is the reason why even ordinary peasants and workers take over the office of preaching, boasting that no study is required because "we are all taught by God." Because they treat scripture without the spirit of prophecy, they bring about countless errors. They despise the old teachers of the church as if now only the uneducated were wise. And most of them also condemn schooling for children so that now schools are neglected. The devil loves to see this kind of negligence, but God is very displeased.

I ask you: twenty years from now where will the church find ministers of the word to call? From what source will cities and princes obtain their jurists? People will be illiterate and stupid brutes. Germany will become barbaric as it used to be, and we will again fall prey to all kinds of deceivers. Our ability to recognize the antichrist and Roman treachery, along with our freedom in Christ, has been wrought in us by God through the study of languages and of a more genuine theology.

Because some preachers talk about satisfaction without sufficient care, the untaught common folk think they are completely exempt from the exercise of good works and from bearing the cross.

Virginity assuredly receives praise in scripture, but it is scorned by some preachers with shameful words that wound many innocent hearts. They go to the extreme in both directions and are unable to stay on the royal road.[4] Without doubt one should give marriage the highest praise, but do it without insulting virginity.

I also hear that some pastors think little of confession. They fail to examine their flock diligently in confession or to require the catechism. Instead, when a large group is present for confession, they instruct all of them at one time and then absolve them. This practice does not build up anyone but rather destroys the churches of Christ.

Many preachers of the same stripe prattle foolishly about human traditions: "One must run from all human traditions; they are from the devil. One is not bound to obey them." That is a scandalous and misleading way to talk. On this subject one should carefully teach how human traditions are defined and how many different kinds there are, also how one can distinguish between those that should be kept and those that should be rejected. But the preachers put them all in one category and condemn them without any distinction whatsoever. The common people, therefore, think they have been freed from all laws and are under no obligation whatsoever to obey any human regulations.

They also speak ineptly about fasting: "We do not need fasting. It does not atone for sin or perform satisfaction. Fasting is an invention of the pope, etc." Here the preachers generally stop. Since, however, our flesh by nature flees the cross and self-restraint and seeks pleasure instead, such sermons will only lead to countless evils. We see that people plainly despise fasting as if it were no use whatsoever, and they indulge themselves without restraint in all kinds of excess. On this point, certainly, the supreme judge will require the blood of those who perish because of such fatuous sermons at the hands of the preachers themselves, as God threatens in Ezekiel (Ezek 33:8).

What shall I say about prayer? Some can think of nothing else to say when they happen to come upon the subject than these unfortunate words: "Frequent praying and jabbering is a pagan error and hypocrisy in which God takes absolutely no pleasure." They cut their remarks too short at this point. As with other topics, they ought to take more time and treat the subject of prayer in orderly fashion, so that people are not distracted by dull and empty comments from this necessary practice of piety.

The way some pastors talk about the invocation of saints is so scurrilous that devoted hearts cannot help being offended by their blasphemies, especially since one should refer to the saints with reverence. Through this wicked slander Satan is trying to arouse contempt for the article of faith, "[I believe in] the catholic church, the communion of saints," so that we have little or no regard for the communion of saints.

Similar foolishness about images is heard from many of the same preachers who understand nothing about Christian freedom.

On the subject of festivals or holy days they spread fanatical opinions that discourage people from hearing God's word and from receiving the sacrament.

They also fail to preach as they should about matters of ritual and worship; in some places one hears only the following: "The rituals are futile; they produce no benefits. Why does one need special vestments in church? They amount only to human trifles."

O foolish people! As if this life could be without ritual! One must wisely distinguish between ruinous rituals and others that are optional. Those rituals that promote order in the church should be retained with propriety and not so rashly rejected, for making abrupt changes in the old rituals has always caused great dissension and discontent in Christendom.

The Satan of the Sadducees[5] and of the Origenists[6] vexes some preachers so much that they speak shamefully about Christian burials and cemeteries. This frivolity undermines faith in the resurrection. Pious hearts are bound to speak respectfully about burial and everything that pertains to it owing to the certain hope of a glorious resurrection that is our unique consolation. It does not allow us to dispose of our bodies without great respect, since we know from God's word that on the last day they will be made like the glorious body of Christ (Phil 3:20–21).

Who can even keep track of all these inept teachings? Lest I appear to lack diligence in this matter, I have composed some brief formulations that I also tend to use whenever I have to preach in church on the subjects listed below. It will be a great help, my dear colleagues, to keep them handy, so that we preachers may give no offense to the laity: repentance, faith, good works, merit, mass, law, free will, predestination, Christian freedom, civil authority, everyone taught by God (John 6:45), satisfaction, virginity, confession, human traditions, fasting, prayer, invocation of the saints, images, festivals, rituals, burial....

How to speak properly about fasting.

Fasting is twofold, daily and spiritual. Daily fasting is the daily sobriety and moderation of Christians. They should always avoid too much drinking and becoming intoxicated, according to the admonition of Christ (Luke 21:34), so that they are able to glorify the name of the Lord with their senses intact. Scripture presses this point everywhere: "Do not get drunk with wine, for that is debauchery; but be filled with the Spirit, as you sing psalms, hymns, and spiritual songs among yourselves, singing and making melody to the Lord in your hearts, giving thanks to God at all times and for everything in the name of the Lord" (Eph 5:18–20). "Let us then lay aside the works of darkness and put on the armor of light; let us walk in an orderly way as in the day, not in gluttony and drunkenness; and make no provision for the flesh, to gratify its desires" (Rom 13:12–14). Let us who are children of God be sober (1 Thess 5:5, 8). "For the grace of God has appeared, bringing salvation to all, training us that we might live lives that are self-controlled, etc." (Titus 2:11–12).

A special kind of fasting takes place, however, when in the face of great calamity or for the sake of prayer people undertake for themselves a day or more of fasting, or when a bishop or civil ruler proclaims a period of fasting, as did Jehoshaphat, king of Judah (2 Chr 20:3). And the apostle [Paul] prescribes such fasting for spouses: "Do not deprive one another except perhaps by agreement for a set time, to devote yourselves to fasting[7] and prayer" (1 Cor 7:5). For this reason I approve of the Lenten fast (although in the early church it was observed in Christian freedom), so that by fasting people might prepare themselves for more ardent and attentive prayer and for giving thanks in the supper of the Lord, both for the most precious death of Christ by which we are redeemed from all evils in eternity, and for his most victorious resurrection, which is the source of our justification and resurrection.

St. Ignatius, the disciple of John the evangelist in Asia and a martyr of Christ, says the following in his epistle to the Philippians: "Do not disregard Lent, for it contains the likeness of life with God."[8] But this holy man did not place burdens on consciences like the burdens of the pope that have encumbered us. The pope commanded this fasting under penalty of mortal sin and prohibited meat, eggs, and butter, but Ignatius makes no mention of such things. In his work against Montanus the heretic, blessed Jerome says: "We fast during Lent every year according to the tradition of the apostles."[9] And St. Ambrose mentions such fasting frequently.[10]

To sum up this topic: Those who are Christians are assuredly moved by the Spirit of God to live every day soberly and moderately, so that the wanton flesh may not overcome the spirit. Whenever they are about to ask God earnestly for something or to partake of the Lord's supper with solemn thanksgiving, at the instigation of the Spirit they will either fast beforehand or live moderately and soberly. If not, they are still carnal and only Christian in name. A thousand years ago the earliest devout Christians observed the forty-day period of fasting as each of them had opportunity. What kind of Christians, then, are we who do not want to fast even once or twice a year when it is time to go to the Lord's table? Still, everything said here about special fasting should be understood as teaching and admonition, not as a commandment, so that consciences may not be ensnared.

12. Thomas Cranmer, A Homily or Sermon of Good Works Annexed unto Faith, 1547

It is very likely, but not certain, that Thomas Cranmer (1489–1556) wrote this homily, the third part of which is printed here. As the reform-minded archbishop of Canterbury since 1533, Cranmer gradually conceived a plan to publish a book of sermons or homilies on major points of Protestant doctrine that were to be read from the pulpits. After the death of Henry VIII in 1547, Cranmer faced the same problem with uninformed preachers in England that Rhegius had found in Germany. He also encountered a shortage of Protestant-minded clergy suitable for preaching the aggressive reform agenda undertaken with his sympathizers under the regency of the new boy king, Edward VI. Part of that agenda was to send visitors or inspectors to all the parishes in order to ascertain their condition. The instructions for those visitors included the order that all the parishes should obtain a copy of the twelve homilies that were published in July 1547. Some may have been prepared during Henry's lifetime, but in all likelihood Cranmer composed the exhortation to the reading of holy scripture and the three homilies on salvation, faith, and good works.[11]

Part III of the homily on faith and good works presents a detailed rejection of late medieval piety practiced by lay Christians in sixteenth-century England. These concrete acts and artifacts of piety constituted their spirituality, and Protestant reformers had difficulty convincing laypeople to replace these acts with a new Protestant spirituality that Cranmer summarizes at the end of the homily. At the heart of the new spirituality Cranmer places obedience to the scriptural command-ments, which are to be regarded with much greater reverence than the rules and traditions of the church. Although its tone is polemical, this text is one of the best summaries of the Reformation battle over true Christian spirituality.

Adapted from *Miscellaneous Writings and Letters of Thomas Cranmer,* ed. John Edmund Cox for the Parker Society, 146–49.

The Third Part of the Sermon of Good Works

Thus have you heard how much the world, from the begin-ning until Christ's time, was ever ready to fall from the command-ments of God and to seek other means to honor and serve him, after a devotion imagined out of their own heads, and how they extolled their own traditions as high or above God's commandments. The same thing has happened also in our times (the more it is to be lamented) no less than it did among the Jews, owing to the corrup-tion or at least the negligence of those who chiefly ought to have preferred God's commandments and to have preserved the sincere and heavenly doctrine left by Christ.

What person, having any judgment or learning joined with a true zeal unto God, does not see and lament to have entered into Christ's religion such false doctrine, superstition, idolatry, hypocrisy, and other enormities and abuses, so as by little and little, through the sour leaven thereof, the sweet bread of God's holy word has been much hindered and laid aside? Never did the Jews in their greatest blindness have so many pilgrimages to images, nor did they practice so much kneeling, kissing, and burning incense to them as has been in our time. Sects and feigned religions were never the forty part so many[12] among the Jews, nor more superstitiously and ungodly abused, than of late days they have been among us. These sects and religions had so many hypocritical works in their state of religion, as they arrogantly named it,[13] that their lamps (they said) always ran over and were thus able to satisfy not only for their own sins but for all their other benefactors, brothers, and sisters of their religion. Thus in a most ungodly and crafty manner had they persuaded the multitude of ignorant people.

They kept in divers places, as it were, marts or markets of merits, being full of their holy relics, images, shrines, and works of supererogation[14] ready to be sold. And all things that they had were called holy: holy cowls, holy girdles, holy pardoned beads,[15] holy shoes, holy rules, all full of holiness. What thing can be more foolish, more superstitious, or ungodly than that men, women, and children should wear a friar's coat to deliver them from agues or pestilence, or that when they die or are buried they cause it to be thrown over them in hope thereby to be saved? That superstition, although (thanks be to God) it has been little used in this realm, yet in divers other realms it has been and yet is used among many people, both learned and unlearned.

But, to pass over the innumerable superstitions in strange apparel, in the use of silence, in dormitory, in cloister, in chapter, in choice of meats and in drinks, and in such things, let us consider what enormities and abuses have been in the three chief principal points that they called the three essentials of religion, that is, obedience, chastity, and willful[16] poverty.

First, under pretense of obedience to their father in religion (which obedience they made up themselves), they were exempted by their rules and canons from obedience to their natural father and mother and from obedience to emperor and king and all temporal power, whom of very duty by God's laws they were bound to obey. And so the profession of their obedience not due[17] was a renunciation of their due obedience. How their profession of chastity was observed—it is more respectable to pass over in silence and let the world judge that which is well known than with unchaste words that would describe their unchaste life to offend chaste and godly ears.

As for their willful poverty, it was such that, when in possessions, jewels, plate,[18] and riches they were equal to or above merchants, gentlemen, barons, earls, and dukes, yet by this subtle and sophistical term, *proprium in communi*,[19] they deluded the world by persuading it that, notwithstanding all their possessions and riches, they observed their vow and were in willful poverty. But for all their riches they were not able to help father or mother or others who were indeed very needy and poor without the permission of their father abbot, prior, or warden. They could take from anybody, but they could not give to anyone, not even to those whom the laws of God bound them to help; and so through their traditions and rules the law of God could bear no rule[20] with them. Therefore of them might be most truly said that which Christ spoke to the Pharisees: you break the commandments of God for the sake of your traditions; you honor God with your lips but your hearts are far from him (Matt 15:3, 8). Likewise, when they used long prayers by day and by night under pretense of holiness to get the favor of widows and other simple folk, so that they [the monks and canons] might sing trentals[21] and services for their [deceased] husbands and friends and admit them into their suffrages[22]—all the more true of them is this saying of Christ: Woe to you scribes, Pharisees, hypocrites, for you devour widows' houses under color of long prayers; therefore your damnation will be the greater; woe to you, scribes and Pharisees, hypocrites, for you go about by sea and by land to make novices and new brethren; and when they are admitted into your sect, you make them the children of hell worse than you are (Mark 12:40; Matt 23:15).

Honor be to God, who did put light in the heart of his faithful and true minister of most famous memory, King Henry VIII, and gave him the knowledge of his word and earnest affection to seek his glory, and to put away all such superstitious and pharisaical sects[23] invented by the antichrist, and to set up again the true word of God and the glory of his most blessed name, just as God gave the same spirit to the most noble and famous princes Jehoshaphat, Josiah, and Hezekiah. God grant us all, the king's faithful and true subjects, to feed from the sweet and savory bread of God's own word and, as Christ commanded, to eschew all the pharisaical and papistical leaven of feigned religion.[24] Although [the religious life] was before God most abominable and contrary to God's commandments and Christ's pure religion, it was extolled to be a most godly life and the highest state of perfection, as though we might be more godly and more perfect by keeping human rules, traditions, and professions than by keeping the holy commandments of God.

To pass over briefly the ungodly and counterfeit religions, let us rehearse some other kinds of papistical superstitions and abuses: beads, lady psalters,[25] rosaries, fifteen O's,[26] St. Bernard's verses,[27] St. Agatha's letters,[28] purgatory, masses satisfactory,[29] stations and jubilees, feigned relics, hallowed beads, bells, bread, water, palms, candles, fire, and others; superstitious fastings, fraternities, pardons, and similar merchandise were so esteemed and abused to the great prejudice of God's glory and commandments that they were made most high and holy things, by which eternal life or remission of sins could be attained. Yea also, vain inventions, unfruitful ceremonies, and ungodly laws, decrees, and councils of Rome were in such wise advanced that nothing was thought comparable in authority, learning, wisdom, and godliness. The laws of Rome, they said, were to be received by all like the four evangelists, and the laws of princes should give way to them. The laws of God were in part omitted and less esteemed, so that the said laws, decrees, and councils with their traditions and ceremonies might be more duly observed and held in greater reverence.

Thus were the people through ignorance so blinded with the goodly show and appearance of those things, that they thought the observing of them was holier and a more perfect service and honoring of God and more pleasing to God than the keeping of God's commandments. We have always had this corrupt inclination superstitiously to make up new ways of honoring God and then to have more desire and devotion to observe them than to search out God's holy commandments and to keep them, and furthermore to take divine commandments for human commandments and human commandments for God's commandments, yea, for the highest and most perfect and holy of all God's commandments. And everything was so confused that only well-learned people, and but a small number of them, knew or at least would know and dared to affirm the truth—to separate God's commandments from human commandments. This confusion produced much error, superstition, idolatry, vain religion, preposterous judgment, and great contention with all manner of ungodly living.

Wherefore, as you have any zeal to the right and pure honoring of God, any regard to your own souls and to the life that is to come, which is both without pain and without end, apply yourselves chiefly above all things to read and to hear God's word. Mark diligently what is his will for you to do, and with all your endeavor apply yourselves to follow the same. First, you must have an assured faith in God and give yourselves wholly to him, love him in prosperity and adversity, and dread to offend him evermore. Then, for his sake, love everyone, friends and foes, because they are God's creation and image and redeemed by Christ as you are. Cast in your minds how you may do good to all to the utmost of your ability and hurt no one. Obey all your superiors and governors, serve your masters faithfully and diligently as well in their absence as in their presence, not from dread of punishment only but for conscience sake, knowing that you are bound so to do by God's commandments. Disobey not your fathers and mothers but honor them, help them, and please them to your power. Oppress not, kill not, beat not, neither slander nor hate anyone; but love every person, speak well of all, help and succor every person as you can, yes, even your enemies who hate you, speak evil of you, and hurt you.

Take no one's goods nor covet your neighbor's goods wrongfully, but content yourselves with that which you obtain truly and also bestow your own goods charitably as need and case require. Flee all idolatry, witchcraft, and perjury; commit no manner of adultery, fornication, or other unchasteness, in will or in deed, with another's spouse, widow, widower, or servant. And travailing[30] continually during your life in observing the commandments of God (in which consists the pure, principal, and direct honor of God and which, wrought in faith, God has ordained to be the right trade and pathway to heaven), you shall not fail, as Christ has promised, to come to that blessed and eternal life where you shall live in glory and joy with God forever. To whom be laud, honor, and impery[31] for ever and ever. Amen.

13. John Calvin, Sermon on Acts 4:32–37, June 1, 1550

Throughout his career in Geneva, John Calvin (1509–64) encountered opposition from the city's old families, who did not like the restrictions imposed on their influence and way of life by the new Protestant regime. Just prior to 1550 that opposition intensified after a new wave of French refugees arrived in the city and the older families gained stronger representation in the city's government. Calvin came under additional stress in March of 1550 when his wife, Idelette de Bure, died. Despite the grief that followed, his workload remained heavy; in addition to his other duties and his large correspondence, Calvin was preaching on Sunday and on some weekdays as well. During that long year from August 1549 to January 1551, he delivered a series of sermons on chapters one through seven of the Acts of the Apostles. The sermon on Acts 4:32–37 presented here belongs to that series.

Like many commentators, Calvin believed that the Book of Acts described the church in its purest state as the earliest embodiment of Christ's kingdom. It was therefore the perfect mirror to hold up to Genevans in order to show them how far they were from the ideal Christian life and to admonish them to reach harder for that spiritual state. The text also enabled Calvin to restate his vision of a successful reformation. It would reach more deeply than the alteration of worship and church structures. A true reformation was the work of the Holy Spirit, who was empowering believers in a united community to purify their faith and to enflame their charity—in other words, to become more like the earliest believers portrayed in Acts. This sermon, delivered in trying times of strife and division, reflects both Calvin's disappointment with the lax Genevans and his unflagging determination to bring them closer to the ideal spiritual community.

Translated from *Supplementa Calviniana* 8, 113–20.

"And the company of those who believed were of one heart and one soul and no one said that any of the things he possessed was his own, but they had everything in common" (Acts 4:32).

The name of faith is honorable indeed and, when one mentions it to us, we say it is an excellent virtue to have. No one, however, wishes to rely on God to the extent that God would consider us truly faithful. We want this reputation in the eyes of others, but in regard to God it does not matter as much to us. For if we had the kind of affection we should, we would realize what is required for faith and what holy scripture is saying about it in order to conform us to it completely. But we do not think about it at all; our nonchalance and laziness are obvious.

It is well to say that we approximate the lives of those whom St. Luke describes in our text when he tells us what has made them such authentic believers, namely, that they are joined together as one and have made confession of their faith. Luke frequently mentions the apostles in particular when he says they have given witness to the resurrection of our Lord Jesus Christ. Although the apostles have given testimony of the resurrection, however, it is obvious that each of us in our own place has not followed them. In fact, we know it is a common matter for all Christians to confess Jesus Christ with the mouth, even though we ought to believe in him from the heart.

Let us therefore note well this passage where St. Luke tells us how the faithful conducted themselves when they gave witness to their faith before God and before the world. He also shows us what the true church is like and how we are brought into it. A genuine union exists among us and everything is so well ordered that all of us make sure we fulfill our duty to our neighbors. In the first place, if we want God to count us among his children, we must have what is declared to us here: we are joined together in one and the same good will, in communion with one another. Next, we should all share the same teaching to which God has borne witness through the Holy Spirit and that he continues to confirm for us every day through the preaching of his gospel. And so it will be when we become the true church!...

In order to gain more benefit from this passage, we should note the following verse: "There was one heart and one soul in the company of believers" (Acts 4:32). As seen above, St. Luke speaks expressly of the multitude of believers. A large assembly of people who can agree with one another is more admirable than only two or three or a dozen who get along. It can happen that the latter might be able to agree. But when a multitude is not governed by the Holy Spirit, there will necessarily be confusion and people will show what they are by nature. We know our natural state. We are all taken with our own desires; in fact, what is the cause of so many troubles and divisions if not the diversity of human affections?[32] One wishes to proceed in one way, another in a different way. Suddenly debate and dissension arise, and the result is always confusion and disorder.

Thus it is a miracle when a great multitude live in peace; the Holy Spirit must have been active and brought it to that point. If we desire above all else to be true believers and have God's approval as such, there must be the same kind of union among us that, according to St. Luke, existed then in the Christian church. What is faith after all? Just as the truth of God is unchangeable and unable to be divided, when we have faith it is necessary for us to be united. For where there is division, people are separated from this truth of God. Consequently, if any persons claim to be faithful, they must say what St. Luke describes here, namely, that they are in accord with the children of God.

St. Luke, however, wished to go further. He not only speaks of the accord that we have in the church of God, but also of that bond that ought to be made visible among us through charity. It is possible that people could be of one accord in matters of doctrine (believe in one and the same God, confess what holy scripture says about Jesus Christ) but nevertheless remain divided among themselves. Why? Because true faith is not in them. There is a great difference between faith in God that ought to be occupied with charity and good works and a belief we have about, for example, a certain story. Many people imagine the story of the gospel to be true, but was that belief put in their heart by the Holy Spirit? We have no such report. In fact, as we said above, if the word of God has taken root in our hearts, the Holy Spirit must have been at work. We know the Holy Spirit is the Spirit of peace and union and that, as long as he remains in us, we must be joined together in true friendship one with another. Thus St. Luke speaks here of the unity and fraternity that ought to exist among the faithful and of the harmony that all of us in the church ought to possess in order to make the same confession of faith and to worship one and the same God as we do. But it behooves us also to know that it is not enough for us to be joined in fraternal love unless God has first brought us to himself and caused a great change in us, namely, established such accord with Jesus Christ that we are joined to him as members of his body.

St. Luke speaks with good reason of this fraternal bond that should exist among us, for later he shows how the faithful demonstrated they had charity among themselves by helping the poor. It is true that, if people boast of having charity but never put it into action, they can be accused of lying. For charity is not a dead thing at all. It will inevitably be visible in external fruits, although it is true that external works are not beneficial unless we have charity. St. Paul says that we can divest ourselves of everything and distribute it to the poor, but if we do not have the love that should go with it, all that we do is like a noise that fades away (1 Cor 13:1–3). You may ask: how does it happen that people can surrender all they have in order to give alms and to aid the poor and still it would happen in vain, like someone batting the air? The answer is: they could be motivated by ambition or by hypocrisy. For if you fathom your heart, you will discover that you do not love your neighbor as you should. Many things are as needful as giving alms. We have to be open to forgiving one another and ready to help one another with every need that arises. Then we have to be ready to endanger our welfare in order to help one another and not even to spare our own persons. When I learn that my neighbors need my aid, I must help them with my possessions and with my body and my person, so that one can see that I do it enthusiastically from the heart.

We mark then the order of St. Luke's remarks. He does not only say that charity is directed toward others, but he adds the fruits that witness to it. He does not start with almsgiving but says that believers were of one heart and soul. Still, here is what we have to do in order to show that we are children of God and have grown in the gospel. Let us remember first that God has called us to the knowledge of his truth and that this bond ties us together in complete charity and brotherhood. Our disagreements do not divide Jesus Christ at all, since he gives himself to us completely. Besides, we know that we have the same Father in heaven and that we are members of one body and heirs of the same legacy. One and the same Spirit of God governs us, so that we are united in one and the same heart and soul. That was the second point. Third, we should demonstrate by helping our neighbors that we have genuine charity in us, especially since extending ourselves toward the neighbor would be nothing if God were not thereby served and honored. We have the teaching of the gospel with a special charge that it be so deeply rooted in our hearts that we never decline to the right or to the left (Deut 5:32). See how our Savior will preserve his church and accept us as his children!

If we now compare to our situation what St. Luke has described, we will recognize how far we are from Christianity! Each of us boasts of being faithful, and we presume not to doubt that we are good Christians; nevertheless it belongs to God to define true Christianity. If we examine ourselves, we will find that we are very far from that which St. Luke says. This passage serves as a touchstone and test for identifying true Christians. We should never think that our Lord could allow his name to be blasphemed thus. For it is certain that whenever we boast of being Christians and then in the next minute do the opposite of what a good Christian should do, we dishonor God and severely blaspheme his name. The more we dare call ourselves Christians with a straight face, the more we bring God's wrath upon us whenever we do not possess the truth of that which we pretend. But if we acknowledge our faults, we must ask God to forgive them and, besides, we are admonished by this passage better to receive the word of God and to prepare our ears for the teaching of the gospel with greater willingness than heretofore.

Why has the gospel made so little headway among us? The majority have not taken a liking to it and are not much concerned with it. True, the gospel is preached well and people come to hear the sermon, but it is only a formality. What do people take home with them after a long sermon? We ought to pose this question every time a sermon is preached so that we give thought to what should be learned and how we should profit from it. It is not a noise that beats the air. One day we will have to give account of all that we have heard, including those times we have taken it lightly. Many others make their profession of the gospel briefly and still wish it were erased and that they had never said anything at all.

Accordingly, when it comes time to separate the sheep from the goats, God will acknowledge only a few of them as his own (Matt 25:32–34). And when the elect finally become visible on that grand day, we will not need to hide as we do now, for our hypocrisy will no longer do us any good.

For the rest, when we see here that the apostles testify to the resurrection of our Lord Jesus Christ, we realize that doctrine must have its beginning in us and then we, increasing in it from day to day, will advance in all good works that proceed from charity. This charity consists of two things. It is the love we have for one another, knowing ourselves to be children of God through Jesus Christ, who has instructed us to support one another and to live together in harmony and union. Each of us should be less concerned with our private affairs and more with mutually extending ourselves toward our neighbors. That is charity. When I say that it consists of two things, however, I mean first charity in itself and second the fact that it must show fruits. The heart cannot contain a charity so restricted that it would not be visible in all of human life or yield any fruits. Then it would not be charity. We are to follow that which St. Luke shows us here. We should not be devoted to ourselves but instead procure the well being and advantage of our neighbors insofar as we are able, as indeed our Lord commands us through his law. Indeed, seeing that each of us is blind insofar as by nature we are disposed to love ourselves too much, our Lord directs us toward our neighbors: "You shall love," he says, "your neighbors as yourselves" (Matt 22:39). It is impossible for us to abide in the union described in this passage if we have no charity inspiring us to help one another. As we said above: we cannot love our neighbors until we have abandoned and forgotten the love of ourselves, and we must fix this fault of esteeming ourselves too highly. Moreover, we must eradicate the disordered desire for our own advantage in order to know how to bear the wrongs that can be committed against us.

To sum it up: where there is no love and affection for the neighbor and no forgetfulness of self, it is impossible for love to reign. The following things are as incompatible as fire and water: dedication to our own advantage and genuine love for the neighbor. I will go so far as to say that those who love themselves hate their neighbors. If they esteem themselves, they look down on others in order to enhance their worth and to get ahead. If they are devoted to their own advantage, they will care only about themselves as if they alone existed. People who are motivated by self-love will have no difficulty deceiving one person and pillaging another, slandering, disparaging, and doing other despicable and illicit things to please themselves and fulfill their evil desires. Whenever we do things like that, regardless of the pretty face we put on it, there is no more charity in us than you find in dogs. Let us learn, then, that after our Lord has shown us that our hearts must be open to our neighbors, he also wishes that our hands be used completely for their good and that we consider the ability we have to help our neighbors. By "hands" I mean everything that God has given us to be used in the service of our neighbors. We should not even dream of holding back anything for ourselves (as if it belonged to us) that God has given for the purpose of sharing with others. St. Luke says precisely that: none of the believers claimed anything as his or her own but regarded everything as common property (Acts 4:32). Even those who owned land and other kinds of property sold them so that those who were in need could be aided and have their needs met (Acts 4:34–35).

When it says "that the faithful had everything in common" (Acts 4:32), Luke means that no one should claim ownership of their property in such a way that would prevent that person from giving some of it to others according to their needs, as will soon be explained more fully. St. Luke does not wish to introduce any confusion that would result in disorder, but he declares that we should not consume what we have in such a private way that we see our neighbors starve around us without coming to their aid, like many who would say: "What I have is mine; let others fend for themselves." We should never do that, but instead we should recognize that God has given us what we have in order to share with others who need it. After all, how does God desire the goods of this world to be used? Is it not that his members be nourished and provided for? Of course! It is evident, then, that wordly goods belong to those who possess them only to the extent that they, as God has given them the ability, must also share those goods with those who obviously have need of them. And this is what St. Luke means when he says that the faithful did not have anything of their own: no possessions should be held back and hoarded so tightly that they would never help anyone else. All here realized that our Lord had exhorted them to this mutual assistance.

It is true, as I have said, that there was no confusion among them, as St. Luke makes clear by adding: "Distribution was made to each as any had need" (Acts 4:35). Note that goods were not just piled up and people allowed to grab whatever they could before someone else got to it. Instead, one person ascertained where there were needs to be met and distributed the goods according to those needs. Indeed, this text has been written for our instruction and not for them. If we desire that God accept us as his children and regard us as the body of his church, then we have to follow their example. We know that our Lord has not changed his purpose since that day! It is necessary for us to have the same union as those of whom St. Luke speaks here. Do we want it to be strong and approved by God? Then we must follow in their steps.

Let us now check how far we are from that union. Very far, in fact. For those who have a lot there is no chance they will do good with it; they fail to help the poor from their substance, nor do they give away any of their surplus, although they could do so without diminishing their principal. Selling one's land and possessions to help the poor is out of the question when one will not donate any of the surplus. On the contrary, people who have twice as much land as they need will never be satisfied until they have amassed still more. For what? To help the poor? Hardly! Rather to make them die of hunger, and still the rich are not content. If truth be told, it is usury, plunder, violence, and extortion: one is pillaged and the other robbed. If inflation comes, their greed will drive them to seize everything. When they see that the poor can no longer make it, they will try to devour them and gnaw them to the bone. Is that our Christianity? Can we then boast that we have something in common with those about whom St. Luke is talking? Certainly not. You can see how remote we are from their way of life and from the charity they exercised toward their neighbors.

As we have seen, fanatics[33] have tried to pervert this passage in order to sow confusion as if everything were mixed up in one batch. "See here the disciples of Jesus Christ," they say, "who sold everything they had; it follows that no Christian should own anything in this world." If that were true, it would follow that what God has said would be useless, namely, that people should work with their hands since they have to eat (1 Thess 4:11; 2 Thess 3:10). How could a person have anything to drink and eat if that person has no land or other possessions? God has declared that his gospel will be preached everywhere and holy scripture be heard by all. Who then will possess anything? No one can. Fields, vineyards, and other properties will lie fallow without cultivation and not produce any crops to sustain us. Thus we should take note of this passage whenever we see such fanatics try to turn it to their advantage against the true meaning of St. Luke.

We see as well how monks under the papacy have distorted this passage. Under the shadow of brotherhood they say they lead an apostolic life and that the disciples held no more in common than they do. As we said! Like pigs in a trough they eat and devour the food of others. They will say, of course, "our cowl, our hood," in pretending they are a community. But they continue to live separately from others and devour every day what poor people have gone to great pains to gather. From this you can see how they abuse this instruction of St. Luke and try to overturn it completely in order to live in leisure and satisfy their desires. From every side we see that what is written here has been given for our instruction. Instead of excessive devotion to ourselves we should know that our Lord has not put us in this world for ourselves but that we are bound to work for the benefit of our neighbors insofar as we are able. Since it is the case that we must work for the benefit of our neighbors and meet their needs from what we have, what will become of those who have the welfare of the poor in their hands and, in place of helping the needy, use their property for their own vain and dissolute ends? That is certainly the opposite of what the disciples of Jesus Christ did. They were selling their possessions in order to relieve the needs of the poor, but these monks would confiscate the money of the poor and turn it into feasting, gluttony, and whatever strikes their fancy. We should fear, therefore, lest God send us a severe punishment when the property that ought to be set aside to help his members is so appallingly misused.

Do we think that God does not notice that? Of course he does. Or that God would tolerate such a waste of the goods that should be offered to members of Jesus Christ? We should call this passage frequently to mind, and if we desire to be united and joined with those who have preceded us and have been the true church of God, it is necessary for us to follow their lead so that we may have the same heart and courage and exercise the same charity toward our neighbors. As we are able we will reach out to those who are in need and not be bad children who deceive one another. Let us remember that others have a part in those things we hold to be rightfully ours, especially since we have the same Father in heaven, the same confident basis on which to confess our Christianity, and we are all joined to the same head, who is Jesus Christ, in order to share in the same glory with him.

PART FOUR

Admonishing and Consoling

Introduction

Seeking consolation in difficult times is one avenue that leads people to religion and a deeper sense of the spirit. That was as true in the sixteenth century as it is today. Pamphlets that consoled people in the midst of adversity and admonished them to repent and improve their lives were a significant genre of literature produced by Protestants and Catholics. Sometimes a specific crisis like war or an epidemic was the occasion for writing such pamphlets, but often it was the ever present struggle with illness and death that confronted pastors and their people with the need for resources that brought comfort and reassurance. Two of the selections presented here were prompted by crises: the treatise by Rhegius was a response to an outbreak of the plague in Augsburg, and the letter from Katharina Schütz Zell sought to comfort the Protestant women of Kentzingen, who had been harassed and mistreated by the soldiers of their Catholic overlords. Of the two remaining selections, one was a sermon for Easter Day, and one a guide for pastoral ministry to the sick.

Seeking and finding consolation seem to be in harmony with spirituality, but admonitions and warnings are not so commonly associated with the spiritual life. Reformation pamphlets are full of them, however, because people believed that adversity was brought by God both as punishment for sin and as stimulation for improving their moral and religious conduct. This belief was common to both Catholics and Protestants, but, because of their immersion in scripture and reliance on its authority, Protestants were armed with an abundance of Bible passages that threatened divine punishment for human sin and misbehavior. Hence the call for repentance and amendment of lives that marks the treatise of Rhegius and also finds mention in the other selections. Early Protestants believed strongly in the reality of human sin. Staying aware of its power and keeping it at bay were therefore important features of their spirituality.

Protestants had, however, fewer religious resources to which they could look for consolation than did late medieval believers. They could no longer turn to the saints or to private masses and works of satisfaction to assuage their fear and guilt. In place of them, preachers and pastors offered four primary resources: (1) prayer directly to Christ and meditation on the complete satisfaction that the death of Christ had made for everyone's sin; (2) the resurrection of Christ and the assurance that all believers would enjoy eternal life; (3) the consoling words of scripture that were contained in the Old and the New Testaments; and (4) the community of believers and the sacraments that were offered in the church. All these resources appear in the following selections, but it is remarkable how many of these resources are, as it were, more external than internal. Prayer and meditation are readily included in the concept of spirituality, but preaching, intensive reading of scripture, and the careful and faithful use of the sacraments also marked the spiritual life of early Protestants. For them, the spiritual life was Christ-centered, scripture-centered, and church-centered, or at least their leaders wanted it to be. With hope and confidence they offered those resources to people as the most effective religious means of enduring adversity, strengthening their faith, and renewing their lives.

14. Katharina Schütz Zell, Letter to the Suffering Women of the Community of Kentzingen Who Believe in Christ, Sisters with Me in Jesus Christ, 1524

The marriage of Katharina Schütz (c. 1498–1562) to the priest Matthew Zell in 1523 was a demonstration of the Christian freedom being preached by Zell, Strasbourg's first Protestant reformer. Katharina Schütz, a devout daughter of the city who regarded her marriage to Zell as a partnership in the gospel, wasted no time in adding her public voice to that of her husband. Within a year she had published a defense of clerical marriage and a justification of her husband and their marriage after they had come under attack. Over the course of thirty-four years, six of her works were either published or circulated in addition to her extensive correspondence. As a laywoman not from a noble family, she stands out among the small number of women writers of the sixteenth century whose works are extant.

Though not ordained, Schütz Zell possessed a strong pastoral sensitivity that manifested itself in her appreciation of hymnody (see text no. 27 below), her hospitality to refugees and others in need, the words spoken to mourners at her husband's burial in 1548, and her letters of consolation. One of the latter was written in 1524, the year after she was married, to the women of Kentzingen, a small town near Freiburg across the Rhine from Strasbourg. When the Catholic overlord of the town tried to stop Protestant preaching that had been endorsed by the citizens, around 150 men together with their preacher fled to Strasbourg. In Kentzingen soldiers burned bibles and Protestant literature, executed the town secretary in front of his wife and children, and mistreated the women who had been left behind. While providing housing and food for a large number of the men, Schütz Zell managed to reach the women with a letter of consolation that offered comfort in the midst of persecution and encouragement to remain steadfast.

The English text is taken from Katharina Schütz Zell, *Church Mother*, ed. and trans. Elsie McKee, 47–62; the German critical edition is published in McKee, *Katharina Schütz Zell*, vol. 2, *The Writings*, 1–13.

May God, the Father of all mercy, send and grant you grace, peace, salvation, strength, and longsuffering patience in overflowing fullness, through the merit of Jesus Christ, in your distressing suffering and trouble sent by God, O believing Christian women of the whole community at Kentzingen, and my sisters especially beloved in God.

All of us, I and those who are united with me in Christ, know and consider well, with compassionate hearts, your great distress, which you suffer for Christ's sake. Yet we also rejoice with you because of it with inward feelings of happiness when, because of this suffering, we hear and sense your God-given faith, which you demonstrate in this trial. I also ask God day and night with all of you that he may increase that same faith, as also Christ's disciples prayed: "Increase our faith" (Luke 17:5). By that faith I also exhort you with friendly request and exhortation, as your sister in Christ Jesus, that you not let the invincible word of God go out of your heart but always meditate on that word, which you have had with you for so long and heard with all earnestness and faithfulness. And may you also receive these sufferings with great patience and thankfulness, as special fatherly gifts sent from God, which he does not give to any but his best-loved children (Prov 3:12).[1]

For indeed to an unbeliever it would look strange that God should give such gifts to the children whom he loves. Such an unbeliever would much rather not be God's child but a child of the world, which does not treat its children that way: the world disciplines its children softly and tenderly. It is true, as Paul says, that faith is not everyone's thing, and the worldly (that is, the carnal) person cannot understand what is godly, but the spiritual (that is, the believing) person understands (1 Cor 2:14–15) that God deals surprisingly with his own, completely contrary to the world and its children. As also he says in the prophet Isaiah: "My thoughts are not your thoughts, nor are your ways my ways" (Isa 55:8). Therefore, he says at another place in the prophet: "The one whom I want to make alive, that one I cause to die; the one whom I want to make well, that one I strike" (Deut 32:39). In sum, he wills that those whom he has eternally chosen and whom he has written as his children in the book of his heirs should also be won away from this world, and he wants to teach us to depend only on him in one strong faith and not expect or take anything from anyone else but only from him.

But the world's children he will not recompense; therefore, he allows them to be given the world, honor, happiness, goods, and whatever the world has. That is their recompense and inheritance and with that he casts them out—just as Abraham, the man of great faith, cast out the illegitimate son Ishmael born of his maid Hagar with a gift of his goods and excluded him from his [Abraham's] inheritance, when his legitimate wife, Sarah, spoke: "Cast out this slave woman with her son; for the son of this slave woman shall not inherit along with my son Isaac" (Gen 21:10). Truly this Ishmael signifies the children of the world, who will undoubtedly be excluded from the inheritance of the eternal Father, and they are established as rulers and owners of this world as also Ishmael was, for they must also have some recompense. But to Isaac, the legitimate son, Abraham gave nothing, but led him up to a mountain and wanted to kill him there with a sword and so sacrifice him to God. In the opinion of the world that was truly an unfatherly thing to do, but Abraham believed and knew that his heir was invisibly kept safe for him and that God could also bring him back to life (Gen 22:1–19; Heb 11:17–19).

So I beg you, loyal believing women, also to do this: Take upon you the manly, Abraham-like courage while you too are in distress and encounter all kinds of insult and suffering by which you are abused. When you meet with imprisonment in towers, chains, drowning, banishment, and the like, when your husbands and you yourselves might be killed, meditate then on the strong Abraham, father of us all (Rom 4:16), and imitate him as a good child should follow his father in a faith like the father's. Do you not think that Abraham also suffered when God told him to kill his only son, when he told Abraham to do it himself, to kill the son in whom the blessing of human beings was promised? Yes, indeed, he was very grieved, for he was also flesh and blood like all of us, but he knew (as the scripture says) that God could bring his son back to life (Heb 11:17–19).

And so you also, when your husbands are killed, do you not know that Christ said: "I am the resurrection and the life; those who believe in me, even though they die, will live" (John 11:25)? And in the sixth chapter of John he says that whoever eats his flesh and drinks his blood, that is, whoever truly believes that he is redeemed only through the death and shedding of the blood of Christ, that one he will bring back to life on the last day (John 6:54). He says to his disciples: "If you know these things, you are blessed" (John 13:17). So also to you, believing women beloved by God, Christ says: "Those who will not leave father and mother, wife, husband, child, and everything they have, for my sake and the sake of the gospel, are not worthy of me....Those, however, who for my sake do leave father and mother, wife, husband, child, farm and field, to them I will return a hundredfold and in the age to come eternal life" (Matt 10:39, 19:29; Mark 10:29–30).

107

Dear Christian women, if you know and do this, then you also are blessed, as Christ said (John 13:17). Trample your flesh under foot, lift up your spirit, and speak comfortingly to your husbands and also to yourselves the words that Christ himself has said: "Do not fear those who can kill the body; I will show you one who can kill your body and soul and cast them in hell" (Luke 12:4–5). And shortly after that he says: "Therefore whoever confesses me before this adulterous and wicked generation, that one I will also confess before my Father and his angels; whoever denies me, however, and is ashamed of me and my words, I will also deny and be ashamed of that one before my Father" (Luke 12:8–9; Mark 8:38). In another place he also says: "A servant is not greater than the lord, the disciple is not more than the master. If they have persecuted me, they will also persecute you. If they have called the father of the family Beelzebub, they will use that name even more so for members of the household. They will ban you and exclude you from their fellowship, and those who kill you will think they are doing God a service" (Matt 10:24–25; John 15:20, 16:2). And he said to them: "Therefore I have told you that this would happen, so that when it happens you will not shrink back and fall away, because I have told you about it beforehand" (John 16:4).

Therefore, dear sisters, I beg you to meditate diligently on these words, for the scripture must thus be fulfilled, as Christ said to the two disciples going to Emmaus: "You foolish and vexatious hearts, slow to believe all that the prophets have spoken! Must not the Christ suffer such things and so enter into his glory?" (Luke 24:25–26). So you also, if you want to be Christians and to enter into his glory with him, you must also suffer with him, and for this you encounter abuse. Yes, even if you are put in chains for Christ's sake, how happy you are. Would that God would regard me with such grace and favor me with such great honor, that I should have gifts unlike yet also like yours, to suffer such things with his dearest Christ and with you. Then I would be more joyful, proud, and glad than all the nobles at the Strasbourg fair in their golden chains and necklaces. Yes, I would be happier in that suffering than if I were the wife of the Holy Roman emperor and sat in his highest imperial seat of majesty.

For I know and am certain that such things [as persecution] are only signs of his fatherly love and indeed the most trustworthy signs. For there is no doubt that he loved Christ his Son and eternal Word above all. We have come into God's love by Christ, as Paul says to the Ephesians (Eph 1:4). And God also allowed suffering to happen to Christ and left his humanity uncomforted, so that Christ also cried out: "My God, my God, why have you forsaken me?" (Matt 27:46). As I said before, God wants to discipline us and tear us away from the desires of this world so that we may learn to desire only him. He also says through the prophet: "If my people sin against me, I will chastise them with rods, but I will never take my mercy from them" (2 Sam 7:14–15). His rod is temporal torment here, but his mercy is the eternal inheritance that he will not take from us, as he has sworn to our fathers Abraham, Isaac, and Jacob. Therefore David says: "The Lord has sworn and will not change his mind" (Ps 110:4).

Therefore, dear Christians, you should not receive with impatience God's rod and whatever he sends; as the wise man says: "My child, do not despise the Lord's discipline or be weary of his reproof, for the Lord reproves the one he loves, as a father the son in whom he delights" (Prov 3:11–12). And Paul says to the Hebrews: "Endure trials for the sake of discipline. God is treating you as children; for what child is there whom a parent does not discipline? If you do not have that discipline in which all children share, then you are illegitimate and not his children....Now, discipline always seems painful rather than pleasant at the time, but later it yields the peaceful fruit of righteousness to those who have been trained by it" (Heb 12:7–8, 11). Earlier in this chapter he also says: "Let us run with perseverance the race that is set before us, looking to Jesus the pioneer and perfecter of our faith, who for the sake of the joy that was set before him endured the cross, disregarding its shame, and has taken his seat at the right hand of God. Consider him who endured such hostility against himself from sinners, so that you may not grow weary or lose heart" (Heb 12:1–3).

Therefore, dear Christian women, consider these words, which are not mine but are from the Spirit of God, and be thankful and welcome such gifts of God. Christ says: "If any want to become my followers, let them deny themselves and take up their cross and follow me" (Matt 16:24). As it was for the dearest Son of God, so must it also be for those who want to inherit with him. Christ says: "Holy Father, I want my servants also to be where I am" (John 17:24); that is, he wants to have us with him in suffering and in joy. Therefore do not impatiently oppose him. It has pleased God to leave you for a little and also to test you a little, as sad widows without husbands, as he shows reassuringly in the fifty-fourth chapter of the prophet Isaiah, which may be applied properly to this and like matters. He says:

> "Do not fear, for you will not be shamed; and do not be sad with thoughts of your widowhood, for the one who made you, that one will protect you, the Lord of hosts is his name; and the holy one of Israel is your redeemer, he is God of all the earth. The Lord has chosen that you should be sad and an abandoned wife.[2] I have forgotten you for the blink of an eye, a little time, but I gather you again in greater mercy; I have hidden my countenance from you for a little, but I will have mercy on you eternally, for I am your redeemer. O you poor thing, cast out in the storm without any comfort! My mercy and my covenant of peace are not divorced from you." (Isa 54:4–8, 10, 11)

O you women, described so perfectly in this chapter, who could want a better description than this? Are you not now widows called by God? All these things have happened to you for the sake of his word. Has he not hidden himself from you for a little, so that you might think he has forgotten you? So that you could scarcely see him through a window (that is, by faith), for he stands behind the wall, as also the lovesick soul wails in the Song of Songs (Song 2:9). Are you not also insulted and left without comfort in the storm? Yes. Consider, however, what he says here, "Do not fear, you will not be shamed," and he says that his mercy and covenant of eternal peace will not be divorced from you in such a storm, for he will not divorce himself from you as he does from the ungodly. As he said to his disciples: "I will not leave you orphaned; I am coming to you. In a little while the world will no longer see me, but you will see me; because I live, you also will live" (John 14:18–19). These words are a reminder that he will not abandon you or forget you, as he also says in the prophet: "As little as a mother may forget her suckling child, so little may I forget you; and if she does forget her child, still I will not forget you" (Isa 49:15).

Therefore David says: "I will not fear what others do to me, and even if they set all their company and armor against me, still my heart will not fear" (Ps 27:1–3). God will not have us fear other people, as he says through Isaiah: "Do not fear, for I am with you," and before that he said three times to the believers: "Fear not, for I your God am with you. All those who fight against you will be shamed" (Isa 41:10–11, 13), with yet many other glorious words. Are those not comforting golden words to a believer? That God, who cannot lie, promises believers his manifold help with the highest oath, that is, he swears by himself that he will not leave them (Isa 41:17; 45:23). Therefore Paul says in First Corinthians: "God is faithful, and he will not let you be tested beyond your strength, but with the testing he also provides an increase of grace so that you can bear it" (1 Cor 10:13).

So, dear Christian sisters, trust God. He does not lay on you more to bear than is good and necessary for you. He will prove your faith as he did for Abraham, when he told him to kill his only son and yet had promised to bless the people through this same son. However, Abraham obeyed God, so God said: "Now I know that you fear me and believe me" (Gen 22:12). Not that God did not know beforehand, but he wanted to demonstrate Abraham's faith and make it certain to Abraham himself and to all of us, as Peter says: "The outward works of love make us certain that we believe" (2 Pet 1:5–11). So also God wants to show you, those who come after you, and all of us that you believe and that he loves you.

Dear sisters, even though sometimes your faith may be discouraged and the flesh may fight against the spirit (1 Pet 2:11), do not therefore be frightened away. It is a holy struggle, it must be thus: faith that is not tempted is not faith. Therefore Job says: "Human life is a tournament" (Job 7:1). God will not reckon what you do as impatience, if only the spirit does not remain under the flesh or the flesh overcome the spirit. Therefore you should constantly pray with the father of the sick child: "Lord, help my unbelief" (Mark 9:24). Christ himself was frightened when he considered

111

the horrors of his impending death, saying, "Father, if it is possible, take this cup from me," but soon he said, "Not what I will but what you will" (Matt 26:39).

So, dear Christian women, I cannot now comfort you more and exhort you better than to counsel you to accept such suffering with appropriate patience and spiritual joy, for these are fruits of the Spirit (Gal 5:22), so that God may be glorified in you above all others who are called but may not yet have been so greatly tried as you are. Consider the words of Christ where he says: "Blessed are those who mourn, for they will be comforted. Blessed are those who are persecuted for righteousness' sake, for theirs is the kingdom of heaven" (Matt 5:4, 10). And he exhorts you and all his own to accept such things with patience and love, saying: "Love your enemies. Bless those who curse you. Do good to those who hate you. Pray for those who afflict and betray you, that you may be children of your Father in heaven." He concludes: "If you love and do good to those who also do good to you, do not the unjust also do that? Therefore you should be perfect as your Father in heaven is perfect" (Luke 6:27–28; Matt 5:44–48). None can do this, however, unless he or she has the Spirit, whom Christ will send according to his promise (John 14:16–17); he himself wants to be your comforter, trustworthy one, and protector. Amen.

Given Friday, the day of St. Mary Magdalene,[3] in the year one thousand five hundred twenty-four.
Katharina Schütz, wife of Matthew Zell, preacher of the word of God to the Christian community in Strasbourg, your fellow sister in Christ.

15. Caspar Huberinus, A Comforting Sermon on the Resurrection of Christ, Useful for Those Weak in Faith to Read, 1525

Caspar Huberinus (1500–1553) was an unusual reformer. Prior to the Reformation he was neither a priest nor a monk, and although he studied theology in Wittenberg, he began to publish pamphlets before he became a pastor in Augsburg, the largest city in southern Germany near his birthplace. Despite his lay status Huberinus repre-

112

sented the city at an early Reformation debate, and in 1535 he and a colleague were sent to confer with Luther about the controversy over the Lord's Supper between Lutheran and Zwinglian clergy in Augsburg. Not long after becoming a pastor in the early 1540s, Huberinus accepted a call from the counts of Hohenlohe to become the preacher in Öhringen. The same religious compromise that favored Catholics and drove Martin Bucer out of Strasbourg, the Augsburg *Interim* of 1548, was accepted by the counts in Hohenlohe, but Huberinus still managed to offer a Protestant celebration of the Lord's Supper in place of the mass. Before he died in 1553, Huberinus equipped Hohenlohe with a constitution for its new Protestant church.

Huberinus was a prolific and popular author of edifying works that were reprinted frequently during the sixteenth century. The most widely distributed pamphlet, *The Wrath and the Kindness of God* (1529), appeared in over forty editions and translations. The sermon presented here may have been delivered in Augsburg on Easter Sunday, 1525, but it is uncertain how the unordained Huberinus was able to preach it. He may have written it for someone else to deliver, but in any case, it is the only stand-alone printed sermon by Huberinus that has survived. Its message of consolation is strongly theological and requires for its effectiveness that believers be troubled by God's wrath against their sin and be confident of the nearness of Christ in adversity.

Translated from *Ein tröstlicher Sermon von der Urstend Christi den Schwachen im Glauben nutzlich zu lesen*, Augsburg: Heinrich Steiner, 1525.

A SERMON FOR EASTER SUNDAY ON CHAPTER 16 OF THE GOSPEL OF MARK

Our gospel reading for today contains one of the twelve articles of Christian faith: the resurrection of Christ from the dead. This article provides immense consolation to every believer, namely, that Christ is risen from the dead and has overcome eternal death for us through his suffering and dying. He has risen for our benefit and is alive for our sake. He has been set upon the throne of David (Luke 1:32) and now rules our consciences with the Holy Spirit. Power to be Lord of heaven and earth is bestowed upon him.

He is our strong, mighty, and powerful king who has preceded us in death and every misery and has overcome them all for us.

Whoever does anything to us does it to Christ himself. He has made us rulers together with him over all creation, so that nothing in heaven and earth can harm us. Death and the devil can do nothing to us because he has conquered both through his death. After all he died for us. For himself he did not need to die, but he died in order to defeat death for us and now he rules over both of those enemies, as indicated by the prophet Hosea: O death, I will be your death; now [I have] become a vanquisher and a victor (1 Cor 15:54–55; Hos 13:14).

Through his wonderful resurrection, therefore, we have become sovereigns and conquerors of hell and sin. He has promised this to us, and for our sake went down into the depths in order to preserve us from this cruel and horrible descent into hell. Through his joyous resurrection he has also become a great high priest for us, who has obtained direct access to the Father and has reconciled us to the Father through his suffering and dying. By his merits and good works he has earned for us a welcome access to the Father and abolished our eternal death; in its place he has given us through his rising eternal resurrection and endless life.

Christ is the true high priest, our real bishop, who has taken away from us the Father's anger and, together with our sin, placed it on himself and thereby reconciled us and God to one another. In place of God's robust justice and his potent anger, Christ has obtained for us the abundant gift of the Father's mercy. For God's righteousness is so stern and exacting that it is unable to leave any sin unpunished, especially since in Adam's fall we also became subject to this terrible judgment of God and became children of wrath and of eternal damnation, although from the beginning of the world we were ordained to become children of God and were destined for eternal life (Eph 1:4, 5). In order for God's justice to remain intact and to provide a way to punish sin as the justice of God demands, Christ loved us so much—while we were still enemies of God and could merit nothing through our works, for we were children of wrath and mired in our sins—Christ loved us so much, I say, that he freely gave himself for us amid this misery and took upon himself the wrath of his Father. He quieted it and removed the wrath of God his Father from us. In this way the justice of God, which cannot let any evil go unpunished, retains its integrity.

So that we did not have to bear the punishment of our sins, God allowed his beloved child to be scourged for us: because of the transgression of my people I have "struck down" my son (Isa 53:4–5). For our sake God cast him down to hell, and therefore God's wrath against us has been stilled and abolished. Through his beloved Son he has become so fond of us that he restored us to favor and has become a merciful Father.

Through this high priest we may boldly approach the Father (Heb 4:14–16), for he is our reconciliation (1 John 2:1–2). Whenever we are weak and stumble into sin, he is there to help us up and to intercede for us with the Father. On the cross Christ offered the true sacrifice for our sin and also prayed for us, "Forgive them, for they do not know what they are doing" (Luke 23:34).

This Christ is our true paschal lamb, as Paul says (1 Cor 5:7). He has accomplished everything for us through his joyful and merciful resurrection. As a result, today we gladly sing: Christ is risen, we should all be joyful, Christ will be our comfort.[4] He is indeed our true consolation who comes to our aid and comforts us in all suffering, just as here (Mark 16:6–7) he comes to the aid of the women and the apostles, announcing to them through the angel that he is risen; that he had overcome torture, death, and hell; and that power in heaven and on earth had been given to him (Matt 28:18).

As a consequence of his resurrection all of us who believe have become priests with him. Because the Father has become so fond of us through his Son, we may joyfully approach the Father and make requests for ourselves, and not only for ourselves but also for our neighbors. We may also teach and instruct them and proclaim to them the glad tidings of the gospel. Now we see what the resurrection of Christ has gained for us: we have become rulers and priests with Christ (Rev 5:10), and he has stilled the horrible wrath of God and removed it from us.

Which good work of ours was so costly and powerful that it could have quelled God's great anger? The righteousness of God needed to be satisfied and to punish sin, and that required something that was precious and acceptable, something effective and pleasing to God, namely, his own beloved child. If our work had been able to accomplish this, then Christ would be an insignificant God who died and rose for no reason at all. If, however, for nine hundred years Adam was not able to make up for his sin with any good work (Gen 5:5), then he had to depend on this Christ alone, believe in him, and be freed from sin. No one climbs up to heaven but he who descended from heaven, Christ our head (John 3:13). If we want to ascend, we have to become one with this Christ and be carried up on his back. Our works cannot accomplish that, because our righteousness is nothing but a filthy cloth (Isa 64:6).

Hence we must let go of our works and comfort ourselves solely with this joyful resurrection of Christ. He is truly the one accepted and loved by the Father, yes, the one with whom he is well pleased (Matt 17:5). The Father has regard for his merits alone, not for our good works or our hypocritical, invented works that reason thinks are good. Honor, glory, and praise belong to Christ alone (1 Tim 1:17). He wants to be our only true helper, the way to heaven, and the door to the Father, yes, our merciful Savior. He will not pay tribute to anything else, not to us, or to our opinions, or to our actions. Such honor does not belong to the creature but only to the almighty, merciful God. He will prove himself alone to be just, true, all powerful, and merciful, who can also go down to Hades and back again: "For you have power over life and death; you lead mortals down to the gates of Hades and back again" (Wis 16:13). You are also the one who kills and makes alive, as scripture indicates to us (1 Sam 2:6).

Because we have such a powerful king who has preceded us in death and every misfortune and has conquered all that for us, who will harm us? If he is with us, who shall be against us and whom should we fear? Who will hold us guilty and accuse us of sin when Christ has already taken it away (Rom 8:31–34)? Hence neither death nor the devil, heights nor depths, neither present nor future can turn us away from this Christ (Rom 8:38–39). He has taken on our weakness and was tempted from every side but, in contrast to us, without sin (Heb 4:15), so that he could bestow faith on our weakness, come to our aid, and represent us to the Father as often as we need it.

Who, therefore, will charge us with sin when we have this priest, who for our sake offered the unique sacrifice that is more precious than heaven and earth? He intercedes for us, protects us, so that nothing can harm us no matter how versatile and powerful sin and the devil turn out to be. Christ is risen in order to help us in every situation, listen to us, and be close to us at all times. Before he died, he could not be with everybody everywhere at once. Since he is risen, however, he can give to all aid and counsel all the time, also fortify them so that the weak are raised up and those already strong confirmed in their strength. He has entered the kingdom of the Father so that he can always be near to help us (Matt 28:20) and to protect us from violence. For he sits at the right hand of the Father with all power and authority, and every force in heaven and earth must be subject to him (Phil 2:9–11).

We receive this genuine benefit from his joyous resurrection when we believe that he has done everything for our sake and has become our own. Because we could not make satisfaction for sin, we have one who is our surety and paid everything for us. If death tries to destroy us with eternal death, he has conquered death and suffered it for our sake with the result that for us it is no more. If hell opens its jaws and tries to devour us, Christ has already been there for us, closed its jaws and worn down its might. If the multitude of our sins tries to make us lose heart and give up hope, we have one who was given for us and has given us all things with himself: all righteousness, godliness, and everything that accompanies them. He is our spouse who has taken us to himself in marriage. Whatever belongs to us—death, sin, and unrighteousness—they are now his. And everything that he has—righteousness, eternal life, everything—is now ours.[5] We can now say to him with great joy: You are mine, and I am yours, and whoever harms you harms Christ himself, for "whoever lays hands on you touches the apple of my eye" (Zech 2:8).

He cannot and will not allow any of his faithful ones to be harmed. He may look on for a while, stand behind the wall and watch us through the crack; he may let us swim for a while but without drowning. For a time he lets us suffer onslaughts and vexations so that our faith and confidence in him become that much stronger and we learn to trust him boldly in the face of all opposition. In a way he is testing his own grace that he has poured into us so that it takes root and grows strong, but he remains near us and takes wonderful care of us. We have become exceedingly dear to him, for we cost him dearly and he had to pay a high price for us, namely, his own rose-colored blood. He will not let us go to ruin or because of us let his own blood count for nought.

It is our fault that we do not trust him with our whole heart and cast ourselves on him with complete confidence. He cannot bear for anyone to do us harm and considers that harm done to himself. We have a splendid example of that in the Acts of the Apostles. When Saul wanted to persecute the Christians, Christ spoke to him: "Saul, Saul, why do you persecute me?" (Acts 9:4). Christ did not say "my Christians" but "me," my very self. It is magnificent consolation for us that Christ identifies himself so closely with us.

We should not allow the world, death, sin, hell, or the devil to make us afraid or despair, because we have a powerful, strong, and mighty Lord. We should boldly look to him for everything good in life and in death. Although he sometimes acts as if he were angry with us, it does not last forever. He lets up and remembers his mercy and comes back to us. Although he sometimes scares us by seeming to abandon us, he only does that in order to keep our reverence and respect, to give us reason to ask for his grace and to strengthen, motivate, and practice our faith. He wants our faith to be strong so that we let nothing in heaven, hell, or on earth separate us from the love that is in Christ our Lord. Amen.

16. Urbanus Rhegius, Apothecary of the Soul for the Healthy and the Sick in These Dangerous Times, 1529

Before he left Augsburg in 1530 (see text no. 11 above), Urbanus Rhegius composed this archetype of Protestant solace literature; it appeared in the same year as the first version of a consolatory pamphlet by Huberinus, who was also living in the city. Both works became enormously popular: *Consolation from Divine Scripture* by Huberinus was printed sixty-eight times and Rhegius's *Apothecary of the Soul* sixty-four times. Beginning in 1542 the two treatises were supplemented with woodcuts of the dance of death by Hans Holbein, and in that form they appeared in more than fifty additional printed versions. Altogether, the two consolatory works by Huberinus and Rhegius were printed over 120 times in ten to twelve different languages!

Apothecary of the Soul is the longer of the two, and for that reason only the first two parts are presented here. These parts address the fear and anxiety caused first by sin and then by death; the third part offers remedies against the fear of hell. The advice is directed to both sick and healthy people, because the sudden onset of illness and impending death might not leave time for proper repentance, absolution, and the Lord's Supper, which would forgive sin and bolster faith. In fact, as this treatise was being written, the sweating sickness was raging in Augsburg. In the last two months of 1529 it claimed more than twelve hundred victims. Epidemics were, however, only one cause of shorter life spans for sixteenth-century people and death was an ever-present threat to them. The copious use of scripture is typical of works by Rhegius.

Translated from *Seelenärtzney für die gesunden und kranken zu disen gefärlichen zeyten, durch Urbanum Rhegium,* in Gunther Franz, *Huberinus—Rhegius—Holbein,* 241–60.

Jeremiah 26:13: "Now therefore amend your ways and your doings, and obey the voice of the Lord your God, and the Lord will change his mind about the disaster that he has pronounced against you."

Bodily illness and death are terrible indeed, but sickness and death of the soul are the most horrible things that can happen to us. If we fear punishment, illness, and dying, all the more should we fear sin, guilt, and God's anger. If we seek medicine for the body, why not also find medicine for the soul? What good is it to possess all the world's goods, live for a thousand years, and have no physical illness, if our soul is poisoned by the deadly malady of sin, ruled by the devil's might, out of favor with God, and has nothing more imminent than the eternal death and damnation of body and soul?

Christ says: "Keep awake, therefore, for you know neither the day nor the hour in which the son of man is coming" (Matt 25:13).[6] In order that we do not chase after the least important thing and neglect the greatest, he teaches us the sure path: "But strive first for the kingdom of God and his righteousness" (Matt 6:33). Day and night we worry about food and other things that will not always help or stay with us; we fail to rank them below eternal possessions, and that is a dangerous blind spot. We seldom think seriously about the life to come and our physical death. Only when it finally hits us

119

do we decide to prepare ourselves. All of that is a sign that our faith is weak and untried. May God have mercy upon us. Amen.

Still, no repentance comes too late if it happens before we die. No one, however, should wait until the last minute. Even those who prepare for death while they are healthy can hardly bear the end, so what happens to those who have led a contemptible and evil life without any fear of God or repentance at all?

Since there are so many parishioners, and the servants of the gospel cannot be everywhere, I have written this little instruction for ordinary folk, so that everyone who can read can comfort the sick with the word of God and encourage them in distress. When they are sick, people are visited by various doubts and regrets that must be resisted. First, it is awful to think of dying and leaving behind all those who are related to us. Second, we remember all the sins that we have committed against God; they loom before us afresh and ruthlessly terrify our consciences. Third, death, divine judgment, and fear of hell and damnation stir up a monstrous dread in our old selves, and we need a constant faith to withstand the attacks. All those things appear horrible to us because our faith is weak and unpracticed and has not fully comprehended the riches of the children of God: the assured forgiveness of sin through Christ, the true and certain resurrection of the flesh, the wonderful company of the elect and eternal life. We have all these in and through Christ.

We should daily remind ourselves of these parts of our faith and go as often as we can to the Lord's table after necessary instruction and earnest preparation. For some years now the Lord's Supper has been dishonored, neglected, even scorned by many. That is a serious sin, as indeed the present epidemic indicates and as St. Paul predicted (1 Cor 11:29). May God enlighten us so that we regain our wits and put error behind us. We should long for the Lord's table and seek there the renewal and deepening of our faith and love. We should have all the articles of Christian faith fresh in our minds, but in times of peril we should concentrate on these four: the communion of saints, forgiveness of sin through the blood of Christ, resurrection of the flesh, and eternal life.

As death is a punishment for sin (Rom 6:23), illnesses often strike for the same reason (John 5:14; Ps 89:31–32; Deut 28:20–24; 2 Sam

24:10–17). We are also victims of calamities for the purpose of trying and testing our faith, for then we learn how much God means to us and how well we trust in him. Above all, therefore, you should direct your heart, soul, and mind to God and with penitent hearts bewail the sin for which all of us have deserved divine wrath and punishment. When you do this, the Gospel of John prescribes comfort, absolution, and forgiveness in the Christian assembly, and this treasure is available to you every day. "Receive," Christ says, "the Holy Spirit. If you forgive the sins of any, they are forgiven them; if you retain the sins of any, they are retained" (John 20:22–23). Accordingly, after we have prayed to God our Father to forgive our sin, the punishment or the illness will either come to an end or, through the merciful will of God, promote the salvation of the sick person.

You should realize and never doubt that punishment is a bitter yoke for the flesh, even if it is only a father's discipline used by God to draw the child to himself and shield it from sin. He means well by us, "for the Lord disciplines those whom he loves" (Heb 12:6), so that they will not have to suffer eternal punishment. You should confidently consider God to be your loving and faithful Father even when he appears angry (Ps 89:32–33). It is the wrath of our dear Father, who does not desire our ruin but only our improvement, welfare, and salvation. That is so true—if only we could believe it!

Ask first of all, therefore, with repentant hearts for grace and forgiveness of all your sin through Christ so that you and God are again reconciled. Then you may ask God to free you from this evil, as written in Sirach, "My child, when you are ill, do not delay, but pray to the Lord and he will heal you" (Sir 38:9). The psalmist also prayed: "Restore us again, O God of our salvation, and put away your indignation from us" (Ps 85:4). The psalmist first desires forgiveness of sin so that he may become holy through God, and then he asks God to be angry no more. Always add to that, however: "May your holy will be done." For we are unable to arrange anything better than our faithful, almighty, and omniscient God, who always looks after us, worries about us, and has counted the hairs of our heads (Matt 10:30). He nourishes, bolsters, upholds, and supports you better than any creature could hope to do (1 Pet 5:7, 10).

Three things torment and terrify us during this plague: sin, death, and hell. First, there is sin, which has caused us so dreadfully to waste this life against God and our neighbor. From sin have arisen fear and agony, as Paul says, wrath, fury, anguish, and distress for all souls who do evil (Rom 2:8–9). Second, death. Our nature does not willingly depart from this life. Our hearts tremble with greater distress and misery than any tongue can express. Our weak and timid nature is always afraid it will perish and never reappear, in other words, that all is lost. Third, hell, eternal damnation. We are afraid that we must be cast out of God's sight where there is nothing but eternal death. At this point we must be strong so that timidity and despair do not gain a foothold. Eternal God, grant that in times of prosperity I keep you before my eyes and with proper fear not forget the solemn conflict to come (Eccl 7:14). May we remain watchful and God-fearing in all we do and leave undone.

(1) What to do when sin causes anxiety to the conscience.

Remember that God's son came from heaven and became human to take upon himself your sin and the sin of the world. For that he died willingly on the cross, did penance for sin, made satisfaction for it and thus [in our stead] became the one who paid. This priceless death and bloodshed of Jesus Christ are assuredly your own, if you now believe that Christ died as much for you as for Peter and Paul. You should not doubt that you have been baptized into the death of Christ (Rom 6:3), and do not underestimate the potential consolation. The death of Christ is comfort and help for you because through his death you have died to sin, receive with certainty the forgiveness of sins, and will see resurrection and eternal life. Christian baptism is a covenant or grace-filled transaction in which you and God have agreed that you will forever have a good conscience by virtue of the forgiveness of sin through the resurrection of Christ. Christ also assures you of this in the Lord's Supper, when he says that his blood is shed for the forgiveness of sin (Matt 26:28). If you have led an evil life, hasten to call upon the name of God and you will find help (Rom 10:13). Say:

"O merciful God, Father of our Lord Jesus Christ, be merciful to me, a poor distressed sinner, for the sake of the bitter suffering and death of Jesus Christ, your only begotten Son, my only redeemer, Amen. Lord, do not deal with me on the basis of my guilt but of your infinite mercy, for I am a poor creature and stand under your almighty hand. Almighty God, dearest Father, do not forsake me. I am yours; you are the only one who can comfort and deliver me. You are the true savior in all tribulation. 'Lord, I hope in you; let me never be put to shame.'" (Ps 25:2; 69:6; Rom 10:11)

Remind the sick that they should not merely ponder their sins but concentrate on the saving death of Christ. Let them recall that their sins no longer rest on them but on Christ; he has removed their sins from all the faithful and paid for them himself (Isa 53:6). We ourselves confess that in the creed: "I believe in the forgiveness of sins."

Hold before the sick what the word of God says about the forgiveness of sin through Christ: "Here is the lamb of God who takes away the sin of the world" (John 1:29). We are not ransomed with perishable things like silver and gold but with the precious blood of the unblemished lamb Christ (1 Pet 1:18–19). My brother, you are a Christian; Christ always bears your sin. As long as you do not doubt that, you are free from sin and a child of God. "For God so loved the world that he gave his only Son, so that everyone who believes in him may not perish but have everlasting life" (John 3:16). "For I have come to call not the righteous but sinners" to repentance (Matt 9:13). "Come to me, all you that are weary and are carrying heavy burdens, and I will give you rest" (Matt 11:28). "But God proves his love for us in that while we still were sinners Christ died for us. Much more surely then, now that we have been justified by his blood, will we be saved through him from the wrath of God" (Rom 5:8–9).

Brothers and sisters, God your dear Father wants this comforting gospel proclaimed to you, for all has been done for your benefit and is meant to help you eternally. Now believe it and entrust yourself to Christ, your redeemer. "For if while we were enemies, we were reconciled to him through the death of his Son, much more surely, having been reconciled, will we be saved by his life" (Rom 5:10). Christ "became for us wisdom from God, righteousness, sanctification, and redemption" (1 Cor 1:30). If you are a sinner and unrighteous, confess it and bring your lament to Christ, adhere to him as your only sanctifier; then the righteousness of Christ is your own and covers all your sin so that it cannot harm you. For us Christ became a sacrifice for sin so that we in him would become righteousness that can stand before God (2 Cor 5:21). Christ "gave himself for our sin to set us free from this present evil age according to the will of God our Father" (Gal 1:4). "In him we have redemption through his blood, the forgiveness of our trespasses, according to the riches of his grace" (Eph 1:7).

"Christ Jesus came into the world to save sinners" (1 Tim 1:15). Look confidently to him as well as Paul did and you will be holy and blessed. Christ Jesus "gave himself a ransom for all" (1 Tim 2:6). Trust firmly in that, sisters and brothers, and you are certainly one of the saved. "We have been sanctified through the offering of the body of Jesus Christ once for all" (Heb 10:10). In the Lord's Supper you hear how Christ speaks with you and offers food and drink for eternal life. He says: "Take and eat, this is my body," which is given for you. "Drink from it all of you; this is my blood of the new covenant, which is poured out for many for the forgiveness of sins" (Matt 26:26–28; 1 Cor 11:24–25). Receive these words. Christ is talking to you. All this is for you as much as for Peter and Paul. "He himself bore our sins in his body on the cross" (1 Pet 2:24). "Christ also suffered for sins once for all, the righteous for the unrighteous, in order to bring you to God" (1 Pet 3:18). "The blood of Jesus" Christ "cleanses us from all sin" (1 John 1:7). "If anyone does sin, we have an advocate with the Father, Jesus Christ the righteous, and he is the atoning sacrifice for our sins, and not for ours only but also for the sins of the whole world" (1 John 2:1–2).

Use many of these verses or only a few according to the condition of the sick person. Hear these words of the Holy Spirit: God the Father, who does not desire the death of a sinner, but his conversion and life (Ezek 33:11), out of love for you has taken your sins from you and laid them upon his dear Son, Christ. That one has already borne and paid for them. They can no longer condemn you, for God has counted the death of his Son as full penance and payment for all your sins if you will only believe in Christ. Since your sins have been placed on Christ and were not able to confine and condemn him in death, they have surely been forgiven. Believe that firmly and you will live eternally. Christ has borne your sin and has died for you. But he rose again, and thus the sins of the faithful have all been more than paid through the death of Christ and the strict righteousness of God more than satisfied through Christ (Rom 5:18–19). Christ now belongs to you and to all the Christian faithful with his benefits, his death, resurrection, ascension, life, merit, and glory. The devil has no more power and claim over you, for you have been made righteous through Christ, freed from all your sin and a child of God. He has become your dear Father for the sake of Christ who has reconciled you.

Persevere, therefore, and be joyful in the Lord. You are well preserved in the faithful hand of the almighty God, your Father. Christ is yours; he covers all your sin with his innocence. No one can snatch you out of the hand of your heavenly Father (John 10:28). You are dealing here only with a momentary bit of distress, in which Christ has already preceded you as your head (Heb 4:15). You are to be made like him, dying to sin, leaving behind this sinful life (Rom 6:10–11), and living with Christ, your Lord, forever. Do not allow your sins to bother you; they are already gone and paid for. The evil spirit has been conquered, and God is watching and waiting for you together with all his angels and saints. You cannot be condemned any more than Christ can be condemned as long as you cling to Christ in true faith. If sin, death, and hell cannot hurt Christ, neither can they harm you, because you are in Christ and Christ is in you (John 6:56) and you cannot be condemned. If you had to carry your own sins, they would be too heavy and thrust you down into the abyss of hell. But Christ, truly divine and truly human, carries them for you, as he says: "What I did not steal I must now restore" (Ps 69:5).[7] You are the one who sinned, but Christ has paid for your guilt, makes you free, unbinds you and sets you loose when you believe this gospel.

Even if you had committed all the sins in the world, more than enough grace is still available. God has blessed you in Christ and promised you grace, and this same grace has been secured and applied in Christ your Lord. The matter of your salvation is certain, for the same Christ is God's Son by nature in the divine being, the truth itself. As a human being he has our flesh and blood. Who can be a more reliable giver and payer of the promise of grace than the one who is the truth of the promise himself and loves us so deeply that he would rather die than have us find the promise in any way defective? It is impossible, therefore, that you believe in Christ but are not blessed by God, freed from sin, and made an heir of God and co-heir with Christ eternally. For heaven and earth will pass away, but the word of God remains forever (Matt 24:35; Isa 40:8; 1 Pet 1:25). Believe firmly and do not doubt. The Almighty has become a man who was born, died on the cross, rose from the dead, ascended to heaven, and has delivered to us all that was promised. "For in him every one of God's promises is a 'Yes'" (2 Cor 1:20). Desire and expect from God through Christ nothing but grace and mercy. Outside Christ there is no consolation or help; in Christ consolation, help, and salvation are abundantly greater, higher, and richer that anyone can imagine or want. May God give us then a solid faith!

In this form, longer or shorter according to the condition of the sick, speak with them and turn their eyes away from the harsh appearance of sin and death and direct them with full hearts toward Christ alone. In him they have nothing but innocence, godliness, life, and blessedness, and all of those are their own when they acknowledge Christ as their sanctifier and savior. Do not allow the sick to concentrate on their sin; alter their focus as best you can, so that they place only the crucified Christ before their eyes and fill their hearts so full with him that they can withstand the gates of hell, no matter how horrifying they may be. Remind them how throughout the gospels Christ always received sinners mercifully when they asked for grace and confessed their sins. As examples hold up Mary Magdalene,[8] the thief on the cross, the tax collector, the publican, Zacchaeus, and others who experienced pure grace. In short, Christ is pure grace and mercy, help, consolation, life, joy, and blessedness to all who expect these things from him. God has said so, and it can never fail.

You may well remember, in times of crisis, the way you mistreated others by taking away their honor and possessions. Then do what Christ did on the cross: From your heart pray for all those who have done you wrong and pardon all those who have injured you or taken something from you. Let it all go. If you have taken another's goods, return them if you can or see to it that the person is repaid. Confess and say you are sorry. If you cannot return anything, then forgive those who have taken something from you or who have damaged your honor and be consoled. It is impossible for God not to forgive those who forgive others. He has taught it to us himself: "If you forgive others their trespasses, your heavenly Father will also forgive you" (Matt 6:14). That is God's word; heaven and earth must pass away before it could ever prove untrue.

(2) What to do when death terrifies.

If Christ himself were not there, death would be an unbearable ordeal and dread; it would be hell. Through Christ, however, death has already been abolished and conquered. The soul does not suffer eternal death (Matt 10:28); it goes to Christ (Phil 1:23), just as the thief on the cross in his distress hears Christ say: "Truly I tell you, today you will be with me in Paradise" (Luke 23:43). The body rests in the certain hope of blessed, immortal life and on the last day it must rise with honor and glory, so that body and soul will be eternally with Christ and all the elect—those unknown and those known to you on earth, along with those related to you. Scripture calls the death of Christians a sleep because this frail body, which is now mortal and corruptible, will be raised at the last day like someone awaking from slumber; the death already in Christians will itself be slain and their bodies will rise immortal, glorified, powerful with eternal vigor, and completely pure and spiritual (1 Cor 15:42–44). The psalm says therefore: "Precious in the sight of the Lord is the death of his faithful ones" (Ps 116:15). Listen, brothers and sisters, the world thinks that we expire and disappear into the ground, the body will disintegrate, and it is all over. Not so. The world is wrong; the body is not so contemptible to God. He has already prepared his honor and blessing for the body. The very body you now inhabit and that becomes ill is destined to live eternally with the soul. If we were to lose the body and never receive it back, death would be terrible instead of valuable and precious. Remember, therefore, and do not doubt that the body of Christ lay in the grave and rose again on the third day (1 Cor 15:4) into a new, eternal life and will never die again (Rom 6:9). The bodies of all Christians will also, once they have fallen asleep, rest a while in the grave in the certain hope of a joyful resurrection, and they must rise again into a new, eternal life at the last day, when there will be no more sin or death but only godliness, life, joy, and blessedness forever and ever. God almighty has spoken and it must take place; count on it with rejoicing.

At this point comfort the sick with the word of God concerning the resurrection of the body, for Paul teaches that we should encourage one another with these passages (1 Thess 4:18). It is genuine encouragement, because we do not use human words but the word of God himself, who without doubt can and will bring to pass what his word says. No one can stop him. He is all powerful, true, and inexpressible grace and mercy; no one should doubt that. "The righteous will shine like the sun in the kingdom of the Father" (Matt 13:43). The same thing is said about the faithful after the resurrection: "Very truly, I tell you, anyone who hears my word and believes him who sent me has eternal life, and does not come under judgment, but has passed from death to life" (John 5:24). "This is indeed the will of my Father, that all who see the Son and believe in him may have eternal life; and I will raise them up on the last day" (John 6:40). "Very truly, I tell you, whoever keeps my word will never see death" (John 8:51). In the eleventh chapter of John, Christ said that Lazarus sleeps, the one who has died and whose body lies in the grave (John 11:11, 14, 17). But Christ, "who gives life to the dead and calls into existence the things that do not exist" (Rom 4:17), says further: "I am the resurrection and the life; those who believe in me, even though they die, will live, and everyone who lives and believes in me will never die" (John 11:25–26). Immediately thereafter, he raised Lazarus, who had lain four days in the grave and whose body had begun to stink and decay.

Our despondent and timid natures could use more support for believing firmly in the resurrection from the many stories of those who rose from the dead at the time of the prophets and apostles. Christ raises the widow's son at Nain (Luke 7:11–17), the daughter of a leader of the synagogue (Luke 8:49–56), and Lazarus (John 11:1–44). Peter raises Tabitha (Acts 9:36–42). Paul raises Eutychus (Acts 20:7–12). Elisha the prophet raised from the dead the son of the Shunammite woman (2 Kgs 4:18–37). Elijah the prophet raised the son of the widow of Zarephath from the dead (1 Kgs 17:17–24).

Two holy men, Enoch (Gen 5:24) and Elijah (2 Kgs 2:11), were taken body and soul from this transitory life by God as an indication of that genuine life to come, so that we would not be like pagans and deny that another life would follow this miserable one.

Admonish the sick with little faith to remember how the mighty Lord over life and death said: "Weep no more; the girl is not dead; she is asleep" (Luke 8:52). Faithless reason does not comprehend the secrets of God and laughs, but Christ acts on what he says, for he is God. He says only, "Get up, my child," and her soul returned to the body and she stood up (Luke 8:54). The same Lord Christ now receives your soul and preserves it, and at the last day he reunites body and soul in eternal life. "The time is coming when all who are in the grave shall hear his voice and move forth; those who have done right will rise to life" (John 5:28–29). "Moreover, if the Spirit of him who raised Jesus from the dead dwells within you, then the God who raised Christ Jesus from the dead will also give new life to your mortal bodies through his indwelling Spirit" (Rom 8:11). "God not only raised our Lord from the dead; he will also raise us by his power" (1 Cor 6:14). The fifteenth chapter of First Corinthians is full of comfort and pure gold. Paul ties our resurrection inseparably to the resurrection of Jesus in this way: Christ rose from the dead; that is certain. We will also certainly rise again, for Christ is our head and we are his members. The head does not leave its members behind. We must go where he is, for we are the members of his body, flesh and bone (Eph 5:30).

Who can adequately praise the glorious riches of his grace? God came from heaven and became a mortal human being so that mortal human nature, through union with the immortal divine nature, would be elevated to eternal life by the endless power of the godhead. If we believed this to be our own treasure and blessed destiny, how could we grieve? The human nature of all people who have ever lived, before or after Christ, has assuredly put on immortality in Christ, the epitome of all humanity and true God. Hence Paul comforts the Corinthians resolutely with the resurrection of Christ and says: "Christ is risen from the dead, the first fruits of the harvest of the dead. For since it was a human being who brought death into the world, a human being also brought resurrection from the dead. As in Adam all die, so in Christ all will be brought to life;

129

but each in his or her proper place: Christ, the first fruits, and afterward, at his coming, those who belong to Christ" (1 Cor 15:20–23).

After this Paul offers an illustration from nature through which we can clearly see our bodily resurrection: a seed placed in the ground dies and decays; it does not disappear completely but rises forth with a handsome form and body, quite new and fresh (1 Cor 15:35–44). In this way our body will also come forth, no longer feeble and decaying as now, but with adornment, strong and immortal in eternal life. That is the passage through death as we know it into our true everlasting life and homeland. Flesh and blood cannot inherit the kingdom of God where there is nothing but life. The perishable body must put on the imperishable, and the immortal body must put on immortality (1 Cor 15:53), and the scripture is fulfilled, "Death is swallowed up in victory" (1 Cor 15:54; Isa 25:8). Christians have become rulers over sin, death, and hell. They are bold in Christ and say: "Death, where is your sting? The sting of death is sin, sin gains its power from the law. But thanks be to God who has given us the victory through our Lord Jesus Christ" (1 Cor 15:55–57).

There is comfort beyond measure also in other passages. "For we know that he who raised the Lord Jesus to life will with Jesus raise us too" (2 Cor 4:14). "We are citizens of heaven, and from heaven we expect our deliverer to come, the Lord Jesus Christ, who will transfigure the body belonging to our humble state, and give it a form like that of his own resplendent body, by the power that enables him to make all things subject to himself" (Phil 3:20–21). "You died, and now your life lies hidden with Christ in God. When Christ, who is our life, is manifested, then you too will be manifested with him in glory" (Col 3:3–4). "We want you not to remain in ignorance, brothers and sisters, about those who sleep in death; you should not grieve like the others (unbelievers), who have no hope. We believe that Jesus Christ died and rose again; and so it will be for those who died as Christians; God will bring them to life with Jesus" (1 Thess 4:13–14)....

Dear children of God. I ask you not to scorn this little instruction with which I, a weak member, wished to serve you, my co-members in the Lord, in haste and great weakness through divine grace. I prefer to have comforted you all orally in person if I had been able. Please allow my prayer for you this time to replace my service. May our proven physician and bountiful apothecary Christ cause these prescriptions for the soul, drawn from the medicine chest of holy scripture, to fortify our hearts so that we now and forever may persevere and be constant in true Christian faith, heartfelt love of God and neighbor, patient endurance of the cross, obedient following of Christ, and in the firm hope of eternal life through Christ. Amen.

Pray also for me a poor sinner.
Augsburg, eighth day of the winter month
[December 8], in the year 1529.

17. Martin Bucer, A Brief Statement or Instruction on How the Sick Should Be Visited by the Ministers of the Church and the Procedure to Be Followed in Their Homes, about 1549

After Martin Bucer and his wife were allowed to establish residence in Strasbourg (see text no. 4 above), he was invited to become the pastor of St. Aurelius parish and soon emerged as the leader of the evangelically minded clergy. Once a new church order was adopted in 1534, the city council shared oversight over spiritual life with the church assembly, a council of clergy that met weekly and chose Martin Bucer in 1541 to be its first president. By that time Bucer and his colleagues were trying to impose a system of public church discipline that would move the town closer to his ideal of a Christian city. Their proposal required a yearly confession of faith by adults that would be followed by private confession and absolution prior to communion. Bucer's proposal was never able to gain the council's approval, however, and when he offered it to voluntary groups of laity called Christian fellowships, it was not enthusiastically received.

The main elements of Bucer's system are also present in the *Order for the Visitation of the Sick* that was adopted in 1537 and in the *Brief Statement* that Bucer wrote at a later date. After the instructional section of a *Brief Statement,* which is presented here, Bucer attached "A

Form and Method for Imparting Absolution and the Sacrament of the Supper to the Sick," so that clergy would have a liturgical form to follow at the sickbed. Bucer's emphasis on the sacraments as instruments of pastoral care may seem more material than spiritual and more similar to Luther's views than to Zwingli's. The *Wittenberg Concord* of 1536 between Lutherans and South Germans indicates that Bucer did embrace a notion of Christ's real presence in the Lord's Supper even though Bucer's conception of that presence may not have been as physical as Luther's. Regardless of their differences, however, most Protestants regarded scripture, preaching, and the sacraments as means of the Holy Spirit's work and therefore as essential parts of the spiritual life. In the *Brief Statement* Bucer declares his strong appreciation for the church as a sacramental community, and he reveals the way in which he was led to this point by the course of religious reform in Strasbourg. The *Brief Statement* was almost certainly composed before Bucer left for England in 1549.

Adapted from *Common Places of Martin Bucer,* trans. and ed. David Wright, 430–51.

VISITATION OF THE SICK

Under the papacy, when the sacrament of the body and blood of our Lord Jesus Christ was presented to the sick and they were in this manner (as was then claimed) catered or provided for, two abuses obtained among the people. First, outside the festival of Easter they very largely neglected to receive this sacrament and put off receiving it for ages until they fell ill and arrived at the point of death. Second, when they had reached a critical condition and were breathing their last, they placed more confidence in the external reception of the sacrament than in the death and holy communion of Christ our Lord—about which in any case they were told very little.

Now in order to remove these two abuses and corruptions, at the commencement of our ministry in the holy gospel we diligently exhorted the people, as we must do even now, to receive the sacrament in the church of God while they were still in good health, so that if perchance they were seized with adverse health, they would nevertheless have learned to receive the Lord by true faith even if the opportunity of sacramental reception was not granted them.

And since the error of placing one's trust in the outward act had itself taken much deeper root at that period than at present, so much more urgently did we exhort people to receive by faith and to receive the sacrament in the church.[9]

But we now observe how successfully Satan has deflected and diverted our teaching and exhortation, directed only against an empty confidence in the external ministry of the word and sacraments, and still daily deflects and diverts them, so that great numbers of people are despising and forsaking the entire ministry of the church—the word and the sacraments, the comfort of absolution, the prayers, in fact the whole communion of the church. They falsely claim they can receive by faith with the result that, not only when they are ill at home but even when fit and well at church, they never trouble themselves about the sacraments. They are becoming totally estranged from the communion of the church and—this is the inevitable outcome—lapse piteously from true faith in Christ and all obedience to the holy gospel and are perishing. On us surely lies the obligation to endeavor with all faithfulness to overcome Satan by the word and might of the Lord on this front, to resist with the utmost zeal the ruin of so many people in such a grievous and open manner, and by employing every godly means to invite, admonish, and exhort all to the proper use of the sacraments no less energetically than we have hitherto striven (and shall strive hereafter) to deliver them from a vain trust in the external performance of the sacraments.

Since the Lord inflicts illnesses for the very purpose of drawing us to himself out of a lost world and moving us to seek him afresh with our whole heart, and by means of an illness often urges a whole family to repentance, we should spare no effort in our dealings with the sick to lead them together with their families fully back to the Lord and to guide them to the point of acknowledging and accepting him with genuine faith as their only Savior. But since none can acknowledge and accept the Lord as their only Savior unless they acknowledge and are ready to make use of his word and all its comfort along with the sacraments, just as the Lord ordained, we must always diligently teach the sick and others we find with them how the Lord has designed to effect our salvation in the communion of his body, the church, through his word and sacraments,

133

and how it behooves us to receive it in the very means that he has appointed.

In visiting the sick, then, we should always request that as far as possible the whole family be assembled. First, we must point out to them from the scripture that God our heavenly father created us all in the beginning upright in body and soul, healthy and good, and partakers of his own divine, blessed, and eternal life; but through sin we fell away from all such blessings, and thenceforward from our first parent on, all of us have been born not only in ignorance of God our creator but also rebellious at every point against his will, which alone is good. This blind and rebellious nature subsequently leads us into every kind of sin and unrighteousness and arouses the righteous wrath of God upon us eternally. Hence all our sickness, death, and eternal damnation.

Our next point must be that nevertheless God in his mercy and kindness has taken pity on us. Since all of us from our first parent on are totally corrupt and depraved and condemned to eternal death with not one of us, nor any creature in heaven or on earth, able to help another, he has freely given us his only begotten Son to assume our flesh. By his bitter suffering and death the Son has made satisfaction for our sins and procured for us the grace of restoring to the divine image and nature all whom the Father gives him, so that they truly acknowledge, love, and worship God the Father and him whom the Father sent and so live in him that they do not experience death. For whoever believes in the Lord abides in him and the Lord in him, and therefore he cannot die but has passed through death into eternal life. Thus does the Lord restore to participation in his own eternal, blessed, and divine life all who were lost in the first Adam and born to eternal death.

In the third place we must make plain that the Lord effects this work of our restoration or renewal and salvation through his word and sacraments in his church. In sacred baptism we are buried into his death for the washing away and destruction of all our sins and the putting to death of our sinful flesh; we are ingrafted and incorporated into him—receiving full favor, love, adoption as children of God along with newness and holiness of life—so that we live in him and he in us, he our head and we the members of his holy body, which is his church.

For this church he has appointed his regular ministry, entrusting to it the keys of his kingdom and the power of binding and loosing, of retaining and remitting sins. In this church we must, in complete obedience toward the Lord and genuine love and fellowship with all its other members in the Lord, persevere to the very end of this life and present ourselves to the regular ministers of Christ for daily edification and instruction in all the commandments of the Lord. For we heed him when we heed them, and we reject him when we reject them. At their hands we ought to accept rebuke when we sin willfully, and, if for our sins we are bound by them to display repentance, we must not doubt that the Lord himself will regard us as bound, as surely as he will regard us as loosed once the church through its regular ministry has loosed us. Therefore we should prize most highly his comfort concerning the remission of sins, which the church offers to those who are penitent and seek pardon. We should also in real and effectual love manifest our common participation in Christ to all the members of the church by teaching, reproof, exhortation, and comfort and even by material assistance, and receive the same from them with full gratitude.

Since we can do no good thing of ourselves, our flesh and blood cannot enter upon the inheritance of the kingdom of God and assume a heavenly and spiritual nature. The Lord, therefore, out of his great and ineffable love, has ordained and appointed for us a sacred supper in which he gives us his body and blood, in order that we through him and in him may become a new and divine flesh-and-blood and ever more fully live in him and he in us, with a life truly divine.[10] We should receive these great and precious gifts as frequently as possible with sincere devotion and utter thankfulness, and in the act of receiving commit ourselves ever more completely to him and proclaim triumphantly and declare to others by word and deed his death and our redemption. So we shall increase daily in his life, that is, in genuine faith toward him, in love toward our neighbor, in self-control and forbearance, and in the blessed hope and expectation of his coming in salvation.

Fourth, after all this instruction we should carefully point out to the sick and the others present that when we evince no gratitude for this grace, become negligent and undisciplined in the Christian life, and have an excessive love for the world, the Lord in his matchless grace and mercy punishes and chastises us with illness and adversities of every kind. Scripture asserts this throughout and especially in Paul's words in 1 Corinthians: his purpose is not to abandon us but to draw us back to himself, "so that we may not be condemned along with the world" (1 Cor 11:32). We must therefore diligently warn the sick and their companions to have no doubt that they have fallen ill because of their sinful ingratitude to the Lord in return for his manifold and precious gifts and because of their sinful devotion to their own flesh and the world rather than to the Lord.

However, we must admonish those present around the sickbed not to imagine that those afflicted with illness by the Lord are therefore worse sinners than the rest of us. On the contrary, the Lord often makes a spectacle of his dearest children in order to summon us to repentance through the hardness of his judgment on the elect. For he begins his judgment at his own house and disciplines the one he loves (1 Cor 4:9; 1 Pet 4:17; Prov 3:12).

This body of teaching we should compress or expand, sharpen or soften, on every point or on selected points, according to what we ascertain is opportune and necessary for each sick individual or other person present. For people well instructed in these truths need only to be reminded of them very briefly. Those, however, who are conscious of the hand of the Lord and are terrified by his judgment must be given correspondingly greater comfort, and any discovered to be still unacquainted with the Christian life and lacking repentance and acknowledgment of their sins should receive a lengthier and more serious exhortation. Finally, pastors who with all diligence are aiming to build up and comfort the sick and their companions in Christ as perfectly as possible will also take into account their physical strength and their every convenience.

Fifth, following such admonition and exhortation we should ask the sick if they acknowledge and believe all they have heard and if they have kept it all or not, and we ought to offer them a chance to receive instruction and comfort in private. But whether they request it or not, we must give careful attention to ascertaining the sick persons' faith and knowledge of Christ, whether they are well-instructed and devout or untaught and lacking Christian experience, whether prior to that time they belonged to the church's communion or not, whether they neglected that communion out of ignorance and carnal carelessness or out of a marked contempt for God and his church or hatred of his ministers, or finally because of entanglement with sects and false doctrine. Also we must ask whether they have been forbidden to partake of the sacraments, and if so by whom, and whether it was done in the name of the whole church or through particular ministers. Then our treatment of them must be dictated by the kind of persons we discover them to be.

If we find them to be well-instructed and devout Christians who have faithfully honored the communion of Christ, we should therefore mostly comfort them and encourage others present to emulate their example. In addition, whether they confess privately or not, they should be urged after being counseled and comforted to make public confession and a request for absolution before all present. The recital of their confession should come first, and afterward the imparting of absolution. If there is cause to fear a dangerous or prolonged illness, the comfort of the sacrament should also be offered and imparted to them at their request. But if we discover that the sick persons have previously revealed themselves to be ignorant and irreligious, whether or not they made use of the sacraments, we must not impart to them either absolution or the sacrament unless we perceive in them genuine repentance and some danger of death. For where we see no true repentance or acknowledgment of sin, we ought of course to speak of it and set it before them. But if there is some evidence of repentance but no danger of death, then the matter should be again deferred, and the persons concerned urged to receive absolution and the sacrament in the sanctuary after recovering their health. But if there is a real danger of death and some indication of repentance, then we should impart absolution and the sacrament.

Next, if we encounter sick folk who previously have never bothered about the communion of the church at all, for whatever reasons, we must vehemently and earnestly rebuke their denial of their baptism and their desertion of Christ and proceed to deal with them further in such measure as they give signs of repentance and the danger of death presses hard. Where there is no pressing danger of death, then only after they have recovered should they be reconciled with the church, absolved, and admitted to the sacraments. In the meantime, during their illness, they should practice the continual repentance that the Lord himself imposes on them.

In addition, whatever has caused their estrangement from the communion of Christ—whether carnal carelessness and living with abandon, or contempt for the church, or hatred of its ministers, or the sects and their errors—must be sternly exposed and rebuked in each individual case, but with the requisite moderation so that the rebuke makes for the awakening of true repentance and a desire for Christ's forgiveness and redemption, not despair. But if the sick in danger of dying have been publicly excommunicated by the church, they must also receive absolution from the council of the chief ministers and then be admitted to the sacrament.

If, on the other hand, sick persons are encountered who, while enjoying good health, were unconcerned about God and even when ill and in danger of death evinced no acknowledgment of their sins or desire for Christ, they must be committed to the judgment of the Lord. But they should have the seriousness of such ruinous obduracy straightly laid before them and be urged as diligently as possible to a timely repentance. Such persons should also not be buried among other Christians and even after death are to be regarded as excommunicated and excluded from the church.

We have frequently made mention of the danger of death: where it is present, no one who seeks the reconciliation and propitiation of Christ is to be denied,[11] but where it is not, absolution must be deferred. We ministers of the grace of Christ ought not to wait until the last second to decide, so that no one who seeks the church's reconciliation and absolution, as far as it is in our power, should depart this life without it. Rather, we should from time to time absolve and comfort a number of sick folk at their request and admit them to the communion of Christ, though they appear more likely to recover from their illness than to die, than allow anybody who requests it to die without having been reconciled or strengthened by the communion of Christ.[12]

Similarly, even though we must take special care after our instruction to distinguish between those who truly desire the grace of Christ and those who do not, those who reveal true repentance for their sins and those who do not, nevertheless we should not make the recognition of true repentance and desire for Christ a matter for the most precise and definite calculation anymore than we should the danger of death. We must give a charitable appraisal of every situation, since we can see into nobody's heart, and the Lord is well able to discover and judge any who request and receive his grace from the church with empty words and an insincere attitude. Nevertheless, seeing that we are the servants of Christ, who can endure no hypocrisy or pretense and will deal only with reality and honesty, we must faithfully press home their sinfulness and Christ's redemption, even though the danger of death be such that reconciliation cannot be put off till a return to health. Indeed, where there is room for delay, we should also put off the requested reconciliation for a time, if enough is available, in order to arouse in the sick by this delay a stronger desire for grace. Often in the hour or night after, the admonition and exhortation work wonders and kindle such a desire in the sick that they long wholeheartedly to receive absolution and the sacraments.

Since, then, we are bound to give account to the Lord for all his sheep that we neglect and abandon to destruction, it is our duty, when we learn of sickness, not to wait until we are summoned. We should offer our ministry, even though not called for, and discharge it as faithfully as we can.[13]

PART FIVE
Living the Faith

Introduction

It is much easier to study what Protestant theologians thought than to discover how Protestant laity lived during the Reformation. Our sources are overwhelmingly literary, and even when they urge a certain way of practicing the faith, they are more hortatory than descriptive. Nevertheless, theologians wanted their hearers and readers not only to believe differently from their ancestors but also to practice their faith in a different way. Protestant spirituality, as the reformers envisioned it, was more about action than contemplation, or, more accurately stated, it was the new theology in practice.

Convincing people to change their religious ways was not simple, however. Pre-Reformation Christians were very good at practicing their faith, in part because their devotion—so they had been taught—would earn them a place in heaven. After Protestant reformers eliminated from their doctrine salvation by merit, they were confronted with this question: If religious performance and charity would not earn the laity eternal life, how could they be motivated to go to church and to love their neighbor? This dilemma posed a special challenge to preachers, as we saw in Part Three, and it became the subject of Protestant pamphlets, including those sermons that were printed and circulated among the laity.

Martin Bucer's earliest work attacked the problem head on: "Since true faith unfailingly produces true love, which makes us overflow with good works toward others and live not for ourselves but for the eternal glory of God, and since faith comes from God's grace through hearing the word of God (Rom 10:17), we must above all things adhere to the divine word, listen to it, read it, meditate on

141

it with diligence, and act accordingly." This sentence contains three typical elements of the Protestant solution. First, the ability to live for others and not only for oneself comes spontaneously from true faith and issues in concrete acts of love for the neighbor. Second, faith itself cannot be earned or merited; it is a product of divine grace and is generated in us through God's word. Third, Christians must therefore zealously pay attention to the divine word, reading it if possible, hearing it proclaimed, and meditating on it. The goal, of course, was to act upon what one read and heard.

The remaining selections in this part offer variations on these fundamental themes. Andrew Karlstadt argues that the commandments to love God and neighbor, taught by Jesus, are inseparable, and he draws on mystical theology to explain how the soul can be prepared to receive and to give love. It would have been easy to infer from Bucer's words that Christians could not love themselves at all while learning to live for others, but Karlstadt, refusing to dodge the issue, carefully shows how one can love oneself so that loving the neighbor is also done in the way that Jesus intended when he said, "Love your neighbor as yourself." In a sermon that was published under the title "The Strength and Increase of Faith and Love," Martin Luther reaffirms the link between faith and love that he had forged in his 1520 treatise on Christian liberty; on the basis of Ephesians, he also voices the expectation that both faith and love would grow stronger as believers are united with Christ and filled with the fullness of God.

Finally, claiming disagreement with Luther, Ulrich Zwingli argues that the kingdom of Christ—and therefore Christian living and spirituality—is not only an internal matter but quite public and external. Luther did, in fact, deny that the kingdom of Christ was from this world (John 18:36), but only in order to emphasize the primacy of faith over worldly merit and power as the way of salvation. Neither theologian, however, would disallow the claim that living the faith calls for public and external actions that go beyond personal devotion and prayer. In his urban setting Zwingli's actions made clear that Protestant spirituality, including the personal activities illustrated in this book, had public, even political, consequences.

142

18. Martin Bucer, How to Live for Others and Not for Oneself, 1523

The full title of Martin Bucer's first Reformation treatise is stated as a proposition: "That we should not live for ourselves but for others and how we might achieve that goal." It summarizes the Reformation message that Bucer intended to present to the people of Strasbourg once he was granted permission to speak publicly (see text no. 4 above). In the preface Bucer notes that some hearers of his early lectures asked him for a fuller account of his teaching. He provides that account in two parts. In the first, not printed here, Bucer bases the ideal of mutual service on the divine order of creation and shows how the human fall into sin has turned us instead into self-seekers. In the second, translated here in full, he argues that only faith in Christ can restore us to that created ideal of living for others. The preface to this work shows that Bucer's proposition is not only a theological argument but that he expects it to be realized in Strasbourg and to "become more than mere talk among us."

Translated from the German text in *Martin Bucers Deutsche Schriften,* vol. 1, *Frühschriften 1520–24,* 44–45, 59–67.

PREFACE

Grace and peace to you from God, our Father, and the Lord Jesus Christ. I thank and praise God our Father through our Lord Jesus Christ for so igniting in you the love and desire for his word that now you avidly seek and request it. Indeed, it is the word of faith through which righteousness and salvation come to us. Therefore, St. Paul aptly calls the word a "power of God for salvation to everyone who has faith" (Rom 1:16).

Since you eagerly hear it and diligently inquire about the word, you are certainly born of God (John 1:13) and constitute a true assembly of Christ. As the city belongs unquestionably to the empire, in which the emperor's word is heard and his commands obeyed, so must it certainly be the kingdom of Christ and the true church where the word of Christ is so eagerly heard and diligently kept. His word can never return to him empty (Isa 55:11), but some people must always be caught by it. Without a doubt it will not be lacking in you.

My dear fellow-citizens, according to the grace bestowed on me I gladly offer to do more (as all of us are obligated to do for one another) in order to meet the request of some who were not satisfied with what I said in the lectures I delivered. On the basis of scripture I am submitting a short admonition and description of the way in which we can live for others and not for ourselves, and I am suggesting how we might reach that goal, which is a state of perfection that is possible in this life. May the Father of grace grant through our Savior, Jesus Christ, that this perfection become more than mere talk among us; for "the kingdom of God depends not on talk but on power" (1 Cor 4:20). May the Father also stop you from being content with human admonitions like these; instead, as faithful sheep of your true and only shepherd Jesus Christ, study divine scripture and listen to his voice so that you may advance in faith, become perfect in love, and live not for yourselves but for your neighbors. Through them live also for Christ and through him for the all-powerful Father, to whom be praise and glory forever. Amen. Strasbourg, August 1523.

PART ONE: WE SHOULD LIVE FOR OTHERS AND NOT FOR OURSELVES....

PART TWO: HOW WE CAN ACHIEVE THIS GOAL

Let me now describe how we may return to the life for which we were originally created, that is, living not for our own benefit but for that of others and for the glory of God. In brief, only faith can bring that life to us. As all things were created through Christ Jesus our Savior, so it pleased God through him to restore all things to the order in which they were created. The revealing of God's children (Rom 8:19), that is, the appearance of those who are true believers, will benefit other creatures. The restoration of humanity to its earliest and essential being will begin now, although here it will not reach perfection. That will happen when they believe in Christ, that is, when they trust that by his blood Christ has recon-

144

ciled them to the Father and brought them again into his favor. Those who believe will also know that by his Spirit Christ has restored them among all the creatures to the original order of creation, which, as I said above, is very beneficial and discernible to everyone who is receptive.

For Christ is to each of us and does for each of us according to our trust. He said to the blind men: "Do you believe that I am able to do this for you?" They said to him: "Yes, Lord." He then said: "According to your faith let it be done to you" (Matt 9:28–29). Now apply those words to us. Through our sin we have fallen from that original state in which we lived to serve others and to praise God. Owing to our corrupt nature we love only ourselves and seek only our profit. As a result, we ruin ourselves, injure our neighbor, insult God, and disgrace our creator. At the same time, however, we can believe the following: by making our Lord Christ head of his community, God has reconciled and united all things through him (Col 1:18, 20); that is, God has restored all things to their true purpose— to live for the glory of God and to serve all creatures, especially humanity. Yes, if we will only believe that this restoration through Christ, this reconciliation and new disposition, pertains to us as well, then without a doubt the spirit of true love will come upon us, a love that is considerate and seeks not its own welfare but the welfare of others. His word must prove true: "According to your faith let it be done to you."

True faith, moreover, enables us to believe all the words of God, the entire scripture, which exhibits to us Christ Jesus our Savior and shows us that we have been washed clean by his blood and through the Father's grace transferred from the power of darkness into his kingdom (Col 1:13). Now we are not only free but also true children of God for, when we believe in his name, he has given us power to become children of God (John 1:12). The Father has sent into our hearts his Spirit, which cries: "Abba! Father! So you are no longer a slave but a child, and if a child, then also an heir of God through Christ" (Gal 4:6–7). Paul writes the same thing to the Romans (Rom 8:15–17). Since, however, it is now clear that through faith we become children of God and have the Spirit of adoption, which also assures us that we are God's children (Rom 8:14–16), and since through that Spirit we acknowledge and call upon God as a father, then it must follow that we acknowledge all people as sisters and brothers and place ourselves at their service. The Father is especially pleased at this, because he created us for this purpose and pointed the way by means of his entire law and all the prophets (Matt 7:12). We can say with certainty that faith alone is able to draw us away from ourselves and present us as children to God the Father. Then, when we have become true children, our highest priority must be to follow the will of our dearest and kindest Father and in everything to live according to his law. As the law is fulfilled in this one command, "You shall love your neighbor as yourself" (Gal 5:14), let us immediately pour out ourselves and place ourselves completely at the service of others to the delight and glory of our dearest heavenly Father.

This is easy for all those who have true faith because, as we said, faith brings with it the Spirit of adoption, the Spirit of God that witnesses to "our spirit that we are children of God, and if children, then heirs, heirs of God and joint heirs with Christ" (Rom 8:16–17). If we acknowledge ourselves to be children and heirs of God and believe it with certainty (nothing is more certain than what we believe on the basis of God's word), we must also acknowledge and deem it most certain of all that we have and shall have for ourselves enough of everything. Indeed, we must consider ourselves as nothing other than already blessed, although now only in hope, and we shall receive God's eternal inheritance in full only when we are revealed with Christ in the glory of God and become like God (Col 3:4; 1 John 3:2). As a devoted and faithful father that has the ability to help cannot leave his dear children in want, our eternal Father will never let us suffer want. He will do more for us than any father can do for his children, and he also knows everything. The word of the prophet is definitely true: "Those who fear him have no want" (Ps 34:9); it applies only to those who are dear children of God through faith.

Our nature, however, is so attached and dedicated to worldly goods that it is preoccupied with obtaining enough of them and thus unable freely to help others unless it has first been served. There is no help for our nature, nor will it obtain enough unless it believes that it is a child and heir of God and that it will have what it needs now and in the future. The heart is satisfied only when true faith is present, for then the heart realizes with certainty that it will

146

lack nothing. The heart will then think like Paul: "He who did not withhold his own Son, but gave him up for all of us, will he not with him also give us everything else?" (Rom 8:32). The meaning is: If God has sacrificed for us that which was best and most precious, his only and beloved Son, which sin of ours will he not forgive? What good could he withhold from us? His love is too vast. As soon as through faith the heart apprehends this truth, it is immediately saturated with love and fully prepared to do good to everyone and, above all, to lead others to this blessed satisfaction by proclaiming the surpassing goodness of God. According to its nature, true goodness cannot hold back but must pour itself out as far and wide as it can. No good tree can be without fruit, and it must bear good fruit (Matt 7:17–18).

Faith plants in us complete trust in Christ, and it restores us to the proper divine order in which we were created. Through this faith we also obtain and receive his Spirit, which assures us that we are children of God. As a result, we gladly serve and please him with every kind of loving deed toward our neighbors, which is the utmost that he demands of those who belong to him. Inasmuch as we are blessed in and for ourselves as children and heirs of God (it is certain that we will lack nothing now and in the future), we also have this challenge to serve our neighbors faithfully with that unfeigned love that springs from faith. From scripture we learn that by nature we were children of wrath (Eph 2:3) and hence unworthy to be served by anyone, but the Lord has promised that he will accept as done unto him what we do for the least of those who belong to him (Matt 25:40), and that mercy, which the Lord demands in place of sacrifice (Hos 6:6), will abound for all those who show mercy toward their neighbors (Matt 5:7). Our hearts are therefore glad that serving our neighbors and showing them mercy are required of us, so that we can show at least a little gratitude to our most gracious Father and Savior and with confident hearts expect further mercy, since we are now trying in some way to do his will.

Since the inestimable sacrifice bestowed by our Lord and redeemer, Jesus Christ, is recognized and appreciated by faith alone, it keeps that sacrifice fresh and present in the mind. Consequently, those who have faith will acquire the same attitude they see in Christ, "who, though he was in the form of God, did not regard equality with God as something to be exploited, but emptied himself, taking the form of a slave, being born in human likeness and being found in human form, he humbled himself and became obedient to the point of death, even death on a cross" (Phil 2:6–8). When a believing heart meditates upon those words, it will be so inflamed with love for its Savior and Lord that it will completely divest and renounce itself, thinking: If the eternal Son of God, your Savior and Lord, did not come to be served but to serve others, if he has given his soul for you and for the deliverance of many, if he gave up the divine form which he had and took the form of a servant, if he became obedient unto death, even to death on the cross, what will you then make of yourself? Oh, that I might to some extent follow my Lord and deliverer out of gratitude for what he has done, even though I am nothing and can do nothing! Everything I have is through him from the Father's grace, and I will gladly offer all I have for the service of others without taking anything from them. I shall also be obedient to death, even death on a cross, that is, dying amidst manifold suffering and disgrace. Then it will come to pass that we deny ourselves, take our cross upon us, and follow our Lord, master, king, and Savior (Luke 9:23), and on the basis of that humility, service, and obedience we, like him, shall pass into the eternal glory and blessedness of the kingdom. Amen.

Finally, love for the honor, fortune, and pleasures of this life keeps some from exercising genuine love and service to their neighbor. True faith, however, frees us from all that, because in Christ faith presents to our eyes an eternal, heavenly Father, who is gracious and ready to give us everything good. Then temporal things become a burden that oppresses and repulses us to the point that we prefer to die and be with Christ (Phil 1:23), where we would be free of worldly things and therefore also free from sin and no longer cause our dear heavenly Father to be angry. We, therefore, regard this life and all its demands more as a burden than a benefit. For true believers to give their lives for others is a small matter, not to mention giving up their honor, possessions, or pleasures. After all, out of his boundless love Christ also gave his life for us (John 3:16).

Although brief, these words confirm that only faith restores us to the original and true divine disposition in which we were created, praise God, to dedicate ourselves to the service of all creatures, and to seek no gain for ourselves, because our Father and creator, the all-powerful God, has already provided enough for us. This faith is genuine righteousness in which the righteous live as they should toward God, other people, and all creatures (Hab 2:4). They give due honor and praise to God and practice toward others the love that fulfills all the commandments (Gal 5:14). In this way we indicate that we are disciples of Christ, keeping his new commandment (John 13:34) and through it the entire law and all the prophets, and we shall surely pass from this godly and Christian way of living into eternal life.

In comparison some will learn more accurately what kind of faith they have. Faith leads to self-denial, dedication to the service of others, sacrifice of self, and living to the praise of God wholly for others. If faith does not issue in these things, it is not true and legitimate faith; it is a dead faith, that is, no faith at all. If faith produces the above fruits only weakly and imperfectly, then faith is also weak and imperfect, and with few exceptions, unfortunately, this is the faith we all have. If faith were whole and if the heart were yielding completely to scripture and in reality, without any pretense, were trusting it alone in everything, it would be impossible for believers to seek their own advantage or to live only for themselves. Scripture would teach them for certain that self-seeking would ruin them and cause them to lose their lives and everything else (Luke 9:24; John 12:25). With complete trust and their whole heart true believers have to yield to that unspeakable goodness that scripture describes as prepared for them through Christ in God the Father (1 Cor 2:9) and visibly bestowed on them as soon as they believe. Through faith they are made entirely new; they no longer worry about themselves because they are assured that the eternal God and Father cares for them as dear children. Like a gushing fountain, believers must pour out the goodness granted them by God the Father through Christ for the welfare of everyone, but especially for their companions in the faith, who, unlike others, are receptive not only to material goods but to spiritual benefits as well.

In conclusion, I will use a clear text from St. Paul to show that people with true faith have become altogether different from what they were, new creatures in Christ, who can no longer live selfishly but are compelled to live for the benefit of others and the glory of

God: "For by grace you have been saved through faith, and this is not your own doing; it is the gift of God, not the result of works, so that no one may boast. For we are what he has made us, created in Christ Jesus for good works, which God prepared beforehand to be our way of life" (Eph 2:8–10). See how clear it is that, if we believe, we are saved through faith, that is, we have everything that is necessary, not from ourselves and our good deeds but as a free gift from God? We are thus a work of God, created through Jesus Christ for doing good deeds, not however for ourselves but in the way God prepared them to become our way of life. These works are without question those which God everywhere commands, namely, deeds by which we serve our neighbors. God demands no other works from us, and Christ has taught us no others, alluding therefore frequently to the prophet Hosea, "I desire mercy and not sacrifice" (Hos 6:6), and declaring that he will judge us accordingly. If believers are a work of God created for deeds of that kind, they cannot ignore such deeds and pursue solely their own advantage. What God has created through Christ Jesus must be good and right and accomplish the purpose for which it is created, just as all other works and creatures of God attend to that for which they were created: birds to flying, fish to swimming, and humans to speaking. No creature or work of God can disregard that for which it was created unless prevented by an accident. Likewise, no true Christians and believers can live without doing good works unselfishly for all people according to their disposition.

By now it should be clear in the first place that true faith is that through which we come to live not for ourselves but for others to the glory of God and to be diligent in genuine good works. In the second place, we should also understand that whoever preaches faith also teaches the source of all good works and that nothing is farther from the preacher's mind than forbidding good works. In the third place, we must also pay attention to this: if we are not diligent in doing the good works in question, it is certain that we have little faith; and if we undertake no such works and remain self-serving, we have no faith at all. According to Paul, even if we spoke in the tongues of mortals and angels and if we could prophesy and comprehend every mystery and thing to be known, and even if we possessed faith great enough to move mountains—that is, the gift of working miracles, given at times to people who do not have true faith, like those who have performed miracles in the name of the Lord yet shall hear him say "I have never known you" (Matt 7:22–23)—and even if we distributed all our possessions to the poor and gave our bodies to be burned, yet we would be nothing if we had no love (1 Cor 13:1–3). So it is for those striving for nothing but their own interest, because love seeks no advantage for itself. We also are nothing if we have no faith, for through faith we are not only made something but are made blessed, as the passage above emphasizes. Indeed, we are God's work, which must not only be something but something good.

Since true faith unfailingly produces true love, which makes us overflow with good works and live not for ourselves but for others and the eternal praise of God, and since faith comes from God's grace through hearing the word of God (Rom 10:17), we must above all things adhere to the divine word, listen to it, read it, meditate on it with diligence, and act accordingly. No one must keep us from the word of God; for it we must risk honor, life, possessions, and all that God has given us. The word of God alones makes us whole and blessed. The word brings faith; faith brings love; love brings forth the fruit of good works. Then follow the eternal inheritance and a thoroughly divine and blessed life. Amen.

In these dangerous times, when faith has disappeared and love has been extinguished because the divine word has not been faithfully and assiduously preached, let us earnestly beseech God to send us the rain of his pure, divine word, give us grace to receive it, and either to convert or to make an end of those who so madly fight against it. Amen.

19. Andrew Karlstadt, The Two Greatest Commandments: Love of God and Love of Neighbor, 1524

Andreas Bodenstein, from the German town of Karlstadt (1486–1541), was the only reformer to identify publicly during his lifetime with Lutheran, radical, and Zwinglian reforms. He was already professor of theology at the University of Wittenberg and archdeacon

151

of the clerical chapter at the Church of All Saints when he presided over the awarding of the doctorate to Martin Luther in 1512. In 1515 he traveled to Rome for additional study; the following year he received the doctorate in both civil and canon law. Returning to Wittenberg, he hesitated at first to join Luther's effort to shift the curricular emphasis from scholastic theologians to the Bible and Augustine, but he soon changed his mind and became one of Luther's staunchest supporters, debating the Catholic theologian John Eck in 1519, as did Luther, at the famous Leipzig Disputation. While Luther was in hiding at the Wartburg fortress after the Diet of Worms (1521), Karlstadt led the movement in Wittenberg to abolish the mass, to put an end to compulsory clerical celibacy and fasting, and to curtail devotion to the saints.

Upset by the civil unrest caused by Karlstadt's aggressive program and its endorsement by the town council, Luther returned to Wittenberg in March 1522, publicly criticized Karlstadt's strategy in eight sermons, and slowed down the reform movement. One year later Karlstadt renounced his academic career and retired as pastor to the village of Orlamünde, where, as Brother Andrew, "a new layman," he instituted the changes he tried to make in Wittenberg. In treatises first published in 1523, Karlstadt expressed the mystical tendencies that increased the distance between him and Luther and pushed him toward more spiritual and radical notions of reform.

One of these works was the sermon on love of God and love of neighbor from which the selections below are taken. The sermon was preached at Orlamünde in March of 1523, but it was not published until 1524. It is only one of ninety publications by Karlstadt, but it is one of the best expressions of his spirituality, which stressed the regenerated nature of the Christian life and its saturation by love of God and neighbor. The sermon also demonstrates Karlstadt's indebtedness to medieval mystical theology that he read during the early 1520s. This newfound appreciation of love and holy living in his mature theology led him, perhaps, in the last decade of his life to accept positions of diaconal service and teaching in the Reformed communities of Zürich and Basel.

Adapted from *The Essential Carlstadt,* trans. and ed. E. J. Furcha, 229–46, and from *Karlstadts Schriften aus den Jahren 1523–25,* ed. Erich Hertzsch, 1, 49–71.

REGARDING THE TWO GREATEST COMMANDMENTS: THE LOVE OF GOD AND NEIGHBOR (MATT 22:36–40). AN EXPLANATION OF HOW THE RIGHT LOVE OF NEIGHBOR IS NOT HUMAN BUT DIVINE AND FLOWS FORTH FROM GOD'S WILL

The gospel of love for God and neighbor teaches in a nutshell about the first work of God that a servant of God must receive and possess above all else. It also tells how a person can prepare for this initial work and become skilled at receiving it.

You should know that the greatest and noblest work of God in the created soul[1] is also the first. All acts of service rendered to God flow from this best and noblest work; they must be governed by it and conform to it. This is true because God places the greatest of all works in the ground of the soul[2] where he dwells, teaches, rests, instructs, and governs—united and in spiritual unity. But since reason differs from divine inspiration, our reason considers it strange, even foolish, that God should place his greatest work first and foremost in the created spirit and then build other works upon the noblest one. It is fitting for reason to consider it foolish so that, insofar as the knowledge of God is concerned, reason too might be deemed a fool and the ground of our soul develop a bitter aversion toward natural reason and flee from it.

One ought to know, however, that God does not establish his greatest work in the soul all at once, as if that work were fully grown at the moment of seizing and occupying it. God's gift begins with saplings. Similarly, God imprints his loving knowledge upon a new heart in subtle and small ways, as one might imprint the form of a seal upon a piece of hard and unformed wax, making it difficult to distinguish the lines of the form and hard to read the letters. This young shoot of the greatest work of God is granted in greater measure to some than to others. God distributes his talents and goods as he wills, desiring that everyone be content with what God gives, provided we are not slothful and bury our talent (Matt 25:18).

153

(1) The nature of the greatest work.

At this point someone may ask: which is the greatest work created by God in his spirits?[3] I respond: The love of God without knowledge and understanding is blind and deceitful. Faith or knowledge of God without love is cold and dead. Hence, the greatest divine work must be the loving knowledge of God, which scripture often calls love and to which it attributes the function and nature of knowing.

This work is also called faith, to which the quality of love is attributed so many times that one could say faith without love is worthless (1 Cor 13:2). Love without faith does not satisfy. Therefore, the right work is loving faith or faithful love. God recognizes and values it, as one recognizes and values a thing that is dear and delightful.

Loving faith is the best and noblest work because eternal life is contained in it (John 6:47; 17:2–3). It is also the first because love does the commandments of God (John 14:15) and because whoever does not believe is damned. Therefore, God's love must be present, or else the commandments remain unfulfilled; and faith and understanding must be present if God is to be pleased by anything a person does (1 John 3:22–23).

That scripture ascribes to love the qualities of faith and attributes to faith the works of love is apparent from the fact that love alone counts for something before God. It is active through faith or, put differently, only faith that is active in love counts for anything before God. Faith without love is worthless (1 Cor 13:2). The godless also know God, as Ezekiel and other prophets kept saying (Ezek 36:23), but they have no regard for God and their knowledge is dead, for they are lacking in love.

In short, John ascribes one work to faith or to knowledge and love of God; that work is to keep the commandments of God (1 John 3:23). He says whoever claims to know God but does not keep his commandments is a liar (1 John 2:4), but those who keep his commandments truly have the love of God. Note how the apostle John instructs us that both faith and love of God keep the commandments and that we can know, from the fulfillment of the divine commandments, faith and love just as we know a tree by its fruits (1 John

154

3:23–24). Therefore, they lie who say, "I know Christ," but do not walk in his commandments. Those also lie who say, "I love Christ," but fail to do his commandments; but those who fulfill God's commandments know God, just as those who keep his word truly have the love of Christ.

Faith and love are known by one work and one fruit. That is why I said that the Holy Spirit apportions one character and quality to these two virtues, and Paul attributes the best to God's love when he says that love is the best or greatest. Faith without love has no regard for what it knows and is a fickle faith that lacks discernment (1 Cor 13:2, 13). Therefore I am on solid ground when I say that the best and noblest work created by God in the soul is a faith abounding in love or a love abounding in faith. It is absolutely true that our love of Christ, as does faith, informs us of Christ and makes Christ known to us.

Again, faith is active and merciful, as is love, and Christ dwells in our hearts through love as much as through faith. For this reason Christ says: "Whoever does not love me does not keep my word," but "those who love me will keep my word, and my Father will love them, and we will come to them and make our home with them" (John 14:23–24). Christ clearly teaches us that God comes to dwell within us through love. For this reason Paul desires that Christ may dwell through faith in the hearts of the Ephesians, as they are "being rooted and grounded in love" (Eph 3:17). Accordingly, Christ dwells in created spirits through his love as much as he does through faith.

In this way he also teaches self-understanding and radiantly implants himself in the hearts of all who love him, as Christ says: "Those who love me will be loved by my Father, and I shall love them and reveal myself to them" (John 14:21). Hence the love of Christ is the root of faith; love receives Christ as he dwells within, and Christ reveals himself to love. I have said all this lest anyone confuse the terms *love* and *faith* or mistake a blind love or a fragile, loveless faith for the greatest work. You should know that the Holy Spirit intends to include faith when the Spirit speaks of love, just as love promised to God embraces faith as well.

Whenever our gospel speaks of love, you must certainly understand [it to mean] a faithful love and not in any way separate faith from love or imagine a denuded love, which neither understands nor leads to understanding. What was said above we wish to demonstrate from the gospel lesson for today:[4] God's faithful love is also the first work that God brings about in his created spirits. All of Moses and the prophets depend on this work, says Christ (Matt 22:40); therefore, God's love has to be the first work, for in God's works there is an order that is also found in his commandments.

Now you might ask two questions. The first is: Christ speaks of the greatest commandment and you speak of the greatest work. How do these tally? The second question is this: Christ says that the law and all the prophets derive from two commandments, while you say that all commandments derive from one, namely, "You ought to love God with all your heart." How do you explain that?

My reply to the first is: God's commandments give us ways of seeing concretely God's work in different ways, and we find the same order in the works that we find in the commandments, so that the highest and greatest commandment reveals and demands externally the greatest and highest work. Now Christ has said that the highest and greatest commandment is: "You shall love the Lord your God" (Matt 22:37–38). Hence love that is rich in faith must also be the noblest work that God has ever made known through his commandments and demanded of us. Consequently, God's love surpasses all other works; it is nobler, better, and more precious than all other gifts, outshining and perfecting them. This is true, for love is purer and more sincere than all of God's works, immersing the lover more deeply and with greater oneness in God than any of God's other works. There is no other work in which the created spirit disregards self more than in the work of love. Love draws us into its object. Lovers do not look to themselves as they do with other gifts, and the soul finds less of itself in love than in other gifts. Moreover, God's love is more courageous, bolder, and more penetrating than the other gifts and works of God. Therefore, it is easily the foremost and noblest work of God and would remain the best, even if our explanations should fail us and force us to rely alone on the words of Christ, in which he set love above all other works and valued it more highly than others: "On these two commandments hang all the law and the prophets" (Matt 22:40).

Indeed, the second commandment and work that concern love of neighbor depend on the commandment and the work of God's love. Love of neighbor must be abandoned whenever it obstructs God's love or when both cannot happen. It is possible to hate, persecute, or kill the neighbor out of love for God (Luke 14:26), but to hate and persecute God is prohibited for eternity. I can imagine no situation in which we are allowed to hate God. Whoever loves father or mother more than God is not worthy of God (Matt 10:37). We have been commanded to love God more than anyone else. We could perhaps taunt our parents with the question: "Who are you?" But it would be demonic to ask God sarcastically: "Who are you?" Therefore, love of God is a work on which love of neighbor depends. For this reason Moses says: "Honor your father and your mother, as the Lord your God commanded you" (Deut 5:16), that is, with the same will, understanding, and manner that God set before you.

Love of neighbor—be it angel, human being, or Christ in his humanity—must be governed by love of God and must be in line with it, just as a carpenter's line must follow the plumb and square. It is impossible for one who does not love God to love the neighbor in a divine manner, for we must love the neighbor as God demands and because this pleases God. This is impossible without love of God. Moses was teaching this in the ten commandments, and he began to explain the first commandment with love for God when he spoke of "those who love me and keep my commandments" (Deut 5:10).

Now I have already done justice to the second question: How can all the law and the prophets depend on two commandments? It is true, however, for all commandments and prohibitions deal with love of God and love of neighbor. It is not sufficient not to hate; love is also required. You must love your neighbors and speak well of them, and not harm them or treat your neighbors as if there were no God who seeks (or might seek) those who belong to him. You must love your neighbors, whenever you plan to fast, pray, sing, and do good works in the sight of God. Without love of neighbor, God abhors you and your alleged good works. Even then you cannot love your neighbor unless, of course, you love God, who has shown you how to love with a love abounding in faith.

Paul's assertion that love of neighbor fulfills the whole law (Rom 13:8) only applies if love of neighbor fulfills all the commandments that concern our relationship to the neighbor. That is exactly what Paul intends to show in the verses that follow (Rom 13:9–10). Hence, love of neighbor must above all else give attention to love of God, flow from it, and be guided by it. Christ never calls love of neighbor the highest or first but makes it secondary and like the first. Now the first must always be ahead of the second, or else they happen at the same time. There can be no second commandment and work of God unless the first commandment and work of God already exist. Where love of God is lacking, love of neighbor is also lacking. Love of neighbor is like love of God, as Christ says. Thus it must orient itself to love for God and follow it. It is futile for us to speak a great deal about love of neighbor when we ignore the love of God.

Our love for one another is carnal and human when we muster a godless love, that is, our love for one another is selfish. We love the neighbor for the sake of profit, assistance, or gain—motivated by our needs or by self-indulgence—as do the Gentiles and those who have forgotten God (Matt 6:32; 1 Cor 13:4–5). But when love of neighbor is pure and genuine (as Christ exemplifies it in the Gospels and demonstrates its likeness to divine love), it surely flows from divine love. That is why love of neighbor comes after the first and is like the first; it cannot help but have the same manner, nature, habit, and form as love of God—the second must, as it were, be shaped by the first.

Since love of neighbor follows love of God and is like the love of God, it is above nature and has supernatural powers. It has no place, therefore, in the spirit that does not love God, for as John says: "Everyone who loves is born of God and knows God" (1 John 4:7). When the apostle says: "For those who do not love a brother or a sister whom they have seen cannot love God whom they have not seen" (1 John 4:20), he does not contradict himself but strengthens and supports what he previously said. For love of God brings out love of neighbor every time it meets or hears brothers and sisters in Christ. Therefore, the same apostle says: "The commandment we have from him is this: those who love God must love their brothers and sisters also" (1 John 4:21).

The cause and origin of love of neighbor is that God is love itself. His love is an autonomous and uncreated loving power that touches the ground of the soul, that is, the innermost being. This loving power discloses itself and reveals God, teaching the created spirit to understand God and itself. It is like the rays of the sun, which reveal themselves to the eye on which they shine, teaching the eye to understand itself and the sun. An essential feature of the uncreated nature of divine love is God's love for his chosen creatures; God proved it by sending his Son as the incarnate Christ. Therefore, whenever divine love is revealed and poured out into the human heart, it also teaches love of neighbor and makes us love all that God loves, just as faith has regard for everything that is God's, namely, the poor and the forsaken.

It is impossible, therefore, that we love God whom we cannot see when we hate brothers and sisters whom we see. The above-named apostle says: "Beloved, let us love one another, for love is from God. Everyone who loves is born of God and knows God" (1 John 4:7). Mark well that everyone who loves the neighbor knows God; John spoke about this earlier (1 John 4:1–6). In other words, God has made himself and his love known to us, and it is impossible for anyone to love God before his divine, autonomous love has been revealed in the ground of the soul. But when God's love has given understanding to the heart, it must love God and all the children of God. Accordingly John says: "By this we know that we love the children of God, when we love God and obey his commandments" (1 John 5:2). In short, it is impossible for anyone who does not love God to love brothers and sisters in Christ or the children of God. We can see, however, that someone loves the children of God when that person loves God. The love of God, which is grasped by intuition, is a sure and unerring testimony to love for the neighbor, just as the Spirit of God is a witness and seal of divine gifts. Now if someone who envies a child of God were to say, "I love God," he would make God into a false witness and a liar.

It remains true, therefore, that love for God is the noblest and highest divine work, revealed through God's own love, and love of neighbor must be measured by and adjusted to it. Love of neighbor cannot possibly be right and good as long as it does not flow from and exist within the love of God. The love of which I speak is sometimes God's own love that makes itself known to the heart; sometimes it is the effect that this same love (that is, God himself) leaves in the ground of the soul after it has revealed itself, just as we call the eternal remembrance of a light once seen also a light. This illustration may dispel the darkness of what has been written and indicate which kind of love is meant....

(2) How we must be prepared to receive God's noblest work....

A person must be prepared and made ready above all else to receive the noble work of God. Christ and Moses point to this preparation when they say: "You shall love the Lord your God with all your heart, and with all your soul, and with all your might" (Deut 6:5; Matt 22:37).[5] How then are the heart and soul prepared, and what is this preparation called?

I reply: this preparation is called wholeness of heart or soul. When soul or heart is made whole, it is prepared for the work. Wholeness is the preparation. Division is the opposite and an obstacle to it. If you wish to know why God allows himself to be kept from creating a small spark of his very best work in your soul, it is because your heart or soul is not whole but divided and fragmented. For where there is multiplicity, simplicity has no room, and where that which is manifold dominates, that which is simple cannot rule. The soul is unable to serve two masters (Matt 6:24).

There are many creatures; God alone is one. Whoever clings to creaturely things is incapable of the great work of God and finds it incomprehensible. That work binds us to the one, and through it the one is unified; that work is the love of God. Moses, wishing to speak of the love of God, said: "Hear, O Israel, your God is one" (Deut 6:4).[6] After offering a short preface about God, namely, that God is the only true one, Moses places thereafter the commandment regarding love (Deut 6:5), so that everyone knows God's love pertains to the one. If we come to hate multiplicity and dismiss all that fragments and divides the soul, we become whole, acquiring our own unified interior and integrity, and become capable of receiving the noble work of God.

If you cannot understand this, note that the heart must divest itself of all creaturely clothing or images. In other words, the heart must be circumcised if it is to receive divine love. God must remove the foreskin of the heart (Deut 10:16) along with other impediments and circumcise the soul until it is just soul. It is then nothing but soul, an undivided ground, which God finds and uncovers by turning the sod and casting off all creaturely things.

The soul resembles the things it loves. Those who attach themselves to a harlot in order to love her, become like a harlot, one flesh and one body (1 Cor 6:16), for God ordained that we must become like the things we love. In God's sight and in truth, all who love contemptible and useless things, blind idols, deaf stones, or anything abominable become contemptible, useless, deaf, blind, and odious (Hos 9:10; Jer 2:4–11). Then the soul does not remain soul, but becomes an idol with the idol it loves, a deaf ear and a blind eye, just like the stone or block of wood that it loves and trusts in vain (Ps 115:4–8).

All these things break and destroy the soul, cover up the ground, and harden the heart so solidly that God cannot accomplish his work. Neither does he intend to plant his paternal works in that covered ground before it has been cleared. Hence, the soul must first be circumcised and swept clean and attain its clarity and inwardness before it is capable of receiving the noble work. Moses taught this in clear words when he said: "Moreover, the Lord your God will circumcise your heart and the heart of your descendants, so that you will love the Lord your God with all your heart" (Deut 30:6). Do you see that God must circumcise your heart?…

Note how clearly God's Spirit teaches that you must first be circumcised and swept clean before you can receive God's gifts. You may laugh or get angry [at what I say], but it is true, and that is why I claim that we cannot fulfill any of God's commandments on earth, not even the least. You need not despair, however. While it is true that we cannot enter the kingdom of God unless we believe, love God, and do his commandments as Christ says "with all one's heart," the consoling savior Christ Jesus has reassured us: in this vale of tears we may believe and love God and do his commandments in recognition of his abundance, even though we have not been wholly circumcised and have not reached complete wholeness and nakedness of our heart.

All who like branches have been grafted onto the vine that is Jesus Christ receive from God through the vine heavenly waters by which they are sprinkled and cleansed and made fit to receive God's love, faith, and work. This is illustrated by the story of the discovered treasure that led the finder to sell everything in order to acquire the field (Matt 13:44). From Christ Jesus living waters flow into us; they pervade our souls and gush up to eternal life (John 4:14). The spirit of awe that Christ had in great measure allows his powers to flow through himself to all the branches that grow on Christ the vine, creating a total aversion to all that is evil....All desire and love for our life is torn out and replaced by displeasure and weariness with this life and with our abilities and desires, so that we shy away from all things which prevent heart and soul from receiving the work of God.

When we have taken on the nature of the vine and begin to loathe and dread all creaturely desires, we open up a little and thirst for heavenly waters, just like arid ground that is cracked open because of drought. When we are thus opened, we too are prepared, empty, and free to be filled with God as he has promised. He is a helper in need. When we are prepared to receive divine gifts like faith and love, God gives as much as we are able to receive. If our capacity to receive is great, God gives great gifts. To all who wish to receive, God gives according to their capacity. If we are in every way prepared to receive God's work, God gives us everything in rich measure.

But if the created spirit is not sufficiently circumcised (and it never is), the consolation of Christ is available nonetheless, so that in Christ we may bear fruit as if we were branches on a fruitful vine. Although our works (or fruits) never reach maturity before the final circumcision, they are present in the soul nonetheless. Moreover, the Father prunes the branches daily and cleans them out, so that they bear more abundant and perfect fruit. It is a pleasant consolation, full of joy and delight, that God the Father implants his work and his fruits in our soul, even when our souls have not been fully circumcised and still show coarseness and blindness.

God first gives to the heart that has put on Christ and stands in Christ small treasures, tiny pearls, and subtle sparks, like an intense longing for God and his love. Or he grants us deep sighs for God until the heart is more fully swept clean. When it is well prepared and trimmed and quite new (as an old moss-covered tree becomes new when trimmed), God gives it the full love that he has commanded and requires.

At the outset God's noblest work is small and so insignificant that many people are unaware they possess it. It grows daily, however, and becomes larger and more obvious, filling out and making its presence known; but this growth happens within the six days that are full of labor and great unrest. On the seventh day, when the sprinkling has been completed, God's work remains at rest, without labor, and in perfection; then it is a love with all one's heart, soul, and strength. We lose ourselves in the snow-white cloth that comes from heaven and enfolds us so effectively that we can no longer find ourselves—in the will, desire, strength, or in the soul—once surrender of self[7] is complete....

How the heart is prepared and fitted to receive God's love is seldom explained or discussed. The same is true of the great effort that is required for us to become skilled at taking upon ourselves the love of God, for it means that one must teach and want the harsh purgatory that engenders an ardent longing for that love.

I should now speak about love of neighbor, which alone brings forth external works pleasing to God, but the topic is extensive and difficult to grasp for the simple reason that the commandment, "Love your neighbor as yourself," has to this day been poorly explained. God our Lord has explained it frequently enough, but the great masters have barely touched on it. I shall make a tentative beginning for you; you may then pursue the matter further and test whether or not you can grasp its secret and hidden meaning in the depth of your hearts.

Love of neighbor requires two things: it must be like love of God and also like love of self. Love of neighbor must be like the love of God just as the second commandment is like the first. Accordingly, Christ says: "This is the greatest and first commandment; and a second is like it: 'You shall love your neighbor as yourself'" (Matt 22:38–39). The other likeness requires that love of neighbor be equal to love of ourselves. If we want to love our neighbor aright, we must understand both these comparisons and know to what extent love of neighbor resembles divine love and how it resembles love of self. Otherwise, love of neighbor cannot be right and good, because all the works of God must issue forth in the manner and with the motivation that God intended when he commanded them. Likewise Moses said you should do the commandments of God as he commanded them, whenever the manner of doing them is portrayed by the commandments; that is one reason why God gave us his law (Deut 5:32–33). Thus we should observe diligently how God commanded love of neighbor and how it resembles love of God and love of self.

We should also know who our neighbor is; for Christ, our example, did not say in vain: "You shall love your neighbor as yourself" (Matt 19:19). To the brood of vipers he said: "An evil and adulterous generation asks for a sign, but no sign will be given to it except the sign of the prophet Jonah" (Matt 12:39). To the Pharisees and hypocrites Christ said: "Those who are well have no need of a physician" (Luke 5:31). He forbade us to throw precious pearls before swine (Matt 7:6), and he said to let the blind leaders go (Matt 15:14) and to beware of the sourdough of the Pharisees (Matt 16:6). Paul, too, forbade us to have fellowship with those who teach and live contrary to God (2 Cor 6:14–15). Another apostle says: "Do not receive into the house or welcome anyone who comes to you and does not bring the teaching of Christ" (2 John 10).

If we are not to have a friendly chat with those who do not have Christ's teaching, neither greet them nor invite them to our homes, then we are not allowed to love such people as our neighbors. Moreover, if I am not to provide food or drink to anyone who strives against Christ, that person cannot be my neighbor. If I am not to throw the little pearl before swine, it follows that no animals that have a human skin and the form of a human being may be regarded as my neighbor but rather as swine to whom I must not extend the good works owed to a neighbor. One must therefore carefully consider the identity of the neighbor whom we are to love as ourselves, so that we do not act contrary to God's love at the very moment that we are passionately practicing love of neighbor. For we would only create a love of neighbor that is more unlike love of God than a beam is unlike a human being....

The second commandment is like the first in that love of neighbor must be as upright and serious as love of God. For just as our love for God must be upright and serious, our love of neighbor must involve an upright and earnest will and desire. Just as love of

God implies an uncoerced obedience that is upright and desires nothing but God, love of neighbor also implies an uncoerced obedience toward God that is pure and must have the upright intention to love and serve and benefit the neighbor for God's sake, without desiring remuneration or reward.

The term *upright* means that we must walk and look straight ahead. The opposite of this is looking to expect something in return. Christ's words about the banquet explain this: I should invite the poor to be my guests for the sake of the one who commanded me to do so rather than invite the rich who are able to return the favor (Luke 14:12–14). The latter kind of love is not upright; instead, it turns back to me, finds my soul, and seeks what is mine and my pleasure. Were I to love the neighbor in that manner, I would corrupt my soul, because at the cost of my soul I am not to seek myself in any of the commandments or works of God. Yet, that is just what I do when I love the neighbor for the sake of something other than God. I must seek no reward nor should I allow the neighbor to repay me. My love must be without reward; only then is it upright.

Let me give another example. If I invite a poor official to my table or render other works of love while refusing food from him in return, I am not justified just because I invited a poor person, and my love is not upright if I expect the poor official to put in a word for me with my lord or to reward me for the food by overlooking something or making certain concessions. No love that hopes for a reward can be upright; rather, it is bent over and returns to what is mine. When you love the poor and show your love through external works, as when you feed or clothe them, and if you want to receive praise from people, you have already received your reward and by no means are you without reward. Your will toward your neighbor is not upright. Indeed, your will calls attention to your own praiseworthiness, honor, and glory; thus it returns to you, for when your love is not oriented to God's will and to the neighbor, so that God alone is praised and the neighbor alone helped by you, your intention is not upright but crooked and bent on profit as you aim at yourself and what is yours.

It is somewhat like that with upright desire. Where desire is upright, you are unaware of it and do not find yourself in it, but the person whom you love and benefit with an upright desire senses it. From this you can learn the meaning of earnest love or desire. When you have an earnest desire, it does not titillate you or puff you up, but you experience great fear of evil and you keep within the limits of God's work and are a simple servant and tool of the work of love. You have a swift and serious desire simply to fulfill the commandment of the great ruler. This earnestness is the fruit of the spirit of fearing God and grows from hatred of evil and love of good. When your love of neighbor shows the neighbor that your works are upright and earnest, it is like love of God and very close to it, as you may deduce from what was said above.

You must never forget what I have said all along: love serves and benefits the neighbor for God's sake; love of God must fill the heart and love of neighbor must spring forth from divine love. This is why we have a divine and not a human commandment to love the neighbor. I owe obedience to God and not to the neighbor. When I serve the neighbor, I must heed God's will and render the required obedience to God alone. From this you can understand again how the second commandment is close to and like the first, and you can understand how love of neighbor equals and resembles love of God, not least because of the sound reasons found in both the Gospels and Moses.

Now, for a brief summary of the similarity between our love of neighbor and the love of self. It seems strange and unpleasant that we should love ourselves, for love of self has been clearly forbidden and uprooted. In its place envy and hatred have been implanted.

It has always been impossible for humankind to understand what contributes to our true nature. We may well choose whatever we consider to be good, but it does not become good or useful simply because we consider and value it to be good. Take for example a person with a fever who chooses wine as if it were good for him. As soon as he satisfies his desire and realizes that the wine was harmful to him, he must revise his opinion and his choice and admit that the wine is not good for him. Now, as it is with the wine, so it is with other created things that a person chooses as if they would benefit a good life and nature. Experience proves, however, that we do not know what is good for us and that we especially fail to understand what benefits us for eternity.

Since we cannot see what is eternally good for us, we are unable to love ourselves any more than we are able to love others for their benefit. Hence, we are unable really to love either ourselves or the neighbor in a way that brings true and eternal benefits rather than in a way that seems good now but turns out to be harmful and evil. Nonetheless, God has given us one commandment for love of neighbor and of self and bound us to love the neighbor as ourselves. God would be fully in his right to damn us if we were to neglect that commandment, but his mercy is immeasurable and cannot stop doing good. Therefore, God made known his commandments that we might learn what is always and eternally to our benefit and that our well-being derives from keeping God's commandments. For this reason Moses frequently says: "Keep the commandments of the Lord your God and his decrees that I am commanding you today for your own well-being" (Deut 10:13). We must learn how God has decreed through his commandments that which contributes to our well-being and is truly good for us. We learn from them to make good choices and sound judgments and how all of us can love ourselves rightly and for lasting benefits. By the same token we must also engender love of neighbor.

I must not begrudge my neighbors any gifts that God has given me, so that they might enter with me into a divine community and receive an eternal good. I am obliged to want them to walk in all of God's commandments and to become strong, wise, and holy in God. To this end I must spare no labor or expense. Rather, I must stretch out my hand and provide food, drink, and clothing, teach and do everything that I want done to me, in order to receive my just deserts.

Now we can see how passages of scripture that ask us to avoid certain people, neither greeting them nor eating with them, agree with passages that urge us to accommodate neighbors who are not close to us and even to seek their advantage, help them, and be at their disposal. The latter are close to us in God; they are our siblings and children of God, who are redeemed by the precious blood of Christ. The others do not confess Christ, but, if they wish to hear about him, they also are close to me, even without the title, name, and baptism of Christians. Love is shown to all creatures when we follow God our Father and do good to people—be they good or evil—since he lets his sun shine on them all without distinction. And this is also a work of love toward the neighbor: to do good to one's enemies and pray for one's persecutors, as Christ and Stephen did (Luke 24:34; Acts 7:60). Still, we must not be blind and foolish in these matters. We should not eat with those who are hostile to Christ or associate with those who entice us away from God, lest they become our downfall (2 John 7; Deut 13:6–8). You ought to know, too, that Christ refused to pray for those who belonged to the world (John 17:9). Love without salt is foolish and dumb and belongs underfoot. Note from this that brotherly love is a carnal and devilish love when it displaces the love of God.

You now understand how we can love ourselves for our own benefit and then love the neighbor as ourselves. The little word *as* means equality or sameness, as if to say: we should love the neighbor in the very same way we love ourselves. For now, this is all that needs to be said on the commandments to love God and neighbor. God willing, you shall hear more and I shall say more to God's glory at a more appropriate time. Amen.

Preached at Orlamünde in the year 1523.
Printed at Strasbourg in the 1524th year.

20. Martin Luther, A Sermon on the Strength and Increase of Faith and Love, 1525

The date on which Luther delivered this sermon is not certain because it is extant only in seven printed editions, most of which appeared in 1525. The biblical text for the sermon is the epistle lesson for the sixteenth Sunday after Trinity, which fell on October 1 of that year. Whether the sermon was preached on that day or not, 1525 is likely the correct year, and it was a busy one in Luther's life, full of controversy and significant events. Until June of 1525 the peasants' revolution was raging and Luther wrote his notorious reply to their rebellion; the man who had protected Luther and the Reformation in Saxony, Elector Frederick, died; in June, Luther and Katharina von Bora were married; during the autumn, besides lecturing on the Old Testament prophets, Luther labored over *Bound Choice*, his reply to Erasmus.

The sermon as we have it, however, contains no direct reference to those events but instead applies the text of Ephesians in a general way to spiritual and devotional themes like internalizing the word and deepening faith and love, themes that were summed up in the title attached to the printed editions. Luther is nonetheless answering a charge that was frequently made against the young Protestant movement by Catholic theologians and by radical preachers like Thomas Müntzer. The charge was simple but persistent: Protestants claimed they were saved by faith, but they did not put that faith into action and produced no more visible fruit than believers had shown prior to the beginning of the Reformation.

After replying to this charge, Luther explains the meaning of verses 17–19 in a spiritual tone that contrasts sharply with the polemical language used against Erasmus. His explanation of being filled with the fullness of God (Eph 3:19) is one place in his writings where Luther speaks of becoming godlike. Although he tempers this expression by acknowledging the sin and imperfection that mark all human life, his positive description of the change that true faith effects in believers indicates that for him life in the fullness of Christ is substantially different from life under the power of sin.

The portions of the sermon presented here have been translated from the German text in WA 17/1, 428–38. The English translation of a later and longer (but less reliable) form of the sermon from Luther's Postils has also been consulted; it can be found in *Complete Sermons of Martin Luther*, ed. J. N. Lenker, 7, 259–80.

THE EPISTLE LESSON FOR THE SIXTEENTH SUNDAY AFTER TRINITY (EPHESIANS 3:14–21)

"For this reason I bow my knees before the Father, from whom every family in heaven and on earth takes its name. I pray that, according to the riches of his glory, he may grant that you may be strengthened in your inner being with power through his Spirit, and that Christ may dwell in your hearts through faith, as you are being rooted and grounded in love. I pray that you may have the power to comprehend, with all the saints, what is the breadth and length and height and depth, and to know the love of Christ that surpasses knowledge, so that you may be filled with all the fullness of God. Now to him who by the power at work within us is able to accomplish abundantly far more than we can ask or imagine, to him be glory in the church and in Christ Jesus to all generations, forever and ever. Amen."

Up to this point in the epistle Paul has praised the office of preaching, which in the New Testament proclaims the gospel. With lofty words he has recounted the utility, power, and wisdom of the office, and above all how God through preaching has showered us with all the strength, wisdom, and goodness of which he is capable in heaven and on earth. For the gospel proclaims life from death, justification from sin, redemption from hell and all evil, and brings the kingdom of God out of the kingdom of darkness. It is all too magnificent for Paul to describe adequately in words, yet he extols it to the highest degree possible.

Now Paul adds his wish that this message not only be preached and reverberate externally in the ears, but that it also enter the heart and have the same effect inwardly that the sound does outwardly. Otherwise it remains a poor husk that is only preached with the mouth and heard with the ears but never enters the heart with force or leads to any action—which would be all the more regrettable in light of Paul's saying: "The kingdom of God depends not on talk but on power" (1 Cor 4:20). To believe inwardly with the heart and to demonstrate that faith outwardly with love are in essence one thing, the result of which is acting, not just talking, and living, not just chattering. The word should not remain stuck on the tongue or in the ears but have force and lead to actions and deeds. In the Old Testament Moses talked a lot, but no one acted on those words; here the reverse should be true: few words but much doing. Paul desires that the gospel not be preached in vain but accomplish the purpose for which it is proclaimed.

See how he comes to the aid of Christendom and gives a lesson, especially to preachers, as to how they might improve people. Whenever we hear the gospel and could be passing it on, we carelessly dismiss it, because by then we have heard enough and content ourselves with knowing it without giving any force or momentum to what we know. Sighing day and night, we should unceasingly plead with God that he would empower the word to become effective in our hearts, as David says: "Listen, he sends out his voice, his mighty voice" (Ps 68:33). This lesson is not only for preachers. All Christians should prevail upon God, who has given us comprehension of the word, also to bestow strength to put that word into effect so that it does not remain a matter of mere talk....

"That you may be strengthened in your inner being with power through his Spirit" (Eph 3:16). What is it that Paul asks for? Not only that the word be with them, although it is a great gift when amply provided, but that it also delight their hearts and have force in their lives. For that reason he contrasts word and strength: many have the word but few experience its impact on their lives and see the results that are claimed for it. Our adversaries cannot scold or ridicule us more harshly than to say that we preach and listen to much that is good but go no further. We do not act on what we hear or improve our lives by listening to it; in fact, we become worse than we were before, and it would be better if we had stayed as we were.

How shall we respond to this criticism? First, because we see that the word is not taken seriously and that its potential force is not actualized, we have all the more reason to pray as Paul teaches here. Second, although our adversaries see little fruit and improvement, they are hardly the ones who should be passing judgment. They assume we should be performing miracles and waking the dead. They think only roses grow where Christians walk and that nothing but pure holiness is found there, but if this were true, what need would there be for us to pray? I cannot pray for what I already have but only thank God for it. Because Paul and scripture command us to pray, however, we must be lacking in strength; otherwise, why would scripture promote such useless talk? Paul himself, therefore, confesses that the Ephesians are weak, and he makes the same complaint in other letters, especially to the Corinthians, and everywhere he urges them to act and live as they have learned to do. What would compel him to be so insistent other than observing then what we also see now: people everywhere coming up short and nothing going as it should. Even if all do not act according to the gospel, nonetheless some improve and produce the kind of fruit that gives many people a good conscience and prevents much of the evil that used to take place....We confess that we are not all strong, but if there were no weakness among us, then there would be no need for constant prayer or urgent preaching....

Our third response: we are certain that the preaching of God's word must produce fruit. Since we have God's word, God's Spirit must also be with us, and wherever the Spirit is, faith is also present—however weak it may be and hard at first to recognize. Among us there are to be sure Christians who pray daily, although no one may be aware of them....

"That Christ may dwell in your hearts through faith" (Eph 3:17). The Holy Spirit brings Christ into the heart and teaches us to recognize him. The Spirit warms the heart and gives it courage. Paul everywhere implies that no one is able to come before God without Christ, who is the only mediator. When Christ dwells in the heart and rules my entire life, it makes no difference if my faith is weak, for Christ is not mere bone but also flesh with its distensions, growths, and sins of which he is not ashamed. Wherever he dwells, all fullness is there, regardless of whether the person is strong or weak.

For Christ to dwell in the heart means nothing other than to know him, to understand who he is and what we can expect from him—that he is our Savior, through whom we may call God our Father and receive the Spirit, who gives us courage in the face of misfortune. We can only lay hold of Christ where he dwells with us, in our hearts, because he is not an inanimate thing but the living God. But how do we in fact embrace him in the heart? Not through ideas or thoughts but only through living faith. Christ does not allow himself to be grasped with works or caught with the eyes but to be held only with the heart. If your faith is genuine and rests on a good foundation, you can tell that you have Christ in your heart; you are aware of all his intentions and actions in heaven and on earth. You also observe how he rules through his word and Spirit, and you discern the attitudes of those who have Christ and those who do not.

In this passage Paul wishes Christ to be so efficacious in our hearts that he informs us of what the word can bring: liberation from sin and death and assurance of grace and eternal life. It is impossible for the heart that feels that power to be other than firm and courageous when confronted by the terrors of the devil and the world. Those who have not yet arrived at this point are here advised what course to take, namely, to ask God for such faith and strength and to ask for the prayers of others to the same end. That much about faith; now follows what Paul says about love.

"As you are being rooted and grounded in love" (Eph 3:17). This is an unusual way of speaking. Are we not rooted, engrafted, and grounded through faith? Why, then, does Paul attribute all these effects to love? It is true that we are rooted through faith, but love shows whether or not faith is solid and the heart joyful and confident in God. In those who have absolute confidence that God is their Father, however weak their faith may be, it will find expression in word and deed and they will serve their neighbors with instruction and helping hands. When Paul says we are "rooted and grounded in love," he means that we can see and feel that we have genuine faith. Love is the test that determines the quality of faith, as Peter says: "Be all the more eager to confirm your call and election" (2 Pet 1:10); that is, do good works and the exercise of them will help you become certain of your faith. Until you do, you will always be uncertain, irresolute, and shallow, not rooted and grounded. In the two parts of this verse, therefore, Paul teaches first that we should have in our hearts genuine faith toward God and, second, that faith should break forth and express itself in loving service to the neighbor.

"I pray that you have the power to comprehend with all the saints what is the breadth and length and height and depth" (Eph 3:18). These words represent another feature of the apostle's wish for the Ephesians to be heartened and confident in God through faith and rooted and grounded in love for their neighbors. "When you are thus strengthened," he intends to say, "and permeated and reinforced, you will be able to grasp with all the saints the four dimensions, to grow with their aid, and to understand them more and more." Faith alone brings about this growth and understanding; love is not a primary force, but it does help to make faith certain.

Some teachers have applied the four dimensions to the shape and size of the holy cross, but Paul does not mention the cross. He says in effect: "That you may comprehend all things including the length, breadth, height, and depth of Christ's kingdom." When my heart has been granted that degree of comprehension, Christ cannot make his kingdom too long or too wide for me to traverse, or so high and so deep that I would be separated from him or his word.

I see now with certainty that, wherever I go, he is already there and that he rules in all places, however long or broad, deep or high they may be, now or in eternity. No matter how great the distance, I find him everywhere, as David says: "Where can I go from your spirit? Or where can I flee from your presence? If I ascend to heaven, you are there; if I make my bed in Sheol, you are there" (Ps 139:7–8). Christ rules eternally. His length and breadth, depth and height, are unlimited. Even if I descend to the depths of hell, my heart and my faith tell me that Christ is also there.

The sum of the matter is this: Humiliate or exalt me, judge me as you wish, pull me hither or thither, I will still find Christ. He holds in his hands everything in heaven and earth, and all things are subject to him: angels, the devil, the world, sin, death, and hell. Therefore, as long as he dwells in my heart, I still have confidence, and, wherever I go, I cannot be lost. I dwell where Christ my Lord dwells. Reason cannot possibly be confident in this way. If reason were to rise a yard above the earth, it would despair. Through Christ, however, we Christians receive extraordinary confidence. We are assured that he dwells everywhere: in the presence of honor and dishonor, hunger and sorrow, illness and imprisonment, death or life, blessing or affliction. Paul asks God to give the Ephesians the blessing and healing they need in order to know that assurance deeply in their hearts, and he concludes the prayer in these words:

"And to know the love of Christ that surpasses knowledge, so that you may be filled with all the fullness of God" (Eph 3:19). He means: "In addition to having faith and apprehending the four dimensions of Christ's kingdom, I want you to know the love of Christ that we should have: the love that Christ bears toward us and the love that we owe our neighbor. This knowledge transcends even familiarity with the gospel, for, even if you have a great deal of information, your knowledge will avail little or nothing without love."

To sum it up: Paul wants our faith to increase to the point that it is strong and efficacious, our love is warm and fervent, and we are filled "with all the fullness of God." To be filled in that way means, if we refer to the Hebrew language, to be filled in all the ways that God's bounty makes possible: full of God, showered with all his gifts and grace, and filled with his Spirit, who gives us courage, illuminates us with his light, lives in us with his life, saves us with his salvation, and enkindles love in us with his love. In short, everything that God is and can do is completely in us and so effective that we are entirely made like God—not in such a way that we have just one part or a few pieces but "all the fullness." Much has been written about the way we are to become godlike. Some have constructed ladders on which we can climb to heaven, and others have written similar things. All they propose is piecemeal. This passage shows us the truest way to become godlike: be filled to the utmost with God, lacking in no part but having it all together, until every word, thought, and deed, your whole life in fact, becomes utterly divine.

No one should imagine, however, that such fullness can be attained in this life. We may indeed desire it and pray for it, as Paul does here, but we will not find any person alive with that perfect fullness. We must rely alone upon our desire for such perfection and our deep sighing for it. As long as we live in the flesh, we are filled, alas, with all the fullness of Adam. Hence we must pray unceasingly for God to remove our weakness, put courage and spirit[8] into our hearts, and so to fill us with grace and strength that God alone may rule and be fully at work in us. Let us all desire this for one another, and to that end may God grant us grace. Amen.

21. Ulrich Zwingli, Letter to Ambrosius Blarer, May 4, 1528

The text below belongs to the longest extant letter from the pen of Ulrich Zwingli. It was addressed to Ambrosius Blarer, a former Benedictine monk who was an evangelical preacher in the German city of Constance, also Blarer's birthplace. Under the leadership of Blarer and John Zwick (c. 1496–1542), Constance was gradually establishing a Protestant form of Christianity similar to that which Zwingli had instituted in Zürich, and Blarer was exchanging letters with the Zürich reformer. By 1527, all clergy had been instructed to preach the gospel, and they were required, like all other citizens, to swear allegiance to the city. Most of the clergy who had remained loyal to Rome had left the town, but there were controversial reforms still to be made: altering or abolishing monasteries, removing statues and pictures from the churches, ending celebration of the mass, instituting a welfare system and new regulations for marriage. Zwingli's letter reveals that there was resistance to some of these "external" changes and, prompted by statements of Luther with whom he was now at odds over the Lord's Supper, he addresses the issue head on.

In this letter Zwingli makes the notable statement that "the kingdom of Christ is external." By this he means that changes in worship, law, and piety that agree with the word of God are essential to establishing the kingdom—just as essential, in fact, as right attitudes of the heart like faith and love. Although Luther had supported many of the same changes in German towns, he did emphasize that the right kind of faith and love were more important than externals and could co-exist with some externals like the images and statues that Zwingli insisted must be removed. This difference of opinion, along with their disagreement over the presence of Christ in the supper, would lead to a permanent division between Lutheran and Reformed confessions.

In spite of their differences, however, Luther would agree in principle with Zwingli that Protestant spirituality involved not only the heart but also external matters of worship and piety. They would also agree that the faith which justified believers before God should produce works of love that were external and quite visible to the people who benefited from them. For Zwingli, love had backbone; it could make the hard decisions about changing externals even if nonviolent coercion must be used.

English translation of the German version in *Reformatorenbriefe*, ed. G. Gloede, 269–73.

Grace and peace from the Lord!

I thoroughly acknowledge your apprehension, my dear Ambrosius,[9] and I sense it so strongly in your letter that it has rubbed off on me and I am quite concerned. In our century many novel teachings are set forth in a haphazard manner; and while we should be wary of them, we must also be careful not to fall into an even greater error. We have therefore chosen to proceed with caution, and this caution is just as important as the frankness that should prevail in our discussion of important problems, so that falsehood will not be treated as truth.

Luther has served up a paradox that most of us have swallowed: the kingdom of Christ is not external....That assertion is mainly supported by the statement, "My kingdom is not from this world" (John 18:36), but also by other passages in which Jesus withdrew from those who wanted to make him either king or judge (John 6:15; Luke 12:14). In those cases, however, the context is not taken into consideration, and other places where Jesus both speaks and acts differently are ignored. For example, when it is suggested that a Christian magistrate may not command anything that would injure weak consciences (1 Cor 8:12) because the kingdom of Christ is not external, then I understand "external things" to mean precisely those requirements that formerly bound our consciences: fasting, restrictions on certain foods, obligatory places and times [for religious matters], holy days, and similar rules. People fail to notice that Christ himself, the first and best authority to whom I can appeal, did not place much importance on those externals; otherwise, he would have made his disciples fast. They were not fasting, although the Pharisees and the disciples of John the Baptist did, and it caused a scandal (Mark 2:18–20). For Christ, however, superstitious people were a lower priority than securing the liberty of the children of God (Rom 8:21). Fasting was clearly an external issue, was it not?

I am trying to point out two things: First, Christ certainly meant for people to be free from ritual washing before meals and to eat whatever they wanted without worrying about laws or traditions or the criticism of the people who heard him. Second, even though the kingdom of Christ is not external in the sense that his critics understood it, why did he nevertheless defend the disciples against the traditional rules? And why did Christ then prohibit them from taking along food and clothing on their journeys to proclaim the good news (Matt 10:7–10)?…You see, I am trying to demonstrate that the kingdom of Christ is in some way external. Taking no bag, no change of clothes—that is certainly an external matter. Christ intended to set the standard and make the rules in outward things, and his kingdom is therefore quite external.

Apostles, elders, and the whole church set guidelines about everything that concerned circumcision, blood, and strangulation (Acts 15:19–20). Why is it forbidden, therefore, for the Christian senate and people of Constance to decide an external matter that involves religion when the decisions measure up to scripture—even if some people disapprove?[10] No parish has ever been so lucky as to have no one who disagreed with the word and its servants. Of course, moderation allows for some exceptions when applying external guidelines. Paul circumcised Timothy, for example, because otherwise he would have had a revolt on his hands (Acts 16:4). As the number of believers increased, however, he no longer felt forced to circumcise Titus because he realized there would no longer be an uproar (Gal 2:3).

As long as peace is maintained, everything that is directly opposed to the word of God and to devout consciences must be abolished. Even in everyday affairs you will never do anything right if you wait until no one is offended.

Some people will object: "The senate of Constance is not the church!" I know we are not speaking here of the church when the senate is not in agreement with your entire community.[11] In Constance, however, you have the guild assemblies with their delegates from all the crafts and trades. As long as they are asked for their decision, there is no need to seek a larger consensus from the church community. It is also possible to entrust an especially difficult matter to a few people or to one person alone. When the issue of circumcision was being debated, the entire Christian community of Antioch did not go to Jerusalem but sent Paul and Barnabas as their delegates to decide the matter (Acts 15:2). True, the Christians at Antioch were examining a question they had in common with the church at Jerusalem, but in Antioch they took the initiative to decide the matter. Every member of your church community would have an opportunity to consult with the pastors if a council of guild representatives were to be held. Why then could you not allow the senate to give the order to remove the statues and images still in our churches and to abolish the mass, that intolerable atrocity! By that time all the apostles, elders, brothers, and sisters—indeed the entire community—would have a part in the decision.

After all, Christ quickly fashioned a few cords into a whip and applied substantial force to drive the dealers, buyers, and money-changers out of the Temple because that kind of business was not permitted in the holy precinct (John 2:14–15). It was proper for Christ to proceed with force against those offenders; why is it not right for us to use force against those who commit the offenses in our day? If he had merely overturned the dove pens and tossed the scales out of the Temple, it would be enough to refute the Anabaptists,[12] who declare that civil officials have no right to interfere in external matters that offend the conscience. But since he also threw the changers' money on the floor and whipped the dealers and their customers, he taught us that force has to be considered when the occasion demands. I want "force," however, understood very carefully. It does not include violence associated with cruelty and injustice but should be applied with intelligence, control, and compassion. This use of force is nothing other than the exercise of just and pious authority....If the two Catos,[13] Camillus,[14] and Scipio[15] had not been so devout, they would never have been so generous. Back then religion did not stop at the Palestinian border, for the heavenly Spirit had not only created and sustained Palestine but the whole world. The Spirit also allowed piety to flourish among those whom he chose no matter where they lived....

The Lord's Supper should not be considered an external matter to be tolerated for the sake of the weak,[16] but it belongs to those essential teachings without which a pure and unshakeable Christian faith cannot be transmitted. Another essential teaching concerns the head of the church. The following sentences are contradictory, are they not: "Christ himself is head of the church" and "The Roman pope is the head of the church of Christ"? And these two sentences: "Sins are forgiven alone through the death of Christ" and "Sins are forgiven through the bodily eating of the body of Christ"? As a consequence, the Lord's Supper should not be downgraded to an external matter but considered one of those essential teachings that genuinely instruct inward faith and, at the same time, cut off and purify everything that resists that faith. No mortal has the right to resist with power and force anything that promotes the pure deliberation and knowledge of faith, unless it involves people who have been clearly refuted but still refuse to be converted and appear godless in the eyes of every devout person. Today, however, as true doctrine increases steadily, it is an audacious act of violence for rulers to suppress with force the most powerful thing of all, the truth.

Love, therefore, has to decide which things must be done and which left undone, not just any Bible verse chosen at random, for we are not under the law but under grace (Rom 6:14). Love does

179

not shy away from hard decisions and it follows divine precedents—even if it means getting rid of an opponent who has been convicted of heresy or blasphemy, refuses to repent, and stubbornly repeats the same offenses that endanger and damage religion. For such action to be taken, there must be a real threat to religion itself, not just to us personally. If you and I were to be offered up but religion remained unharmed for our followers, then we should bare our throats even for a Caiaphas or Annas (John 18:13–14, 24, 28). If, however, true religion can be defended and upheld by Hezekiah (2 Kgs 18:1–6), Elijah (1 Kgs 18:20–40), and Josiah (2 Kgs 23:1–25),[17] why not allow them to do it? If they can keep the peace by themselves with the aid and consent of everyone else, we should not hesitate a second....

If our opponents ask whether or not we should force certain people to faith, tell them: "Not at all." We want to protect the faithful against violent people who lash out as soon as some authority is given to them. That is the first duty of a just and objective judge....A Christian is to the church what a good citizen is to the city. Hezekiah and Elijah are not binding for us; instead, a common love and the same Spirit obligate us to follow their examples insofar as religion, the commonweal, and peace require.

This is the end of my jumbled remarks; they are hard to read and not very orderly. I have expressed myself openly and given you material for critical appraisal. Now you have to read it carefully and select what is useful.

Your brother Thomas has come to us.[18] I exchanged a few words with him as he left, and they reeked a little of Luther's teaching. Be careful and, if at all possible, do not let him take offense at this letter. I can tell that he is thin-skinned about his respect for Luther. I wish that Thomas could assess Luther as well as we do, but that's the way it is.

I have stolen a few hours for myself, but I had to take them from my much-needed afternoon nap and my work. Ask yourself now what is right and fair in these matters and discuss it all with Zwick.[19] Without piety no one knows what is truly right and fair, but I do not have to remind you what piety and devotion are. Then abolish everything that appears to be useless and unfair! Farewell!

Your Ulrich Zwingli

180

PART SIX

Singing

Introduction

It is hard to overestimate the importance of singing to the Reformation. All Protestant traditions made use of chant, psalms, and hymns to enrich their worship and to express their devotion. In the German town of Joachimsthal, according to Christopher Brown, "the most telling aspect of the Reformation's success…was the use of Lutheran hymns within the home."[1] Texts by Martin Luther and others were widely printed and found their way into the houses and the hearts of the laity. In the French Reformed churches the metrical psalms of the poet Clément Marot (d. 1544) and translations by Theodore Beza, John Calvin's Genevan successor, were set to music and sung in place of hymns and liturgical chants. The psalter that Calvin published in 1539 for the French congregation in Strasbourg included six of his own translations.[2] The Radical Reformation also produced distinctive music, such as the rich and powerful songs about its martyrs. These songs were especially popular among Dutch Anabaptists, who published them together with prose accounts in their martyrology (*Het Offer*, 1563; 1570). German Anabaptists published their own songbook, the *Ausbund*, which is still used by the Hutterites today.[3] The course of the English Reformation can be traced by its music. The English Latin liturgy was replaced by the vernacular service in *The Book of Common Prayer*; congregations began to participate actively in worship by singing parts of the liturgy and the psalms in English. Except for the revival of Latin church music during the brief reign of Mary Tudor (1553–58), the vernacular texts of the liturgy, psalms, and anthems formed the core of a new English Protestant identity.

Early Protestant music served many purposes. It often called worshipers back to the center of Protestant theology and faith, Jesus the Christ, as did the hymn by Elisabeth Cruciger, "The Only Son from Heaven." Songs were also employed in public confrontations, even when they were not battle hymns, as in the German town of Göttingen in 1529. As a procession organized by Catholics went from church to church to pray for protection against the sweating sickness, it was interrupted by evangelical laity, who blocked them at one intersection and sang Luther's version of the 130th psalm, "Out of the Depths." When the procession reached the last church and monks and clergy sang the *Te Deum*, the Protestant crowd pressed in from the back and tried to drown them out with a German version of the same ancient hymn, *Herr Gott, Dich loben wir* (Lord God, we praise you).[4] Except for its appeal to Christ in the first stanza, the poem composed by Ulrich Zwingli after his serious illness in 1519 or 1520 reads like a prayer of lamentation and thanksgiving from the Book of Psalms. It is an expression of deep piety that could have been written in almost any era. Some hymns were composed as catechetical devices. "Salvation unto Us Has Come" by Paul Speratus is a summary of Lutheran teaching that other Protestants might have claimed as their own. It not only emphasizes justification by faith alone, but it also underlines the vitality of that faith manifested in service to others. Other songs and hymns in this section express the desire for peace in turbulent times, thanksgiving for God's faithfulness at the beginning of a new day, faithful submission to the will of God to direct one's life, and absolute devotion to God, as expressed in the introduction to every verse of the beautiful hymn by Leo Jud, "My Heart Shall Be Yours and Yours Alone."

Katharina Schütz Zell conveyed the versatility of Protestant music when she commented about the songbook of the Bohemian Brethren that she published in Strasbourg: "Indeed, I ought much rather to call it a teaching, prayer, and praise book than a songbook, although the little word 'song' is well and properly spoken, for the greatest praise of God is expressed in song." The last phrase can be applied to both contemporary praise music and sixteenth-century hymns. Indeed, when sermons are long forgotten and Bible verses—their power weakened by competing translations—fade from memory, favorite hymns and songs are still remembered, prized, and sung. When new hymnbooks and new forms of worship are introduced, the danger of change is an acute threat because there is no deeper well of spirituality than music. The early Reformation was just such a period of change; in order for its music to sustain the new evangelical movements as it did, that music must have been even more moving and profound than most Protestants today can recognize.

22. Ulrich Zwingli, A Christian Song Written When He Was Attacked by the Pestilence, 1519

Despite the title and section headings given to this poem in the Zürich hymnbook of 1552, Ulrich Zwingli did not compose it during the illness he suffered in late 1519 and early 1520, soon after his arrival in Zürich. It could have been written in late 1520, but some scholars believe the text that Zwingli, an accomplished musician, also set to music was not composed until 1525. Either way, the hymn recalls the thoughts and emotions that seized Zwingli after he became a victim of the plague in September 1519. The poem also suggests that his near-death experience confirmed Zwingli's call as an evangelical preacher and steeled him to resist opposition fomented by the Reformation.

The original German text contained three stanzas of twenty-six short lines each, a form that was already favored in learned circles of the era. As a hymn of consolation for the sick it appeared in Swiss hymnals of the sixteenth century and again in modern collections of German hymns.

The English text is based on *Ulrich Zwingli: Early Writings*, ed. Samuel Macauley Jackson, 56–57. Also consulted: the German text in ZS 1, 3–11.

(1) Help, Lord God, help in this trouble!
I think death is at the door.
Stand before[5] me, Christ, for you have overcome him.
To you I cry: If it is your will, take out the dart that wounds me,
nor lets me have an hour's rest or repose.

Will you, however, that death take me in the midst of my days,
    so let it be.
Do what you will, nothing shall be too much for me.
Your vessel am I, to make or break altogether.
For if you take away my spirit from this earth,
you do it, so that [my spirit] may not grow worse,
or spot the pious lives and ways of others.

(2) Console me, Lord God, console me, the illness increases;
pain and fear seize my soul and body.
Come to me then with your grace, my only consolation.
It will surely save all who set their heartfelt desires and their
    hopes on you,
and who besides despise all gain and loss.
Now all is over. My tongue is dumb, it cannot speak a word;
my senses are all blighted.
Therefore it is time that you conduct my fight hereafter,
since I am not so strong,
that I can bravely make resistance to the devil's wiles and
    treacherous hand.
Still my spirit will constantly abide with you,
however he may rage.

(3) Sound, Lord God, sound! I think I am already coming back.[6]
Yes, if it please you, Lord, that no spark of sin
rule me longer on earth,
then my lips must bespeak more thy praise and teaching than
    ever before,
in every way possible, in simplicity and without guile.
Although I must sometime endure the punishment of death,
perhaps with greater anguish than would now have happened,
since I came so near to death's door;
so will I still bear joyfully, for the sake of the reward,
the spite and boasting of this world by your help,
without which nothing can be perfected.

23. Paul Speratus, Salvation unto Us Has Come, 1523

The German text of this hymn (*Es ist das Heil uns kommen her*), one of the earliest and most popular Reformation songs, may have been written in 1523 during the Moravian imprisonment of Paul Speratus (1484–1551). A well-educated priest who eventually earned a doctorate in Vienna, Speratus converted early to the Protestant cause, married, and served in Austria before his strong evangelical views led to his banishment. After he was released from prison, Speratus and his wife went to Wittenberg, and in 1523 he helped Martin Luther prepare the first Lutheran hymnal called the *Book of Eight Songs* because it contained only eight hymns, one of which had this text by Speratus. Upon Luther's recommendation Speratus became court chaplain to the duke of Prussia in Königsberg and oversaw the organization of the church in that territory.

The text of the hymn summarizes the theology on which early Lutheran spirituality was based and enabled laypeople to internalize it by singing the message of Luther and other preachers like Speratus. The original tune, an anonymous melody, became familiar to generations of German Protestants. It appeared in the earliest hymnals, and J. S. Bach used the tune in five cantatas and one chorale prelude for organ.

English text from the *Lutheran Book of Worship* (1978), no. 297.

(1) Salvation unto us has come by God's free grace and favor;
Good works cannot avert our doom, they help and save us never.
Faith looks to Jesus Christ alone, who did for all the world atone;
He is our mediator.

(2) Theirs was a false, misleading dream who thought God's law
    was given,
That sinners might themselves redeem and by their works gain
    heaven.
The law is but a mirror bright to bring the inbred sin to light
That lurks within our nature.

(3) And yet the law fulfilled must be, or we were lost forever;
Therefore God sent his Son that he might us from death deliver.

He all the law for us fulfilled, and thus his Father's anger stilled,
Which over us impended.

(4) Faith clings to Jesus' cross alone and rests in him unceasing;
And by its fruits true faith is known with love and hope increasing.
For faith alone can justify; works serve our neighbor and supply
The proof that faith is living.

(5) All blessing, honor, thanks, and praise to Father, Son, and
  Spirit.
The God who saved us by his grace, all glory to his merit.
O triune God in heav'n above, you have revealed your saving love;
Your blessed name we hallow.

24. Elisabeth Cruciger, The Only Son from Heaven, 1524

The text and the tune of this German hymn (*Herr Christ, der einig Gotts Sohn*) first appeared in a collection published in Erfurt in 1524, the same year that Elisabeth von Meseritz (1500?–35), author of the text, married Caspar Cruciger, one of Martin Luther's favorite students. Two years earlier Elisabeth, a nun at Belbuck near Treptow (Pomerania), had fled the suppression of Protestant sympathies at the cloister and sought out Luther's new Wittenberg colleague, John Bugenhagen, who had been a teacher in Treptow and lector at Belbuck. After marrying Caspar, Elisabeth Cruciger spent three years in the Lutheran town of Magdeburg, where her new husband served as preacher and school principal, but she returned to Wittenberg in 1528 when Caspar began to teach at the university. Elisabeth, probably the first Protestant woman to write hymns, became a close friend of Luther's wife, Katharina von Bora, who also escaped from a convent and came to Wittenberg.

"The Only Son from Heaven," similar to the fourth-century Christmas hymn "Of the Father's Love Begotten," was attributed publicly to "Elisabeth M." (Meseritz) for the first time in 1528 and one year later to Elisabeth Cruciger. Well regarded by hymnologists, it is one of three songs written by her and perhaps the first newly composed

Protestant poem dedicated to Jesus as the Son of God and second person of the Trinity. The tune to which it is still sung is the folk melody that Cruciger chose for its first publication in 1524.

The English translation, made around 1850 by the Anglican priest and tunesmith Arthur Tozer Russell (1806–74), is from the *Lutheran Book of Worship* (1978), no. 86.

(1) The only Son from heaven, foretold by ancient seers,
by God the Father given, in human form appears.
No sphere his light confining, no star so brightly shining
As he, our morningstar.

(2) Oh, time of God appointed, Oh, bright and holy morn!
He comes, the king anointed, the Christ, the virgin-born,
Grim death to vanquish for us, to open heav'n before us
And bring us life again.

(3) Awaken, Lord, our spirit to know and love you more,
In faith to stand unshaken, in spirit to adore,
That we, through this world moving, each glimpse of heaven
    proving,
May reap its fullness there.

(4) O Father, here before you with God the Holy Ghost,
And Jesus, we adore you, O pride of angel host:
Before you mortals lowly cry: "Holy, holy, holy,
O blessed trinity!"

25. Michael Weisse, Praise God Above on the Highest Throne, 1531

Born in Silesia, Michael Weisse (c. 1488–1534) studied at the University of Cracow before becoming a monk in Breslau. In 1518 he left the monastery and sought refuge in Moravia (now the Czech Republic) among the Bohemian Brethren, an independent Protestant community that originated among the followers of the fifteenth-century Czech reformer and martyr John Hus. Weisse was also influenced by the writings of Martin Luther, whom he visited at least twice in Wittenberg and who called him an excellent poet. Two years before Weisse died, he was ordained and served as a pastor among the Brethren.

Weisse is best known for editing in 1531 the first German-language hymnbook of the Bohemian Brethren.[7] In addition to twenty hymns translated into German from Czech and Latin, Weisse wrote, revised, or adapted 137 additional hymns, one of which is presented here. According to Weisse, the words belonged to the community and could not be altered, but they could be sung to different melodies. The hymns were divided into eighteen sections, an arrangement kept by Katharina Schütz Zell when she published an edition of the collection in 1534 for the Protestants in Strasbourg (see text no. 27 below).

The text presented here was one of the Easter hymns; it is a translation of *Gelobt sei Gott im höchsten Thron*, in *Evangelisches Gesangbuch Niedersachsen/Bremen* (1994), no. 103.

(1) Praise God above on the highest throne, together with his
    only Son,
who for us enough has done. Hallelujah, Hallelujah, Hallelujah.

(2) Very early on the third day, while the stone on the grave still lay,
he rose free of any stain. Hallelujah, Hallelujah, Hallelujah.

(3) The angel said: "Do not fear; I know why you came,
but Jesus whom you seek is not here." Hallelujah, Hallelujah,
    Hallelujah.

(4) "He is risen from the dead, has overcome all want and dread;
come see where he lay." Hallelujah, Hallelujah, Hallelujah.

(5) Now we pray, O Jesus Christ, because you have risen from
    death,
give us our salvation. Hallelujah, Hallelujah, Hallelujah.

(6) So that we, free from sin, may sing to your blessed name
    forever!
Hallelujah, Hallelujah, Hallelujah.

26. Wolfgang Capito, Give Peace in Our Time, O Lord, 1533

Wolfgang Capito (1478–1541) belonged to the team of reformers in Strasbourg when he wrote this hymn in 1533. By then, as a pastoral colleague of Martin Bucer for ten years and as a Hebrew scholar and lecturer on the Old Testament, Capito had helped to shape the Protestant church and civic community in Strasbourg. Like Bucer, he was an irenic spirit who strove for the reconciliation of Swiss Protestants and German Lutherans, but he also was in the thick of religious conflict between Catholics and Protestants after 1530. It is no surprise that Capito would dedicate one of his two hymns to the end of religious strife and to spiritual renewal. At the same time, the words make clear that Capito was devoted to Protestant reform against the "enemies of Christ" who would "shame his name."

The text below is a translation of *Gib Fried zu unsrer Zeit, O Herr,* from the *Evangelisches Kirchengesangbuch...Niedersachsens* (1986), no. 389. It was sung to an early Wittenberg tune.

(1) Give peace in our time, O Lord, we stand in greatest need;
the enemy desires to shame Christ's name and stifle our worship
     with deceit.
Defend it with your might, for only you can help us through the
     dangerous night.

(2) Give us the peace that we have lost through lack of faith and
     evil life;
we resist your word with foolish force and push away our salvation;
without good reason, we confess, we live with lukewarm dedication.

(3) Give peace and send your Spirit to renew our hearts in Jesus
     Christ through heartfelt sorrow for our sin; take from us all
     disgrace and fear, warfare, risk and blame,
so that every land may honor your great name.

27. Katharina Schütz Zell, Foreword to Her Edition of the *Hymnbook of the Bohemian Brethren*, 1534

Three years after the first German-language hymnbook for the Bohemian Brethren was printed in 1531 (see text no. 25 above), it was edited and republished in Strasbourg by Katharina Schütz Zell, the lay reformer and author (see text no. 14 above). As her preface indicates, Schütz Zell was motivated by the collection's religious content and its potential utility for the faithful: "I found such an understanding of the works of God in this songbook that I want all people to understand it. I ought much rather to call it a teaching, prayer, and praise book than a songbook." Her aim was to create a new spirituality or piety in the town. By offering hymns that would "convey the whole business of Christ and our salvation in song," Schütz Zell hoped to replace popular songs, which she regarded as bawdy and scandalous, with good Christian hymns that would nurture faith and appreciation for the work of Christ. To this end, she divided the hymns into groups and published them in several booklets that could be purchased for pennies apiece.

Schütz Zell also wanted these Protestant hymns to teach concrete lessons that would express the new piety. First, they should enhance for laity the significance of their daily tasks and labor. Those tasks were just as precious to God as the religious rituals of monks and clergy. Second, these hymns should teach the proper significance and observance of holy days like the birth of John the Baptist, which was celebrated near the summer solstice and was criticized by reformers for fostering superstition and misbehavior. Schütz Zell was well aware of the importance that congregational singing had for Protestant spirituality and contributed to its nurture in Strasbourg and beyond.

English text from Elsie Anne McKee, *Reforming Popular Piety in Sixteenth-Century Strasbourg: Katharina Schütz Zell and Her Hymnbook*, Studies in Reformed Theology and History 2:4 (1994), 65–67. German edition in McKee, *Katharina Schütz Zell*, vol. 2, *The Writings*, 58–64.

Out of special love and friendship a songbook was given to me to read. It was printed in Bohemia and sent to good people in Landskron and Fullneck by a godfearing man, indeed, a man who knows God. His name is Michael Weisse.[8] I do not know him personally, but as the Lord says: "By their fruits shall you know them" (Matt 12:33). When I read this book, I had to conclude that, so far as I understand the scriptures, this man [Weisse] has the whole Bible wide open in his heart. Indeed, he has the same knowledge and experience as the two dear men Joshua and Caleb had of the promised land, when they had faithfully visited and walked through it by the command of the Lord given through Moses (Num 13:25–29).

I found such an understanding of the works of God in this songbook that I want all people to understand it. Indeed, I ought much rather to call it a teaching, prayer, and praise book than a songbook, although the little word "song" is well and properly spoken, for the greatest praise of God is expressed in song, as when Moses sang a glorious song of praise to God when the Lord brought him and his people through the sea (Exod 15:1–18). And the holy Hannah in the same way sang thanks and praise to God the Lord when he had given her Samuel (1 Sam 2:1–10). As also David made so many glorious Psalm songs and often used the expression, "we should to sing to the Lord," and such like (Ps 95:1; 96:1–2; 98:1, 5). Thence have also come all the songs of the church, where they have been kept in the right way and with the right heart, as they were by the first singers.

Since, however, so many scandalous songs are now sung by men and women and also children throughout the world, songs in which all slander, coquetry, and other scandalous things are spread through the world by young and old (and the world likes to have such things sung), it seemed to me a very good and useful thing to do as this man has done, that is, to convey the whole business of Christ and our salvation in song, so that the people may thus enthusiastically and with clear voices be exhorted regarding their salvation, and the devil with his songs may not have any place in them. Also so that good parents may say to their children: "Up till now we have all sung bad songs, to the scandal [vexation] of our souls and our neighbors' souls." But so that you may not complain, "So may we never sing? Must we become like sticks and stones," therefore now sing these songs, which express so admirably God's love towards us and exhort us so faithfully not to neglect the salvation offered to us.

Wherefore also St. Paul teaches us that we should not allow anyone to hear from us avaricious or insulting words, raillery, or foolish things, and should not be full of wine but full of the Spirit, and that we should exhort one another with psalms and hymns and spiritual songs (Eph 5:4, 18–19; Col 3:16). And St. James says whoever is anxious should pray, and whoever is in good spirits should sing psalms, that is, all kinds of praise of God (Jas 5:13), as also this man of God [Weisse] has divided up the songs in his book into eighteen groups of songs about the works of God. This book was a concern to me [because of its size]; there were too many songs to be printed all together; that would be too expensive for people to buy. So I took the book in hand for the use and service of children and the poor, and divided it into several small booklets costing two, three, and four pennies. However, in the first booklet I put a little index of the order and titles of all the songs of the whole book, and in the next booklet I indicated what follows in the other [book], so that if anyone wanted to buy all of them and put them together in order in one book until perhaps it is complete as it has been printed [that would be possible].

For there are to be found here many attractive songs about the feast days: the coming and the work of Christ, such as the angelic salutation, Christmas, Easter, Ascension, Pentecost, and so on, and the true dear saints. So that many good people may not complain: "The holy remembrances themselves will all be forgotten, if no one ever celebrates the feasts of Christ and the saints." Therefore, dear Christian, whoever you are, since you have until now allowed your children and relatives to sing false scandalous songs at the country dances and elsewhere, and even much more on the feasts of Christ and the saints—as on St. John the Baptist's day,[9] when it would be more fitting for all Christians to be sorrowful that things in the world were in such bad shape then (and are still so), that one who spoke and taught the truth [John the Baptist] had to die for doing so (Matt 14:3–12). So now (in response to this clear call which God makes to the world) encourage them [your children and relatives] to sing godly songs in which they are exhorted to seek knowledge of their salvation.

Teach your children and relatives to know that they do not serve human beings but God, when they faithfully (in faith) keep house, obey, cook, wash dishes, wipe up, tend children, and similar work that serves human life, and that (while doing this very work) they can also turn to God with the voice of song. And teach them that in doing this, they please God much better than any priest, monk, or nun with their incomprehensible song in the choir, where they lifted up some foolish devotion of useless lullaby to the organ. A poor mother would so gladly sleep, but at midnight she must rock the wailing baby and sing it a song about godly things. That is called, and indeed it is, the right lullaby (provided it is done in faith), which pleases God and not the organ or the organist. God is no child, and you may not silence him with piping and singing! But silence yourself; he requires something else.

The seven holy times, mass, vespers, and matins, will be sung thus: the artisan at his work, the maidservant at her dishwashing, the farmer and vinedresser on the farm, and the mother with the wailing child in the cradle—they use such praise, prayer, teaching songs, psalms, or similar things, provided it is all done in the faith and knowledge of Christ, and they devoutly order their whole lives with all faithfulness and patience towards everyone.[10] These will also praise God with and in Christ the everlasting priest, with his angels, before God's throne (Rev 7:9–12). But the others, who only use scandalous knavish songs and rotten, wanton sayings and have let their children and relatives learn, sing, and say them, will have to weep, wail, and gnash their teeth forever with the devil (Matt 8:12).

Here let everyone choose which one they want; they will receive final judgment according to that choice. But I wish for all people knowledge of the good and everlasting salvation. Amen.

28. Leo Jud, My Heart Shall Be Yours and Yours Alone, 1540

Leo Jud (1482–1542), Alsatian by birth, was the closest colleague of Ulrich Zwingli and co-leader of the Zürich reformation. Jud and Zwingli had been friends since their university days, but after Zwingli's death in 1531 Jud refused the invitation to become Zwingli's successor. His public duties were the pastorate of St. Peter's parish in Zürich and the instruction of Hebrew at the *Prophezei,* the budding seminary in

Zürich. Through his facility with languages, he also made lasting contributions to the Zürich Reformation and the Reformed tradition of Protestantism. Several popular catechisms and the first German liturgy for baptism used in Switzerland were written by Jud, and he supervised the scholarly team that translated the scriptures into German and published the Zürich Bible in 1531. Jud also translated the Old Testament into Latin and the *First Helvetic Confession* of 1536 from Latin into German. Works by other theologians were also translated and edited by Jud: Augustine, Luther, Erasmus, his colleague Zwingli, and Thomas à Kempis.

The Imitation of Christ by à Kempis expresses the straightforward personal piety of the *devotio moderna* (modern devotion), the late medieval movement that influenced Jud as shown by the text of the hymn presented here. It was written two years before his death and demonstrates that this scholar of languages and confessions was also a poet with a deep personal spirituality. The English translation is made from the German text of *Dein, dein soll sein das Herze mein*, no. 431 in *Evangelisches Kirchengesangbuch Niedersachsen* (1952).

(1) My heart shall be yours and yours alone, my dearest
    Lord and God.
You have clad and led me safely in the way of your commandments;
as long as you allow, no force or favor will draw me away,
and even when the flesh gives way, my heart will ever with you
    stay.

(2) My heart shall be yours and yours alone, O Christ the
    chosen One.
You give true joy, make sorrow flee, without you I'd be lost;
All my longing is for you from the bliss within my heart,
you are my refuge, and your word forever gladness does impart.

(3) My heart shall be yours and yours alone, help and comfort of
    the poor.
Look at the trouble I must endure and grant me all your mercy.
Stop the foe, quiet the sin, and do it to your praise,
Keep me in tow and boost my faith in you for all my days!

29. Martin Luther, Lord, Keep Us Steadfast in Thy Word, 1541–42

Martin Luther, who was the author and adapter of many hymns, probably wrote these words when the Ottoman Turks seemed to threaten Germany after Austrian troops were defeated at Budapest in 1541. In its second line, the original text implores the Lord to "curb the Turks' and papists' sword," a pairing of adversaries that caused such offense in Catholic parts of Germany that later Lutherans began to change the line into milder forms like the translation below. The future of the Protestant Reformation looked bleak in the 1540s owing to political ineptness, the impatience of Emperor Charles V, renewed Catholic strength, and Turkish advances. In Luther's eyes, all of these forces were a threat to the gospel, that is, the Lutheran reform of Christianity that was now more than twenty years old. In spite of these time-bound polemical circumstances, however, the hymn expresses a universal spirituality that is useful to all believers under hostile pressures, and for that reason it has been perhaps the most popular of Luther's hymns in all eras.

The earliest source of the hymn is Joseph Klug's Wittenberg hymnal of 1543, in which the text was set to a melody by Bishop Ambrose of Milan (340–97)—a melody that was adapted for the words by Luther himself. The English translation presented here, made by Catherine Winkworth (1829–78), is no. 230 in the *Lutheran Book of Worship* (1978) and is set to the same tune.

(1) Lord, keep us steadfast in your word; curb those who by deceit or sword
Would wrest the kingdom from your Son and bring to nought all he has done.

(2) Lord Jesus Christ, your power make known, for you are Lord of lords alone;
Defend your holy church that we may sing your praise triumphantly.

(3) O comforter of priceless worth, send peace and unity on earth;
support us in our final strife and lead us out of death to life.

30. John Zwick, The Morning Is All Fresh and New, before 1542

Like Ambrosius Blarer (see text no. 21 above) John Zwick (c. 1496–1542) was a pastor and reformer in the south German city of Constance, his hometown. Educated in law and ordained a priest, Zwick earned in Italy a doctorate in civil and canon law and taught legal studies at the University of Basel. There he became acquainted with Erasmus and gradually, after marrying secretly and taking a post as parish priest, he established contact with Swiss and South German reformers and made their ideas the subject of his own evangelical preaching. Ousted from the pulpit in Basel, Zwick returned to Constance and worked with Blarer and the city council to make Constance a Protestant town.

Zwick was not only a good organizer but also a talented spiritual and pastoral leader. He composed a prayer book for young people and drafted a new school order (educational plan and policies) for the city. For the well-regarded Constance hymnal that appeared in 1540 Zwick wrote an extended introduction and contributed seventeen of his own compositions. The text presented here is still a popular hymn and describes the life of faith that Zwick wished for himself and his people. Several months after answering a call to preach in the Thurgau region of Switzerland that had been struck by the plague, Zwick caught the disease himself and died before reaching the age of fifty.

English translation of *All Morgen ist ganz frisch und neu,* no. 440 in *Evangelisches Gesangbuch Niedersachsen/Bremen* (1994).

(1) The morning is all fresh and new; his grace and faithfulness
    stay all day long
and remain trustworthy for everyone.

(2) O God, you beautiful morningstar, grant from your love what
    we desire;
may our hearts ne'er lack your grace; ignite in us your heavenly fire.

(3) Drive away all darkness, you blessed light; protect us from
    fault, blindness, and shame;
day and night, O blessed Lord, offer us your hand by your great
    name.

(4) Then we shall always walk in light no matter what may be our part,
we remain in faith until the end and never stray from where thou art.

31. Johann Freder, O Dear Lord Jesus Christ, around 1555

Johann Freder (1510–60?), a native of Pomerania, studied and lived in Wittenberg from 1524 to 1537 before serving as a pastor in four different cities of North Germany. In Wittenberg he lived for a time in Luther's house and married a relative of one of Luther's colleagues. In 1545 he composed *Dialogue in Honor of Marriage* in order to refute a collection of proverbs disparaging women and marriage that had been published four years earlier. Accomplished in languages, Freder translated German works by Urbanus Rhegius (see text no. 11 above) into Latin, and he composed poetry in his native Low German dialect.

Although his ministry as pastor and overseer was stalked by controversy, he found time to write this baptismal hymn, which celebrates the beginning of lifelong spiritual journeys under divine favor and angelic protection. Although sixteenth-century Protestants rejected the cult of the saints, most of them continued to believe in the shelter of guardian angels, as Freder demonstrates in verse five.

It is a translation of *Ach lieber Herre Jesus Christ,* no. 203 in *Evangelisches Gesangbuch Niedersachsen/Bremen* (1994).

(1) O dear Lord Jesus Christ, purely born of a virgin you became a child,
that we might never be lost.

(2) You have never despised the children brought to you;
you laid your hand on them, gathered them round and said:

(3) "Let the children come to me and do not hinder them;
the kingdom of heaven belongs to those who are brought to me, both poor and rich."

(4) I pray, O Lord, that you will protect this little child and all
    Christians
from sorrow and distress.

(5) Through your angels guard us against danger and calamity;
have mercy upon us and gently bestow your blessing.

(6) Give grace so that all may be done to your honor and well-
    pleasing,
in true piety now on earth and afterward in eternal life.

32. Albert, Duke of Prussia, Let My God's Will Prevail Always, 1554

It is instructive to consider the words of this hymn in light of the author's life. It was written by a layman, albeit a high-ranking noble-man, Duke Albert of Prussia (1490–1568), when he was sixty-four years old. The Duchy of Prussia was created in 1525, when young Albert was still the Grand Master of the Teutonic Knights; he joined the evangelical movement and transformed the lands of the order into a secular duchy. From that point on, Prussia became a stronghold of the German Reformation, especially after Paul Speratus (see text no. 23 above) helped Albert to consolidate the movement. Albert remained beholden to the Reformation in spite of political risks and theological storms, one of which started under his nose.

This hymn celebrates the divine will, but Albert's life demon-strates the active human dimension of Protestant spirituality, the human effort expended in faith to improve the practice of Christianity and the conditions of human life. At the same time, the text of the hymn could describe Albert's own conviction about his conversion: it was God's will that he could not and would not resist. Although Albert did not write stanza four, it is not unlikely that he found great comfort in the conviction that God's will would finally prevail, even over death and hell, as have generations of believers after him for whom the hymn has remained popular.

The English text is a translation of *Was mein Gott will, das g'scheh allzeit*, no. 364 in *Evangelisches Gesangbuch Niedersachsen/Bremen* (1994).

(1) Let my God's will prevail always; his will is ever best.
He stands ready to help those who believe in him.
God is just, fills every need and comforts the world beyond
    measure.
He will never leave those who trust in him and build on his good
    pleasure.

(2) God, my assurance and comfort, my hope and also my life;
I shall never resist your will for me.
Your word is true; you have counted all the hairs on my head;
You look out for us so that we lack nothing alive or dead.

(3) I, a sinner, must leave the world according to God's will;
When it pleases him, I will go to my God; for him I will keep still.
In my last hour I commend to him my poor and sinful soul,
for you, my God, on my behalf have conquered sin, death,
    and hell.

(4) One more request I have, dear God, please do not deny me:
when the devil attacks, keep me steadfast in you.
Help, guide, defend, O precious Lord, to the honor of your name,
Because those who desire your aid will receive it,
I can joyfully say, Amen.

PART SEVEN
Praying

Introduction

The relationship of prayer to spirituality is obvious—perhaps so obvious that it needs hardly any comment. Alongside public worship, personal prayer to God the Father and Jesus Christ has always been at the heart of Christian devotion. It may come as a surprise to learn, therefore, that prayer was a controversial spiritual practice when the Reformation began. Late medieval people prayed often and earnestly, to God, to Mary, and to the saints, using manuals and mnemonic devices like the rosary. In the preface to his 1522 *Personal Prayer Book*, however, Martin Luther sharply criticized medieval prayer guides:

> Among the many and harmful books and doctrines which are misleading and deceiving Christians and give rise to countless false beliefs, I regard the personal prayer books as by no means the least objectionable. They drub into the minds of simple people such a wretched counting up of sins and going to confession, such un-Christian tomfoolery about prayers to God and his saints! Moreover, these books are puffed up with promises of indulgences and come out with decorations in red ink and pretty titles....These books need a basic and thoroughgoing reformation if not total extermination.[1]

After delivering this broadside, Luther offered his own guide to prayer, insisting that the Lord's Prayer was sufficient at any time and that a persistent and heartfelt turning to God was more important than many words.[2]

201

Sixteenth-century Protestants also objected to prayers for the dead offered at vigils and in private masses by monks and priests, who were paid for that service out of funds set up by devoted family members. In the first text below (see text no. 33), Martin Luther advises an Austrian nobleman who lost his wife not to pay for prayer vigils but to pray in faith once or twice for her and trust that his prayer will be answered as God has promised. Mindful of the Pauline admonition to pray without ceasing (1 Thess 5:17), Protestants did not always oppose frequent or constant prayer, but they were mistrustful of devotional gimmicks and concentrated instead on teaching people the Lord's Prayer and on composing supplications that were appropriate for public worship. Thomas Cranmer, for example, protested late medieval strategies for facilitating private prayer (see text no. 12 above), but he also composed eloquent collects for the Sundays and festivals of the church year that became staple ingredients of English piety. Prayers that were never intended for regular corporate worship can also be recovered from writings of the reformers, where they might be attached to lectures, sermons, and/or meditations on scripture. In the Protestant Reformation the ritual use of prayer by laity migrated in large part from individual devotion to communal worship, but personal prayer remained important in private and was expected at some public occasions.

Instruction about prayer occurred mainly in classes and sermons on the numerous catechisms that were prepared by pastors. Renewed effort was made to explain the Lord's Prayer, which had always been a centerpiece of Christian catechizing, especially after organized surveys and informal samplings of lay piety revealed that many people could not even recite the prayer, much less explain what it meant. Theologians like Philip Melanchthon (see text no. 35 below) also took it upon themselves to publish treatises on prayer that did not shy away from asking hard questions about its effectiveness or naming reasons why young people should be taught to pray. One of those reasons was the perilous and turbulent world of sixteenth-century Europe, which Melanchthon offered as grounds for prayer in much the same spirit that soldiers would say there are no atheists in a foxhole: "It should stir our hearts to pray even if they were made of iron, because this motive grows out of the constant and overwhelming dangers and evil that surround us every day. A well-known saying goes like this: 'Whoever cannot pray should go to sea.'" Like their forebears, early Protestants prayed whenever the horsemen of the Apocalypse (Rev 6:1–8)—pestilence, war, famine, and death, as portrayed in sixteenth-century woodcuts by Albrecht Dürer and Lucas Cranach—made their appearance.

When crises did not call for special petitions, however, Protestants often expressed the core of their theology in prayer. From experience they knew only too well that the twin pillars of their spirituality, faith in God and love of neighbor, were not unassailable or one-time gifts, but that reliance upon God was needed to keep them strong and active. Miles Coverdale (see text no. 37 below) was acutely aware of that need, which he expressed in the following way:

> O merciful Father, give us grace with fervent hearts to consider the unspeakable love of you and of your Son, and never to forget the same—that our faith and trust in you may be strengthened, that love in us towards you and our neighbor may be kindled, that above all things we may love you, the wellspring of all goodness, and that we may serve our neighbors in love, care for them, and do them good, according to the love that your dear Son has bestowed upon us.

33. Martin Luther, Open Letter to Bartholomew von Starhemberg, 1524

Bartholomew von Starhemberg (1460–1531) was an Austrian nobleman who lost his wife, Magdalena von Losenstein, in 1524. A common acquaintance, Vinzenz Wernstdorffer, made Luther aware of the loss and asked the reformer to send Starhemberg a letter of consolation. Intended by Luther as a private communication, the letter was published with an editorial note at Augsburg in 1524, presumably because its content made simple and forceful propaganda for the evangelical cause and, as the editor opined, because "none of Martin's writ-

ings is so small that it does not contain something remarkably useful."
In 1526 Starhemberg became a public supporter of the Reformation.

The consolation offered by Luther sounds strange, even offensive, to modern ears, but it comes straight from the heart of early Protestant spirituality. Trust in God's will and the awareness that earthly blessings, fragile though they be, are God's gifts replaced religious ritual and meritorious acts in the daily practice of faith. Luther's advice to pray for something once and to trust that God has heard the prayer should be read against the backdrop of his polemic against the wrong kind of prayer and the misuse of the mass: the medieval practice of paying for continual prayer for the souls of the dead and for private masses said on their behalf. In other situations, like the threat of Turkish invasion, Luther advised early Protestants to pray unceasingly in harmony with Luke 18:7: "And will not God grant justice to his chosen ones who cry to him day and night?"

The original of this letter is not extant, only a handwritten copy and one printed edition. The words intended for the nobleman himself are preceded in the printed edition by an admonition to the reading public.

English translation from the German text in WA 18, 5–7.

Salvation to the Reader!

Sisters and brothers in Christ. By chance an open letter from Martin Luther to Bartholomew von Starhemberg has come to light. It contains comfort for those who mourn the dead or the sleeping, instruction on how to pray for these souls, and a warning against masses and vigils for the dead. The form is brief, but the content is rich.

It seemed appropriate and well-advised to publish this letter so that devoted Christians should be deprived of nothing, however small, that promotes the word of God and teaches them to be wise. Although it reproaches serious abuses with only a few words, it still speaks clearly enough so that laypersons can easily understand it. None of Martin's writings is so small that it does not contain something remarkably useful.

Grace and peace in Christ, noble sir! The occasion for sending this work to your grace[3] was supplied by the Christian devotion of

Vinzenz Wernstdorffer. Accordingly, I beg your grace to look on this letter with favor.

Wernstdorffer reported to me the passing of your dear wife, who died in God. He described how you are making every effort to help her soul with many religious services and good works, especially with private masses and vigils. Your wife unquestionably earned such attention from you with her life and loving devotion. Wernstdorffer asked me to write about this, and I did not know how to turn him down since he was seeking the best for you. Therefore, I humbly ask your grace to look favorably upon my admonition.

In the first place, I would remind you of what is said in Job: "The Lord gave and the Lord has taken away" (Job 1:21). As it pleased the Lord, so has it happened. You should sing to your faithful, dear God, who gave to your grace such a precious and faithful wife and now has taken her back. For she was God's before he gave her; she was God's as he gave her; she is still God's now that he has taken her back, just as we all are his. Although it hurts us when God takes his own away from us, our heart should find greater consolation in God's most gracious will than in all his gifts. It is much better to hold on to his will than to the best wife in the world, even though we cannot grasp his will as well as we can the wife. Faith can grasp[4] that will, however.

Therefore, your grace, give back to God with joy what belongs to him and accept this just exchange with its suprahuman gain: in place of a dear and tender wife now you have the dear and tender will of God and, in addition, God himself. Oh, how blessed and rich we all would be if we were able to conduct such a trade with God! We could do it if only we truly understood it. God encounters us daily with it; we, however, cannot grasp it.

In the second place, gracious sir, I ask that your grace do away with the masses, vigils, and daily prayers for the soul of your wife. It is sufficient for your grace earnestly to pray once or twice for her. For God has promised that whatever you ask for, believe that you will receive it and you will certainly have it (Luke 11:9–10). In contrast, whenever we pray over and over again for the same thing, it is a sign that we do not believe God and with our faithless prayer we only make him angrier. When I pray repeatedly for the same thing, is it not the same as admitting that my previous prayers were not heard and that I have prayed in contradiction to his promise? True, we should constantly pray, but always in faith and certain that we are being heard. Otherwise the prayer is in vain. There are always plenty of different things for which to pray.

In particular, I ask your grace to do away with the vigils and the private masses for the dead. Both are unchristian practices that provoke God to hot anger. It is obvious that neither earnestness nor faith are present in the vigils; they amount only to useless mumbling. How differently we have to pray if we want to get something from God! Such vigils only make fun of God.

Furthermore, God did not institute the mass for the dead but made it a sacrament for the living. It is abominable and terrible how human beings have interfered and turned this and other institutions of God into their own works and transformed the sacrament of the living into a sacrifice for the dead. Your grace should guard against such practices and not become an accomplice in this despicable error, which the priests and the monks have promoted for the sake of their bellies. Christians should do nothing unless they know that God has commanded it. The priests and the monks can produce no such command for their vigils and masses. This practice is their own invention, and they bring in money and property while helping neither the dead nor the living.

Your grace can find out more about all this from the above-named Vinzenz Wernstdorffer. He wants only good for your grace and has persuaded me to write to you. May it please your grace. Do not believe those who say otherwise, who speak without God's word, and offer only their own lies and human rules.

May Christ enlighten and strengthen your grace in true faith and in love toward your neighbor. Amen.

Written at Wittenberg on the day of
St. Giles[5] in the year 1524.

34. Peter Martyr Vermigli, Sacred Prayers Drawn from the Psalms of David, 1545–47

Peter Martyr Vermigli (1499–1562) was an Augustinian regular canon[6] who fled Italy in 1542 and became an effective Protestant theologian in northern Europe. After stopping in Zürich, Martyr lived until 1547 in Strasbourg as a professor of Old Testament at the Strasbourg Academy. He left Strasbourg for England (and was soon followed by Martin Bucer), but after teaching six years at Oxford, he returned to Strasbourg when the Catholic Mary Tudor became queen of England. As Strasbourg became staunchly Lutheran, Martyr, who sympathized with the Reformed theology of Zwingli, Bullinger, and Calvin, left the city in 1556 and taught in Zürich until his death.

The following texts have been selected from the 297 prayers that he wrote on 149 psalms, probably at the end of his first sojourn in Strasbourg. They reflect the pressures placed on Protestants by the Council of Trent, which began in 1545, and by the defeat of Protestant forces in Germany by Emperor Charles V in 1547. Sin and inadequate zeal are frequent themes, although they, like the implied link between laxity and misfortune, may not be exclusively Protestant. Martyr allegedly used some of these prayers with students after each of his lectures at the Strasbourg Academy, perhaps during both of his stays. The prayers, first published in 1564, were reprinted and translated a number of times thereafter.

From *Sacred Prayers Drawn from the Psalms of David,* trans. and ed. John P. Donnelly, SJ, 41, 113, 120, 141.

FROM PSALM 42

There is none, O almighty God, who has really studied your goodness who does not pant and aspire for you night and day, like a stag who is dying from thirst. How could it happen that anyone endowed with true faith should not hasten to the living God? But so far that eagerness has been very slack in us, nor have we sought you, as was right, by good faith in holy assemblies. Because of our sadness and trouble, tears have become for us our food and drink in these difficult times, and enemies far and wide mock the church and say: "Where is their God?" But we beg you, O God, since you are merciful and kind, to put aside your anger which you have rightly conceived against us and, mindful of your promises, grant that we may be made firm in a solid hope and faith, although we have not merited it, so our soul may not be unduly downcast. Although it seems that all the waves, storms, and abysses of temptations have been poured upon your church, may you be appeased by the goodness of your mercy and grace so that the solid joys of heart and conscience may not be taken away from us. Make it happen that stirred by the Holy Spirit we may continually encourage ourselves to hope and trust in your help, because henceforward we are going to glorify your name and give thanks for being restored to salvation and tranquility. Through Jesus Christ, our Lord. Amen.

FROM PSALM 112

O almighty God, the fear of you, namely inborn godliness, makes those truly happy who are touched by no concern except the immediate execution of your will. Thereby we are led to request your mercy so that you may be pleased to restore your dilapidated church. For there is no other way that her posterity, which is your posterity, can ever emerge either illustrious or powerful. There is no other source from which to expect an abundance of spiritual gifts, nor can light burst forth any other way amidst errors and the darkness of calamities. Besides, if as we pray, godliness revives in her, our sincere duties of charity toward our neighbors will be carried out without fail. Instead of themselves, people will look after their sisters and brothers. They will govern their actions not by chance or impulse but by a spiritual standard. We therefore request this as a chief priority: that you solidify our confidence in you, from which neither storms of troubles nor the pleasure of good fortune can tear us in any way. Through Jesus Christ, our Lord. Amen.

FROM PSALM 119:17–32

Since our strength depends on you, O great and good God, and without your help we cannot accomplish anything that pleases you, we rightly take refuge in you so that by the help of your grace we may indeed conform our actions to your laws. That can in no wise happen if you do not remove from our eyes the curtain that evil desires keep putting between us and sound teaching. The result is that we pay no attention to the beneficial things it commands us to do. Also keep far away, we pray, the swelling of the mind and the elation of the heart by which we are sometimes inclined to overestimate human institutions and inventions so that compared to them your institutions seem vile to us. That happens mainly when we fear to undergo the contempt and hatred of this world. Therefore, when we find our hearts so torn between opposites, do, O God, refresh us with your word and be pleased to calm the cares of our hearts and our excessive anxiety with spiritual tranquility and to prevent us from being deceived by the lies of this world, which otherwise are so enticing. For if you shall have once enlarged our anguished heart with your Spirit, nothing shall be able to block us from running as fast as we can to carry out your commands. We beg you with all the intensity we can that we may be able to attain this in the end. Through Jesus Christ our Lord. Amen.

From Psalm 128

Nothing good or joyous can happen except to those who fear and reverence God and who walk faithfully in the ways of God's commandments by upright living. That fact now shows us the reason why we are undergoing disasters. In your supreme mercy, almighty God, you gave us your salutary teaching, but the last thing we have carried through is worshiping you in the proper way. We ranked fear and reverence for your name behind our own desires, and we discarded the discipline of your commandments. We have no reason then to complain that sufferings are sometimes laid upon us unfairly. Disregard, we pray, our iniquities and wicked deeds and because of your mercy reestablish within us fear, devotion, and holy behavior. Finally shine down from Zion, that is, from your lofty and inaccessible light, upon your suffering church and rescue her when she is beset by such dangers. Through faith you have taken her unto yourself as a wife; grant that she be increased by the fecundity of her holy children. May she be like a vine which spreads out widely and cannot be cut down, regardless of how antichrist strives to do so. We urgently ask that we obtain this especially from you, good Father: that you deign to grant good and salutary things to your Jerusalem and to send peace and tranquility to the true Israel. Through Jesus Christ, our Lord. Amen.

35. Philip Melanchthon, On Prayer, 1552

After Martin Luther's death in 1546, his younger colleague Philip Melanchthon (see text no. 9 above) became the leading Lutheran reformer and professor in Wittenberg. The next fourteen years prior to his own death were tumultuous in every way. Emperor Charles V captured Wittenberg in 1547, and the capitulation was followed by eight years of conflict and negotiation until the Peace of Augsburg (1555) awarded Lutherans political legitimacy and security in Germany. Melanchthon was attacked relentlessly by other theologians who believed that he had betrayed Luther's theology. Moreover, he struggled with poor health while mourning the death of his twenty-three-year-old daughter in 1547 and of his wife ten years later. In other words, during these years Melanchthon had a lot to pray about and good reason to reflect on the nature and power of prayer.

Melanchthon delivered at least two public addresses on prayer. The occasions for these addresses are not known, but it was typical for Melanchthon, the humanist and educator, to be concerned about the religious education of young people and to address this topic at academic convocations. The formal nature of the address should not be allowed to minimize the highest regard in which he held prayer or the personal intensity with which Melanchthon himself prayed.

The address below was given in 1552 on the second of those occasions and is translated from *Melanchthon Deutsch*, 2, 102–15.

God gives to the church in every age many marvelous blessings. Often he liberates her, and he protects and preserves her in times of great peril. Nevertheless, we should first recall our recent blessings, commend them, and constantly thank God for them.

For a number of years God has heaped kindness after kindness upon our city[7] and our church by restoring to us the light of the gospel and providing us with sufficient tranquility that, despite the upheavals in Germany, theological studies can be pursued. At every public occasion that calls for a speech it is fitting to give thanks to God for preserving both church and university. The gratitude we offer only in words is, to be sure, not enough. Yet we do nothing more important than employ all the natural abilities supplied to us from heaven in order to return to God some of what he has given us—alien goods, as it were, instead of our own possessions—and to render thanks to the giver of all good gifts. We know that God desires this service from us and that he accepts it as honor and reverence for the sake of his Son.

Furthermore, prayer appeals to the unlimited goodness of God on our behalf. We know that everything rests in God's hand. In the last few years, however, who could have foreseen that within our region God would preserve a small enclave, in which young people could be educated, and a safe haven, so to speak, in which the heavenly message about the divine will and God's Son, our redeemer, could be proclaimed? May it be a good omen for our convocation and for my presentation that we now join our hearts and desires in prayer and thank God for his preservation of the entire church in every age and especially for the way in which he watches over and protects us amid the storms and floods of our day:

"Eternal God, Father of our Lord Jesus Christ, with your Son and the Holy Spirit who proceeds from both of you, you have created heaven and earth and from the beginning of the world you have chosen for yourself a people from the whole human race. We thank you first, as much as our hearts can muster, for your readiness to liberate us and all people through your Son, whom you willed to be sacrificed for us. You have revealed your kindness in many places where you appeared, and above all at the center of the world, yes, in Jerusalem. We thank you as well for restoring the light of the gospel in this needy and uninviting region to the north.[8]

"In the second place we are grateful that your gracious favor has protected us from the might and the snares of our enemies, who wish to destroy doctrine and to bring ruin upon the lands that harbor the church and upon the learning that brings salvation.

"We implore you graciously to shield and preserve us, especially those to whom you have entrusted the instruction and guidance of your flock, so that they might profitably hand over to posterity the true and saving doctrine of your glory and the salvation of all people. May they spread that message, so that we do not suffer the devastation or barbarianism that has already afflicted many nations previously adorned with the honor of your name and the praise of your glory. Now hardly a trace of their past reputation remains.

"Shelter us, we pray, our families and our descendants, and direct us so that we proclaim and extol you as true God in all eternity. Then we will delight in your goodness with endless joy and enter ever further into the infinite knowledge of your being."

According to tradition, however, I must now speak on a specific topic. Since I did not want to torment myself by searching feverishly for a theme, I decided on a subject that was near to hand and gave me something definite to say. I would like for young people to consider for a moment the subject of prayer and to hear my brief reasons for encouraging them readily and frequently to call upon God. We know that God counts this service as an exceptional form of reverence since the text of the prophet admonishes us to offer God "the sacrificial calves of our lips" (Hosea 14:2).[9]

Pious people will think of many reasons for praying regularly and conscientiously. It is enough for me, however, to suggest three reasons to young people. I am speaking to them alone, and I ask everyone else who may enjoy excellent reputations based on their learning and experience to bear with me for the sake of the youth— out of public courtesy and their own upbringing—until I have finished my address.

First, I will argue that we should encourage our heart and spirit to pray because God has commanded it. Second, [we should pray] because of his promise and especially since our requests never lack success. Finally, [prayer is necessary] because daily needs in public and in private require that in our suffering we seek and implore help and relief from God.

(1) The first reason, God's command, should be very effective in causing us to pray. We have often been charged with this form of reverence: to honor God with trust in Christ and with persistent requests for the forgiveness of our trespasses and freedom from our guilt, and finally to ask for everything we need for our salvation and for supporting our lives. You are familiar with the texts: "Call on me in the day of trouble" (Ps 50:15) and "Ask and you will receive" (John 16:24). Paul says to "pray without ceasing" (1 Thess 5:17). Even if no other dangers of body and soul move us to prayer, these directions oblige us to demonstrate our obedience in prayer because God desires and requires this service from us.

This command to pray must be set against the many obstacles that make us less conscientious about showing our reverence in this way. Those who fear God are often discouraged by a feeling of unworthiness or by a notion of special election that would cause God to hear only the prayers of a few. Since I am speaking to young people, however, I urge them also to remember this command to pray and not to be put off by their own obstacles, to wit, their carefree life and on occasion their all too lackadaisical attitude. Since young people live more from their inner desires than from thoughts about God or their duties, they pray less regularly because they fear God less. They suppose that God fails to notice their happy-go-lucky existence and is not angry when they dishonor God by failing to call upon him or not performing other obligations as God desires.

We should obey the command to pray so that those who are faint and afraid do not become pessimistic about prayer because they fear their unworthiness. They should be assured that their petitions are dear to God, who insists on hearing them. We are emphasizing this command, however, in order to counter the carefree and sensual outlook and the almost epicurean neglect among young people, as if it were not important for them to pray and to commend us and the church to God with pious petitions and godly requests.

Let superstitious persons save themselves the trouble of lecturing me with the following idle argument: the faithful ought not to be intimidated with an earnest command to pray, for they will spontaneously fulfill the obligation of praying and thereby demonstrate their faith to God and to others. It is unnecessary, so the argument goes, to push people to act properly with commands that are like edicts of a Roman praetor or to compel them with force, since right action will arise from a heart that has been enlightened by faith. Just as it is absurd to claim that three plus seven would have to equal ten, since in fact they already equal ten, so is it redundant to claim that we owe reverence to God in prayer because those who have been reborn through the Holy Spirit do this very thing already without compulsion.

I grant it is true that the faithful pray voluntarily. Nevertheless, we need to issue the command for the sake of both good and evil people. For the latter, so that they will not imagine there is no fault or impiety in failing to do their duty; for the former, so that good people will be reminded of God's will and perform more readily, zealously, and cheerfully what they know God desires by acknowledging the obligation imposed by God's will and command. Observe the arrogance of the human heart! If worldly-minded people did not imagine they could manage their own affairs without divine aid, they would not be so carefree but instead more diligently seek counsel and success from God. Because they trust their own cleverness and ability as sufficient to help them finish what they begin, asking God for help is a mark of superstitious and unlucky people. Ajax said that other people might gain victory with the support of a god, but he would do great deeds without a god.[10] The Gentiles, however, believed just the opposite, namely, that those without divine support were the unfortunate ones. Therefore Homer said: "All people pray and need God."[11]

In our effort to render full obedience, we should first call upon God as the demonstration of our reverence and service. Invocation of God is counted among the excellent forms of reverence and honor, and we in the church must acknowledge this. Do not think it is optional for you to bring petitions to God out of a full heart. On the contrary, if you never pray or pray only seldom, you are guilty of effrontery and rouse God to anger, drawing down on yourself and your family severe punishment in the form of both public and private misfortune! Here one should give more detail about God's wrath and the penalties for nonchalance and neglect. Even if these penalties overlap with those for disobeying the ten commandments, they are still the particular consequences for neglecting prayer. To keep my comments brief, however, I will move on to the second reason that should instill in us the inclination to pray more conscientiously.

(2) Like a thunderbolt God's will and command should stir us to acknowledge with humility his right to have us call upon him for help and relief from our distress. The second reason, however, should also entice us to call upon him: our requests are always effective and attain something from God. He always hears them, whether he fulfills our wishes immediately or delays that fulfillment, as he is wont to do, to keep our faith active. A worldly frame of mind will undeniably contribute to our laziness in prayer because it considers praying to be an

ineffective waste of energy. We often doubt that God hears us, either because we speculate about predestination or fear that we are too unworthy to be heard, or for other reasons.

Against these new hindrances you should remember the promise that is behind the command to pray and the fact that you will never ask in vain because you will always attain something from God. We never receive an outright rejection, so to speak, whether God grants our requests right away or whether he delays it for a while. This very reason has often caused me to push other hindrances aside, to lift up my spirit and my eyes to God, and to open my mouth in prayer, because I remembered the promise that never disappoints, even if the fulfillment came later or in a way that was not anticipated.

The promise of grace and reconciliation is certain and given to everyone who prays. Many texts indicate this: "As I live, says the Lord God, I have no pleasure in the death of the wicked" (Ezek 33:11); "[Righteousness] depends on faith, in order that the promise may rest on grace and be guaranteed to all his [Abraham's] descendants" (Rom 4:16). The statement of Basil is also to the point: "If you will it, God is already there."[12] All can testify how they experience consolation and relief from anxiety and God's wrath when they pray earnestly to the Father through the Son of God.

Time and again we hear that this assurance of grace and reconciliation must be distinguished from the promise of physical benefits. Prayers for these benefits, however, are never offered in vain. To be sure, God has never promised anyone a specific outcome that will benefit their corporal existence, like a healing or relief from some other pressing misfortune. It is nevertheless certain that God hears our petitions and answers them even when the results are delayed or never come to pass. For this is also true: when we do not attain that for which we pray, God sees to it that we receive something much better. God may not take away your distress or illness, but he gives to you and your family other material blessings, or he enriches you with a deeper knowledge of God and, as Psalm 4 points out, puts "gladness in your heart" (Ps 4:7) and reinforces your readiness for eternal life.

The church teaches us that God hears his people and all those who honor God by calling upon him. Nevertheless, for many reasons that cannot be named here, God wills that the church endure sundry afflictions and be marked with the cross. God also wishes to discipline the church, instruct the godly, and call them to repentance. He supplies witnesses to the immortality of that life which comes after this one. There we receive the true reward for our devoted service and for all the other reasons that are cited and should be obvious to us. God does not always give us protection and the comforts of this life but heaps upon us much greater blessings: the heavenly light of the gospel, righteousness, and a foretaste of eternal life. He compensates for our physical suffering with more splendid blessings; for example, he did not prevent Joseph from going to jail (Gen 39:19–23), but later he offered Joseph the opportunity to ascend to the pinnacle of power (Gen 41:37–57). Although material promises are fulfilled at first for the entire body of the church, individual members of the body also receive from God exactly what they requested. For God intends for the church to thrive in this life and to be preserved. He desires our faith to grow through our petitions for material goods. God also wants us to remember that the comforts of our existence do not by chance fall into our lap but that we possess them because he gives and offers them to us, as the psalm says: "When you give to them, they gather it up; when you open your hand, they are filled with good things" (Ps 104:28).

Your wishes or requests are in no way fruitless or made in vain. The saying is true: God hears our prayer for material things not exactly as we wish but in a way that promotes our salvation. Under these conditions, why do we delay or fear to carry our pain and sighs in supreme confidence to God for him to heal them privately and publicly?

(3) Now I come to the third reason that I gave earlier. It should stir our hearts to pray even if they were made of iron, because this motive grows out of the constant and overwhelming dangers and evil that surround us every day. A well-known saying goes like this: "Whoever cannot pray should go to sea." It reminds us that people are not so impassive or sophisticated that they refuse to ask God for help or deliverance when they find themselves in peril and terrifying situations. We should therefore stay aware of our public and private perils. We obviously face a great deal of public mischief and abuse. No one who has contributed to these will escape his or her

share of public penalties. We can see the dangers to which the church is exposed; it is threatened not only by enemies from outside but also by adversaries on the inside, who obstruct the dedicated and pious efforts of their teachers.

The sounds of war over religion will not cease, for Christ says: "I have not come to bring peace but a sword" (Matt 10:34). Our schools and parishes also have to endure punishments and danger from internal foes, homemade problems so to speak: extravagance, political ambition, insatiable greed, irresponsibility and quarrels, outbreaks of hate, and other blights. So much confusion and uncertainty plague our governments that no one can predict where the church will later find a home and hospitality. No father would fail to consider where on earth he should seek his children if suddenly he awoke after ten years of slumbering.

History tells us that Pompey and his two sons were buried in three different parts of the world: Asia, Africa, and Europe. Civil wars had caused this dispersal of the sons and their father over a vast area even after their deaths.[13] Examples from the history of the church are more instructive. When Jacob was already old, he was taken to Egypt and died there far from his homeland (Gen 49:29–33). Think about the diaspora and the conflicts that have afflicted all his descendants thereafter! As far as our children are concerned, can we predict where this political unrest and disturbance will take them after a few years? By God's grace there are still a few quiet regions that I pray God will preserve, but the political situation almost everywhere else reminds me of the old verse: "Peace comes for a while, but you can never rely on it."[14] The public dangers that threaten us are so ominous they cannot be portrayed.

Some people think that public dangers do not affect their private lives and therefore should not concern them, as if they were hoping to remain whole and secure when the world was on fire around them, or as if they were sure they would emerge unscathed from the sea while watching their ship go under. They are like the onlookers at the time of Noah, who were unconcerned for their safety as the entire earth was inundated (Matt 24:37–39). Every person experiences eternal punishment because of his or her sins in the private sphere, but beyond that consider how many bad things happen in daily life! How much anxiety there is in every heart owing to

217

the crises of our day! So many tragedies occur one after the other and form an unbroken chain of misfortune. God afflicts humankind daily in order to remind us of our duty, our sins, and our repentance, and ultimately to drive us to prayer, since otherwise we snore loudly and would live an epicurean and carefree life.

We are beset not only by outward dangers, however, but our adversary also sets traps for those who fear God, in order to lead their intentions and their thoughts into sin and mischief from which they cannot be extricated. You will never be able to spot these traps ahead of time unless you ask heaven to grant you the shield of the Holy Spirit to keep you from stepping into them and falling victim to the wiles of the adversary, even when you are engaged in a deed that appears proper on the surface. I will pass over the daily problems that afflict everyone in matters of health, property, and the hazards that endanger ourselves and those we love.

Even if everything at home and outside is peaceful and orderly and nothing bad is happening to us, we still have to beware of the adversary who sneaks up and is most likely to snare us in the absence of misfortune. At these times people are especially careless, disregard God, and succumb to many amusements, so that the risk is greater that they fall easily into ruin. Thoughtful people are instructed by the Roman poet Ennius that contentment is the greatest reason to be afraid: "When he has succeeded, a Roman trembles in his heart."[15] It would be appropriate for the faithful to be uneasy and on guard against the tricks of the adversary, especially when God has granted a period of repose. Holy scripture admonishes us frequently not to forget God when times are quiet; for example: "And the people sat down to eat and drink, and rose up to revel" (Exod 32:6).

Above all, peace and quiet require prayer to God in order to guide and keep us on the right path, so that we do not lose our reverence for him and thoughtlessly neglect his will. For the faithful there is never a moment when prayer is not needed; we pray either that God will preserve us in dark times or watch out for us when things do not look so bad, so that we do not abuse his goodness. That abuse is a rampant disease in humanity.

In order not to ramble I will draw my remarks to a close by challenging young people to establish early the habit of offering

God the daily service of prayer. First and foremost they should strive to perfect their way of life and moral conduct. They should also strive to educate themselves in the knowledge of heavenly doctrine taught by the church, in order to learn that every invocation of God must be illuminated ahead of time by faith. God is not pleased by the prayer of a worldly-wise, carefree, irresponsible, and flippant hypocrite who lacks faith in the Son of God, as Solomon says: "Lying lips are an abomination to the Lord" (Prov 12:22).

Let us keep before our eyes all the motives that lead us to pray, and especially the three I have treated: God's command, the power and efficaciousness of prayer, and our ever-present public and private emergencies. May God, the Father of our Lord Jesus Christ, direct our thoughts, so that we call upon him with a true heart and live in a way that pleases him and redounds to his glory! Amen.

36. Philip Melanchthon, Prayers for Morning and Evening and Prayer in Time of War, 1540, 1551, 1547

Philip Melanchthon not only analyzed prayer, but he also prayed frequently and intensely. We may have more prayers from him than from any other reformer in the sixteenth century. Some of them are no more than short yearnings interspersed in his correspondence, but we also have several hundred long prose prayers inserted into his other writings, such as his essay on prayer (see text no. 35 above). His candid admission that God does not always answer prayer in the way we expect did not discourage him from praying. Prayer was still commanded and beneficial; as he advised his audience in 1552: "Your wishes or requests are in no way fruitless or made in vain."

A prayer might include thanksgiving, confession of sin, or acknowledgment of God's gifts, but it always contained a request. Whether the prayer was short or long, Melanchthon was not shy about asking God for that which would benefit his people and preserve his church.

The following prayers are translated from the German texts in *Ich rufe zu dir: Gebete des Reformators Philipp Melanchthon,* ed. Martin H. Jung, Gerhard Weng, and Klaus-Dieter Kaiser, 18–20, 55.

Morning Prayer (1540, on a Trip to Weimar)

Father, I owe you thanks and praise for raising up the light of the sun and causing day to follow night in endless succession. Make our hearts, I pray, bright with the word that in the divine breast streams forth always from you.

Evening Prayer (1551, Based on Luke 24:29)

Evening is already here, so stay among us, O Christ. Make sure, we pray, that your light is extinguished nevermore.

Prayer in Time of War (1547, at the End of the Schmalkald War[16])

Almighty, eternal and true God, Father of our Savior Jesus Christ, creator of heaven and earth, with your dear Son, Jesus Christ, and the Holy Spirit.

We give you heartfelt thanks that you have revealed yourself to us and sent to us your Son, Jesus Christ. You have disclosed the marvelous hidden plan for our redemption. You gather to yourself an eternal church through your gospel and the Holy Spirit. You also mercifully supply governments and nourishment.

We acknowledge that these and other goods are your gifts that have been given to us and preserved for the sake of your Son. We also confess that we have become unclean through many known and unknown sins. We are sorry that we have acted against your just will.

We ask you to turn our hearts to you and forgive us all our sins for the sake of your Son, Jesus Christ, as you have promised out of your immeasurable mercy. Through your Holy Spirit awaken in us true faith and obedience and establish your rule over us. We earnestly intend to improve ourselves and to live in obedience to you.

For the sake of your Son we also implore you to gather always your church in these lands and preserve genuine Christian doctrine so that we may call upon you, live in true obedience, and praise and love you in eternity. For this purpose give us faithful teachers and preachers who will contribute to our blessedness and praise of you through their doctrine and good example.

For the sake of your Son, we also ask you to give these lands peaceful and Christian governments that promote good fortune; mercifully preserve them and direct them through the Holy Spirit, so that they may live and rule to your glory and for the peace and salvation of their subjects.

In your mercy give us the fruit of the earth so that our bodily life is nourished and we learn to acknowledge and call upon you. Give us our daily bread and bless it.

You know the weakness of human nature. Soften your anger with mercy on account of the intercession of your Son. Lighten our well-deserved punishments, and comfort with your Holy Spirit all who grieve. Help them to persevere in true faith and prayer and to extol your mercy forever.

37. Miles Coverdale, Meditation and Prayer Recalling God's Unspeakable Love, between 1540 and 1547

This meditation and prayer are found in a lengthy series of lessons drawn from the passion story as told in the gospel accounts. Those lessons are part of an even longer series that was published in Marburg, Germany, from 1540 to 1547, during one of Coverdale's sojourns on the continent. The texts for this meditation are the prayer of Jesus in Gethsemane, which asks for his cup of suffering to be taken away, and the scolding of the disciples Peter, James, and John for falling asleep while Jesus prayed (Mark 14:32–42).

Miles Coverdale (1488–1568), a former Augustinian friar, is best known for the first complete edition of the English Bible, which was printed on the continent in 1535 and became the foundation of the so-called Great Bible of 1539. By 1528 Coverdale had become a staunch Protestant and a good friend of Tyndale and Cranmer; as a result, he went into exile several times when Protestant reforms fell into disfavor. Prior to Mary Tudor's reign he served three years as bishop of Exeter, and during her reign he lived again on the continent where he contributed to the Geneva Bible, the English Bible of the Protestant Marian

221

exiles. Although he translated more works than he wrote, the "Fruitful Lessons" appear to be his own production, even though the plan of the work came from a similar treatise by Ulrich Zwingli.

Adapted from "Fruitful Lessons upon the Passion, Burial, Resurrection, Ascension, and the Sending of the Holy Ghost," in *Writings and Translations of Myles Coverdale, Bishop of Exeter,* ed. George Pearson for the Parker Society, 262–63.

For here we are instructed and certified of the kindness of our loving Father, that he is not angry or takes it evil when we complain to him of our present trouble, so that we give over our will to his. All those who are in afflictions, adversity, and temptations must set this example of the Lord directly before their eyes and ponder it in their hearts. Not only is the Father not angry when we complain to him in our necessity, but in all trouble he sends us his own help and comfort either by his angel, or inwardly by his Spirit, or outwardly by some other means. He sends us strength, gives us his hand, draws us, delivers us, and suffers us not to be tempted above our power, or else in the midst of our adversity he gives us consolation and strength to overcome it.

Oh, what great comfort this brings to our afflictions in life and death, if we ponder, weigh, and consider the exceeding love of God our heavenly Father, who gives his dear Son into such great trouble that we might be delivered from eternal adversity and sorrow! If we also remember the love of our Lord Jesus toward us, who for our sake takes upon himself so great a fear and passion, how can we not look for all good things at his hand? What thing is so great that we his members would not suffer for his sake, if we behold the head in such anguish and trouble? And inasmuch as he suffers all this for the satisfaction of our sins, we ought to apply great diligence that we fall not again into sin for which Christ suffered this and from which Christ with so great a passion has delivered and cleansed us.

We learn here also to love our neighbors, to care for them, to pity them, even if they are impotent and slow, to pray for their infirmity, seeing that we are all weak and feeble. We are to have respect for such weakness, so that we do not become arrogant or hold much of ourselves, when we see that Peter and the others are so full of sleep and sluggishness that all the admonitions and exhortations of

Christ could at that time do little with them. But we ought to stand always in humbleness of mind and in the fear of God, ascribe all good things to him, and be direful[17] and watch, lest the devil draw us into temptation.

O merciful Father, give us grace with fervent hearts to consider the unspeakable love of you and of your Son, and never to forget the same—that our faith and trust in you may be strengthened, that love in us toward you and our neighbor may be kindled, that above all things we may love you, the wellspring of all goodness, and that we may serve our neighbors in love, care for them, and do them good, according to the love that your dear Son has bestowed upon us. Oh, give us patience and steadfastness in adversity, strengthen our weakness, comfort us in trouble and distress, help us to fight;[18] grant unto us that in true obedience and peace of mind we may give over our own wills unto you, our Father, in all things, according to the example of your beloved Son, so that in adversity we grudge not but offer up ourselves to you. Give us strength constantly to subdue the rebellious and stubborn flesh and to make it obedient to the Spirit, to cast away all temporal and carnal fear, to resort oft unto prayer and to be earnest and fervent therein, to mortify all our own wills and lusts, and utterly to give them their leave. O give us a willing and cheerful mind, that we may gladly suffer and bear all things for your sake. Amen.

38. Thomas Cranmer, Original Collects for *The Book of Common Prayer*, 1549

A collect is a short prayer used in a liturgical service of Western churches. Normally, it has one petition in addition to an acknowledgment of God's power or mercy and a conclusion in which the prayer is offered "through Jesus Christ our Lord," the only mediator as far as Protestants were concerned. Collects originated in the early church and were gradually assigned to specific Sundays and holy days alongside the scripture readings or pericopes for those days. These collects became a fixture of medieval worship, and during the Reformation they were adopted by German and English Protestants, who used liturgies based on the mass. Although Lutherans and Anglicans eliminated some parts of the mass objectionable to them, they rewrote other parts to suit their theology of worship and devotion.

Most of the collects that had come from the sacramentaries (worship books) of the fifth and sixth centuries were acceptable to Thomas Cranmer (see text no. 12 above) and his colleagues who produced the *English Book of Common Prayer* (1549). Cranmer did, however, compose some original collects that are presented here. They emphasize typical Protestant themes. The prayer for the Second Sunday in Advent asks for the internalization of "all the holy scriptures" that were so important to Cranmer and the other reformers. The collect for Ash Wednesday emphasizes repentance in place of ritual fasting. The prayer designated for the First Sunday after Easter was originally the collect for the second communion service on Easter Day. The body of the prayer is taken almost entirely from biblical verses (Rom 4:25; 1 Cor 5:8). Cranmer based the collect for the Sunday after the Ascension on an antiphon that was used in the late medieval church at Vespers (the evening service) on Ascension Day:[19] "O king of glory, Lord of hosts, who today ascended in triumph far above all the heavens, do not leave us orphans, but send the Spirit of truth promised to us by the Father. Alleluia." These prayers are still used in the liturgical services of some Protestant churches, but not necessarily at the same point in the church year.

The collects printed here are in the form in which they appeared in *The Book of Common Prayer 1559: The Elizabethan Prayer Book,* ed. John E. Booty, 79, 108, 156, 167.

THE SECOND SUNDAY OF ADVENT

Blessed Lord, which hast caused all holy scriptures to be written for our learning: Grant us that we may in such wise hear them, read, mark, learn, and inwardly digest them; that by patience and comfort of thy holy word, we may embrace and ever hold fast the blessed hope of everlasting life, which thou hast given us in our Savior Jesus Christ.

ASH WEDNESDAY, THE FIRST DAY OF LENT

Almighty and everlasting God, which hatest nothing that thou hast made, and dost forgive the sins of all them that be penitent: Create and make in us new and contrite hearts, that we, worthily lamenting our sins and knowledging[20] our wretchedness, may obtain of thee, the God of all mercy, perfect remission and forgiveness; through Jesus Christ.

TUESDAY IN EASTER WEEK

Almighty Father, which hast given thy only Son to die for our sins, and to rise again for our justification: Grant us so to put away the leaven of malice and wickedness, that we may alway serve thee in pureness of living and truth; through Jesus Christ our Lord.

THE SUNDAY AFTER THE ASCENSION

O God, the king of glory, which hast exalted thine only Son, Jesus Christ, with great triumph unto thy kingdom in heaven: We beseech thee leave us not comfortless, but send to us thine Holy Spirit to comfort us, and exalt us unto the same place whither our Savior Christ is gone before; who liveth and reigneth with thee and the Holy Ghost, now and ever. Amen.

PART EIGHT

Reconstructing Sacraments

Introduction

Because by definition they contain earthly or material elements, sacraments appear to be the antithesis of spirituality. Prior to the Reformation, however, theologians had already distinguished *sacramentum* from *res sacramenti*, that is, the external or material sign from the spiritual substance or grace conferred by the sacramental act. Among the seven rites that were designated sacraments by the late medieval church, the material signs were most discernible in baptism (water), confirmation (oil), the eucharist or mass (bread and wine), and extreme unction or anointing the dying (oil). Even in those sacraments, however, the material element was not as important as the grace that was conferred by the sacramental act itself. Moreover, the source of sacramental grace was Christ himself, who was the sacrament par excellence and whose death and resurrection made available through sacraments the saving grace for believers. According to this congenial theology, any preoccupation with the material elements themselves or superstitious beliefs about them was clearly unorthodox and decidedly an obstacle to the spiritual benefits that sacraments bestowed.

Although well versed in this theology, early Protestants were convinced that the sacramental world in which they had been raised did not promote genuine spirituality. The obstacles lay both in the theology and in the practice of sacraments. Protestants agreed that sacraments would not be sacraments without material elements, but if the elements became the vehicles of sacred and spiritual power, they could also become objects of superstition and bearers of magical influence. Reformers agreed that people had already succumbed

227

to these temptations and that an overhaul of sacramental theology and practice was necessary. With his *Babylonian Captivity of the Church* (1520), a draconian pruning and reinterpretation of sacraments, Martin Luther was again in the vanguard of this movement, but he was soon joined by equally earnest and efficient reformers. Reducing the number of sacraments from seven to two was not as important to these minds as redefining the purposes of the remaining sacraments, baptism and the Lord's Supper, in the lives of believers. Protestant reformers disagreed in some cases about how these purposes were accomplished, but they agreed that the material elements of water, bread, and wine were signs by which the Holy Spirit brought people to faith in Christ and nurtured that faith throughout their Christian journey. The faithful, therefore, needed to hear about that purpose through continual teaching and preaching, in order to take advantage of these signs—commanded by Jesus and attached to his promises—and maintain the vitality of their faith and love.

Protestant church bodies that originated in sixteenth-century Europe (Lutheran, Reformed, Baptist, Anglican or Episcopal, Mennonite) owe their distinctiveness largely to their different views of the sacraments. All but Baptists and Mennonites baptize infants and small children, but they have divergent interpretations of what happens in baptism. Only Lutherans and some Episcopalians believe in the real bodily presence of Christ in the Lord's Supper, but the relationship of Christ to the bread and wine is also debated by the other churches. In the texts below, however, these differences play a small role. Instead, all these Protestants could identify with Luther's Pauline emphasis on baptism as dying and rising; on the need for repentance and confession in the way they are redefined by Zwingli; on the importance of rearing children in the faith as proposed by the reformers in Strasbourg in their reconception of confirmation; and finally, despite his unambiguous disagreement with Luther, on the purposes of both sacraments as carefully explained by Henry Bullinger, the successor of Zwingli and the long-term shaper of the church in German-speaking Switzerland. The importance of the sacraments for early Protestant spirituality could scarcely be stated with greater clarity and contrast to late medieval practice than in the following summary by Bullinger: "If our minds are not confirmed, they waver on every side. God, therefore, framed himself according to our weakness and by his sacraments, as much as may be, upholds us, yet in such a way that we refer all benefits of our confirmation to the Spirit and to its operation rather than to the elements." Only those very few who rejected sacraments completely would have disagreed.

39. Martin Luther, A Sermon on the Holy and Noblest Sacrament of Baptism, 1519

The following sermon was the second part of a trilogy on the sacraments that was in all likelihood not preached but written solely for publication. All three sermons—on penance, baptism, and the Lord's Supper—were written in November 1519, two years into Luther's conflict with the Roman curia, but almost one year before his critique of the medieval sacramental system: *The Babylonian Captivity of the Church* (1520). Nevertheless, Luther was well aware that these sermons contained both criticism and fresh ideas, and none more so than this sermon on baptism. In the dedication to Duchess Margaret of Brunswick-Lüneburg, a German territory that would become a stronghold of the Reformation, he complained that the true meaning and use of these sacraments had been so concealed by false teaching that people were ignorant of the grace and comfort they provided.

The main difference between Luther's view of baptism and the medieval view is Luther's emphasis on the lifelong use and effectiveness of the sacrament. Baptism became a much stronger and enduring spiritual resource than it was for late medieval Christians. In the pre-Reformation period, when primarily the infants of European Christendom underwent baptism, it was thought to forgive original sin, whereas the sacrament of penance, which could be repeated as often as necessary, was used to acquire remission of the actual sins committed over a lifetime. In the text below Luther makes clear that baptism itself both initiates a lifelong struggle against sin and commits God to forgive our sin as we fight against it until our death removes it completely. Believers can always appeal to the covenant of their baptism for forgiveness and for strength to carry on the struggle.

English translation from the 1519 German version of *Ein Sermon von dem heiligen hochwürdigen Sakrament der Taufe,* in Clemen 1, 185–95.

A SERMON ON THE HOLY AND NOBLEST SACRAMENT OF BAPTISM

(1) In Greek, baptism is *baptismos* and in Latin, it is *mersio.* It means to submerge something so deeply that it is covered by the water. It is no longer a common practice to immerse infants but to scoop water from the font and pour it over them. We should restore the practice of immersion, however, because it agrees with the meaning of the word *Taufe:*[1] the infant or whoever is to be baptized should be submerged in the water and drawn out again. In the German language the word *Taufe* comes undoubtedly from the word *tief;*[2] therefore, those who are baptized should be dunked.[3] Immersion is also suggested by the significance of baptism, for baptism, as we shall hear, signifies that the old person and our sinful birth from flesh and blood are to be altogether drowned by the grace of God. We should therefore do justice to its meaning and make the act of baptism an accurate and perfect symbol.

(2) Baptism is an external sign or token that separates us from all who are not baptized and makes us recognizable as people of Christ, our leader, under whose banner, the holy cross, we continually fight against sin. In this holy sacrament we must pay attention to three things: the sign, the meaning, and faith. The sign is being plunged into the water in the name of the Father and of the Son and of the Holy Spirit; however, we are not left there but drawn out again. Accordingly, people use the common expression "to be lifted out of baptism [or the font]." The sign must have both parts: the dipping and the drawing out.

(3) The meaning of baptism is a blessed dying to sin and a resurrection in the grace of God, so that the old person, conceived and born in sin, is drowned there and a new person, born in grace, emerges and rises. Thus St. Paul calls baptism a "water of rebirth" (Titus 3:5), for in this washing a person is born again and made new. Christ also says: "Unless you are born a second time of water and the Spirit (of grace), you may not enter into the kingdom of heaven" (John 3:5).[4] Just as a child is lifted out of the mother's womb, born,

and through this fleshly birth becomes a sinful person and a child of wrath (Eph 2:3), so we are lifted out of baptism and born spiritually and through this spiritual birth become children of grace and justified people. In baptism sin is drowned and righteousness rises to take its place.

(4) This meaning of baptism, the dying or drowning of sin, is not finished in this life and will not be completed until we die physically and turn completely to dust. As we see, the sacrament or sign of baptism is quickly performed, but what it stands for—the spiritual baptism and drowning of sin—lasts as long as we live and is perfected only in death. Only then are we completely submerged in baptism and that which baptism signifies finally comes to pass.

Our entire life, therefore, is nothing but a spiritual baptism that does not cease until death, and those who are baptized are condemned to die, as if the priest who baptizes were to say: "Behold, you are sinful flesh, and in the name of God I drown you and condemn you to death, so that all your sin may die and perish with you." Therefore St. Paul says: "We have been buried with him by baptism into death" (Rom 6:4). The sooner after baptism we die, the sooner our baptism is completed, for sin never ceases as long as the body is alive. Our bodies are so wholly conceived in sin that sin is their nature, as the prophet says: "Indeed I was born guilty, a sinner when my mother conceived me" (Ps 51:5). Sinful nature cannot be remedied unless it dies and perishes with all its sin. The life of Christians from baptism to the grave is nothing other than the beginning of a blessed death, for God will make them new and different at the last day.

(5) Likewise the lifting out of the baptismal water is quickly done, but its meaning— spiritual birth, the increase of grace and righteousness—though beginning in baptism lasts until death and even until the last day. For the first time we will see the fulfillment of that which the lifting out of baptism signifies: we will arise from death, sins, and all evil, pure in body and soul, and we shall then live eternally. We will be truly lifted out of baptism and impeccably born, and we shall put on the baptismal garment of immortal life in heaven, as if the sponsors, lifting the child out of baptism, were to say: "Behold, your sins are now drowned, and we receive you in God's name into an eternal life of innocence." In this way the angels

will raise up at the last day all Christians—all devout and baptized people—and will fulfill what baptism and godparents signify, as Christ declares: "And he will send out his angels with a loud trumpet call, and they will gather his elect from the four winds, from one end of heaven to the other" (Matt 24:31).

(6) At the time of Noah baptism was foreshadowed in the flood, when the whole world was drowned except for Noah with his three sons and all the wives—eight souls—who were saved in the ark. The drowning of all those people on earth signifies that in baptism sins are drowned, but the preservation of those eight people in the ark with animals of every sort signifies, as St. Peter says, that people are saved through baptism (1 Pet 3:20–21; 2 Pet 2:5). Baptism is by far a greater flood than the one Noah survived. It drowned people for no longer than a year, but baptism drowns people throughout the world from the birth of Christ until the day of judgment. That was a flood of wrath, but this is a flood of grace, as declared in the psalm: "God will make a continually new flood" (Ps 29:10).[5] For many more people have undoubtedly been baptized than were drowned in the flood.

(7) From all this it follows, to be sure, that those who come forth out of baptism are pure, without sin, and wholly guiltless. Still, this is not perfectly understood by many people. Thinking that sin is no longer present, they become lazy and neglect to slay their sinful nature, as some do even after they have gone to confession. For this reason, as I said above, we should understand and know for a fact that our flesh, as long as it is alive, is by nature wicked and sinful.

To aid the flesh God devised a plan to make it altogether new, as Jeremiah shows: "The vessel he was making of clay was spoiled in the potter's hand," and he thrust it again into the lump of clay and kneaded it, "and he reworked it into another vessel as seemed good to him....[Just like the clay in the potter's hand], so are you (says God) in my hand" (Jer 18:4–6). In the first birth we are flawed; therefore he thrusts us into the earth again by death and reworks us at the last day, so that we become perfect and without sin.

This plan, as I said, begins in baptism, which signifies death and resurrection at the last day. As far as the sacrament's sign and its meaning are concerned, sin and humanity are already dead and we have risen; in this sense the sacrament has taken place. The work of the sacrament, however, has not yet been fully done insofar as death and resurrection at the last day are still before us.

(8) Baptized people are therefore sacramentally altogether pure and guiltless, that is, they have none other than the sign of God, baptism, which indicates that all their sins are to be killed and that they, too, are to die in grace and at the last day are to rise again to everlasting life, pure, sinless, and guiltless. With respect to the sacrament, it is true that they are without sin and guilt; yet because all is not yet completed and they still live in sinful flesh, they are not without sin or pure in all things, but have begun to grow into purity and innocence.

When people grow up, the natural and sinful appetites— wrath, impurity, lust, greed, pride, and the like—begin to stir; there would be none of these if all sins were drowned in the sacrament and were dead. The sacrament, however, only signifies that they are to be drowned through death and resurrection at the last day. Wherefore St. Paul and all the saints with him lament that they are sinners and have sin in their nature, even though they were baptized and holy (Rom 7:14–25). The reason is that the natural and sinful appetites remain active as long as we are alive.

(9) You may ask: "How does baptism help me, if it does not cover and eliminate sin completely?" To answer this question a true understanding of baptism is necessary. The noble sacrament of baptism helps you because God is bound and united to you in a gracious covenant of comfort.

[Here is how it works.] First, you acquiesce in the sacrament of baptism and what it means, that is (as I said and the sacrament indicates), you wish to die together with your sins and to be made new at the last day. God accepts this desire, has you baptized, and immediately begins to make you a new person. God pours into you his grace and Holy Spirit, who begins to slay nature and sin and to prepare you to die and to rise at the last day.

Second, you pledge to abide by this desire and to slay your sin more and more as long as you live, until you die. God accepts this pledge as well and trains you throughout life with many good works and all kinds of suffering. In this way God accomplishes what you wished for in baptism: to be free of sin, die, rise anew at the last day, and thus complete your baptism. Accordingly, we read how bitterly God has allowed his saints to be tortured and suffer, so that on the brink of death they might finish the sacrament of baptism, die, and be made new. When none of that happens and we neither suffer nor experience testing, evil nature gains the upper hand and makes our baptism ineffectual, so that we fall into sin and remain the same old people we were before.

(10) As long as you keep your pledge, God in turn gives you grace and promises not to impute to you the sins that remain in your nature after baptism, having no regard for them or condemning you because of them. God is satisfied and pleased that you willingly and constantly strive to slay these sins and to be rid of them at your death. Although evil thoughts and appetites may appear and you at times may sin and fall, as long as you rise again and enter once more into the covenant, these sins are already removed by the power of the sacrament and its covenant, as St. Paul says (Rom 8:1–4). No one who believes in Christ is condemned by the evil inclination of sinful nature, as long as he or she does not follow it and give in to it. In his epistles St. John the evangelist writes: "But if anyone does sin, we have an advocate with the Father, Jesus Christ the righteous, and he is the atoning sacrifice for our sins" (1 John 2:1–2). All this takes place in baptism, where Christ is given to us, as we shall hear in the next sermon.[6]

(11) Now if this covenant did not exist and God did not mercifully wink at our sins, no sin could be so small that it would not condemn us, for divine judgment cannot tolerate sin. There is thus no greater comfort on earth than baptism, through which we come under the judgment of grace and mercy that does not condemn our sins but expels them by much testing. St. Augustine puts it eloquently: sin is altogether forgiven in baptism, not in the sense that sin is no longer present but that sin is not imputed.[7] As if he were to say: "Sin stays in our flesh until death and stirs itself continually, but as long as we do not give our consent to it or remain stuck in sin, baptism keeps it in check so that it does not condemn us and is not harmful to us. Instead, every day sin is more and more demolished until our death."

We should therefore not be frightened if we detect lust and love that are bad, nor should we despair even if we fall; rather, we

234

should remember our baptism and let it cheer and comfort us because in it God has promised to slay our sin and not allow it to condemn us, as long as we do not consent to sin or abide in it. Moreover, do not let these raging thoughts and desires, or even committing a sin, become an occasion for despair; consider them instead to be a warning from God to remember our baptism and the words spoken there, so that we are led to call upon God's mercy and exert ourselves in the battle against sin, even to welcome death so that we may be rid of sin.

(12) Here is the place to discuss faith, the third part of the sacrament. It means that one firmly believes all this: the sacrament not only signifies death and resurrection at the last day, when a person is made new to live without sin eternally, but also begins to bring it about and to establish a covenant between us and God. Our part is to struggle with sin until we die and to slay it, and God's part is to look favorably upon us, deal graciously with us until we are purified by death, and not judge us with severity because we are not sinless in this life.

Now you understand how in baptism we become guiltless, pure, and sinless while remaining full of evil inclinations, so that we are said to be pure only in the sense that we have begun to become clean and have a sign and covenant of that same purity and are indeed to become more pure. On that account God will not hold our residual impurity against us, and thus we are pure by the gracious imputation of God rather than by virtue of our nature. Accordingly the prophet says: "Happy are those whose transgression is forgiven, whose sin is covered; happy are they to whom the Lord imputes no iniquity" (Ps 32:1–2).

This faith is the most necessary thing of all for it is the ground of all comfort. Those who do not have it must despair in their sins, because the sin that remains after baptism makes all good works unclean before God. We must therefore cling to our baptism boldly, hold nothing back, and set it against all sin and terrors of conscience, saying with humility: "I know full well that I cannot do a single thing that is pure, but I am baptized and through my baptism God, who cannot lie, has obligated himself not to count my sin against me but to slay and abolish it."

(13) We see then that the innocence we have from baptism is solely because of divine mercy, which has initiated our innocence, bears patiently with our sin, and regards us as if we were sinless. Now we know why Christians are called in the scriptures children of mercy, a people of grace and of God's good will[8]—because through baptism they have begun to be pure and by God's mercy are not condemned because of leftover sin, until through death and at the last day they become wholly pure, as baptism demonstrates with its sign.

People make a big mistake by assuming that through baptism they have become wholly pure. They go about in their ignorance and do not slay their sin; in fact, they do not admit it is sin and persist in it, making their baptism of no effect. They hang onto a few good deeds, while pride, hatred, and other evils in their nature, which they disregard, grow worse and worse. No, it is not right to think that way. The inclination to sin must be recognized as real sin, but it does not harm us and should be committed to the grace of God, who will not count sin against us as long as we struggle against it through many trials, labors, and sufferings until we slay it at death. Those who do not respond this way will receive no forgiveness from God, for they do not live according to their baptism and covenant with God, and they hinder the work that God and their baptism have started.

(14) Those who presume to put away their sin by satisfaction[9] are the same sort of people. They disregard their baptism as if they had no need of it beyond the fact of having once been baptized. They do not know that baptism is effective throughout life, until our dying and, as I said, even to the last day. They presume to find another way of eliminating sin, namely, by works, and for themselves and others they create evil, terrified, and uncertain consciences that despair at the hour of death, thinking that through sin they have lost their baptism and that it is no longer of use.

By all means guard yourself against this error. As I said, those who have fallen into sin should all the more remember their baptism, by which God is obligated to forgive all their sins if they will resist them until death. They must joyfully rely upon this truth, upon this alliance with God; then baptism is in force and goes to work again and their heart is once more happy and content, not with their own works or satisfaction, but with the mercy of God promised in baptism, a mercy that God will sustain forever. They must hold so firmly to this faith that they would be able to cling to it even if they were to be ambushed by every sin in creation. Those who allow themselves to be forcibly separated from this faith make God a liar about the divine obligation incurred in the sacrament of baptism.

(15) Faith like this is subject most of all to the devil's attack. If he overthrows it, he has won the battle. The sacrament of penance (already treated)[10] also has its foundation in this sacrament, inasmuch as sins are forgiven only to those who are baptized, that is, to those whose sins God has promised to forgive. The sacrament of penance thus renews and points again to the sacrament of baptism, as if the priest would say in the absolution: "Behold, God has now forgiven your sin as he promised earlier in baptism and now commanded me, by the power of the keys, to assure you that you are forgiven and again benefit from what baptism is and does. As you believe, you have, but if you doubt, you are lost."

Sin may hinder the work of baptism in forgiving and slaying sin, but only the failure to trust in its work can rob baptism of its power. Faith removes the obstruction to the operation of baptism, and consequently everything depends on faith. To put it plainly: it is one thing to forgive sin and quite a different thing to lay it aside or drive it out. Faith attains the forgiveness of sin even though sin is not entirely expelled. To drive out sin is to exercise ourselves against it and finally to die, for in death sin is extinguished at last.

Both the forgiving and the expelling of sin are the work of baptism. Accordingly, when the apostle writes to the Hebrews who were baptized and whose sins were forgiven, he tells them to lay aside the sin that clings to them (Heb 12:1). As long as I believe that God will not reckon my sins against me, my baptism is working and my sins are forgiven, even though most of them may remain. They may then be driven out through suffering, death, and the like. We confess this very article [in the creed]: "I believe in the Holy Spirit... the forgiveness of sins." Here we find a clear reference to baptism, in which forgiveness takes place through God's binding himself to us. Therefore we must not doubt this forgiveness.

(16) As a consequence, baptism renders all suffering and death in particular beneficial and helpful. They have no choice but to serve the work of baptism, namely, the elimination of sin, for there is no other way for it to happen. Those who desire to give baptism its full due and be rid of sin must die. Sin, however, does not die gladly, and thus it makes death so bitter and terrible. God is so gracious and powerful, however, that sin which has brought about death is banished by its own work, that is, by death itself.

Many people intend to live in a way that makes them pious and say outright they wish to be pious. There is no shorter means or path to piety than through baptism and the work of baptism, which is suffering and death. Their unwillingness to take this path is a sign of their ignorance of the proper way to become pious. For that reason God organized life into several estates[11] in which we are to train ourselves and learn to suffer. For some he has commanded the estate of matrimony, for others the ministry, for others authority in the civil realm; and he has ordered toil and labor for everyone, in order to slay the flesh and familiarize it with death. In the case of those who are baptized, the ease, comfort, and contentment of this life have become poisonous and pose an obstacle to the work of their baptism; in comfort and contentment they do not learn to suffer and die gladly in order to be liberated from sin and thus to comply with their baptism. Instead, love of this life only increases, along with disdain for eternal life, fear of death, and the refusal to eradicate sin.

(17) Many people engage in exercises like fasting, praying, and undertaking pilgrimages, imagining that they are accumulating merit and gaining for themselves the highest seats in heaven. They no longer bother with learning to kill their wicked vices. Fasting and all such exercises, however, should be directed toward suppressing the old Adam, our sinful nature, teaching it to do without the pleasures of this life and preparing it daily more and more for death. In that way we accomplish the purpose of baptism. The proper dose of these exercises and efforts should be determined not by their quantity or magnitude but by the demands of baptism. We should take upon ourselves as much of them as is sufficient and useful for suppressing our sinful nature and preparing it for death. We should add to or subtract these works as we see sin increasing or decreasing. Now it happens that people take upon themselves this or that task, engage in this or

that exercise, on the basis of how it looks and what it might accomplish. Later they quickly drop it and become so fickle that finally they amount to nothing. Others rack their brains and ruin their health over these exercises and become of no use either to themselves or to others. Why? Because we have been possessed by the teaching that after repentance or baptism we have no sin and that good works are to be accumulated for their own sake or to make up for sins already committed, but not for the elimination of all sin.

This way of thinking is encouraged by those preachers who unwisely teach the legends and feats of the precious saints by holding them up as examples for everyone to follow. The uninformed laity easily fall for these stories and end up destroying themselves by trying to emulate the saints. God has indeed given every saint a special means and grace for living out that saint's baptism. For everyone, however, God has set a common standard for baptism and its meaning, so that all of us, in whatever state we are, can examine ourselves and discern the best way to comply with the purpose of our baptism, that is, the best way to slay sin and to die so that the burden of Christ may become light and easy (Matt 11:30) and not heavy with worry and care. About the latter Solomon says: "The toil of fools wears them out, for they do not even know the way to town" (Eccl 10:15). For as anxiety seizes those who wish to go to town but cannot find their way, so it is for those whose entire life and effort leave them bitter and accomplish nothing.

(18) Here is the place to discuss the common question whether or not baptism and the vow we make to God at baptism are something more or greater than the vow of chastity or the vows required for the priesthood and the clergy. Since baptism is common to all Christians, the clergy are thought to have taken a special and a higher vow.

It is easy to answer this question on the basis of what we have said to this point. In baptism we all make one and the same vow: to exterminate sin and to become holy through the action and grace of God, to whom we surrender and offer ourselves as clay does to the potter (Jer 18:4–6). One vow is no better than another. For complying with the purpose of our baptism, however, for exterminating sin, the same means or station in life is not right for everyone. For that reason I said that each of us must determine which station best enables us to exterminate sin and keep our nature in check. The truth is, therefore, that no vow exists which is higher, better, or greater than the vow of baptism. What more can we promise than to banish sin, to die, to despise this life, and to become holy?

Over and above this vow, people may bind themselves to an estate that is best suited to accomplish the purpose of their baptism. It is like two people who travel to the same town, one by the foot-path, the other by the highway, just as each deems best. Those who bind themselves to the state of matrimony undergo the struggles and sufferings which belong to that estate and take on those burdens, so that they grow accustomed to pleasure and sorrow, avoid sin, and prepare themselves for death better than they could outside that state. Those who seek more suffering and more intense training in order to prepare quickly for death and to reach the goal of their baptism should bind themselves to chastity or to a clerical order. The spiritual estate,[12] properly exercised, should be full of so much suffering and torment that it would offer more training for the application of baptism than the estate of matrimony and through such torment quickly accustom those in the spiritual estate to accept death with joy and thus attain the goal of their baptism. Now above this estate is yet a higher one that governs others in the spiritual order: the estate of bishop, priest, and so forth. Those who occupy these offices should be thoroughly trained in labor and suffering, and they should be prepared for death every minute—to die not only for their own sake, but also for the sake of those under their care.

In all these estates, however, the standard set down above should never be forgotten: to direct our efforts only toward the abolition of sin and not the accumulation of noble deeds. Alas, we have failed to remember our baptism and its meaning, the vows we made there, and the manner in which we should live out our baptism and arrive in the end at its goal. At the same time we have forgotten the right direction and the estates themselves to such an extent that we hardly realize for what purpose these estates were created or how to live in them in order to fulfill our baptism. They have become an ostentatious show; little remains of them besides worldly glitter, as Isaiah says: "Your silver has become dross, your wine is mixed with water" (Isa 1:22). May God have mercy! Amen.

(19) If then the holy sacrament of baptism is so noble, gracious, and full of comfort, we should earnestly remember to offer God joyful and heartfelt thanks, praise, and honor for it. I am concerned that our ingratitude has made us blind and unworthy of recognizing such grace. The entire world has been full of baptism and the grace of God, and still is, but we have been misled into an uncertain and disquieting reliance on our own deeds and then on indulgences and similar false comforts. We have imagined we should not trust God until we were righteous and had made satisfaction for our sin, as though we were trying to buy grace or pay God for it.

Truly, if we are not convinced that God's grace bears with us sinners and will save us but instead head only for God's judgment, we will never rejoice in God nor be able to love or praise him. If we hear, however, that through the covenant of baptism God receives us sinners, spares us, and makes us pure from day to day, and if we firmly believe that, then our hearts will inevitably be joyful and they will love and praise God. In this way God speaks through the prophet: "I will spare them as parents spare their children" (Mal 3:17). Hence we must give thanks to our praiseworthy majesty, who shows this grace and mercy toward us poor, condemned little worms, and we must magnify and acknowledge God's works that are already impressive by themselves.

(20) We should beware, however, lest a false security sneak in under the following pretext: "If baptism is so gracious and effective that God will not count our sins against us, and if, as soon as we have turned back from sin, everything is made right by virtue of baptism, then for now I will do as I please. Later, or when I am about to die, I will recall my baptism and remind God of his covenant, and then I will accomplish the purpose of my baptism." Baptism is indeed so powerful that, if you turn back from sin and appeal to the covenant of baptism, your sins are forgiven. But watch out! If you wantonly sin and presume on God's grace, his judgment might come upon you before you are able to turn your back on sin. Even if you wished at that point to believe or trust in your baptism, the attacks on your faith allowed by God would be so strong that your faith would not survive them. If those who do not sin or those who fall because of sheer weakness barely survive, what will happen

because of your wanton sin, which has risked provoking God and mocked his grace (1 Pet 4:18)?

Let us therefore conduct our lives with fear and reverence, so that we may retain the riches of God's grace with a firm faith and joyfully give thanks for his mercy forever and ever. Amen.

40. Ulrich Zwingli, Repentance and Confession, 1525

In 1525 the Reformation in Zürich reached a noteworthy plateau with the celebration at Easter of the Lord's Supper in evangelical form. For almost two years Zwingli and his colleagues had sought the council's approval for this step, but it was too late in coming for the most radical of his followers. In January 1525 they performed the first rebaptisms and gave birth to the Anabaptist movement, which posed an enduring challenge to mainline Protestants. Moreover, Catholic opponents of reform were still active in the city, and the controversy between Zwingli and Luther over the Lord's Supper was getting under way. Even though by this time the city council had approved most of the religious changes that Zwingli and his colleagues requested, the Reformation was by no means secure. The time was therefore right for a summary of evangelical teaching that would clarify and support the changes that were now in place. Between December 1524 and March 1525, therefore, Zwingli composed this summary in Latin and dedicated it to King Francis I of France, who—some Protestants hoped—would become an advocate of the Reformation.

Although the *Commentary* was not written for a lay audience, it did make a trenchant case for evangelical teaching on twenty-nine topics by offering scriptural support and clearly distinguishing evangelical teaching ("true religion") from the Roman Christianity ("false religion") it was replacing. Although Zwingli no longer considered repentance and confession parts of a sacrament of penance, he did consider both to be an essential part of Christian spirituality after they had been interpreted and appropriated in an evangelical way. Believers needed to confess and repent of their sin in order to become certain of God's forgiveness and to produce the fruits of repentance in the new life to which they were called. For, according to Zwingli's expectations, "it ought to be altogether foreign to Christians to waste away in the same sins from which with joy they had been delivered."

The English text has been adapted from *Commentary on True and False Religion,* 131–37 and 253–56. Also consulted: the modern German text in ZS 3, 144–52 and 322–26.

REPENTANCE

We have till now regarded repentance as a forced and feigned pain for sins committed, and as the paying of the penalty set upon a sin by the judge, that is, the father confessor.[13] We repented of our evildoing only when the pope ordered, or when the celebration of Easter was approaching,[14] or when our health demanded it. What was this but hypocrisy? From what source did it arise if not from ignorance of ourselves? For those who have attained knowledge of themselves see such a vast slough of wickedness that they are driven not only to grieve but to shudder, to despair, to die. For what lust is so filthy, what greed so bold, what self-esteem so high, that each of us does not see it in our own hearts, scheming or working or hiding something? Since no one can deny this, how has it happened that we have not felt the pain that is born of this sight? It has happened because, as was said above, we do not try to go down into ourselves, not one of us. When, therefore, we do go down, real pain and shame immediately follow. This was by no means earlier the case with the repentance of the popes. For how should any be disgusted with themselves when none knew themselves, but thought rather that they were righteous either through their own works or through the hired efforts of others?

The second part of the gospel, then, is repentance,[15] not that which takes place for a time, but that which makes those who know themselves blush and be ashamed of their old life, for one reason because they are greatly dissatisfied and pained at themselves, and for another because they see it ought to be altogether foreign to Christians to waste away in the same sins from which with joy they had been delivered. When, therefore, Christ, John and the apostles preached "repent," they certainly did not speak of that feigned and counterfeit repentance that I mentioned at the beginning, nor of that which is felt once and for all and straightway thinks it has license to sin; this kind, as has been sufficiently set forth, is just as spurious as that performed by order of the popes.

Christ and the apostles spoke of the repentance in which we go into ourselves and diligently investigate the reason for all our acts, pretenses, and dissimulations. When we have done this honestly, we are driven by the vast extent of our disease to despair of our own righteousness and salvation, just as the person who has received a mortal wound keeps expecting black and everlasting night. Then, if some Machaon[16] should bid us be of good cheer because the wound could be sewn up and made good again, I think nothing more acceptable and cheering could happen to us.

We sinners, too, having thus probed our wounds and despaired of safety, beg for mercy and, after seeing Christ, understand that all things are to be hoped for. "If God is for us, who is against us?" (Rom 8:31). Those rise up who had lain prostrate. Those live who had learned and felt to their horror that they were dead. But neither Christ, nor John, nor the apostles implied that this repentance could last only a certain length of time and then be put aside. It is to last permanently, as long as we carry about this pitiful burden of the body. For this body is so given over to vanities that it never stops teeming with evil growths, which, as soon as they spring up, must be crushed, cut off, and stifled as things highly unbecoming a Christian. This labor, this struggle, this watchfulness—what is it if not repentance? Therefore, when Christ and John and the apostles preach, saying "repent," they are simply calling us to a new life quite unlike our life before; and those who had undertaken to enter upon this life were marked by an initiatory sacrament, to wit baptism, by which they gave public testimony that they were about to enter upon a new life.

Now I will come to the testimony of the word, lest I seem to anyone to have brought forward my own rather than heavenly testimony.

Christ called a certain man to the service of the gospel, but he replied: "'Lord, first let me go and bury my father.' Jesus said to him, 'Let the dead bury their own dead; but as for you, go and proclaim the kingdom of God.' Another said, 'I will follow you, Lord; but let me first say farewell to those at my home.' Jesus said to him, 'No one who puts a hand to the plow and looks back is fit for the kingdom of God'" (Luke 9:59–62). These words of Christ are per-fectly clear in themselves, for they plainly require that we neglect everything else, follow God at once, and not look back. Although they seem to apply to those only to whom the ministry of the word is entrusted, they do apply to all, as do also those two parables in which Jesus teaches that those who determine to follow him must examine their strength: one about the man who wished to build a tower, the other about the king who was going to make war against a foe. Each of them before starting upon his undertaking counted the cost and his resources, lest he might be forced to leave every-thing unfinished. Finally, Christ makes this application: "So there-fore, none of you can be my disciple if you do not give up all your possessions" (Luke 14:33). But what advantage is gained by renounc-ing riches unless you have renounced those sins on account of which we are taught that riches should be scorned?

The same is taught by the parable of the man who had been cordially invited to a marriage feast but failed to wear a wedding garment and was therefore cast into outer darkness. Thus those who are called to the marriage feast of the heavenly bridegroom should make sure that they clothe themselves and walk so as not to disgrace themselves and insult the bridegroom (Matt 22:11–13).

Again Christ says: "If you continue in my word, you are truly my disciples" (John 8:31). They are disciples, therefore, who abide in his word. Elsewhere he speaks in like fashion (John 14:21–24).

Paul most clearly teaches that those who have enlisted under Christ must begin a new life, saying: "Do you not know that all of us who were baptized into Christ Jesus were baptized into his death? Therefore we have been buried with him by baptism into death, so that, just as Christ was raised from the dead by the glory of the Father, so we too might walk in newness of life" (Rom 6:3–4). What else is Paul teaching but that all who have been baptized have been admitted to the death of Christ, as the act of baptism bears witness? It first plunges us into the water to recall the death and burial of Christ and then draws us out again, signifying nothing else than this: as Christ rose again from the dead to die no more, so we while buried in baptism are dead to the world and our former life, but when drawn out begin a new life, that is, one worthy of Christ. This the apostle himself expounds in the following verses, saying:

For if we have been united with him in a death like his, we shall certainly be united with him in a resurrection like his. We know that our old self was crucified with him so that the body of sin might be destroyed, and we might no longer be enslaved to sin. For whoever has died is freed from sin. But if we have died with Christ, we believe that we will also live with him. We know that Christ, being raised from the dead, will never die again; death no longer has dominion over him. The death he died, he died to sin, once for all: but the life he lives, he lives to God. So you must also consider yourselves dead to sin, but alive to God in Christ Jesus. (Rom 6:5–11)

In these words of Paul, clearer than the sun as they are, there is nothing which everybody cannot easily grasp except the one expression "to be dead unto sin." This expression is used by Paul in different senses. When he teaches that Christ died to sin, he means that Christ died because of sin, in order that sin might be slain. But when he says that we are dead to sin, he means that we are freed from sin and hence no more subject to it....

All the writings of the apostles are filled with this conviction: the Christian religion is nothing other than a firm hope in God through Christ Jesus and a blameless life based on the pattern of Christ as far as he gives it to us. It is plain, therefore, that repentance is not only knowledge and denial of self, but watching out for the self, so as always to have something to hope for while you walk in hope and to have something to fear, namely, a relapse into sin.[17] This also is clear: it is not repentance but hope in Christ that washes away sin, and repentance is being on guard lest you fall back into the ways you have condemned.

Many obstacles seem to prevent us from hoping that blamelessness can be preserved. First: "Everyone is a liar" (Ps 116:11), and where lying flourishes all things are depraved. Then: "For all of us make many mistakes" (Jas 3:2), and as many as offend, also sin (Luke 17:1–2). Therefore, since we all offend in many ways, we all sin in many ways. Furthermore John declares: "If we say that we have no sin, we deceive ourselves, and the truth is not in us" (1 John 1:8). How, therefore, can we be saved, even when Christ has been given to us, since he demands a new life and different behavior, whereas we find ourselves constantly falling back into our old ways?

Here it is a hard task to satisfy some wise and learned persons. They have the clearest testimony of scripture on both sides: first, that the redemption brought by Christ is mighty and effective for all that pertains to salvation, and second, that blamelessness is so uniformly demanded. Two difficulties appear then to follow: one, that those who dauntlessly and constantly inculcate faith in Christ seem to be traitors to a zeal for blamelessness; the other, that seeing blamelessness so insistently demanded, they begin to doubt how much Christ can do. These persons, therefore, are very hard to satisfy; they do not possess that understanding which faith in Christ has given to the pious, and hence they do not grasp that which is spoken spiritually. For piety is a matter of fact and experience, not of speech or knowledge.

Abraham knew that the voice of God which bade him slay the son through whom a holy posterity had been promised was the voice of him who had made the promise (Gen 22:1–14). Even though human reason might fairly have maintained something else (namely, that it was the voice of the tempter, the devil, saying: "How could it be that he should bid you slay him whom he had just given you for raising up a posterity?"), he girds himself with unshaken faith, arranges the wood for the fire, though inexperienced as either lector or priest he binds the loved and tender form, draws the sword with hardly less pain surely than if he were drawing it through his own heart, and raises it (oh, with what trouble of soul) over the blameless neck so often covered with his kisses. All of that was the work of God alone, that he might be marvelous in our eyes. For if God had not so impressed himself upon the understanding of Abraham that he had no doubt the voice was God's, the command would have been given in vain.

As that voice was known to Abraham alone as the voice of God, while everybody else would have thought it the voice of an impostor, so the things that I am going to say about faith in Christ and Christian blamelessness will not be understood by those whose faith is a matter of teaching rather than of experience. For I see them at once scoff and say: "I have faith; it is you who lack it; why do you judge me?"...When Paul magnified grace so highly, there were not lacking persons to snarl, as some also do today: "If the goodness and bounty of the grace of God are made manifest in my sin, what forbids my sinning almost without limit, that the bounty of God may become known to all?" And again: "Should we continue in sin in order that grace may abound?" (Rom 6:1). He replied to them in the way I quoted a little while ago from chapter six of Romans. On the other hand, when he saw that some were beginning to have confidence in themselves because the law so emphatically demands blamelessness, he says that Christ is of no use to us if righteousness come from our works (Gal 2:16) and that grace through Christ is of no avail if salvation be due to works (Rom 11:6). Placed, therefore, in this dilemma, he shows his true self and gives us an example from which we can learn what really happens to those who trust in Christ: through faith they are sure of salvation but through the weakness of the flesh are constantly sinning, though their sins are not imputed to them as such because of their faith....

CONFESSION

The truly sacred writings know of no other confession than that by which we come to know ourselves and to throw ourselves upon the mercy of God, according to the word of the prophet: "I said, I will confess my transgressions to the Lord; and you forgave the guilt of my sin" (Ps 32:5). As, therefore, it is God alone who remits sins and puts the heart at rest, so to God alone ought we to ascribe the healing of our wounds, to him alone display them to be healed. For who would ever uncover a wound to anyone but the physician or the person from whom they hoped to obtain helpful advice? So is it with confession: it is God alone who heals our hearts; to him alone, therefore, is the wound to be disclosed.

If you do not yet know the physician or you are unsure where he dwells, no one forbids you to unbind your wound before a wise counselor and to beg for advice. If the counselor is wise and faithful, you will be referred to a physician skilled enough to sew up your wound. I will now explain the parable. Those who do not know the physician are those who have not yet come to a right knowledge of grace through Christ and yet, owing to the nemesis of conscience, are seeking to lay down the burden by which they are oppressed.

The sage and faithful counselor is the minister of the word of God who, like the good Samaritan, pours wine and oil into our wounds (Luke 10:34). The wine signifies the sharpness of repentance that we feel when we are set before our own eyes in order to learn about ourselves or when we are dragged in spite of our resistance to a knowledge of our hypocrisy. It is a bitter and sharp thing to realize that you are evil within to the very core; it is a still more bitter thing that you cannot deny your wickedness; it is the most bitter thing of all when you realize that you are dead and that your hopes have failed. Then the wound begins to burn. At this moment the minister of the word should pour in oil, that is, Christ, who is anointed beyond all with the oil of gladness. The minister should show us that which grace has bestowed upon us through Christ. When we have learned this, we can no longer be kept from hastening to Christ.

Auricular confession,[18] then, is nothing but a consultation, in which we receive from the ones appointed by God to offer us the law from their lips advice as to how we can secure peace of mind. Behold the keys,[19] therefore, behold the gospel, of which enough has been said. The minister of the word evangelizes you; and when you have been evangelized, that is, when you have received Christ, you are absolved and delivered from the burden of sin, and this relief you feel in your heart even if no priest pronounces the words of any formula over you. Nonsense and sheer trumpery, therefore, are the promises of the papists concerning the keys. In the same category belong the doctrines of certain reckless persons[20] who have asserted that you are made certain [of forgiveness] by the keys. Unless you are certain within yourself through faith, the minister will say in vain that you are free. For the minister can no more make a person sure by words alone than the minister can make an elephant of a fly by saying to the fly: "You are an elephant." You or the minister may teach and expound the meaning of the gospel, but it is done in vain unless the Lord gives inward teaching. For how many are there who hear and do not receive it!

What is the reason they do not receive it? God has not drawn them (John 6:44). As soon as God draws them, they leap over to him without your help. Unless we have this certainty of faith, we will be absolved a thousand times by the priest in vain because afterward we remain in despair and unbelief....In a word, those make sufficient confession who trust in God,...who praise him and give thanks for blessings bestowed,...who acknowledge their sins and deplore them before the Lord,...and who fervently pray for forgiveness with the help of other faithful believers. Those make sufficient confession who are so minded and have no need of any priest....Let us, therefore, confess frequently to the Lord, let us begin a new life frequently, and if there is anything not clear, let us go frequently to a wise scholar who looks not at the pocketbook but at the conscience!

41. Oldest Order for Confirmation in Strasbourg, after 1549

Confirmation was not considered a sacrament by Protestant reformers as it had been in the Middle Ages, but a rite of confirmation was nonetheless introduced by Martin Bucer in Strasbourg and Hesse. From there it spread to other Protestant areas, including England, where an order for confirmation was printed in *The Book of Common Prayer.* The exact date of its origin in Strasbourg is not known, and documents testifying to its practice in that city come from the period after Bucer was forced to leave for England in 1549. The oldest document is an order for confirmation from the parish of St. Nicholas, whose pastor, Johann Marbach, was president of the church assembly from 1552 to 1581.

For Protestants, the purpose of confirmation was to acknowledge the ability of older children to make a public declaration of their faith and thus to demonstrate their readiness to receive the Lord's Supper. In some locations the ritual included a blessing of the Holy Spirit that was conveyed by an act that was also part of the medieval sacrament, the imposition of the minister's hands on the heads of the confirmands. Bucer was not the first reformer to advocate the catechetical instruction of children, but his advocacy of a regular confirmation ceremony and his designation of this service along with the blessing of marriages and the setting apart of ministers as "sacramental ceremonies" have connected his name historically to the Protestant adaptation of confirmation. The church orders (constitutions and directives) written in 1539 for Hesse under Bucer's leadership contain a rationale and guidelines for confirmation that antedate the oldest extant order from Strasbourg. From all of these texts it is clear that the introduction of a Protestant confirmation was one response to the demand of radical reformers like the Anabaptists for a more committed and disciplined Christian community.

The oldest Strasbourg order is translated from Hubert, *Die Strassburger liturgischen Ordnungen im Zeitalter der Reformation*, 132–39.

THE CONFIRMATION OF CHILDREN

Among other reasons why the Anabaptists reject the baptism of infants and young children is this: because of it, discipline and order have deteriorated in the churches and cannot be restored until infant baptism is abolished. They argue as follows: Although everyone was baptized as a child, faith is not something for everybody (Matt 22:14: "For many are called but few are chosen"). Therefore, willing obedience and submission to the discipline of the churches have been lost and no distinction can be made between committed true Christians and false believers, who are Christians in name only. They live openly in sin and with vices that have been forbidden, but they cannot be excommunicated as the custom was formerly in the churches. As a consequence, everyone wishes to be called a Christian because of the baptism they have received. If, however, baptism is held in reserve and delayed until every one reaches the age of understanding and if only those are baptized who beforehand make a public confession of their faith and submit willingly to the discipline and penalties of the church, they could be held accountable from that point on and warned and then punished according to the teaching of Christ if they fall into sin and wrongdoing.

Infant baptism, however, is precious and unjustly blamed by them. The fault lies not with it but with the papacy and with we who are called evangelicals, and even with the Anabaptists themselves, all of whom have neglected the catechism and failed to require its use. Now when children are grown and have reached the age of understanding, they are not required to make a public declaration of their faith before the church or to submit to the discipline of the church with all other Christian people. As a result, young people have been spoiled and reared with no fear of God. They do not know the fundamentals of the Christian religion, nor can they recite them. With such coarse and untrained people the pastors are able to establish only a minimum of order and discipline so that public vices and sins can be prevented.

For the people of God in the Old Testament and for the earliest Christian churches after the time of the apostles, it was the custom, after children were circumcised or baptized, before they came of age diligently and earnestly to provide for their instruction, either in the law by the Levites in their synagogues or in the main articles of Christian doctrine by catechists as soon as the children could understand. Then either during the three great festivals at the temple in Jerusalem, or for the baptized children in the parishes and churches where they had been baptized, they made a public profession. After that, Jewish children through the sacrifices and ceremonies and Christian children through the imposition of hands and Christian prayer were received into the people of God and the Christian community and confirmed therein.

We should again establish this Christian and necessary ceremony in the churches. After baptized children have learned the catechism, they should be publicly presented to the church; after they have made their profession and willingly submitted to the discipline and obedience of the church, they should be commended to the Lord our God and to his beloved congregation through the imposition of hands and solemn prayer. So it has been done previously in the parish church of St. Nicholas.

ORDER FOR THE CONFIRMATION OF CHILDREN IN THE PARISH OF ST. NICHOLAS

(1) In the week before the Sunday on which the children are to be presented, they should all come to the church for an hour every day and recite the entire catechism in order, so that with so much practice they will not stumble. Then on Sunday during the sermon the pastor shall announce that in the afternoon some children who have learned their catechism will make public profession of their faith. The congregation should make every effort to attend, but especially the parents and the godparents, who promised on behalf

of the children at their baptism that they would make this public profession before the congregation when they had grown up and reached the age of understanding.

(2) At one o'clock in the afternoon a first signal is given by sounding the bell for fifteen minutes. After that the minister reads from the altar two or three chapters of the Bible with the summaries of Veit Dietrich.[21]

(3) After the reading, the gathering bell is sounded. Meanwhile the boys and girls who are to be presented have arrived, and they should now take their place in orderly fashion as decided earlier in the week.

(4) When the gathering bell has fallen silent, the whole congregation that is present sings the hymn "Come Holy Spirit." From the altar the pastor then offers the opening prayer: "Almighty God, merciful Father, who has given your holy angels...," followed by the Lord's Prayer.

(5) The pastor says: "Dear friends, you heard in the morning sermon why we are gathered here. We are presenting your children to make a public profession of their faith, that is, what they believe about God and the true Christian religion. If their profession is correct and conforms to the divine scripture, then we will commend them with our prayer to almighty God, the Father of our Lord Jesus Christ. Therefore, let us sit quietly without disturbing anyone and listen intently."

(6) The pastor moves then from the altar to where the children are and addresses them together: "My dear children, you were born of Christian parents, who through holy baptism have incorporated you, like all other children, into the church and our Lord Jesus Christ and together with your godparents promised that they would bring you up in the fear of God. They also promised to teach you, as soon as you were capable of understanding, the ten commandments, the creed, the Lord's prayer, and all other matters it is necessary for a Christian to believe and know. After learning all these things, they would present you to the church to make public profession of your faith and willingly submit yourselves as godly children to the discipline and justice of the church. Since the people present today have gathered to hear all of this from you, please

answer properly those things which I now ask you in order. Now, my dear child, tell me: Are you a Christian...?"

First, the pastor asks for direct answers without elaboration to the first six questions as they are printed at the beginning of the catechism. After seven or eight boys and girls have recited these, each in order, the pastor starts over with the ten commandments and also asks for the explanations of each one.

(7) After the boys and girls have recited correctly all parts of the catechism with their explanations, the pastor addresses them as follows: "My dear children, you have now correctly put into words the sum and the main articles of the Christian faith, but do not think that you know everything and have nothing further to learn or no need to study. You have merely made a beginning and laid the right groundwork for coming to the knowledge of God and true blessedness. In the first place, therefore, it is necessary for you to keep attending regular catechism instruction on Sunday so that you learn to practice what you have professed and beyond that become familiar with the list of household duties.[22] If such things are not practiced, they are easily forgotten. Once they are truly comprehended, however, they remain exceptionally useful in everything you undertake. You will be able to understand all the sermons much better, profit more from your reading of holy scripture at home, and be able to recognize and evaluate any teachings that are strange to you.

"In the second place, since there is only one Christian church that has the pure word of God and the right use of the sacraments, and seeing that through holy baptism you have been incorporated into this church and now through the laying on of hands are to be confirmed as true members of it, you will also promise to stay with the same church forever, to despise and flee the papists, and to avoid all the other sects that are opposed to sound teaching.

"In the third place, my dear children, according to the apostle, not the hearers of the law but doers of it are justified (Rom 2:13). Therefore, it is not enough for you only to know the catechism and the main articles of Christian faith, but you must do all in your power to see that everything you do or leave undone conforms to the law, so that you give no offense to anyone or set a bad example, but always be found as true and productive members of the Christian church and obedient children of God.

"Finally, since no one is without sin and even the holy children of God from time to time struggle and fall, and especially since during the growing years inexperienced youngsters are most of all in need of direction and help to keep on the straight and narrow, you should willingly and readily accept instruction and guidance at home from your parents and elders and show them due obedience and respect in all things. Whenever you sin and do wrong (may the Lord God protect you from that), you should subject yourselves to the warning and discipline of your lawful authorities and also of the church and its elders and ministers. If you are willing to do this, then answer one after the other: 'Yes sir, with the help and grace of our Lord Jesus Christ.'"

(8) The pastor turns away from the children and addresses the congregation: "Dear friends, you have now heard the profession of faith by the children presented here, and it has conformed to scripture in every way. They have also willingly submitted themselves to the church and to all of you. Therefore, from this point on accept and acknowledge them as your fellow members and as heirs of the Christian church and of that eternal life to come. Because you are ahead of them in age and understanding, you should exercise special care to see that they faithfully live out and fulfill what they have promised today before the church. Guard yourselves against any offense or careless living that would cause them to sin and lead to wrongdoing; instead, when they do sin, earnestly punish and correct them and keep them on the right path.

"If we the ministers with our office can be of help to you with appropriate passages of encouragement or admonition out of God's word, we stand always at your service. Now, so that God will bestow his grace and Holy Spirit upon all this, let us now call upon him from our hearts with solemn prayer."

The pastor with the two assistants now kneels before the altar and says aloud: "Almighty, merciful God, you alone begin all good things in us, confirm...."

At the end of this prayer, the pastor turns around toward the children, stretches out his hand over them, and says: "O Lord Jesus Christ, Son of God, you have said that we, though evil, can give good gifts to our children...."

After this prayer, the service concludes with a psalm, such as "Lord, keep us steadfast in your word,"[23] or with the Magnificat,[24] "My soul does magnify the Lord," or with something different. Then a benediction is addressed to the people and they are dismissed.

The children, however, who have been presented, are detained until all their names and the names of their parents are recorded in the parish register. Afterward they are admonished once more faithfully to attend catechism class and to learn the table of household duties and the six parts of the catechism.

This service of confirmation for children is commonly held twice a year, once in spring and once in autumn, if a sufficient number of children have learned the catechism by then.

42. Henry Bullinger, Sermon on the Purpose of the Sacraments, 1551

Not long after the death of Ulrich Zwingli in 1531, Henry Bullinger (1504–75) became the chief pastor of the young Protestant church in Zürich. Zwingli had served the town for a period of twelve years, but Bullinger presided over the Zürich church for almost half a century before he died in 1575. It was Bullinger and his colleagues who molded the German-speaking Protestants of Switzerland into a Reformed church which, after the 1549 agreement with its French-speaking counterpart in Calvinist Geneva, became a continental force in the European Reformation. Bullinger conducted an international correspondence with Protestant leaders while preaching regularly in Zürich and hosting a number of prominent exiles from the Marian persecution of English Protestants in the 1550s. His leadership and his writings became well known in England and, after the establishment of a Protestant church in England in 1559, some of his works were translated into English.

One of those works was a collection of sermons known as the *Decades* because the fifty sermons it contained were divided into five groups of ten. The first part of the *Decades,* published in Latin in 1549, was dedicated by Bullinger to his Zürich colleagues, who may have heard earlier forms of the sermons preached in the *Prophezei,* an early morning colloquium of Zürich scholars who read and exposited the

Bible in Hebrew and Greek. The first complete Latin edition of 1552 was obviously intended for well-educated readers, and it served as a theological compendium that could become a resource for the sermons of clergy who consulted it.

It was not long, however, before the *Decades* were translated into vernacular languages and began to shape Reformed belief and practice for laity as well as clergy. One subject that was especially pertinent to spiritual practice was the sacraments, and on this topic Bullinger integrated into the last decade a treatise that he had written earlier.[25] In the selection offered here Bullinger endeavors to explain the purpose of sacraments in general and illustrates that purpose specifically in the cases of baptism and the Lord's Supper.

The text is an abridged, modernized version of the English translation in the 1840 Parker Society edition of *Sermons on the Sacraments*, 100–140. That edition was in turn based on the third English edition published in 1587. A modern German text is available in BS 5, 332–91.

The chief end of sacraments is this: they are testimonies to confirm the truth. By the sacraments, the Lord in his church visibly testifies that the things now uttered by preaching the gospel and by the promises assured to the faithful from the beginning of the world are in every point brought to pass and are just as certainly true as they are declared and promised in the word of truth. Baptism is the heavenly and public witness in the church of Christ, and by it the Lord testifies that he receives us freely into favor, cleanses us from all blemishes, and in short makes us partakers and heirs of all his goodness. After the same manner, circumcision in times past was a public and heavenly testimony that God purges and adopts us; therefore Moses said: "Moreover the Lord your God will circumcise your heart and the heart of your descendants, so that you will love the Lord your God with all your heart and with all your soul, in order that you may live" (Deut 30:6). In the same way, the Lord himself, instituting the holy supper in his church, by the present signs is openly our witness that his body was certainly given for us and his blood truly shed for the remission of our sins, so that he is also that living food that feeds us to eternal life....

As the gospel is called a witness and the preachers of the gospel witnesses, even so we call sacraments witnesses of the same truth. Although the sacraments do not speak, yet are they visible, and for that reason St. Augustine calls them "visible words."[26] The preaching of the gospel, consisting of words heard with the ears, is a speaking witness, but sacraments, which consist of signs and are seen with the eyes, are speechless witnesses and, as it were, remnants and remembrances of the preaching of the gospel. Indeed, sacraments were instituted by God to the end that they might visibly confirm the ready good will of God toward us, the preaching of the gospel, and all the promises of life and salvation. In addition, sacraments were instituted as seals set and fixed to the gospel and promises made by God, seals that would testify and confirm that faith in Christ is true righteousness.

I will confirm what I have said by the writings of the apostles. Earlier I taught that there is one ground of all the sacraments in the Old Testament and in the New—with a few exceptions. Now is the time to compare both, in order to judge the force and use of our sacraments. Paul said to the Romans:

> We say "faith was reckoned to Abraham as righteousness." How then was it reckoned to him? Was it before or after he had been circumcised? It was not after, but before he was circumcised. He received the sign of circumcision as the seal of the righteousness that he had by faith while he was still uncircumcised. The purpose was to make him the ancestor of all who believe without being circumcised and who thus have righteousness reckoned to them, and likewise the ancestor of the circumcised who are not only circumcised but who also follow the example of that faith that our ancestor Abraham had before he was circumcised. (Rom 4:9–12)

All these are Paul's words, which first of all, must be expounded. Then we must seek the sense and meaning of the apostle's words and, last of all, apply them to the purpose of the sacraments.

The apostle here uses two words: "sign" and "seal." *Signum*, "sign," is more general and stretches very far; but "seal" is a word that properly pertains to the sacraments, which are seals and confirmations. All signs do not seal, because some by signification alone accomplish their purpose. But σφραγιζειν indeed means to seal for assurance and to confirm for the sake of faith or credit. For that reason σφραγις is a seal that is set to keep and to confirm our faith and promise with no danger of deceit. Here, as elsewhere very often, the Lord imitates human customs, for by setting seals we are wont to confirm our writings, covenants, and faithful promises, which beforehand we had made by words. Testimonies of scripture show that seals have always been used for this purpose. For example, when the children of Israel made a covenant with the Lord, by and by they set down their covenant in writing and sealed the writing to be a testimony of the truth as we read: "Because of all this we make a firm agreement in writing, and on that sealed document are inscribed the names of our officials, our Levites, and our priests" (Neh 9:38)....Sacraments have a greater and more effectual force than any sealed charters can have. For privileges that princes give are written on parchment and their seals are set to the parchment thus inscribed, but God imprints his seal into the very bodies of those that are his....

We may apply these things further to our sacraments. Christ, the anointed of the Lord, after he had by a guiltless and undeserved death redeemed the world from the power of Satan and was ready to ascend into heaven to the Father, called his disciples and said: "Go into all the world and proclaim the good news to the whole creation. The one who is baptized will be saved" (Mark 16:15). The preaching of the gospel lays open and abroad the great, precious, healthful, lively, bountiful, royal, and divine privilege that from children of the devil we are made the children of God, the heirs (I say) of God and joint heirs with Christ, who by the shedding of his blood purchased for us this inestimable salvation. From this grace of God none is excluded, except those who through disobedience, by their own corruption and fault, exclude themselves. Referring to the children and infants of believers, the Lord in the gospel says: "Let the little children come to me, do not stop them; for it is to such as these that the kingdom of God belongs" (Mark 10:14). Wherefore that royal, ample, and divine privilege is first by the very preaching of our Lord Christ and then by the doctrine of his apostles revealed to the world. Afterward, at the Lord's command, the same privilege was set down by the apostles and evangelists in writing. Now the Lord himself added this sacrament as a sign and seal unto his preaching and to the scriptures, ordaining baptism in the place of circumcision. Because the latter was a bloody thing and, to conclude, a sign of the blessed seed that was to come and was then revealed, it ought to be abrogated. Baptism itself, therefore, succeeding circumcision, is also a seal of the righteousness of faith, an evidence and sealed charter that God assuredly cleanses us and make us heirs of eternal life and that the whole grace of baptism pertains to them that are baptized, if they stand steadfast in true faith.

But, you will say, the infants of Christians that are to be baptized do not believe. I grant you that, but neither did the infants of the Jews believe, who nevertheless were circumcised and were in league with God and made partakers of all good gifts. True godliness bids us attribute the same to our infants. When the offspring of the Jews waxed in age and did wickedly transgress, they fell from the covenant of God. Likewise, the infants of Christians, when they come of age and commit wickedness, fall from the grace of the gospel, yet they are received again by faithful repentance into the same grace from which they fell.

Now back to our theme. Baptism, the seal of the righteousness of faith, is not set to parchment or to the writing of the gospel, but it is applied to the very bodies of the children of God and is, as it were, marked and imprinted on them. For we are wholly dipped with our bodies or wholly sprinkled with the water of baptism; it is truly a visible sealing, confirming that the true God is our God, who sanctifies and purifies. That purification and every good gift of God are owed to us as the heirs of God. Pertaining to this matter is the evident statement of Paul in his letter to the Galatians: "For in Christ Jesus you are all children of God through faith. As many of you as were baptized into Christ have clothed yourself with Christ" (Gal 3:26–27).

The supper of the Lord has the same basis: it is also a seal of the righteousness of faith. For the Son of God died, by his death redeemed believers, and his body and blood are our meat and drink unto eternal life. Indeed, this singular and excellent privilege given to the faithful is declared and set down in writing by the apostles, but it is consecrated and sealed by the Lord himself in the sacrament of his body and blood. By it he seals for us an assurance that we are justified by faith in the death of Christ, that all good gifts of Christ are communicated to us, and that we are fed and strengthened by Christ. Moreover, that the sealing might be all the more lively, he does not set the seal to written parchment, but it is brought and given to be eaten by our bodies, so that we might have a witness within ourselves that Christ with all his gifts is wholly ours if we persevere in faith. In the Gospel the Lord himself says: "So whoever eats me will live because of me" (John 6:57). But the one who eats also believes, because in the same chapter the Lord says: "I am the bread of life. Whoever comes to me will never be hungry, and whoever believes in me will never be thirsty" (John 6:35).

Now we can sum up the matter: the sacraments seal up the promises of God and the gospel. For that reason the church often mentions evidences, letters patent or charters, and seals of the preaching, the gospel, and the promises of God. The whole mystery of our salvation is renewed and continued whenever those actions instituted by God (I mean sacraments) are celebrated in the church....

If our minds are not confirmed, they waver on every side. God, therefore, framed himself according to our weakness and by his sacraments, as much as may be, upholds us, yet in such a way that we refer all the benefits of our confirmation to the Spirit and to its operation rather than to the elements. Wherefore, as we attribute confirmation to doctrine and to teachers, we likewise attribute sealing to the sacraments. In the Book of Acts we read: Paul and Barnabas returned and "there they strengthened the souls of the disciples and encouraged them to continue in the faith" (Acts 14:22). And in the first letter to the Thessalonians: "We sent Timothy, our brother and co-worker for God in proclaiming the gospel of Christ, to strengthen and encourage you for the sake of your faith" (1 Thess 3:2). Nevertheless, unless the inward force of the Spirit draws and quickens the hearts of the hearers, the outward persuasion of the teacher, though it be ever so forcible and vehement, shall avail nothing. But if the Holy Spirit does show forth might and works with the word of the preacher, the souls of the hearers are most mightily strengthened. So it is with the mystery of the sacraments. If the inward anointing and sealing of the Holy Spirit is wanting, unbelievers will consider the outward action nothing but a toy and the sacraments will perform no sealing at all. When faith, however, the gift of the Holy Spirit, precedes, the sealing of the sacraments is very strong and sure. So far I have spoken of the principal virtue of sacraments: they are testimonies of God's truth and of his good will toward us, seals of all the promises of the gospel, sealing and assuring us that faith is righteousness and that all the good gifts of Christ pertain to them that believe.

There is also another end and use of sacramental signs, namely, that they signify and in signifying represent something.... Now to signify is to show and by signs and tokens to declare and point out something. To represent, however, does not mean (as some dream[27]) to bring or to give or to make now corporally present that which was formerly taken away, but to resemble it in likeness and by a certain imitation to call it back again to the mind and to set it, as it were, before our eyes. We say that a son represents or resembles his father when, after a fashion, he expresses his father in favor and likeness of manners, such that those who see him may think they are seeing the father. In this manner sacraments stir up and help our faith, while we see outwardly before our eyes that which stirs up the mind, works in us, and warns us of our duty. Indeed, everything that we earlier comprehended in our mind is now visibly offered to our senses in a similitude, parable, type, or figure to be viewed and weighed in our minds so that mutually they help one another....

Purely out of mercy the bountiful and gracious Lord receives us into the partaking of all his good gifts and graces and adopts the faithful, so that now they are not only joined in league with God but also become the children of God. This thing is made visible to all by representation in the holy action of baptism, being instead of the sign or the very sign itself.[28] At the holy font stands the minister of God, to whom the infant is offered to be baptized and who receives and baptizes the infant into the name, or in the name of the Father, of the Son, and of the Holy Ghost. We may use both "into the name" and "in the name," for to be baptized "into the name of the Lord" is to be sealed into his virtue and power (for the name of the Lord signifies power) and into the favor, mercy, and protection of God, indeed to be grafted and as it were to be fastened, to be dedicated, and to be incorporated into God. To be baptized "in the name of the Lord" is by the commandment or authority of God to be baptized;

that is, by the commission or appointment of God the Father, the Son, and the Holy Spirit, to be received into the company of the children of God, and to be counted of God's household, so that they who are baptized are, and are called, Christians and are named with the name of God....Those, therefore, who before by grace invisibly are received by God into the society of God are visibly now by baptism admitted into the self-same household of God by the minister of God. At the same time they also receive their name, so as always to remember that in baptism they gave up their names to Christ and in like manner also received a name. In this way, by a most apt analogy, the sign itself resembles the thing signified.

In short, baptism is done by water, and water ordinarily has a twofold use: it cleanses filth, and it renews a person as it quenches thirst and cools. Thus it represents the grace of God when it cleanses the faithful from their sins and regenerates and refreshes us with the Spirit. Besides this, the minister of Christ sprinkles or rather pours water on them, or takes those who have been dipped out of the water. Those actions signify that God bountifully bestows gifts upon the faithful and that we are buried with Christ into his death and are raised again with him into newness of life. Pharaoh was drowned in the Red Sea, but the people of God passed through it safely (Exod 14:28–29). Our old Adam must be drowned and extinguished, but our new Adam must be quickened day by day and rise up again. Therefore, mortification and vivification of Christians are excellently represented by baptism.

Now in the Lord's Supper bread and wine represent the very body and blood of Christ. The reason is this: As bread nourishes and strengthens us and gives us ability to labor, so does the body of Christ eaten by faith feed and satisfy our souls and equip the whole person for all the duties of godliness. As wine is drink to the thirsty and cheers our hearts, so does the blood of our Lord Jesus drunk by faith quench the thirst of the burning conscience and fill the hearts of the faithful with unspeakable joy. In the action of the supper, the bread of the Lord is broken, the wine is poured out, for the body of our Savior was broken, that is, by all means afflicted, and his blood gushed and flowed plentifully out of his gaping wounds. We ourselves are at fault that he was torn and tormented. Our sins wounded him and we ourselves crucified him, that is, he was crucified for us, that by his death he might deliver us from death. Furthermore, we take the bread in our hands and we likewise take the cup in our hands because he said: "Take this and divide it among yourselves" (Luke 22:17). We do not lay them aside or hide them, nor do we give them immediately to others, but when we have received them, we eat and drink them, swallowing them into our bodies, and then afterward we communicate and offer them to others. Those who lawfully celebrate the Lord's Supper not only believe that Christ suffered for others but that Christ suffered also for them and liberally communicates, and has already communicated, to them all his gifts.

Therefore, as the substance of bread and wine, passing into the bowels, is changed into the substance of the body, even so Christ being eaten by the godly by faith is united with them by his Spirit, with the result that they are one with Christ and he is one with them. As meat plentifully prepared, daintily dressed, and merely observed on the table does not assuage hunger, even so, if you hear Christ reverently preached but do not believe that Christ with all his good gifts is yours, then neither the word reverently preached nor the board abundantly stored will profit you at all. It adds greatly, moreover, to the reconciling, renewing, and maintaining of friendship that we all are partakers of one bread, that we offer bread to others, and that we drink of the cup that we receive from their hands. For no other reason did the ancient fathers seem to call the supper a synaxis, that is, a communion....

From this short treatment of the analogy, I think it is plain that sacraments stir up and help the faith of the godly. As our minds comprehend and consider the benefits of God, the blessing of Christ, our redemption, and other good gifts, and while they enjoy those gifts with great pleasure of the spirit,...sacraments are also outwardly given. They visibly represent to our eyes all that the mind inwardly comprehends and upon which it meditates, and they cause it to enter all our senses. Because the entire action, which consists of the words and the rite or ceremony, is counted with the sign, our eyes see the signs and everything that is done in the whole action of the signs, all of which, as it were, do speak. Our ears hear the words and institutions of Christ; indeed, our very touching and tasting also feel and perceive how sweet and good the Lord is. Now the whole person, as if both body and soul were caught up into heaven, feels and perceives that faith is stirred up and supported and that the fruit of faith in Christ is passing sweet and comfortable.

All these things take place in those who believe, but in those who fail to believe the signs remain as they are, without life. These things are thus brought to pass by the virtue or power of faith and by the Spirit working through the lawful use of the sacraments; without faith and the Holy Spirit they are not felt or perceived. A similar efficacy or force is present in the preaching of the word of God. Where this word by parables, by examples, and by description is set forth to the hearers, the Spirit and faith shining in their minds cause them not only to hear things expounded but to see them with their eyes. In this vein Paul said: "You foolish Galatians! Who has bewitched you? It was before your eyes that Jesus Christ was pub- licly exhibited as crucified" (Gal 3:1). It is certain that Christ was nowhere either exhibited or crucified among the Galatians. Paul refers instead to the plainness of his preaching, by which things indeed were shown but with such force and efficacy as if they were laid before their eyes. The same efficacy is present in sacraments, which for that very reason were of old called visible words....

We read that St. Augustine, disputing against the Manichees, said: "People cannot be gathered together into any name of reli- gion, either true or false, unless they be knit together in some fel- lowship, or visible signs, or sacraments."[29] We acknowledge that this opinion of St. Augustine, taken from the scriptures, teaches that by sacraments we are gathered and knit together into the unity of the body of Christ and are separated from all other religions, fellow- ships, and assemblies. In addition, we are bound by them, as by an oath, to the true worship of one God and into one sincere religion, to which we openly profess that we agree and give our consent with all those who partake of the sacraments. We should mark chiefly that the gathering or knitting together into the unity of the body of Christ is twofold. Either we are joined with Christ so that he is in us and we live in him, or we are coupled with all the members of Christ, that is, with Christ's faithful servants, the catholic church itself. Furthermore, we are knit together with Christ in spirit and faith, but we are joined to the church or to the members of Christ by the unity of faith and of the Spirit and by the bond of charity, all which are the inward gifts of the Spirit that are freely bestowed on us by the Lord only, not by any creatures and not by any elements. Sacraments, therefore, visibly graft us into the fellowship of Christ and his saints—we who were invisibly grafted by his grace before we were partakers of the sacraments; but by receiving the sacraments, we do now make manifest of whose body we should be, and are, members. The Lord with his signs or marks, by his ministers, also visibly marks us for his own household and for his own people. By the scriptures we will make these things clearer.

Those who in time past became the people of God by the force of the covenant and by the grace, mercy, and promise of God were also by circumcision visibly gathered together into one church and knit together into one body. For the apostle Paul says to the Ephesians: "So then, remember that at one time you Gentiles by birth, called 'the uncircumcision' by those who are called 'the circumcision'—a physical circumcision made in the flesh by human hands—remember that you were at that time without Christ, being aliens from the commonwealth of Israel and strangers to the covenants of promise" (Eph 2:11–12). This text demonstrates that the Jews by circumcision were distinguished from other religions and fellowships, and for the same reason in another place (Rom 2:8) the word "circumcision" stands for those who are circumcised. It also explains why the name "uncircumcised" was reproachful: those that were uncircumcised were counted for ungodly and unclean persons, who had no fellowship or part or inheritance with God and the saints.

Of baptism, which was ordained in the stead of circumcision (Phil 3:2), something is said in my former sermons. The apostle sets forth plainly: "For just as the body is one and has many members, and all the members of the body, though many, are one body, so it is with Christ. For in one Spirit we were all baptized into one body—Jews or Greeks, slaves or free— and we were all made to drink of one Spirit" (1 Cor 12:12–13). We are, therefore, knit together by the sacrament of baptism into the unity of the body of Christ, so that to have broken this bond and to yield ourselves into another fellowship of religion may worthily be called sacrilege and treason. To this the apostle seemed to refer when he [implicitly] asked the Corinthians: "Were you not all baptized into the name of Christ?" (1 Cor 1:13). He was declaring that those who are baptized into the name of Christ have openly sworn and bound their faith before the church of Christ, so that now they neither can nor ought to rejoice in any other name than in the name of Christ, into whose household they are received by baptism. Therefore we are separated by baptism from all other religions and are consecrated only to Christian religion.

In the same letter Paul makes all these points regarding the supper of the Lord (1 Cor 10:14–21). When the apostle would declare to the Corinthians that it is far from all godliness, unseemly, and sacrilegious that Christians should eat in the temples things offered to idols and be partakers of the Gentiles' sacrifices, he appeals to the nature of the Lord's Supper, saying: "Flee from the worship of idols. I speak as to sensible people; judge for yourselves what I say. The cup of blessing that we bless, is it not a sharing in the blood of Christ? The bread that we break, is it not a sharing in the body of Christ? Because there is one bread, we who are many are one body, for we all partake of the one bread." In that we are partakers of one bread, he says, we do openly testify that we are partakers of the same body with Christ and all his saints....

Now note the following about what Paul says. First, for those to whom he referred as many or a multitude he now uses a word that expresses better what he means: *communion*. A communion, therefore, is nothing else but a multitude or congregation. First he said: "The bread is the partaking of the body of Christ," but now he says, "We who are many are one bread, one body," and he means we who are a multitude and a congregation or church, redeemed by the body of Christ that was given and by his blood that was shed for us. When he says "we who are many are one body," he does not say "we...are made one body," for we are not first grafted into the body of Christ by partaking of the sacraments, but instead we who were earlier ingrafted by grace invisible are now also visibly consecrated.

The sacraments, therefore, separate us from all other worship and religions; they bind and consecrate and, as it were, make us of the same body with one true God and sincere Christian religion. We, being partakers of them, openly profess that we are the members of Jesus Christ and no sane person will think to make us members of fornication and of idols.

267

That learned man Zwingli wrote something pertinent to this matter: "Sacraments stand in place of an oath, for *sacramentum* with the Latins is used for an oath. Those who use the same sacraments are one peculiar nation and a holy sworn congregation; they are knit together into one body and one people. Whoever betrays a fellow member shall perish."[30] This makes it easy to understand that sacraments put us in mind of our duty, especially if we mark in the writings of the apostle how, considering the manner of sacraments, the apostles frame their exhortations....Trees are pruned and all that which is dry, barren, and superfluous in them is cut away. Similarly, those who were circumcised were put in mind to cut away with the knife of the Spirit whatever grew up in the flesh against the law of God. This is what Moses meant when he said: "Circumcise, then, the foreskin of your heart and do not be stubborn any longer" (Deut 10:16). Likewise Jeremiah: "Circumcise yourselves to the Lord, and remove the foreskin of your hearts" (Jer 4:4). Those things that Paul taught about the celebration of Passover are so plain that there is no need to rehearse them here, and I have already treated them in the sixth sermon of my third decade. The very same apostle says: "Do you not know that all of us who have been baptized into Christ Jesus have been baptized into his death? Therefore we have been buried with him by baptism into death, so that, as Christ was raised from the dead by the glory of the Father, so we too might walk in newness of life" (Rom 6:3–4). So we are put in mind by the mystery of baptism to renounce and forsake Satan and the world, to mortify and subdue the flesh, and to bury the old Adam, so that the new person may rise up again in us through Christ.

Furthermore, the supper of the Lord reminds us of brotherly love and charity and of the unity that we have with all the members of Christ. It also warns us about the need for purity and sincerity in faith. Because we have openly professed that we are united to Christ and to all his members, we should have a special care and regard that we are not found faithless and untrue to our Lord Christ and his church and that we should not defile ourselves with foreign and strange sacrifices. We are also admonished of thankfulness, to magnify the grace of God who has redeemed us, according to that saying: "For as often as you eat this bread and drink the cup, you proclaim the Lord's death until he comes" (1 Cor 11:26).

PART NINE
Worshiping

Introduction

Although early Protestants worshiped in diverse ways, they emphatically understood public worship as a form of spirituality. Reformers could have applied to all believers that admonition which Martin Bucer addressed to those who were sick:

> But since none can acknowledge and accept the Lord as their only Savior unless they acknowledge and are ready to make use of his word and all its comfort along with the sacraments just as the Lord ordained, we must always diligently teach the sick and others we find with them how the Lord has designed to effect our salvation in the communion of his body, the church, through his word and sacraments, and how it behooves us to receive it in the very means that he has appointed.[1]

Late medieval laypeople, having turned Protestant, needed this admonition, because their spirituality had not included frequent attendance at public worship but focused instead on acts of private devotion. Protestant clergy tried to change that focus, but with limited success, if the reports of worship attendance that we have from sixteenth-century parishes are reliable indicators. In spite of disappointments, however, reformers prepared new forms of public worship that shaped the spirituality of Lutheran, Reformed, and Anglican believers for generations thereafter.

In most cases these liturgies were offered in a spirit of Christian freedom that did not require every parish or congregation to adhere without deviation to the new order. Most reformers agreed with Zwingli's introductory remarks in the first text below: "Concerning the ceremonies that accompany the supper: some people may think we have done too much, others that we have done too little. In this matter, however, every congregation may hold its own opinion, for we will not quarrel about them with anyone."[2] The challengers who thought Zwingli was doing too much were cousins of those young preachers whom Urbanus Rhegius accused of denouncing all ritual and to whom he responded: "O foolish people! As if this life could be without ritual! One must wisely distinguish between ruinous rituals and others which are optional. Those rituals that promote order in the church should be retained with propriety and not so rashly rejected, for making abrupt changes in the old rituals has always caused great dissension and discontent in Christendom."[3] That dissension would continue in Protestant churches as clergy discovered over and over the truth of Rhegius's words. Changing the order of public worship belonged to the essence of reformation, but once these changes were accepted, Protetsants handled further alterations and new ceremonies no better than their ancestors. In spite of the freedom and moderation urged by reformers, laity and clergy found it difficult to stray from the prescribed rituals without conflict and discontent.

It was important, therefore, to get the new orders right, explain them clearly to the people, and urge eager laity and clergy to subject their innovations to the law of love, as Luther tried to do in the preface to his *German Mass* (1526). Evangelical forms of worship were important not only for Protestant adults but for people of all ages, since they were all children in the sense of having to relearn the basics of worship and theology as taught by the evangelical preachers. Hence, public worship involved not only praying and preaching on the biblical text for the day, but also preaching on the catechism for adults and for children. It also included, as we have seen, the composition and singing of hymns that expressed the new theology and sometimes even paraphrased catechetical texts like the creed. Luther also devised a game for teaching children important verses of scripture, and he admonished adults not to think they were too "clever for this child's play." "In order to educate us," he said, "Christ had to become human like us; if we desire to teach children, we also have to become children with them."[4]

The polemical remarks found in these texts, however, demonstrate that the reforming of ritual was more than a child's game. Early Protestants took public worship very seriously, because in their eyes improper ceremonies and ritual had undermined the biblical faith of late medieval believers. Zwingli stated their position concisely and forcefully: "For a long time God's word has boldly and clearly shown that Christ's supper is dreadfully abused; therefore, it will be necessary to remove from it everything that does not conform to the divine word."[5] Most Protestant reformers subscribed in principle to the notion that a good tree produced good fruit, but when it came to the importance of public worship, those same reformers believed the reverse: good fruit made the tree good. Based on their experience, the way one prayed or worshiped appeared to shape belief, according to the dictum that the *lex orandi* preceded the *lex credendi*. The reformers did change worship to fit their theology, but they did so in order that the laity would internalize by worship the theology they had been taught. For the evangelical faith to stick, therefore, the old forms of worship and devotion had to be condemned and new forms created that would sustain the reformation of spirituality, in faith and deed, that early Protestants sought.

43. Ulrich Zwingli, Action or Use of the Lord's Supper, 1525

As indicated above (text no. 40), Easter Sunday 1525 was a turning point for the Reformation in Zürich. For the first time, with the approval of the city council, in place of the mass the Lord's Supper would be celebrated publicly in an evangelical manner. Utilizing the image that Martin Luther had appropriated in 1520 for his rejection of medieval sacramental life, Zwingli characterized the occasion as reclamation of the supper and its proper use after a long period of "captivity." He spared no effort, therefore, to create a new pattern of worship that would turn the medieval ritual into a service of communion that both recalled the death of Christ and engaged the gathered believers in thanksgiving for the benefits of that death. It was new in many ways: the service was held completely in German, there was no chanting or singing of hymns, both women and men had vocal parts in the service, the altar with its silver chalice and paten was replaced by a table with a cup and wooden plates. Many laypeople would have received the wine for the first time—a daunting experience according to reports from other locations. If early Protestant spirituality involved the way faith was practiced, there was no more intense reformation of spirituality than this innovative worship.

English translation of the German text in *Quellen zur Geschichte des evangelischen Gottesdienstes von der Reformation bis zur Gegenwart,* ed. Wolfgang Herbst, 105–12.

To all who believe in Christ, we who administer God's word and are pastors in Zürich offer grace and peace from God.

Dearest friends, after a long period of confusion and darkness we rejoice in the true path and light that God, our heavenly Father, has disclosed to us through his grace. We hold it now in such high regard and embrace it with such ardent desire because formerly we lived in the midst of so much destructive and dangerous turmoil. And although we were beset by countless forms of trickery that undermined both faith and love, in our opinion the worst deceptions involved the abuse of the Lord's Supper. After a long captivity we trust that by the help of God we have reclaimed the supper and reestablished its proper use, just as the children of Israel recovered the passover lamb in the time of the kings Hezekiah (2 Kgs 18:3–4) and Josiah (2 Chr 34:3–7). So much for the supper itself.

Concerning the ceremonies that accompany the supper: some people may think we have done too much, others that we have done too little. In this matter, however, every congregation may hold its own opinion, for we will not quarrel about them with anyone. All believers are well aware of the damage caused by the great number of ceremonies and how they have led many away from God. We therefore think it best to prescribe as little ceremonial and churchly custom as possible for the supper (also a ceremony, to be sure, but instituted by Christ), lest we succumb again over time to old mistakes. Nevertheless, to prevent the supper from being celebrated in a sterile and somber manner and to make concession to human weakness, we have authorized such ceremonies for the supper as you will find here. We have deemed them beneficial and appropriate to enhance to some degree the spiritual memorial of the death of Christ, the increase of faith and love for one another, the improvement of how we live, and the hindering of vices in the human heart. At the same time, we do not condemn the additional ceremonies of other churches—singing and such—which may be appropriate for them and helpful to their worship, since we trust that pastors everywhere desire conscientiously to serve the Lord and to win many people.

Moreover, since this remembrance of Christ's passion and thanksgiving for his death ought to result for Christians in a common way of life that is innocent and devout, we are prepared, in keeping with divine directives, to exclude from this supper all those who besmirch the body of Christ with intolerable spots and blemishes. Because time is short, we will explain how to do this under separate cover.[6] The grace of Christ be with you all.

PREFACE

For a long time God's word has boldly and clearly shown that Christ's supper is dreadfully abused; therefore, it will be necessary to remove from it everything that does not conform to the divine word.

This memorial is an occasion for thanksgiving and rejoicing directed to almighty God for the benefit demonstrated to us through his Son. All those who appear at this feast, meal, or thanksgiving bear witness that they belong to those who believe that they are redeemed by the death and blood of our Lord Jesus Christ. On Maundy Thursday,[7] therefore, let the young people who now faithfully acknowledge God and his word and who desire to celebrate this thanksgiving and supper assemble in front of the chancel, males to the right, females to the left, while the others remain in the archway, the balcony, and elsewhere. After the sermon unleavened bread and wine shall be placed upon a table at the front of the nave, and the action of Christ along with its meaning, that is, the words describing how he instituted this memorial, shall be recited clearly, intelligibly, and in German. Servers designated for this purpose shall carry the bread, placed on large wooden plates, from one seat to the next and allow each person to break off a mouth-sized piece and eat it. They should offer the wine around in the same way so that people do not need to move from their places.

When the distribution is finished, praise and thanks shall be offered to God with clear words in a loud, intelligible voice, and the entire congregation shall conclude the service with "amen." On Good Friday, middle-aged folk shall assemble at the aforesaid place in the nave, and the thanksgiving shall take place in the same way, the men and women separated as above. On Easter Day, likewise the elderly.

The plates and cups are made of wood so that no pomp shall reappear. We shall use this order of service, as long as it pleases our churches, four times a year: Easter, Pentecost, in the fall,[8] and at Christmas.

ACTION OR USE OF THE LORD'S SUPPER MEMORIAL OR THANKSGIVING OF CHRIST AS INSTITUTED IN ZÜRICH AT EASTER IN THE YEAR 1525

The presider or pastor turns toward the people and prays the following prayer in a voice that is loud and clear:

Almighty, eternal God, whom all creatures rightly honor, worship, and praise as their master, creator, and Father, grant to us poor sinners that with genuine devotion and faith we may offer to you praise and thanksgiving, which your only begotten Son, our Lord and Savior Jesus Christ, commanded the faithful to do in memory of his death; through the same Jesus Christ, your Son, our Lord, who lives and reigns with you in the unity of the Holy Spirit, God forever and ever. Amen.

The minister or lector says the following in a loud voice:

A reading from the first epistle of Paul to the Corinthians, the eleventh chapter:

"When you come together, it is not really to eat the Lord's Supper. For when the time comes to eat, each of you goes ahead with your own supper, and one goes hungry and another becomes drunk. What? Do you not have homes to eat and drink in? Or do you show contempt for the church of God and humiliate those who have nothing? What should I say to you? Should I commend you? In this matter I do not commend you! For I received from the Lord what I also handed on to you, that the Lord Jesus on the night when he was betrayed took a loaf of bread, and when he had given thanks, he broke it and said: 'This is my body that is for you. Do this in remembrance of me.' In the same way he took the cup also, after supper, saying: 'This cup is the new covenant in my blood. Do this as often as you drink it, in remembrance of me.' For as often as you eat this bread and drink the cup, you proclaim the Lord's death until he comes. Whoever, therefore, eats the bread or drinks the cup of the Lord in an unworthy manner will be answerable for the body and blood of the Lord. Examine yourselves, and only then eat of the bread and drink of the cup. For all who eat and drink without discerning the body eat and drink judgment against themselves" (1 Cor 11:20–29).

Here the ministers say with the whole congregation: Praise be to God.

Now the pastor says the first line of the following hymn of praise, and the people—men and women—speak the next verses alternately, one after the other.

Pastor: Glory be to God on high!

Men: And peace on earth!

Women: To all people of good will!

Men: We praise you, we bless you.

Women: We worship you, we glorify you.

Men: We give thanks to you for your great glory and goodness, O Lord God, heavenly king, Father almighty!

Women: O Lord, your only begotten Son, Jesus Christ, and the Holy Spirit.

Men: O Lord God, lamb of God, Son of the Father, who takes away the sin of the world, have mercy upon us!

Women: You who take away the sin of the world, receive our prayer!

Men: You who sit at the right hand of the Father, have mercy upon us.

Women: For you alone are holy.

Men: You alone are the Lord.

Women: You alone, O Jesus Christ, with the Holy Spirit, are most high in the glory of God the Father.

Men and women: Amen.

Now the minister or reader says: The Lord be with you.

The people respond: And with your spirit.

The reader says the following: A reading from the Gospel of John, the sixth chapter.

The people respond: Praise be to God.

The reader begins as follows:

"Very truly, I tell you, whoever believes has eternal life. I am the bread of life. Your ancestors ate the manna in the wilderness, and they died. This is the bread that comes down from heaven, so that one may eat of it and not die. I am the living bread that came down from heaven. Whoever eats of this bread will live forever; and the bread that I will give for the life of the world is my flesh. The Jews then disputed among themselves, saying: 'How can this man give us his flesh to eat?' So Jesus said to them: 'Very truly, I tell you, unless you eat the flesh of the Son of Man and drink his blood, you have no life in you. Those who eat my flesh and drink my blood have eternal life, and I will raise them up on the last day; for my flesh is true food and my blood is true drink. Those who eat my flesh and drink my blood abide in me, and I in them. Just as the living Father sent me, and I live because of the Father, so whoever eats me will live because of me. This is the bread that came down from heaven, not like that which your ancestors ate, and they died. But the one who eats this bread will live forever.' He said these things while he was teaching in the synagogue at Capernaum. When many of his disciples heard it, they said, 'This teaching is difficult; who can accept it?' But Jesus, being aware that his disciples were complaining about it, said to them, 'Does this offend you? Then what if you were to see the Son of Man ascending to where he was before? It is the spirit that gives life; the flesh is useless. The words that I have spoken to you are spirit and life. But among you there are some who do not believe'" (John 6:47–64).

Then the reader kisses the book and says: Praise and thanks be to God, who desires to forgive all our sins according to his holy word.

The people say: Amen!

Now the first minister starts with the first line: I believe in one God.

Men: The Father almighty.

Women: And in Jesus Christ, his only-begotten Son, our Lord.

Men: Who was conceived by the Holy Ghost.

Women: Born of the Virgin Mary.

Men: Suffered under Pontius Pilate, was crucified, died, and was buried.

Women: He descended into hell.

Men: On the third day he rose again from the dead.

Women: He ascended into heaven.

Men: And sits at the right hand of God the Father almighty.

Women: From there he shall come to judge the living and the dead.

Men: I believe in the Holy Spirit.

Women: The holy, universal Christian church, the communion of saints.

Men: The forgiveness of sins.

Women: The resurrection of the body.

Men: And the life everlasting.

Men and women: Amen.

Then the minister says:

Dearly beloved, according to the order and institution of our Lord Jesus Christ, we now desire to eat the bread and drink the cup that he has commanded us to use in commemoration, praise, and gratitude for the death he suffered for us and for the blood that he shed in order to wash away our sin. Let everyone recall, therefore, in keeping with the word of Paul, how much comfort, faith, and assurance we have in the same Jesus Christ our Lord, lest anyone who is not a believer pretend to be one and so be guilty of the Lord's death, and lest anyone commit offense against the whole Christian congregation, which is the body of Christ.

Kneel, therefore, and pray:

Our Father in heaven, hallowed be your name. Your kingdom come. Your will be done on earth as in heaven. Give us our daily bread. Forgive us our debts, as we also forgive our debtors. And lead us not into temptation, but deliver us from evil.

The people say: Amen.

Now the minister prays further:

O Lord, God Almighty, by your Spirit you have made us in unity of faith into your one body and have commanded that body to give you praise and thanks for the beneficent and undeserved gift of the death of your only begotten Son, our Lord Jesus Christ, for our sins. Grant that we may receive the same so faithfully that we do not by any pretense or falsehood incite to anger you who are the truth that cannot be deceived. Grant also that we might live blamelessly as becomes your body, your servants, and your children, so that those who do not yet believe may acknowledge your name and glory. Preserve us, Lord, so that your name and honor are never besmirched because of the way we live. Lord, constantly increase our faith, that is, our trust in you, who live and reign, God in eternity. Amen.

The way Christ instituted this supper.

The minister reads as follows:

"Jesus on the night when he was betrayed took a loaf of bread, and when he had given thanks, he broke it and said: 'This is my body that is for you. Do this in remembrance of me.' In the same way he took the cup also, after supper, saying: 'Drink from it, all of you. This cup is the new covenant in my blood. As often as you do that, you do it in remembrance of me.' For as often as you eat this bread and drink the cup, you proclaim the Lord's death."[9]

Then the designated ministers carry round the unleavened bread. The faithful take a piece or a mouth-sized bite with their own hands or let the minister offer the morsel to them. After the ministers with the bread have finished their round and all have eaten a piece, other ministers follow with the cup and in the same manner give it to everyone to drink. All of this should take place with honor and propriety as befits the church of God and the supper of Christ.

After the people have eaten and drunk, thanks are returned according to the example of Christ by using Psalm 113, and the shepherd or pastor begins:

Pastor: Praise the Lord. Praise, O servants of the Lord; praise the name of the Lord.

Men: Blessed be the name of the Lord from this time on and forevermore.

Women: From the rising of the sun to its setting the name of the Lord is to be praised.

Men: The Lord is high above all nations, and his glory above the heavens.

Women: Who is like the Lord our God, who is seated on high, who looks far down on the heavens and earth?

Men: He raises the poor from the dust, and lifts the needy from the ash heap.

Women: To make them sit with princes, with the princes of the people.

Men: He gives the barren woman a home, making her the joyous mother of children.

Then the pastor says: We give you thanks, O Lord, for all your gifts and blessings, you who live and reign, God in eternity.

The people respond: Amen!

The pastor says: Depart in peace!

44. Martin Luther, Preface to German Mass and Order of Service, 1526

As the evangelical movement began to affect parish life in Saxony, Martin Luther and his colleagues finally decided that guidelines for teaching and worship should be available in German to pastors and laity. In November 1524 Luther had written to the pastor in Zwickau, Nicholas Hausmann, that he desired a German mass more strongly than he could promise to work on the project.[10] Luther had already provided Hausmann with a revision of the mass that was mostly in Latin, the *Formula Missae* (1523), which Luther mentions below. By the fall of 1525, however, he had crafted a German order of service that was used for the first time on October 29 in the parish church at Wittenberg. At the end of the year this order was published, and it became the regular form of worship in the town.

The other parishes throughout Electoral Saxony[11] were also ripe for a new German order of service. On October 31, 1525, Luther described the state in which parishes found themselves after the social and religious upheaval caused by the Peasants' War earlier in the year: "Everywhere the parishes are in such poor condition. No one contributes anything, no one pays for anything, mass fees have been abolished, and there are either no rents or they are too small. The commoner pays so little attention and respect to preachers and pastors that in a short time there will not be a parsonage, a school, or a pulpit functioning, and thus God's word and worship will perish."[12] Luther asked Elector John to authorize an inspection of the parishes in order to put them on a firm financial and religious footing, "so that, if it be God's will, the ordinances concerning souls—as, for instance, the higher schools and the worship—will not be obstructed by need and neglect of the poor stomach."[13] Luther's request shows that he was concerned not only about Sunday worship but also about education. For that reason he also began to preach on parts of the catechism, and in 1529 the *German Catechism*, now commonly called the *Large Catechism*, was published as a companion to the *German Mass*.

The concern for education is also expressed in the preface to the *German Mass* and takes up about one-third of the text. Luther's program to repopulate the parishes with more serious Christians depended on both worship and education. Although the general structure of the mass was retained, believers would deepen their faith by hearing and reciting German texts and singing German hymns. Luther expressed the hope that eventually he would have enough "earnest Christians" who would gather for an informal evangelical service and who could also be held accountable for the kind of lives they led. In the meantime, however, Luther contented himself with a German order of service for everyone and encouraged colleagues in other places to create their own.

English translation of the preface is based on the German texts in Clemen 3, 294–99, and in *Martin Luther Taschenausgabe* 3, 116–23. For the order of service in English, see LW 53, 61–90.

First of all, for God's sake I would say to all those who see our order of service and wish to follow it: Do not turn it into an inflexible law that would bind consciences or take them captive, but in the spirit of Christian freedom adapt it as you see fit in whatever way and for however long the circumstances require. We are not publishing this order so that we can be disciplinarians or legislators for others, but because the demand for German masses and services is widespread and people are complaining about the confusing variety of new masses and the fact that every place is creating its own. Some of the authors have good intentions, but others are full of presumption and make innovations so that they stand out and appear to be better than ordinary teachers. That always happens with Christian liberty. Very few use it to promote the honor of God and the benefit of their neighbors; instead, most people exploit it for their own benefit and pleasure.

Although the exercise of this freedom is left to everyone's conscience and is not to be hindered or forbidden, nevertheless we must ensure that this freedom remains a servant of love and of our neighbors. Where people are confused and offended by so many different practices, however, we should limit our freedom and do everything in our power so that we facilitate their worship by what we do or leave undone instead of offending them. Although external orders of service do not affect our conscience before God, they may yet be of use to the neighbor, and as love requires and St. Paul teaches (1 Cor 1:10; Phil 2:2), we should strive to be of one mind and, as far as possible, observe the same rites and ceremonies, just as all Christians have the same baptism and the same sacrament[14] (Eph 4:1–6), for nobody has received a special one from God.

I do not mean, however, that those who already have good orders or by the grace of God can make better ones should give up theirs for ours. I do not think that all of Germany should adopt our Wittenberg order. It has never been the case that all clergy chapters, monasteries, and parishes used the same liturgical rites. Still, it would be well if the worship in every principality would be conducted in the same manner and if the order observed in a given city would also be used in the surrounding towns and villages. Other principalities are free to follow the same order of service or to add something of their own.

In short, we do not prepare this order for those who are Christians already. They need nothing of the kind, and we do not live for their sake. Instead, they live for us who are not yet Christians in order to make Christians of us. Their worship is in the spirit. But this order is necessary for those who are still becoming Christians or need to be strengthened. Insofar as they are Christians, they do not need baptism, the word, and the sacrament, for all things are theirs, but these things are necessary for them as sinners. They are also essential for young and uninstructed folk, who must be trained and educated daily in God's word. They should become so well versed in the Bible that they can account for their faith and with time be able to teach others and to increase the kingdom of Christ. To do this, one must read, sing, preach, write, and compose. And if it would help, I would have all the bells pealing and the organs playing—have everything ringing that can make a sound. The worship of the papists wreaks so much destruction because on the one hand they turn it into laws, works, and merits, while on the other hand they suppress faith. They do not use worship to train the youth and uninstructed people in the scriptures and God's word, but clutch their services to themselves and declare them useful and necessary for their salvation. That is the devil at work! The early Christians did not construct or institute worship for that purpose.

Now there are three kinds of divine service or mass. First, the Latin mass that we published earlier under the title *Formula Missae*.[15] I do not intend to discard or change this service. In the form that we have used it up to now it is available for us to use whenever we please or have reason to do so. In no way do I wish to remove Latin from the service, because I have great concern for our youth. If Greek and Hebrew were as familiar to us as Latin and had as many fine melodies and songs as Latin has, I would (if I could) celebrate mass, sing, and read on successive Sundays in all four languages: German, Latin, Greek, and Hebrew. I strongly disagree with those who cling to one language and despise all others. I would rather train young people and others who could be of service to Christ in foreign lands and be able to converse with people there, lest we become like the Waldensians in Bohemia,[16] who have so entrenched their faith in their own language that they cannot speak understandably with others unless others learn their language first. In the early days of the church the Holy Spirit did not operate this way. He did not wait until all the world came to Jerusalem and studied Hebrew but bestowed manifold tongues on the office of ministry so that the apostles could be understood wherever they went. I prefer to follow this example. Moreover, it makes sense to train young people in many languages, for who knows how God may use them in years to come! For this purpose our schools were founded.

The second is the German mass and the services of worship that we are dealing with here and that were instituted for the unschooled laity. We should allow these services to be celebrated publicly in the churches for all the laity, many of whom do not yet believe and are still not Christians. They stand around and gape, hoping to see something new, as if we were holding a service among Turks or pagans in a public square or in a field. Here there is not yet a well-organized congregation that is certain enough of its faith for Christians to be guided by the gospel. Instead, they have to be publicly attracted to the faith.

The third kind of service is a truly evangelical order that should not be celebrated publicly for just anyone who might attend. Rather, it is for those who want to be Christians in earnest and profess the gospel with words and deeds. They should sign in and meet somewhere in a house to pray, to read, to baptize, to receive the sacrament, and to do other Christian works. Those who do not lead Christian lives could then be discerned, reproved, corrected, cast out, or excommunicated according to the rule of Christ (Matt 18:15–17). One could also solicit a general offering that would be given voluntarily and distributed to the poor, according to St. Paul's example (2 Cor 9:5). There would be little need of elaborate music. One could celebrate baptism and the sacrament in a fine, efficient manner and orient everything toward the word, prayer, and love. A good, short catechism[17] on the creed, the ten commandments, and the Lord's prayer would be useful. In a nutshell, if one had the kind of people who wanted to be Christians in earnest, the rules and rubrics would quickly be in place.

As yet, however, I am not ready to establish or provide directions for such a congregation or assembly. I do not yet have the people for it, nor do I see very many who are pressing for it. If it happens, however, that people push me to do it and I am not able to refuse with a good conscience, I will happily do my part and help as best I can. Until then the two above-mentioned orders must suffice. Meanwhile, besides preaching, I will help to promote the public service, to educate young people, and to call and attract others to the faith, until Christians who earnestly love the word find each other and join together. If I try to force the matter, it might lead to an uproar and more confusion. We Germans are an unruly and uncultured people with whom it is hard to start anything unless it is a dire necessity.

Now let us move on in God's name. First, the German service needs a clear, simple, and effective catechism. Catechism is the instruction by which pagans who want to be Christians are taught what they should believe and know, do and leave undone, according to the Christian faith. For that reason candidates who had been admitted for instruction and learned the faith prior to their baptism were called catechumens. I cannot organize this instruction any better than it has been arranged since the beginning of Christendom and retained until now in these three parts: the ten commandments, the creed, and the Lord's prayer. These three texts contain simply and briefly everything that a Christian needs to know. As long as no separate assembly is set apart [within the parish], instruction should be given from the pulpit at stated times or daily, as needed, and repeated or read aloud evenings and mornings at home for the children and servants in order to train them as Christians. They should not only memorize the words as before, but they should also be asked to tell what each part means and how they understand it. If everything cannot be covered in one session, let one point be taken up today and another tomorrow. If parents or guardians refuse to take on this task, either by themselves or with the help of others, there will be no catechetical instruction unless, as indicated above, a separate assembly is established.

The catechumens should be questioned in the following way:

What do you pray?

Answer: The Lord's prayer.

What do you mean when you say "Our Father in heaven"?

Answer: God is not an earthly but a heavenly Father, who will make us rich and blessed in heaven.

What is meant by "Hallowed be your name"?

Answer: We should honor God's name and use it with care so that it is not profaned.

How do we dishonor God's name?

Answer: When we, who should be his children, do what is evil and teach and believe what is false.

In the same way ask what is meant by the kingdom of God, how it comes, what is meant by the will of God, by daily bread, and so on.

For example, in the creed:

What do you believe?

Answer: I believe in God the Father...from beginning to end.

After that article by article, as time permits, one or two articles at a time, for instance:

What does it mean to believe in God the Father almighty?

Answer: It means for the heart to trust in God completely and confidently to expect from God grace and goodwill, help and comfort, now and forever.

What does it mean to believe in Jesus Christ the Son?

Answer: It means for the heart to believe that we would all be eternally lost if Christ had not died for us. Continue in this way for every article.

Likewise with the ten commandments: ask what is meant by the first, the second, the third, and the other commandments. You may take these questions from our *Little Prayer Book*,[18] in which the three parts are briefly explained, or compose other questions until all Christian teachings are embraced by the heart in two parts, as if they were placed in two purses named faith and love. Faith's purse should have two compartments. Into one we put the teaching that we have all been corrupted by Adam's sin; we are therefore sinners and stand condemned (Rom 5:12; Ps 51:5). Into the other we put the teaching that through Jesus Christ we are all redeemed from that corruption, sin, and condemnation (Rom 5:15–21; John 3:16–18). Love's purse should also have two compartments. Into the first we place the teaching that we should be servants to everyone and do good to all, even as Christ has done for us (Rom 13:8–10). Into the second, the teaching that we should gladly bear and endure all evil.

When children begin to understand this, they should regularly bring home verses of scripture from the sermon and recite them at mealtime for their parents, as they used to do with their Latin. Then they should put these verses into the purses as if they were coins of different value. For instance, faith's purse is for guilders or gold coins. In the first compartment put: "Therefore, just as sin came into the world through one man and death came through sin" (Rom 5:12) and

"Indeed, I was born guilty, a sinner when my mother conceived me" (Ps 51:5). Those verses are two Rhenish guilders for the first compartment, and in the other compartment put these Hungarian guilders:[19] "[Jesus our Lord] was handed over to death for our trespasses and raised for our justification" (Rom 4:25) and "Here is the lamb of God that takes away the sin of the world!" (John 1:29). That makes two good Hungarian guilders for the second compartment.

Love's purse is for silver coins. In the first compartment put the verses about doing good: "Through love become slaves to one another" (Gal 5:13) and "Just as you did it to one of the least of these who are members of my family, you did it to me" (Matt 25:40). That makes two silver coins for the first compartment. In the second put these verses: "Blessed are you when people revile you and persecute you and utter all kinds of evil against you falsely on my account" (Matt 5:11) and "For the Lord disciplines those whom he loves and chastises every child whom he accepts" (Heb 12:6). These verses are two Schreckenberger[20] for the second compartment.

Nobody should think he or she is too clever for this child's play. In order to educate us, Christ had to become human like us; if we desire to teach children, we also have to become children with them. Would to God that we engaged in such child's play more often, for then we would soon notice a precious store of Christians whose souls were rich in scripture and the knowledge of God. They would be adding compartments for all the main topics of theology[21] and putting the whole of scripture in them. Otherwise, people attend church and hear a sermon every day and go home the same as they left. They imagine that hearing the service is enough without learning or retaining anything. Some people listen to sermons for three or four years without knowing how to explain even one article of the creed. I see that every day. Plenty of theology can be found in books, but not all of it has found its way into the heart.

45. Martin Bucer, Public Worship in Strasbourg, 1537–39

During his long period of service in Strasbourg, Martin Bucer proposed many changes in public worship. Until 1537 a great deal of variation was characteristic of the orders of service, but thereafter a more regular schedule of worship and a more standard order for the Sunday liturgy were put in place. These were published in a book that appeared in several editions beginning in 1537: *Psalms and Spiritual Songs, Liturgy and Prayers for the Blessing of Marriage, Holy Baptism, the Lord's Supper, Visitation of the Sick, and Burial of the Dead.* The title indicates that the book contained other services besides a Sunday liturgy. It also included a wide choice of hymns, and the 1539 edition added a number of psalms, twelve of which were among the metrical psalms of Clement Marot, the court poet of France, which Calvin adopted for his French congregation in Strasbourg.[22]

The entire Sunday liturgy is not reprinted here, but only the preface with two forms of public confession and absolution, with which the Sunday service began. An alternate text for confession that describes how each of the ten commandments has been broken is not included. The 1539 edition of this service book and hymnal appeared while John Calvin lived in Strasbourg and influenced the worship that he later introduced in Geneva. The text printed here is translated from Hubert, *Die Strassburger liturgischen Ordnungen im Zeitalter der Reformation,* 90–95.

Three sermons are to be heard every day: (1) At the time of early mass in the morning (after five o'clock in winter and about four o'clock in summer) assemblies are scheduled for all the parishes in such a way that a person can attend two of them. The service begins with a public confession followed by a Christian exhortation based on scripture. Next, a period of time is set aside for silent personal prayer, which is then brought to a close by the minister with an appropriate collect or with a prayer that suits the occasion and spirit. At the end the minister pronounces the benediction. The service is called morning prayer.

(2) About eight o'clock every day in summer and winter there is a sermon in the cathedral.

(3) There is an evening sermon in the cathedral at four o'clock in the summer, or earlier if suitable, and in the winter at three o'clock.

Since holy days are always misused by the common people in deplorable ways, and since God is more disgraced and profaned on those days than on any other, we do not insist that any day but Sunday be observed for the entire day as a holiday. It is desirable for everyone to sanctify the weekly day of rest by worshiping God. The other festivals that commemorate the work of our redemption—the incarnation and birth of our Lord Jesus, his passion, ascension, and the like—are observed with sermons. When those sermons are over, no one is excused from his or her labors. Actually, the community benefits every day from all that makes up a true holy day: Christian assemblies for [hearing the] word, prayer, and other spiritual activities. Nevertheless, Christmas is observed for the entire day, and that is true of a few other days as well.

Sundays are observed in the following way: In the cathedral early morning prayer is conducted as usual. Then, around six o'clock in the other parishes, the assistants deliver a sermon and exhortation to the domestic servants. Soon thereafter, when the people of each parish have arrived at the church, the pastor enters and goes before the altar table,[23] which has been placed closer to the people [than the altar against the wall] so that everybody can understand all the words. The pastor begins the service with words similar to those that follow; they can be longer or shorter as the occasion demands:

[Pastor]: Let everyone make confession to God the Lord and acknowledge with me our sin and offenses:

Almighty, eternal God and Father, we confess to you that we were conceived in unrighteousness and that our lives are full of sin and transgression. We do not perfectly trust your word or obey your holy commandments. Remember your kindness, we pray, and for your name's sake be gracious to us and forgive our iniquity, which sadly is so great.

Another confession:

Almighty, eternal God and Father, we confess and acknowledge that we were conceived and born in sin and that we are inclined to evil and sluggish to do good. We constantly transgress your holy commandments and corrupt ourselves more and more. We are sorry for this and desire your grace and succor. Have mercy on us, most gracious and merciful God and Father through your Son our Lord Jesus Christ. Increase in us your Holy Spirit, so that from the bottom of our hearts we might recognize our sin and unrighteousness, arrive at genuine repentance and regret, die wholly to them, and please you fully in a new and blessed life. Amen....

Absolution or word of comfort:

"The saying is sure and worthy of full acceptance, that Christ Jesus came into the world to save sinners" (1 Tim 1:15).

With St. Paul let all truly acknowledge this in their hearts and believe in Christ. In his name I declare to you the forgiveness of all your sins and pronounce you free of them on earth, that you may also be free of them in heaven for eternity. Amen.

From time to time the pastor may use other passages that assure us of forgiveness and of Christ's payment for our sin, such as John 3:16, John 3:35–36, Acts 10:43, or 1 John 2:1–2.

46. Selections from *The Book of Common Prayer* of the Church of England, 1559

"The Book of Common Prayer and its public worship services both embodied and promoted religious attitudes which made up a distinctly English Protestantism."[24] While most historians would agree with this statement, the question remains: which *Book of Common Prayer*? Although it is still the worship book of Episcopal and Anglican churches, the prayer book has been revised and translated many times since the first version was published in 1549. Composed and promoted in large part by Archbishop Thomas Cranmer (see text no. 12 above), it appeared early in the reign of the young king Edward VI (1547-53) after Cranmer and the reform-minded bishops finally pushed through parliament the approval of both clerical marriage and a new liturgy for communion. Parishes were ordered to use *The Book of Common Prayer* beginning on Pentecost Sunday (June 9) in 1549. Some concessions (like the use of vestments and candles, commemoration of the dead) were made to the conservative clergy who hoped to retain as many Catholic ceremonies as possible, but the prayer book was unmistakably Protestant. Under the influence of Martin Bucer, who had just arrived in England (texts no. 4, 17, 18, and 45 above), Cranmer's view of holy communion, as the mass was now called, had moved away from the Lutheran doctrine of real presence to a more Reformed spiritual view.

EARLY PROTESTANT SPIRITUALITY

Already in early 1550 Cranmer and other clergy began to discuss possible revisions, and that discussion accelerated in 1551 after the prayer book was astutely attacked by the conservative bishop Stephen Gardiner. The advice of both refugee theologians, Martin Bucer and Peter Martyr Vermigli (text no. 34 above), was solicited, and the language associated with the sacrament was substantially altered so that no real presence of Christ was implied. Words addressed to the faithful at the distribution of the elements now admonished them to eat the bread and wine in remembrance that Christ died for them and to "feed on him" in their hearts "by faith, with thanksgiving." The communion prayers were replaced by the simple words of institution, and the possibility of praying for the dead was removed.

It was the 1559 version, however, that remained a fixture of English Protestant culture throughout the religious battles of the seventeenth century when, used by high-church Anglicans and Puritans alike, it had become "a rhythm of worship, piety, and practice that had earthed itself into the Englishman's consciousness and had sunk deep roots in popular culture."[25] This 1559 version had come into use with the Elizabethan settlement after a brief return to the Catholic mass and its ceremonies under Queen Mary and her supporters. For its reinstatement as a Protestant book, the 1552 prayer book was slightly revised in order to support the cautious political stance and conservative religious views of the queen. Some words from the distribution of the elements in the 1549 book were reinserted before the new words that were retained from the 1552 edition, and the so-called black rubric was removed. Introduced in 1552, that rubric had assured communicants that their kneeling to receive the elements did not imply that the elements were being adored.

In spite of the attention given to holy communion, the worship authorized by the 1559 prayer book was noteworthy for three other things: the amount of scripture that was read; the active participation of the congregation; and the regular inclusion of basic Christian elements like prayer, confession, readings from the Bible, and the recitation of creeds.[26] Most churchgoers on Sunday morning, however, would have encountered these elements not in a communion service but in a service that combined morning prayer, parts of the ante-communion service, and a historical collection of intercessions called the litany. Cranmer had intended for English Protestants to commune weekly or at least frequently. That did not happen, even though the words of the communion service became some of the most familiar spiritual texts of the English Reformation. For that reason, part of the communion service is included among the selections below.

From *The Book of Common Prayer 1559: The Elizabethan Prayer Book,* ed. John E. Booty, 18–23, 259–65.

(1) OF CEREMONIES, WHY SOME BE ABOLISHED AND SOME RETAINED

Of such ceremonies as be used in the church and have had their beginning by human institution, some at the first were of godly intent and purpose devised and yet at length turned to vanity and superstition, some entered into the church by undiscreet devotion and such a zeal as was without knowledge. And because they were winked at in the beginning, they grew daily to more and more abuses, which not only for their unprofitableness but also because they have much blinded the people and obscured the glory of God are worthy to be cut away and clean rejected. Others there be which, although they have been devised by human hands, it is thought good to reserve them still, as well for a decent order in the church, for the which they were first devised, as because they pertain to edification, whereunto all things done in the church, as the apostle teacheth (1 Cor 14:26), ought to be referred. And although the keeping or omitting of a ceremony in itself considered is but a small thing, yet the willful and contemptuous transgression and breaking of the common order and discipline is no small offense before God.

Let all things be done among you, saith St. Paul, in a seemly and due order (1 Cor 14:40). The appointment of the which order pertaineth not to private persons, therefore no one ought to take in hand or presume to appoint or alter any public or common order in Christ's church, except they be lawfully called and authorized thereunto.

And whereas in this our time human minds are so diverse that some think it a great matter of conscience to depart from a piece of the least of their ceremonies, they be so addicted to their old customs, and again on the other side, some be so newfangled that they

291

would innovate all things, and so do despise the old that nothing can please them but that is new, it was thought expedient not so much to have respect how to please and satisfy either of these parties, as how to please God and profit them both. And yet lest anyone should be offended whom good reason might satisfy, here be certain causes rendered why some of the accustomed ceremonies be put away and some retained and kept still.

Some are put away because the great excess and multitude of them hath so increased in these latter days that the burden of them was intolerable, whereof St. Augustine in his time complained that they were grown to such a number that the state of Christian people was in worse case concerning the matter than were the Jews. And he counseled that such yoke and burden be taken away, as time would serve quietly to do it.[27]

But what would St. Augustine have said if he had seen the ceremonies of late days used among us, whereunto the multitude used in his time was not to be compared? This our excessive multitude of ceremonies was so great and many of them so dark that they did more confound and darken than declare and set forth Christ's benefits to us.

And besides this, Christ's gospel is not a ceremonial law, as much of Moses' law was, but it is a religion to serve God, not in bondage of the figure or shadow, but in the freedom of the spirit, being content only with those ceremonies which do serve to a decent order and godly discipline, and such as be apt to stir up the dull human mind to the remembrance of its duty to God by some notable and special signification whereby it might be edified.

Furthermore, the most weighty cause of the abolishment of certain ceremonies was that they were so far abused, partly by the superstitious blindness of the rude and unlearned and partly by the unsatiable avarice of such as sought more their own lucre than the glory of God, that the abuses could not well be taken away, the thing remaining still.

But now, as concerning those persons which peradventure will be offended for that some of the old ceremonies are retained still, if they consider that without some ceremonies it is not possible to keep any order or quiet discipline in the church, they shall easily perceive just cause to reform their judgments. And if they think much that any of the old do remain and would rather have all devised anew, then such persons granting some ceremonies convenient to be had, surely where the old may well be used there they cannot reasonably reprove the old only for their age without betraying[28] their own folly. For in such a case they ought rather to have reverence unto them for their antiquity, if they will declare themselves to be more studious of unity and concord than of innovations and newfangleness, which, as much as may be with the true setting forth of Christ's religion, is always to be eschewed.

Furthermore, such shall have no just cause with the ceremonies reserved to be offended. For as those be taken away which were most abused and did burden consciences without any cause, so the other that remain are retained for a discipline and order, which upon just causes may be altered and changed, and therefore are not to be esteemed equal with God's law. And, moreover, they be neither dark nor dumb ceremonies, but are so set forth that everyone may understand what they do mean and to what use they do serve. So that it is not like that they in time to come should be abused as the others have been.

And in these our doings, we condemn no other nations, nor prescribe anything but to our own people only. For we think it convenient that every country should use such ceremonies as they shall think best to the setting forth of God's honor or glory and to the reducing of the people to a most perfect and godly living, without error or superstition. And that they should put away other things which from time to time they perceive to be most abused, as in human ordinances it often chanceth diversely in diverse countries.

(2) THE ORDER HOW THE PSALTER IS APPOINTED TO BE READ

The Psalter shall be read through once every month. And because that some months be longer than some others be, it is thought good to make them even by this means.

To every month shall be appointed, as concerning this purpose, just thirty days.

And because January and March hath one day above the said number, and February which is placed between them both hath only twenty-eight days, February shall borrow of either of the months (of January and March) one day, And so the Psalter which shall be read in February must begin the last day of January and end the first day of March.

And whereas May, July, August, October, and December have thirty-one days apiece, it is ordered that the same psalms shall be read the last day of the said months which were read the day before. So that the Psalter may begin again the first day of the next month ensuing.

Now to know what psalms shall be read every day, look in the calendar the number that is appointed for the psalms and then find the same number in this table, and upon that number shall you see what psalms shall be said at morning and evening prayer.[29]

And where the 119th psalm is divided into twenty-two portions[30] and is overlong to read at one time, it is so ordered that at one time shall not be read above four or five of the said portions, as you shall perceive to be noted in this table following.

And here is also to be noted in this table, and in all other parts of the service where any psalms are appointed, the number is expressed after the great English Bible,[31] which from the 9th psalm unto the 148th psalm, following the division of the Hebrew, doth vary in numbers from the common Latin translation.[32]

(3) THE ORDER FOR THE ADMINISTRATION OF THE LORD'S SUPPER, OR HOLY COMMUNION

[Rubric[33]] So many as do intend to be partakers of the holy communion shall signify their names to the curate[34] overnight, or else in the morning afore the beginning of morning prayer, or immediately after.

[Rubric] And if any of those be open and notorious evil livers, so that the congregation by them is offended, or have done any wrong to their neighbors by word or deed: the curate having knowledge thereof, shall call them and advertise them in any wise not to presume to the Lord's table, until they have openly declared themselves to have truly repented and amended their former naughty lives, that the congregation may thereby be satisfied which afore were offended; and that they have recompensed the parties whom they have done wrong unto, or at least declare themselves to be in full purpose so to do, as soon as they conveniently may.

[Rubric] The same order shall the curate use with those betwixt whom he perceives malice and hatred to reign, not suffering them to be partakers of the Lord's table until he know them to be reconciled. And if one of the parties so at variance be content to forgive from the bottom of the heart all that the other has trespassed against them and to make amends for that they themselves have offended, and the other party will not be persuaded to a godly unity, but remain still in their frowardness[35] and malice: the minister in that case ought to admit the penitent persons to the holy communion and not them that are obstinate.

[Rubric] The table, having at the communion time a fair white linen cloth upon it, shall stand in the body of the church, or in the chancel where morning prayer and evening prayer be appointed to be said. And the priest standing at the north side of the table shall say the Lord's prayer with this collect following:

Almighty God, unto whom all hearts be open, all desires known, and from whom no secrets are hid: Cleanse the thoughts of our hearts by the inspiration of thy Holy Spirit, that we may perfectly love thee and worthily magnify thy holy name; through Christ our Lord. Amen.

[Rubric] Then shall the priest rehearse distinctly all the ten commandments, and the people, kneeling, shall after every commandment ask God's mercy for their transgression of the same, after this sort....

[Rubric] After the creed, if there be no sermon, shall follow one of the homilies, already set forth or hereafter to be set forth by common authority.[36]...

[Rubric] Then shall the priest say to them that come to receive the holy communion:

You that do truly and earnestly repent you of your sins, and be in love and charity with your neighbors, and intend to lead a new life, following the commandments of God, and walking from henceforth in his holy ways: Draw near, and take this holy sacrament to your comfort; make your humble confession to almighty God before this congregation here gathered together in his holy name, meekly kneeling upon your knees.

[Rubric] **Then shall the general confession be made in the name of all those that are minded to receive the holy communion, either by one of them, or else by one of the ministers, or by the priest himself, all kneeling humbly upon their knees:**

Almighty God, Father of our Lord Jesus Christ, maker of all things, judge of all, we acknowledge and bewail our manifold sins and wickedness, which we from time to time most grievously have committed, by thought, word, and deed, against the divine majesty, provoking most justly thy wrath and indignation upon us. We do earnestly repent, and be heartily sorry for these our misdoings. The remembrance of them is grievous unto us, the burden of them is intolerable. Have mercy upon us, have mercy upon us most merciful Father, for thy Son our Lord Jesus Christ's sake; forgive us all that is past, and grant that we may ever hereafter serve and please thee, in newness of life, to the honor and glory of thy name, through Jesus Christ our Lord. Amen.

[Rubric] **Then shall the priest, or bishop being present, stand up, and turning himself to the people, say thus:**

Almighty God our heavenly Father, who of his great mercy hath promised forgiveness of sins to all them which with hearty repentance and true faith turn unto him: Have mercy upon you, pardon and deliver you from all your sins, confirm and strengthen you in all goodness, and bring you to everlasting life, through Jesus Christ our Lord. Amen.

[Rubric] **Then shall the priest also say:**

Hear what comfortable words our Savior Christ saith, to all that truly turn to him:

Come unto me all that travail and be heavy laden and I shall refresh you (Matt 11:28). So God loved the world, that he gave his only begotten Son, to the end that all that believe in him should not perish but have life everlasting (John 3:16).

Hear also what St. Paul saith:

This is a true saying, and worthy of all men to be received, that Jesus Christ came into the world to save sinners (1 Tim 1:15).

Hear also what St. John saith:

If any one sin, we have an advocate with the Father, Jesus Christ the righteous, and he is the propitiation for our sins (1 John 2:1–2).

[Rubric] After which the priest shall proceed, saying:

Lift up your hearts.

Answer. We lift them up unto the Lord.

Priest. Let us give thanks unto our Lord God.

Answer. It is meet and right so to do.

Priest. It is very meet, right, and our bounden duty that we should at all times, and in all places, give thanks unto thee, O Lord, holy Father, almighty, everlasting God.

[Rubric] Here shall follow the proper preface, according to the time, if there be any specially appointed, or else immediately shall follow: Therefore with the angels, etc.

PROPER PREFACES

Upon Christmas Day, and Seven Days After

Because thou didst give Jesus Christ, thine only Son, to be born on this day for us, who by the operation of the Holy Ghost was made very man of the substance of the Virgin Mary his mother, and that without spot of sin, to make us clean from all sin. Therefore, etc.

Upon Easter Day, and Seven Days After

But chiefly are we bound to praise thee for the glorious resurrection of thy Son Jesus Christ our Lord: for he is the very paschal lamb, which was offered for us, and hath taken away the sin of the world, who by his death hath destroyed death, and by his rising to life again hath restored to us everlasting life. Therefore with, etc.

Upon the Ascension Day, and Seven Days After

Through thy dear beloved Son, Jesus Christ our Lord: who after his most glorious resurrection manifestly appeared to all his apostles, and in their sight ascended up into heaven to prepare a place for us, that where he is, thither might we also ascend and reign with him in glory. Therefore with, etc.

Upon Whitsunday, and Six Days After

Through Jesus Christ our Lord, according to whose most true promise the Holy Ghost came down this day from heaven, with a sudden great sound, as it had been a mighty wind, in the likeness of fiery tongues, lighting upon the apostles to teach them and to lead them to all truth, giving them both the gift of diverse languages, and also boldness with fervent zeal constantly to preach the gospel unto all nations, whereby we are brought out of darkness and error into the clear light and true knowledge of thee, and of thy Son Jesus Christ. Therefore with, etc.

Upon the Feast of Trinity Only

It is very meet, right, and our bounden duty, that we should at all times, and in all places, give thanks to thee, O Lord, almighty and everlasting God, which art one God, one Lord, not one only person, but three persons in one substance: for that which we believe of the glory of the Father, the same we believe of the Son, and of the Holy Ghost, without any difference or inequality. Therefore with, etc.

[Rubric] After which preface, shall follow immediately:

Therefore with angels and archangels, and with all the company of heaven, we laud and magnify thy glorious name, evermore praising thee, and saying: Holy, holy, holy, Lord God of hosts; heaven and earth are full of thy glory; glory be to thee, O Lord most high.

[Rubric] Then shall the priest kneeling down at God's board, say in the name of all of them that shall receive the communion, this prayer following:

We do not presume to come to this thy table (O merciful Lord) trusting in our own righteousness, but in thy manifold and great mercies. We be not worthy so much as to gather the crumbs under thy table, but thou art the same Lord, whose property is always to have mercy. Grant us therefore (gracious Lord) so to eat the flesh of thy dear Son Jesus Christ, and to drink his blood, that our sinful bodies be made clean by his body, and our souls washed through his most precious blood, and that we may evermore dwell in him, and he in us. Amen.

[Rubric] Then the priest standing up shall say as followeth:

Almighty God our heavenly Father, which of thy tender mercy didst give thine only begotten Son Jesus Christ, to suffer death upon the cross for our redemption; who made there (by his one oblation of himself once offered) a full, perfect, and sufficient sacrifice, oblation, and satisfaction for the sins of the whole world; and did institute, and in his holy gospel command us to continue, a perpetual memory of that his precious death, until his coming again. Hear us, O merciful Father, we beseech thee; and grant that we receiving these thy creatures of bread and wine, according to thy Son our Savior Jesus Christ's holy institution, in remembrance of his death and passion, may be partakers of his most blessed body and blood; who in the same night that he was betrayed, took bread, and when he had given thanks, he brake it, and gave it to his disciples, saying: "Take, eat, this is my body which is given for you. Do this in remembrance of me." Likewise after supper he took the cup, and when he had given thanks, he gave it to them, saying: "Drink ye all of this, for this is my blood of the new testament, which is shed for you and for many, for remission of sins: do this as oft as ye shall drink it in remembrance of me."

[Rubric] Then shall the minister first receive the communion in both kinds himself, and next deliver it to other ministers, if any be there present (that they may help the chief minister) and after to the people in their hands kneeling. And when he delivereth the bread, he shall say:

The body of our Lord Jesus Christ which was given for thee, preserve thy body and soul into everlasting life; and take and eat this, in remembrance that Christ died for thee, and feed on him in thy heart by faith, with thanksgiving.

[Rubric] And the minister that delivereth the cup, shall say:

The blood of our Lord Jesus Christ which was shed for thee, preserve thy body and soul into everlasting life: and drink this in remembrance that Christ's blood was shed for thee, and be thankful.

[Rubric] Then shall the priest say the Lord's Prayer, the people repeating after him in every petition.

[Rubric] After shall be said as followeth:

O Lord and heavenly Father, we thy humble servants entirely desire thy fatherly goodness mercifully to accept this our sacrifice of thanksgiving, most humbly beseeching thee to grant that by the merits and death of thy Son Jesus Christ, and through faith in his blood, we and all thy whole church may obtain remission of our sins, and all other benefits of his passion. And here we offer and present unto thee, O Lord, ourselves, our souls and bodies, to be a reasonable, holy, and lively sacrifice unto thee, humbly beseeching thee, that all we which be partakers of this holy communion, may be fulfilled with thy grace, and heavenly benediction. And although we be unworthy, through our manifold sins, to offer unto thee any sacrifice, yet we beseech thee to accept this our bounden duty and service, not weighing our merits, but pardoning our offenses, through Jesus Christ our Lord, by whom and with whom, in the unity of the Holy Ghost, all honor and glory be unto thee, O Father almighty, world without end. Amen.

[Rubric] Or this:

Almighty and everliving God, we most heartily thank thee for that thou doth vouchsafe to feed us, which have duly received these holy mysteries, with the spiritual food of the most precious body and blood of thy Son our Savior Jesus Christ, and dost assure us thereby of thy favor and goodness toward us, and that we be very members incorporate in thy mystical body, which is the blessed company of all faithful people, and be also heirs through hope of thy everlasting kingdom, by the merits of the most precious death and passion of thy dear Son. We now most humbly beseech thee, O heavenly Father, so to assist us with thy grace, that we may continue in that holy fellowship, and do all such good works as thou hast prepared for us to walk in; through Jesus Christ our Lord, to whom with thee and the Holy Ghost, be all honor and glory, world without end. Amen.

[Rubric] Then shall be said or sung:

Glory be to God on high. And in earth peace, good will toward all. We praise thee, we bless thee, we worship thee, we glorify thee, we give thanks to thee for thy great glory. O Lord God heavenly king, God the Father Almighty. O Lord, the only begotten Son Jesus Christ: O Lord God, Lamb of God, Son of the Father, that takest away the sins of the world, have mercy upon us. Thou that takest away the sins of the world, have mercy upon us. Thou that takest away the sins of the world, receive our prayer.

Thou that sittest at the right hand of God the Father, have mercy upon us. For thou only art holy: thou only art the Lord: thou only, (O Christ) with the Holy Ghost, art most high in the glory of God the Father. Amen.

[Rubric] Then the priest or the bishop, if he be present, shall let them depart with this blessing:

The peace of God which passeth all understanding, keep your hearts and minds in the knowledge and love of God, and of his Son Jesus Christ our Lord: And the blessing of God almighty, the Father, the Son, and the Holy Ghost, be amongst you, and remain with you always. Amen....

[Rubric] Upon the holy days, if there be no communion, shall be said all that is appointed at the communion, until the end of the homily, concluding with the general prayer for the whole estate of Christ's church militant here in earth, and one or more of these collects before rehearsed, as occasion shall serve.

[Rubric] And there shall be no celebration of the Lord's supper except there be a good number to communicate with the priest, according to his discretion.

[Rubric] And if there be not above twenty persons in the parish of discretion[37] to receive the communion, yet there shall be no communion, except four, or three at the least, communicate with the priest. And in cathedral and collegiate churches where be many priests and deacons,[38] they shall all receive the communion with the minister every Sunday at the least, except they have a reasonable cause to the contrary.

[Rubric] And to take away the superstition, which any person hath or might have in the bread and wine, it shall suffice that the bread be such as is usual to be eaten at the table with other meats, but the best and purest wheat bread that conveniently may be gotten. And if any of the bread and wine remain, the curate shall have it to his own use.

[Rubric]The bread and wine for the communion shall be provided by the curate and the church wardens at the charges of the parish, and the parish shall be discharged of such sums of money, or other duties, which hitherto they have paid for the same, by order of their houses every Sunday.

[Rubric] And note, that every parishioner shall communicate at the least three times in the year, of which Easter to be one, and shall also receive the sacraments and other rites, according to the order in this book appointed. And yearly at Easter, every parishioner shall reckon with his parson, vicar, or curate, or their deputy or deputies, and pay to them or him all ecclesiastical duties, accustomably due, then and at that time to be paid.

NOTES

INTRODUCTION

1. Gwenfair Walters Adams, *Visions in Late Medieval England: Lay Spirituality and Sacred Glimpses of the Hidden Worlds of Faith* (Leiden/Boston: Brill, 2007), 16.

2. Aimé Solignac, "L'apparition du mot 'spiritualitas' au moyen age," ALMA 44–45 (1983–85): 185–206.

3. LW 35, 370–71.

4. Ernest T. Campbell, "What's the Story?" (May 11, 1975), in *Sermons from Duke Chapel*, ed. William H. Willimon (Durham, NC: Duke University Press, 2005), 171.

PART ONE: PERSONAL VOICES

1. A reference to cleaning out the Augean stables, one of the twelve labors of Hercules.

2. Jupiter, the sky god responsible for lightning, is Pope Leo X, who had threatened Luther with excommunication five weeks before this letter was written. The bull of excommunication was not promulgated until January 1521.

3. William a Falconibus was the church official in Switzerland who paid support to Zwingli and other clerics that enjoyed papally endowed positions. In 1520 Zwingli renounced his right to these payments.

4. Hilary, bishop of Poitiers (315–67 CE), prominent defender of Nicean orthodoxy in the West, was exiled to Asia Minor by the emperor Constantius in 356 and allowed to return to France in 360.

5. Lucius I, bishop of Rome (253–54 CE), was sent into exile by the Roman emperor for refusing to sacrifice; after he returned, his steadfastness was praised by Cyprian of Carthage.

6. This textbook on the art of rhetoric written by Philip Melanchthon (1497–1560) was published in Basel in 1519.

7. Xylotectus was the Greek name of the humanist Johannes Zimmermann (d. 1526), a well-educated late medieval cleric in Lucerne who became Protestant and moved to Basel.

8. Johannes Reuchlin (1455–1522), German humanist and Hebrew scholar, published his Hebrew textbook, the *Rudimenta*, in 1506.

9. Heinrich Utinger (1470–1536), a member of the clerical chapter at the Great Minster who had supported Zwingli's election in 1518. *Primiz* is the first mass said by a newly ordained priest.

10. *De votis monasticis Martini Lutheri iudicium* was published in Wittenberg in February 1522.

11. In this case Exodus 20:12: "Honor your father and your mother, so that your days may be long in the land that the Lord your God is giving you."

12. Luther entered the Augustinian cloister in Erfurt on July 17, 1505.

13. Augustine of Hippo, *Confessions* 2.3.6, in CChr–SL 27, 20.

14. Hans Luther was present the first time Luther celebrated mass on May 2, 1507.

15. Luther apparently made the vow during a severe storm in 1505.

16. That is, to entice a person who is unable to keep it to take a vow of virginity by exalting it above marriage.

17. The value of a faithful, chaste, and modest wife was a topos found in classical writings and in Hebrew wisdom literature. Luther could be paraphrasing a saying attributed to Euripides (485–406 BCE): "A man's best possession is a sympathetic wife." Or he might still have in mind Sirach 26:15, Wisdom 3:13, or a verse from Proverbs 31:10–31.

18. See note 10 above.

19. Luther's excommunication was formally pronounced on January 3, 1521.

20. Margaretha Lindemann (1463–1531), born in Eisenach.

21. The Wartburg Castle near Eisenach, where Luther was being hidden by his prince, Elector Frederick of Saxony, after the Diet of Worms.

22. Hosea 4:7: "The more they increased, the more they sinned against me; they changed their glory into shame."

23. That is: do not think that my husband is doing nothing.

24. Perhaps a conflation of Luke 11:13 and Matthew 7:11.

25. Terence (193/183–159 BCE), Roman writer of comedy.

26. Ovid (43 BCE–7 CE), Roman poet.

27. Literally: "The authorities have a fiddle made of the same wood."

28. The imperial diet was the parliament of the Holy Roman Empire that met in Nuremberg in 1524.

29. A wordplay in German: *Reichstag* (imperial diet) and *reich* (rich).

30. When the diet was in session in 1524.

31. A consolidated paraphrase of Isaiah 55:10–11.

32. A reference to the Roman governor's refusal to stand up for the innocence of Jesus and allowing him to be crucified (Matt 27:24–26).

33. The diocese of Würzburg was near the western boundary of Bavaria and the Upper Palatinate.

34. An allusion to Matthew 6:26–30 and perhaps to 1 Kings 17:6.

35. As coadjutant to the bishop of Speyer in 1521, Anton Engelbrecht (d. 1557) released Bucer from his monastic vows. In 1524 Engelbrecht converted to the evangelical side and sought refuge in Strasbourg, where he served as pastor of St. Stephen's parish. Because he opposed the granting of power over religious affairs to the city council, he lost his pastorate and left Strasbourg. In 1544 at Cologne he returned to the Roman Church and two years later published a harsh attack on Bucer. Engelbrecht eventually returned to Strasbourg before his death.

36. Canon 4 of the Synod of Gangra (Asia Minor), c.340 CE, in MPL 56, 788B: "If a person claims that one should not participate in a service where a married priest presides at the sacrament, let that person be anathema." Zwingli also made use of this text (see Barbara Müller, "Zwingli und das Konzil von Gangra," *Zwingliana* 33 [2006]: 29–50).

37. March 22–April 2, 1523.

38. That is: spiritual.

39. Frith's book *A Disputation of Purgatory*, published in 1531.

40. Descendants of Esau, according to Genesis 36, and enemies of Israel that participated in the pillaging of Jerusalem at the time of the Babylonian captivity (see Ps 137:7). Frith is referring to his own enemies.

41. Original obsolete usage, "against you shall come into Egypt."

42. Augustine, bishop of Hippo (354–430 CE). The comment attributed to him has not been located in his works.

PART TWO: INTERPRETING SCRIPTURE

1. The seven passages that Zwingli has just cited in support of his argument: Genesis 6:11–22; 22:2–14; 28:10–17; Exodus 14:11–14; 1 Kings 22:17–21; 18:1, 36–40; Jeremiah 26:7–15.

2. John 1:9 says literally that the light itself was coming into the world.

3. His opponents, the friars, with whom he was debating the necessity of deferring to official interpreters of scripture.

4. Caiaphas and Annas, his father-in-law, were the high priests who condemned the words of Jesus when he appeared before them (Matt 26:57–68; John 18:12–14, 19–23).

5. Zwingli invokes the Vulgate text of Psalm 76:3–4, which is Psalm 77:3–4 in the Hebrew psalter and reads: "My soul refuses to be comforted. I think of God and I moan; I meditate and my spirit faints" (NRSV).

6. Schwenckfeld paraphrases the Vulgate text of Psalm 20:4, which is Psalm 21:3 in the Hebrew psalter and reads: "For you meet him with rich blessings" (NRSV).

7. From a verse of the medieval liturgical sequence, *Veni, sancte spiritus* ("Come, Holy Spirit"): "Sine tuo numine, nihil est in homine."

8. The date of this letter, March 4, was the Monday before Shrove Tuesday and Ash Wednesday in 1527.

9. A town on the Oder River in Silesia.

10. Luther is referring to the chanting of the psalms by priests and monks at masses and canonical hours, as Luther himself had done. In liturgical churches, verses 1–2 and 14–24 of Psalm 118 are still appointed for Easter Sunday.

11. Luther translates Psalm 118:14 into German as "Der Herr ist meine Macht und mein Psalm und ist mein Heil." NRSV: "The Lord is my strength and my might; he has become my salvation."

12. Luther translates the Vulgate version of Psalm 115:10, which is Psalm 116:10 in the NRSV and reads: "I kept my faith, even when I said: 'I am greatly afflicted.'"

13. Psalm 118:6–7: "With the Lord on my side I do not fear; what can mortals do to me? The Lord is on my side to help me; I shall look in triumph on those who hate me."

14. There is no reliable evidence for the circumstances surrounding the death of Jeremiah.

15. The alphabet.

16. See 1 Corinthians 5:6–8.

17. Without thought of earning for oneself special favors, which were expected from some acts of pre-Reformation piety.

18. Hindrance.

19. Teachers.

20. Clergy.

21. A mischievous sprite of English folklore who leads people astray.

22. To find the right direction, like a turn cap, a chimney cap that turns to catch the wind.

306

23. Of the false glosses or teaching.
24. A one-way street.
25. That is: interprets one text in twenty different ways.
26. Anything else.
27. Insipid.
28. Refute.
29. Tyndale alludes to his own repeated challenge that his opponents should cease to attack his translations and instead undertake to translate the Bible themselves.
30. Tyndale's own prologue to Romans.
31. Written by Tyndale and printed in 1531.

PART THREE: PREACHING

1. This paragraph is a paraphrase of Martin Luther's words in the dedication of his 1519 Psalms commentary to Elector Frederick of Saxony (cf. WA 5, 20).
2. Jerome (c. 347–420 CE), *In epistolam ad Galatas* 1.11–12, in MPL 26, 347.
3. Ambrosiaster (late fourth century), *Ad Colosenses* 4.5, in CSEL 81/3, 203–4. Ambrosiaster is the name given by Erasmus of Rotterdam to the anonymous author of this commentary on the Pauline epistles attributed throughout the Middle Ages to Ambrose of Milan (c. 339–97).
4. The happy mean between extremes.
5. The Sadducees were a Jewish party portrayed in the New Testament as opposing the resurrection of the dead (Matt 22:23–33; Acts 4:1–2; 23:6–10).
6. Origenists were supporters of the early Christian theologian Origen (c. 185–251 CE), whose teaching on the pre-existence of souls and the restoration of all things appeared to deny the resurrection of the body and was condemned at the Second Council of Constantinople in 553.
7. Fasting is absent from most versions of the biblical text.
8. *To the Philippians* 12, in *The Apostolic Fathers*, ed. J. B. Lightfoot, 2nd ed. (Grand Rapids, MI: Baker Books, 1981), 2:3, 201. The letter to the Philippians is not an authentic work of Ignatius of Antioch (early second century).
9. Jerome, *Epistula 41 ad Marcellam* 3, in CSEL 54, 313.
10. Ambrose praises fasting in *De Helia et Ieiunio*, a work based on sermons preached during Lent, probably in the years 387 to 390.
11. Diarmaid MacCulloch, *Thomas Cranmer: A Life* (New Haven, CT: Yale University Press, 1996), 372.

12. One-fortieth as many.

13. The monastic and semi-monastic (regular canons) life was called religious, while other clergy not bound by rules of the various orders were called secular.

14. Acts of piety that earned for the religious person doing them more merit than needed; the excess merit could then be transferred to someone else.

15. Beads, like rosaries, to which a pardon or indulgence was attached.

16. Voluntary.

17. Obedience not required, that is, obedience to the pope.

18. Silver and gold plate.

19. Owning in common, that is, belonging to the order or to one of its houses instead of individually to the members, who as a result could claim poverty.

20. Hold no sway over them.

21. A set of thirty requiem masses said on the same day or on different days.

22. Intercessory prayers, especially for the souls of the departed.

23. A reference to the dissolution of the monasteries by Henry VIII between 1536 and 1540.

24. The practices of the papal or Roman church; an allusion to the "old yeast of malice and evil" in 1 Corinthians 5:8.

25. A name for the rosary.

26. The O's of St. Bridget (Birgitta of Sweden, 1303–73), or Fifteen O's, are fifteen meditations on the passion of Christ, each of which begins with "O Jesu" or a similar invocation.

27. St. Bernard's verses belong to a poem ascribed to Bernard of Clairvaux (France, 1098–1153) that honored the members of Christ's body on the cross. It became popular in the fourteenth and fifteenth centuries in connection with a devotional ritual dedicated to the wounds of Christ.

28. Letters written on February 5, the day of St. Agatha (d. c. 250 CE in Sicily) as a charm against fire.

29. A mass celebrated as a good work for the satisfaction of sin.

30. Laboring painfully.

31. Dominion or empire.

32. Strong sentiments, not feelings of fondness.

33. Probably a reference to those sixteenth-century Anabaptists who advocated the common ownership of property.

NOTES

PART FOUR: ADMONISHING AND CONSOLING

1. Schütz Zell not only alludes to biblical passages but also con-flates and paraphrases them, so that introducing a direct quotation from the NRSV would be too great a departure from her own text.

2. In the NRSV Isaiah 54:6 reads: "For the Lord has called you like a wife forsaken and grieved in spirit, like the wife of a man's youth when she is cast off."

3. July 22.

4. From the beginning of the medieval German hymn *Christ ist erstanden*. According to the English version in *Lutheran Book of Worship* (no. 136), the text paraphrased by Huberinus reads: "Christ is arisen from the grave's dark prison. So let our joy rise full and free; Christ our comfort true will be."

5. The marriage between Christ and the faithful culminates in the "marvelous exchange," an image used by Luther and medieval spiritual theologians to explain how the benefits of Christ's work are transferred to believers for their salvation.

6. The NRSV omits the phrase "in which the son of man is com-ing." It is not attested in all the ancient texts, but it is present in the text of Rhegius.

7. The NRSV renders Psalm 69:5 as a question: "What I did not steal must I now restore?" The point of Rhegius's rendering is that Christ pays for sins that he did not commit.

8. The gospels do not label Mary Magdalene a sinner, although Jesus did cast out from her seven demons (Luke 8:2; Mark 16:9). In the Western tradition, however, she was identified with the sinful woman who anointed Jesus and was then absolved by him (Luke 7:36–50).

9. Like all Protestants, Bucer encouraged laity to receive the Lord's Supper in church on a regular basis in place of the medieval practices of attending public mass once a year and requesting a private mass only when people were close to death.

10. Bucer's words are reminiscent of the post-communion prayer: "Almighty God, you provide the true bread from heaven, your Son, Jesus Christ our Lord. Grant that we who have received the sacrament of his body and blood may abide in him and he in us, that we may be filled with the power of his endless life, now and forever."

11. That is: they should not be denied absolution or the sacrament through which the saving work of Christ is transmitted.

12. The "communion of Christ" in this paragraph refers not to the sacrament but to readmission into church fellowship, although that re-

309

admission is accomplished through absolution and the Lord's Supper, also called holy communion.

13. At this point there follows "A Form and Method for Imparting Absolution and the Sacrament of the Supper to the Sick."

PART FIVE: LIVING THE FAITH

1. The human soul.

2. For medieval mystics the "ground of the soul" was the point of contact between human beings and God, which, properly cultivated, led to spiritual ecstasy and mystical union.

3. Human beings.

4. The reading from the Gospel appointed for the Sunday on which the sermon was preached in 1523: Matthew 22:36–40. According to the liturgical calendar, this gospel lesson was read on the eighteenth Sunday after Trinity, which was celebrated in the fall of the year.

5. The last word of the verse in Deuteronomy is "might," while in Matthew it is "mind."

6. The NRSV translation of Deuteronomy 6:4 ("Hear, O Israel, the Lord is our God, the Lord alone") captures the meaning of the verse better than Karlstadt does. The point of the Hebrew is that only the Lord of the Hebrews is God. Karlstadt's more abstract point, made under the influence of his mystical theology, is that God is unified, and there is no dividedness or multiplicity in God.

7. The German word for surrender of self is *Gelassenheit*. For mystics it denoted a state of passivity, surrender, or yieldedness that Karlstadt treated in a separate work.

8. Luther may intend for this "spirit" to be the Holy Spirit, but the text does not say that explicitly.

9. Ambrosius Blarer (also Blaurer; 1492–1564) became an evangelical preacher and reformer in the German city of Constance in 1525. As a Benedictine monk he had received copies of Luther's writings from his brother Thomas, who studied in Wittenberg in 1520. Ambrosius left the cloister of Alpirsbach in 1522 for a period of private study in Constance before he became a pastor in 1525. In 1523 he began to exchange letters with Zwingli, and at Bern in 1528 he also became friends with Martin Bucer, the reformer of Strasbourg. The correspondence of the Blarer brothers is an important source for the Reformation history of Switzerland and southern Germany.

10. Like Strasbourg, Constance was the seat of a bishop. If the city council or senate made a political and religious decision to adopt the

Reformation, they would be defying the Catholic bishop and his supporters. The city council of Zürich had already done this in 1523 and 1525.

11. In typical sixteenth-century fashion, the entire city (and not only the senate) is equated with the church because Constance was considered a Christian community. All its citizens did not support the Reformation, however, and the political issue became this: On what basis should the senate, which did contain some elected members, make a decision for everyone to change the religion of the city? Would some people be forced to go along with the changes, and would that be right?

12. Initially, Anabaptists were radical followers of Zwingli who were not willing to wait, as he was, on governmental approval of religious reform. In 1525 they set themselves apart by rebaptizing one another, and their leaders were soon driven out of Zürich. The Anabaptist movement spread rapidly, but it remained small and suffered severe persecution.

13. Marcus Porcius Cato (d. 149 BCE) and his great-grandson, Marcus Porcius Cato Uticencis (d. 46 CE). Cato the elder ("the censor") was a prominent Roman soldier and senator known for his strict private and public discipline and for his opposition to the corrupting influence of Hellenic culture. Cato the younger was a Roman politician and statesman committed to Stoic philosophy. He became notorious for his stubbornness and his opposition to Julius Caesar.

14. Marcus Furius Camillus (d. 365 BCE), Roman general and statesman who was called the second founder of Rome.

15. The Scipiones were a prominent Roman family whose male members were the conquerors of Spain and Carthage and lovers of Greek culture and learning. Their wealth and extravagance were detested by the family of Cato the elder, who worked hard to ruin Scipio Africanus the elder (d. 183 BCE). Zwingli is probably referring to him or to Scipio Aemilianus Africanus the younger (d. 129 BCE).

16. Zwingli denied that the Roman mass was "merely an external" that would not harm Protestants who were not yet ready for the mass to be changed into the evangelical Lord's Supper. Although Luther agreed that the Roman mass had to be abolished, he argued against Karlstadt in 1522 that it could be celebrated temporarily until more people were ready for it to be replaced by the supper.

17. These biblical figures stand for civil authorities like the senate of Constance.

18. Thomas Blarer (1499–1567) was the brother of Ambrosius and supported the Reformation while serving as mayor of Constance. During his study in Wittenberg (1520) he was very impressed by Luther and read his early works. Zwingli is referring to a recent visit by Thomas to Zürich.

19. John Zwick (1496–1542), a cousin of the Blarers, was another evangelical preacher and reformer in Constance.

PART SIX: SINGING

1. Christopher Brown, *Singing the Gospel: Lutheran Hymns and the Success of the Reformation* (Cambridge, MA: Harvard University Press, 2005), 171.

2. *John Calvin: Writings on Pastoral Piety*, ed. and trans. Elsie A. McKee, Classics of Western Spirituality (Mahwah, NJ: Paulist Press, 2001), 85.

3. *Elisabeth's Manly Courage: Testimonials and Songs of Martyred Anabaptist Women in the Low Countries*, ed. and trans. Hermina Joldersma and Louis Grijp (Milwaukee: Marquette University Press, 2001), 24–25.

4. Georg Erdmann, *Geschichte der Kirchen-Reformation in der Stadt Göttingen* (Göttingen: Vandenhoeck and Ruprecht, 1888), 20–21.

5. In the sense of "protect me."

6. Back to health.

7. Michael Weisse, *Gesangbuch der Böhmischen Brüder 1531*, ed. Konrad Ameln (Kassel: Bärenreiter-Verlag, 1957). Facsimile of *Ein New Geseng Buchlen*, MDXXXI.

8. See text no. 25 above.

9. June 24.

10. The first part of this sentence echoes a familiar passage from the *Paraclesis* of Erasmus of Rotterdam.

PART SEVEN: PRAYING

1. Martin Luther, *Personal Prayer Book* 1522, in LW 43, 11–12.

2. LW 43, 12.

3. Bartholomew von Starhemberg.

4. The English word "grasp" is a translation of the German word *fühlen*. It normally means "to feel," but Luther often uses the verb with "faith" to denote an action both more complex and more cognitive than "to feel." The meaning of *fühlen* as "grasp" comes in general from the German mystical tradition, but Luther has paired it with "faith" in order to express the deep trust that results from the acknowledgment and acceptance of the ways, sometimes mysterious, in which God works. This faith is a gift of the Spirit as well as a human action, and "grasp" seems to

capture its depth and to fit Luther's contrast between the physical holding of a spouse and spiritual holding on to God's will.

5. September 1.

6. Strictly speaking not a monk but a cleric who lived in a community of clergy according to a rule attributed to Augustine of Hippo (354–430), the African bishop who shared a life in common with his clergy.

7. Wittenberg.

8. Saxony.

9. The NRSV reads: "fruit of our lips."

10. Not the correct rendering of what is said about Ajax in Homer, *Odyssey*, 3.48.

11. Homer, *Odyssey*, 3.48.

12. Eusebius, Bishop of Emesa (c. 300–59), *Homilia de poenitentia* 3, in MPG 33, 1482. This homily was formerly attributed to Basil of Caesarea.

13. The last sentence refers to the remarkable fate of the Roman general Gnaeus Pompeius Magnus (106–48 BCE). After his defeat by Julius Caesar in Thessaly, Pompey "the Great" fled with his last wife, Cornelia, to Egypt, where he was murdered, then beheaded, and his corpse incinerated on a funeral pyre. Caesar refused the head of Pompey when it was offered to him but gave the remains to Cornelia, who buried them at their Albano villa in Italy. See *Plutarch's Lives*, ed. and trans. Bernadotte Perrin (London: Heinemann; New York: G. P. Putnam's Sons, 1917), 5:322–25. Pompey's sons, Gnaeus Pompeius and Sextus Pompeius, were defeated by Julius Caesar at the battle of Munda in Spain. After the battle Gnaeus was caught and executed in Spain, but Sextus lived to fight against Augustus in Italy.

14. Ovid, *Tristia* 5.2.71: "Pax tamen interdum est, pacis fiducia numquam."

15. Cicero, *De oratore* 3.42.167: "At Romanus homo, tamenetsi res bene gestat, corde suo trepidat." Cicero does not name Ennius as the author of this saying, but see *Melanchthon Deutsch* 2, 115n118.

16. The Schmalkald War was the conflict between the Protestant Schmalkald League and Emperor Charles V and his Catholic forces. The Protestants lost, and in 1547 Charles V captured Wittenberg and the leaders of the league.

17. Looking out for terrible or dreadful things.

18. To resist the distress and its causes.

19. The festival of Ascension is celebrated forty days after Easter (Acts 1:3) and always falls on a Thursday.

20. Acknowledging.

PART EIGHT: RECONSTRUCTING SACRAMENTS

1. *Die Taufe* is German for "baptism."

2. *Tief* is the German word for "deep," but the alleged derivation of *Taufe* from *tief* is not correct.

3. Luther favored complete immersion but did not insist on it in his 1523 order for baptism, which says the infant should be "dipped in the font."

4. John 3:5: "Very truly I tell you, no one can enter the kingdom of God without being born of water and Spirit."

5. Psalm 29:10: "The Lord sits enthroned over the flood."

6. *The Blessed Sacrament of the Holy and True Body of Christ, and the Brotherhoods* is the last of a series of sermons or treatises that appeared in 1519.

7. Augustine, *On Marriage and Concupiscence* 1.28.25, in NPNF (series 1) 5, 275: "If the question arises, how this concupiscence of the flesh remains in the regenerate, in whose case has been effected a remission of all sins whatever,...the answer to be given is this: carnal concupiscence is remitted, indeed, in baptism, not so that it be put out of existence, but so that it is not to be imputed for sin. Although its guilt is now taken away, it still remains until our entire infirmity be healed by the advancing renewal of the inner person, day by day, when at last our outer person shall be clothed with incorruption" (1 Cor 15:53).

8. Allusions perhaps to Romans 9:8 and Galatians 4:28 ("children of the promise"), Ephesians 5:1 ("beloved children"), 2 Corinthians 4:15, and Luke 2:14.

9. The third part of the sacrament of penance, in which sins are satisfied or compensated for by works of charity and piety.

10. In the first of the three sermons on the sacraments from 1519.

11. Luther frequently divides life into three estates or arenas of human responsibility: matrimony or the household, ministry or public leadership in the church, and civic leadership in the secular realm.

12. To belong to the spiritual estate, in medieval terms, is to belong to the priesthood or to a monastic order. Although Luther in 1520 will redefine the spiritual estate, at this point he is using the medieval definition.

13. The priest to whom confession was made.

14. The law of the Roman church required that confession be made at least once a year before Easter Sunday.

15. In his *Commentary on True and False Religion* Zwingli defined the gospel on the basis of Luke 24:47 as remission of sins and repentance. See ZS 3, 129–30.

16. In Homer's *Iliad*, Machaon was a son of Asclepius and a surgeon for the Greek army at Troy.

17. Medieval theologians subscribed to a similar notion that repentant believers lived between hope and fear, seeking on one side to avoid presumption of salvation and on the other side to prevent despair. Zwingli's position is a subtle but important modification of medieval theology. His notion of fear is closer to a healthy respect for the power of sin than it is to despair, and he emphasizes that not repentance itself but the death of Christ washes away sin.

18. Private confession, called auricular because it is confession entrusted to the ear (*auricula* in Latin) of the priest.

19. The power of the priest hearing confession to forgive or to retain sin, often called the power of the keys in reference to the words of Jesus to Peter (Matt 16:19).

20. Martin Luther and his followers.

21. Veit Dietrich (1506–49) was Luther's close friend and assistant before becoming the pastor of St. Sebald's Church in Nuremberg in 1535. He devoted his scholarship mostly to instructional materials and wrote, among other things, summaries of all the books of scripture.

22. The table of household duties was a list of obligations for each member of the household that can be traced to Greek antiquity and in Christian form to the New Testament (Col 3:18—4:1; Eph 5:22—6:9). A similar table was included in some versions of catechisms by Martin Luther and other reformers.

23. This "psalm" is a hymn written by Martin Luther that was not based on a specific psalm.

24. *The Magnificat* is the song of Mary from Luke 1:46–55.

25. Peter Opitz, *Heinrich Bullinger als Theologe: Eine Studie zu den "Dekaden"* (Zürich: Theologischer Verlag, 2004), 19.

26. Augustine, *Reply to Faustus the Manichaean* 19.16, in NPNF (series 1) 4, 244–45: "For material symbols are nothing else than visible speech, which, though sacred, is changeable and transitory. For while God is eternal, the water of baptism and all that is material in the sacrament is transitory; the very word God, which must be pronounced in the consecration, is a sound which passes in a moment. The actions and sounds pass away, but their efficacy remains the same, and the spiritual gift thus communicated is eternal."

27. Bullinger has Lutherans and probably Catholics in mind.

28. That is: baptism either in place of the sign of circumcision or as itself the sign of adoption by Christ.

29. Augustine, *Reply to Faustus the Manichaean* 19.11, in NPNF (series 1) 4, 243: "There can be no religious society, whether the religion be true or false, without some sacrament or visible symbol to serve as a bond of union. The importance of these sacraments cannot be overstated, and only scoffers will treat them lightly. For if piety requires them, it must be impiety to neglect them."

30. *A Brief and Clear Explanation of the Christian Faith for the King of the Christians*, 1531, in ZS 4, 360–361. Zwingli wrote this treatise for the king of France in hopes of gaining political support for Zürich against Emperor Charles V.

PART NINE: WORSHIPING

1. See text no. 17 above.
2. See text no. 43 below.
3. See text no. 11 above.
4. See text no. 44 below.
5. See text no. 43 below.
6. *Ratschlag betreffend Ausschließung vom Abendmahl*, in Z 4, no. 52 (CR 91, 25–34).
7. Thursday of Holy Week is traditionally celebrated as the evening on which Jesus instituted the Lord's Supper.
8. September 11, *Kirchenweihtag* in Zürich, an important civic and religious celebration. See Thomas Maissen, "'Unser Herren Tag' zwischen Integrationsritual und Verbot: Die Zürcher Kirchweihe (Kilbi) im 16. Jahrhundert," *Zürcher Taschenbuch 1998* (Zürich: Staatsarchiv des Kantons Zürich, 1997): 191–236.
9. These words of institution, based on 1 Corinthians 11:23–26, have been influenced by the accounts of the Last Supper in the Gospels.
10. LW 49, 90.
11. The part of Saxony that was turning Protestant under Luther's prince, Elector John, who had just succeeded his deceased brother, Frederick. The elector of Saxony was one of the rulers who were charged by German law with electing a new emperor. Frederick had participated in the election of Charles V in 1519.
12. LW 49, 135. Mass fees were fees paid to the clergy for saying private masses that were now abolished, and rents were the tithes collected by parishes for use of the land that had belonged to them since the Middle Ages.
13. LW 39, 135.
14. The sacrament of the altar or the Lord's Supper.
15. See LW 53, 19–39.

16. By Waldensians in the sixteenth century Luther means the Bohemian Brethren, a community that descended from the fifteenth-century Czech reform movement led by Jan Hus. The Brethren had received the right of consecrating bishops from the Waldensians, a thirteenth-century movement that started in Italy. The Brethren, who used Czech and Latin, were confined primarily to Bohemia, now the Czech Republic.

17. The *Small Catechism* was published in 1529 and became one of Luther's most popular works.

18. First published in 1522, this *Betbüchlein* contained brief explanations of the ten commandments, the apostles' creed, and the Lord's prayer that had been published earlier. For the text in English, see LW 43, 3–46.

19. In Luther's day Hungarian guilders were more valuable than Rhenish guilders.

20. Schreckenberger were coins made from silver that was taken from a mine in Saxony.

21. Here Luther uses the term *loci communes*, which were the main themes of a subject like theology and also the title of a major work by Luther's colleague Philip Melanchthon.

22. Gerrit van de Poll, *Martin Bucer's Liturgical Ideas* (Assen: Van Gorcum, 1954), 127.

23. The German text reads *altartisch*.

24. Sharon L. Arnoult, "'Spiritual and Sacred Publique Actions': *The Book of Common Prayer* and the Understanding of Worship in the Elizabethan and Jacobean Church of England," in *Religion and the English People: New Voices, New Perspectives*, ed. Eric Josef Carlson (Kirksville, MO: Truman State University Press, 1998), 25.

25. John Morrill, "The Church in England, 1642-9," in *Reactions to the Civil War, 1642–1649*, ed. John Morrill (London/Basingstoke: Macmillan, 1982), 113; quoted in Diarmaid MacCulloch, *Thomas Cranmer: A Life* (New Haven, CT: Yale University Press, 1996), 628.

26. Arnoult, "Spiritual and Sacred Publique Actions," 28.

27. A reference perhaps to Augustine's Epistle 54 to Januarius, in FC 12, 252–60.

28. The 1559 text reads "bewraying of."

29. The table has three columns: one for the days of the month, one for psalms to be read at morning prayer, and one for psalms to be read at evening prayer. For example, on the fifth day of every month Psalms 24, 25, and 26 are read at morning prayer and Psalms 27, 28, and 29 are read at evening prayer. The order of worship for both services is printed in the prayer book.

30. In the Hebrew scriptures Psalm 119 is an acrostic psalm, and each section begins with a new letter of the alphabet.

31. The Great Bible is the English version prepared by Miles Coverdale on the basis of translations by William Tyndale and Coverdale himself. It was published in 1539, and chancellor Thomas Cromwell ordered that a copy be placed in every parish church.

32. The Latin Vulgate text of the Psalter in common use was based on the Greek Old Testament, the Septuagint, which numbered the psalms differently from the Hebrew text.

33. A rubric is a statement that tells the clergy how to lead the service and the laity how to respond at designated places. These statements or directions were called rubrics because they were printed in red (rendered here in bold).

34. In a local parish of the Church of England the curate was an assistant to the rector, who was the primary minister or pastor of the parish. Note how different terms for the pastor are used in the rubric: *curate, minister, priest.*

35. Perversity or contrariness.

36. For example, one of the homilies from the twelve that were published by Cranmer in 1547 (see text no. 12 above).

37. That is, the age of discretion, old enough to realize what the sacrament is.

38. A feature of medieval cathedrals and large churches, to which groups of clergy could be attached in a so-called clerical chapter.

BIBLIOGRAPHY

EDITIONS AND SOURCES

The Apostolic Fathers. Ed. J. B. Lightfoot. 2nd ed. 5 vols. in 2 parts. Grand Rapids, MI: Baker Books, 1981.

The Book of Common Prayer, 1559: The Elizabethan Prayer Book. Ed. John E. Booty. Charlottesville: University of Virginia Press, 1976.

Bullinger, Henry. *Sermons on the Sacraments.* Cambridge: University Press; London: John William Parker, 1840.

Martin Bucers Deutsche Schriften. Ed. Gottfried Seebass, Thomas Wilhelmi, and Stephen E. Buckwalter. 19 vols. Heidelberg: Bucer-Forschungsstelle der Heidelberger Akademie der Wissenschaften/ Gütersloh: GVH, 1960– .

Church Mother: The Writings of a Protestant Reformer in Sixteenth-Century Germany, Katharina Schütz Zell. Ed. and trans. Elsie Anne McKee. Chicago: University of Chicago Press, 2006.

Common Places of Martin Bucer. Trans. and ed. D. F. Wright. Courtenay Library of Reformation Classics, vol. 4. Abingdon, UK: The Sutton Courtenay Press, 1972.

Complete Sermons of Martin Luther. Ed. J. N. Lenker. 7 vols. Reprint of the 1983 (vols. 1–4: Church Postils) and 1996 (vols. 5–7: House Postils) editions. Grand Rapids, MI: Baker Books, 2000.

Corpus Schwenckfeldianorum. 19 vols. Leipzig: Breitkopf and Härtel; Pennsburg, PA: Board of Publication of the Schwenckfelder Church, 1907–61.

English Reformers. Ed. T. H. L. Parker. LCC 26. Philadelphia: Westminster Press, 1966.

The Essential Carlstadt: Fifteen Tracts by Andreas Bodenstein (Carlstadt) from Karlstadt. Trans. and ed. E. J. Furcha. Waterloo, ON; Scottdale, PA: Herald Press, 1995.

Evangelischer Gottesdienst: Quellen zu seiner Geschichte. Ed. Wolfgang Herbst. 2nd ed. Göttingen: Vandenhoeck and Ruprecht, 1992.

319

Evangelisches Kirchengesangbuch. Ausgabe für die evangelisch-lutherischen Kirchen Niedersachsens. Hannover: Schlütersche Verlagsanstalt; Göttingen: Vandenhoeck and Ruprecht, n.d.

Franz, Gunther. *Huberinus—Rhegius—Holbein*. Nieuwkoop: B. de Graaf, 1973.

Grumbach, Argula von. *A Woman's Voice in the Reformation*. Ed. Peter Matheson. Edinburgh: T & T Clark, 1995.

Heinrich Bullinger Schriften. Ed. Emidio Campi, Detlef Roth, and Peter Stotz. 6 vols. Zürich: Theologischer Verlag Zürich, 2004–6.

Huberinus, Caspar. *Ein trostlicher Sermon von der Urstend Christi den Schwachen im Glauben nützlich zu lesen*. Augsburg: Heinrich Steiner, 1525.

Huldreich Zwinglis Sämtliche Werke. Ed. Emil Egli, Georg Finsler, Walther Köhler, Fritz Blanke, Leonhard von Muralt, Edwin Künzli, Rudolf Pfister, Joachim Staedtke, Fritz Büsser, and Markus Jenny. 14 vols. Berlin/Leipzig/Zürich: Institut für schweizerische Reformationsgeschichte, 1905– .

Huldrych Zwingli Schriften. Ed. Thomas Brunnschweiler, Samuel Lutz, Hans Ulrich Bächtold. 4 vols. Zürich: Theologischer Verlag, 1995.

Ich rufe zu dir: Gebete des Reformators Philipp Melanchthon. Ed. Martin H. Jung, Gerhard Weng, and Klaus-Dieter Kaiser. 2nd ed. Frankfurt: GEP Buch, 1997.

Karlstadts Schriften aus den Jahren 1523–25. Ed. Erich Hertzsch. Parts I and II. Halle (Saale): Max Niemeyer Verlag, 1956–57.

Katharina Schütz Zell, vol. 2: *The Writings, A Critical Edition*. Ed. Elsie Anne McKee. Leiden: E. J. Brill, 1999.

Lutheran Book of Worship. Ed. Inter-Lutheran Commission on Worship. Minneapolis: Augsburg; Philadelphia: LCA Board of Publication, 1978.

Luther's Works, American Edition. Ed. Helmut Lehmann and Jaroslav Pelikan. 55 vols. Philadelphia: Fortress; St. Louis: Concordia, 1955–86.

Luthers Werke in Auswahl. Ed. Otto Clemen and Albert Lietzmann. 8 vols. Berlin: De Gruyter, 1959–67.

Martin Luther Studienausgabe. Ed. Hans-Ulrich Delius. 6 vols. Berlin: Evangelische Verlagsanstalt, 1979–92.

Martin Luther Taschenausgabe. Ed. Horst Beintker, Helmar Junghans, and Hubert Kirchner. 5 vols. 2nd ed. Berlin: Evangelische Verlagsanstalt, 1983– .

D. Martin Luthers Werke. Kritische Gesamtausgabe. 105 vols. Ed. J. F. K. Knaake et al. Weimar: Böhlau, 1883– .

BIBLIOGRAPHY

Miscellaneous Writings and Letters of Thomas Cranmer. Ed. John Edmund Cox for the Parker Society. Cambridge: The University Press, 1846.

McKee, Elsie Anne. *Reforming Popular Piety in Sixteenth-Century Strasbourg: Katharina Schütz Zell and Her Hymnbook*. Princeton Theological Seminary, Studies in Reformed Theology and History 2:4 (1994).

Melanchthon, Philip. *Argumentum in Ieremiam Prophetam*. Frankfurt: Peter Brubach, 1548.

Melanchthon Deutsch. Ed. Michael Beyer, Stefan Rhein, and Günther Wartenberg. 2 vols. Leipzig: EVA, 1997.

Plutarch's Lives. Ed. and trans. Bernadotte Perrin. 11 vols. Loeb Classical Library. London: Heinemann; New York: G. P. Putnam's Sons, 1914–26.

Preaching the Reformation: The Homiletical Handbook of Urbanus Rhegius. Ed. and trans. Scott Hendrix. Milwaukee, WI: Marquette University Press, 2003.

Quellen zur Geschichte des evangelischen Gottesdienstes von der Reformation bis zur Gegenwart. Ed. Wolfgang Herbst. Göttingen: Vandenhoeck and Ruprecht, 1968.

Reformatorenbriefe: Luther, Zwingli, Calvin. Ed. Günter Gloede. Berlin: Evangelische Verlagsanstalt, 1973.

Strassburger liturgischen Ordnungen im Zeitalter der Reformation, Die. Ed. Friedrich Hubert. Göttingen: Vandenhoeck and Ruprecht, 1900.

Supplementa Calviniana, vol. 8, *Sermons on Acts of the Apostles 1–7*. Ed. Willem Balke and Wilhelmus H. Th. Moehn. Neukirchen-Vluyn: Neukirchener Verlag, 1994.

Tyndale, William. *Expositions and Notes on Sundry Portions of the Holy Scriptures together with the Practice of Prelates*. Works 2. Ed. Henry Walter for the Parker Society. Cambridge: The University Press, 1849.

Vermigli, Peter Martyr. *Sacred Prayers Drawn from the Psalms of David*. Trans. and ed. John Patrick Donnelly, SJ. The Peter Martyr Library 3. Kirksville, MO: SCJ Publishers, 1996.

Weisse, Michael, *Gesangbuch der Böhmischen Brüder 1531*. Ed. Konrad Ameln. Kassel: Bärenreiter-Verlag, 1957. Facsimile of *Ein New Geseng Buchlen*, MDXXXI.

Work of John Frith, The. Intro. and ed. N. T. Wright. Courtenay Library of Reformation Classics 7. Appleford, UK: The Sutton Courtenay Press, 1978.

Writings and Translations of Myles Coverdale, Bishop of Exeter. Ed. George Pearson for the Parker Society. Cambridge: The University Press, 1844.

Zwingli and Bullinger. Ed. and trans. G. W. Bromiley. LCC 24. Philadelphia: Westminster Press, 1953.

Zwingli, Huldrych. *Ausgewählte Schriften*. Ed. Ernst Saxer. Neukirchen-Vluyn: Neukirchener Verlag, 1988.

Zwingli, Ulrich. *Commentary on True and False Religion*. Ed. Samuel Macauley Jackson and Clarence Nevin Heller. Durham, NC: Labyrinth Press, 1981.

————.*Early Writings*. Ed. Samuel Macauley Jackson. Durham, NC: Labyrinth Press, 1987.

LITERATURE

Adams, Gwenfair Walters. *Visions in Late Medieval England: Lay Spirituality and Sacred Glimpses of the Hidden Worlds of Faith*. Leiden: E. J. Brill, 2007.

Anticlericalism in Late Medieval and Early Modern Europe. Ed. Peter Dykema and Heiko A. Oberman. Leiden: E. J. Brill, 1993.

Architect of the Reformation: An Introduction to Heinrich Bullinger, 1504–75. Ed. Bruce Gordon and Emidio Campi. Grand Rapids, MI: Baker Academic, 2004.

Arnoult, Sharon L. "'Spiritual and Sacred Publique Actions': *The Book of Common Prayer* and the Understanding of Worship in the Elizabethan and Jacobean Church of England." In *Religion and the English People: New Voices, New Perspectives*, ed. Eric Josef Carlson, 25–47. SCES 45. Kirksville, MO: Truman State University Press, 1998.

Backus, Irena. *Reformation Readings of the Apocalypse: Geneva, Zürich, and Wittenberg*. Oxford: Oxford University Press, 2000.

Bainton, Roland H. *Women of the Reformation in Germany and Italy*. Minneapolis: Augsburg Publishing House, 1971.

Bellardi, Werner. "Anton Engelbrecht (1485–1558): Helfer, Mitarbeiter und Gegner Bucers." ARG 64 (1973): 183–206.

The Blackwell Companion to Christian Spirituality. Ed. Arthur Holder. Malden, MA: Blackwell Publishing, 2005.

A Book of Reformed Prayers. Ed. Howard Rice and Lamar Williamson. Louisville, KY: Westminster John Knox, 1998.

Bossy, John. *Christianity in the West 1400–1700*. Oxford: Oxford University Press, 1987.

BIBLIOGRAPHY

Bottigheimer, Ruth B. "Bible Reading, 'Bibles,' and the Bible for Children in Early Modern Germany." *Past and Present* 139 (1993): 66–89.

Bouwsma, William J. *John Calvin: A Sixteenth Century Portrait.* New York: Oxford University Press, 1988.

Brecht, Martin. "Erinnerung an Paul Speratus (1484–1551), ein enger Anhänger Luthers in den Anfängen der Reformation." ARG 94 (2003): 105–133.

Brown, Christopher B. *Singing the Gospel: Lutheran Hymns and the Success of the Reformation.* Cambridge, MA: Harvard University Press, 2005.

Burnett, Amy Nelson. *Teaching the Reformation: Ministers and Their Message in Basel, 1529–1629.* Oxford: Oxford University Press, 2006.

————. *The Yoke of Christ: Martin Bucer and Christian Discipline.* SCES 26. Kirksville, MO: SCJ Publishers, 1994.

Campbell, Ernest T. "What's the Story?" (May 11, 1975). In *Sermons from Duke Chapel*, ed. William H. Willimon, 166–71. Durham, NC: Duke University Press, 2005.

The Collects of Thomas Cranmer. Ed. C. Frederick Barbee and Paul F. M. Zahl. Grand Rapids, MI: Eerdmans, 1999.

Daniell, David. *William Tyndale: A Biography.* New Haven, CT: Yale University Press, 1994.

Diefendorf, Barbara B. *Beneath the Cross: Catholics and Huguenots in Sixteenth-century Paris.* New York: Oxford University Press, 1991.

Duffy, Eamon. *The Stripping of the Altars: Traditional Religion in England 1400–1580.* New Haven, CT: Yale University Press, 1992.

Eire, Carlos. *War against the Idols: The Reformation of Worship from Erasmus to Calvin.* Cambridge: Cambridge University Press, 1986.

Elisabeth's Manly Courage: Testimonials and Songs of Martyred Anabaptist Women in the Low Countries. Trans. and ed. Hermina Joldersma and Louis Grijp. Milwaukee, WI: Marquette University Press, 2001.

Erdmann, Georg. *Geschichte der Kirchen-Reformation in der Stadt Göttingen.* Göttingen: Vandenhoeck and Ruprecht, 1888.

Granquist, Mark. "American Hymns and Swedish Immigrants." LQ 20 (2006): 409–28.

Gregory, Brad S. *Salvation at Stake: Christian Martyrdom in Early Modern Europe.* Cambridge, MA: Harvard University Press, 1999.

Greschat, Martin. *Martin Bucer: A Reformer and His Times.* Trans. Stephen E. Buckwalter. Louisville, KY: Westminster John Knox Press, 2004.

Haemig, Mary Jane. "Elisabeth Cruciger (1500?–1535): The Case of the Disappearing Hymn Writer." SCJ (2001): 24–27.

————. "Sixteenth-Century Preachers on Advent as a Season of Proclamation or Preparation." LQ 16 (2002): 125–51.

Halbach, Silke. *Argula von Grumbach als Verfasserin reformatorischer Flugschriften*. Europäische Hochschulschriften, Reihe XXIII: Theologie 468. Frankfurt am Main: Peter Lang, 1992.

Heinrich Bullinger und seine Zeit: Eine Vorlesungsreihe. Ed. Emidio Campi. Zürich: Theologischer Verlag, 2004.

Heming, Carol Piper. *Protestants and the Cult of the Saints in German-Speaking Europe, 1517–31*. SCES 65. Kirksville, MO: Truman State University Press, 2003.

Hendrix, Scott H. "Angelic Piety in the Reformation: The Good and Bad Angels of Urbanus Rhegius." In *Frömmigkeit, Theologie, Frömmigkeitstheologie: Contributions to European Church History. Festschrift für Berndt Hamm zum 60. Geburtstag*, ed. Gudrun Litz, Heidrun Munzert, and Roland Liebenberg, 385–94. Leiden: E. J. Brill, 2005.

———. "Martin Luther's Reformation of Spirituality," LQ 13 (1999): 249–70.

———. *Recultivating the Vineyard: The Reformation Agendas of Christianization*. Louisville, KY: Westminster John Knox Press, 2004.

Hoffman, Bengt. *Luther and the Mystics*. Minneapolis: Augsburg, 1976.

Hubert, Friedrich. *Die Strassburger liturgischen Ordnungen im Zeitalter der Reformation*. Göttingen: Vandenhoeck and Ruprecht, 1900.

John Calvin: Writings on Pastoral Piety. Trans. and ed. Elsie A. McKee. Classics of Western Spirituality. Mahwah, NJ: Paulist Press, 2001.

Jones, Serene. *Calvin and the Rhetoric of Piety*. Louisville, KY: Westminster John Knox Press, 1995.

Jung, Martin H. *Frömmigkeit und Theologie bei Philipp Melanchthon: Das Gebet im Leben und in der Lehre des Reformators*. Tübingen: Mohr Siebeck, 1998.

Kunz, Ralph. *Gottesdienst evangelisch reformiert: Liturgik und Liturgie in der Kirche Zwinglis*. Zürich: Pano Verlag, 2001.

Leaver, Robin A. *Luther's Liturgical Music: Principles and Implications*. Lutheran Quarterly Books. Grand Rapids, MI: Eerdmans, 2007.

Luther's Spirituality. Ed. and trans. Philip D. W. Krey and Peter D. S. Krey. Classics of Western Spirituality. Mahwah, NJ: Paulist Press, 2007.

MacCulloch, Diarmaid. *Thomas Cranmer: A Life*. New Haven, CT: Yale University Press, 1996.

Maissen, Thomas. "'Unser Herren Tag' zwischen Integrationsritual und Verbot: Die Zürcher Kirchweihe (Kilbi) im 16. Jahrhundert." *Zürcher Taschenbuch 1998* (Zürich: Staatsarchiv des Kantons Zürich, 1997): 191–236.

Matheson, Peter. *The Imaginative World of the Reformation*. Edinburgh: T. & T. Clark, 2000.

McGrath, Alister E. *Roots That Refresh: A Celebration of Reformation Spirituality*. London: Hodder & Stoughton, 1992.

McLaughlin, R. Emmet. *Caspar Schwenckfeld, Reluctant Radical: His Life to 1540*. New Haven, CT: Yale University Press, 1986.

————. "Reformation Spiritualism: Typology, Sources and Significance." In *Radicalism and Dissent in the Sixteenth Century*, ed. Hans-Jürgen Goertz and James M. Stayer, 123–40. Zeitschrift für historische Forschung, Beiheft 27. Berlin: Duncker and Humblot, 2002.

Morrill, John. "The Church in England, 1642-49." In *Reactions to the Civil War, 1642–49*, ed. John Morrill, 89–114. London/Basingstoke: Macmillan, 1982.

Müller, Barbara. "Zwingli und das Konzil von Gangra." Zwingliana 33 (2006): 29–50.

Oberman, Heiko A. *Luther: Man between God and the Devil*. New Haven, CT: Yale University Press, 1989.

Old, Hughes Oliphant. *The Reading and Preaching of the Scriptures in the Worship of the Christian Church*. 5 vols. Grand Rapids, MI: Eerdmans, 1998–2004.

Opitz, Peter. *Heinrich Bullinger als Theologe: Eine Studie zu den "Dekaden."* Zürich: Theologischer Verlag, 2004.

The Oxford Companion to Classical Literature. Ed. M. C. Howatson. 2nd ed. New York: Oxford University Press, 1989.

Ozment, Steven. *Mysticism and Dissent: Religious Ideology and Social Protest in the Sixteenth Century*. New Haven, CT: Yale University Press, 1973.

————. *Protestants: The Birth of a Revolution*. New York: Doubleday, 1992.

Parker, T. H. L. *Calvin's Preaching*. Louisville, KY: Westminster John Knox Press, 1992.

Penitence in the Age of Reformations. Ed. Anne T. Thayer and Katharine Jackson Lualdi. Aldershot, UK: Ashgate, 2000.

Peter Martyr Vermigli and the European Reformations: Semper Reformanda. Ed. Frank A. James III. Leiden: E. J. Brill, 2004.

Peters, Christine. *Patterns of Piety: Women, Gender, and Religion in Late Medieval and Reformation England*. Cambridge: Cambridge University Press, 2003.

Philip Melanchthon Then and Now: Essays Celebrating the 500th Anniversary of the Birth of Philip Melanchthon, Theologian, Teacher, Reformer. Ed.

Scott H. Hendrix and Timothy J. Wengert. Columbia, SC: Lutheran Theological Southern Seminary, 1999.

Poll, Gerrit Jan van de. *Martin Bucer's Liturgical Ideas*. Assen: Van Gorcum, 1954.

Popular Religion in Germany and Central Europe, 1400–1800. Ed. R. W. Scribner and Trevor Johnson. New York: St. Martin's Press, 1996.

Preachers and People in the Reformations and Early Modern Period. Ed. Larissa J. Taylor. Leiden: E. J. Brill, 2001.

The Reformation of Faith in the Context of Late Medieval Theology and Piet: Essays by Berndt Hamm. Ed. Robert J. Bast. Leiden: E. J. Brill, 2004.

The Reformation Theologians. Ed. Carter Lindberg. Oxford: Blackwell Publishing, 2002.

Richard, Lucien J. *The Spirituality of John Calvin*. Atlanta, GA: John Knox Press, 1974.

Rorem, Paul E. "Martin Luther's Christocentric Critique of Pseudo-Dionysian Spirituality." LQ 11 (1997): 291–307.

Russell, Paul A. *Lay Theology in the Reformation: Popular Pamphleteers in Southwest Germany, 1521–25*. Cambridge: Cambridge University Press, 1986.

Scribner, R. W. *Religion and Culture in Germany 1400–1800*. Ed. Lyndal Roper. Leiden: E. J. Brill, 2001.

Solignac, Aimé. "L'apparition du mot 'spiritualitas' au moyen age." ALMA 44–45 (1983–85): 185–206.

Spangenberg, Johann. *A Booklet of Comfort for the Sick and On the Christian Knight* (1548). Trans., ed., and intro. Robert Kolb. Milwaukee, WI: Marquette University Press, 2007.

Spinks, Bryan D. *Reformation and Modern Rituals and Theologies of Baptism: From Luther to Contemporary Practices*. Aldershot, UK: Ashgate, 2006.

Spiritual and Anabaptist Writers: Documents Illustrative of the Radical Reformation. Ed. George H. Williams. LCC 25. Philadelphia: Westminster, 1977.

Steinmetz, David C. "Religious Ecstasy in Staupitz and the Young Luther." SCJ 11 (1980): 23–37.

Stephens, Peter. "The Sacraments in the Confessions of 1536, 1549, and 1566—Bullinger's Understanding in Light of Zwingli's." *Zwingliana* 33 (2006): 51–76.

Strauss, Gerald. *Luther's House of Learning: Indoctrination of the Young in the German Reformation*. Baltimore: Johns Hopkins University Press, 1978.

Taylor, Larissa. *Soldiers of Christ: Preaching in Late Medieval and Reformation France*. New York: Oxford University Press, 1992.

Thompson, Nicholas. *Eucharistic Sacrifice and Patristic Tradition in the Theology of Martin Bucer, 1534–46*. Leiden: E. J. Brill, 2005.

Valentin Weigel: Selected Spiritual Writings. Trans. and intro. Andrew Weeks. Classics of Western Spirituality. Mahwah, NJ: Paulist Press, 2003.

Watt, Tessa. *Cheap Print and Popular Piety, 1550–1640*. Cambridge: Cambridge University Press, 1991.

Weeks, Andrew. *Valentin Weigel (1533–88): German Religious Dissenter, Speculative Theorist, and Advocate of Tolerance*. Albany: State University of New York Press, 2000.

Wengert, Timothy J. "Philip Melanchthon (1497–1560) and His Recently Discovered Prayer for the Church." LQ 11 (1997): 131–42.

Whitaker, E. C. *Martin Bucer and the Book of Common Prayer*. Alcuin Club Collection 55. Great Wakering, UK: Mayhew-McCrimmon, 1974.

Wicks, Jared, SJ. "Living and Praying as *Simul Iustus et Peccator*: A Chapter in Luther's Spiritual Teaching." *Gregorianum* 70 (1989): 521–48.

———. *Luther and His Spiritual Legacy*. Wilmington, DE: Michael Glazier, 1983.

Word, Church, and State: Tyndale Quincentenary Essays. Ed. John T. Day, Eric Lund, and Anne M. O'Donnell, SND. Washington, DC: Catholic University of America Press, 1998.

Worship in Medieval and Early Modern Europe: Change and Continuity in Religious Practice. Ed. Karin Maag and John D. Witvliet. Notre Dame, IN: University of Notre Dame Press, 2004.

INDEX

329

Other Volumes in This Series

Other Volumes in This Series

Other Volumes in This Series

Other Volumes in This Series

The Classics of Western Spirituality is a ground-breaking collection of the original writings of more than 100 universally acknowledged teachers within the Catholic, Protestant, Eastern Orthodox, Jewish, Islamic, and Native American Indian traditions.

To order any title, or to request a complete catalog, contact Paulist Press at 800-218-1903 or visit us on the Web at www.paulistpress.com